Gangland
AUSTRALIA
Colonial Criminals to the Carlton Crew

Darling 12

James Morton
Susanna Lobez

MELBOURNE
UNIVERSITY
PRESS

Imperial to metric conversions

1 pound (weight)	454 grams
1 ounce	28.3 grams
1 stone (14 pounds)	6.4 kilograms
1 inch	2.5 centimetres
1 foot	30.5 centimetres
1 mile	1.6 kilometres

MELBOURNE UNIVERSITY PRESS
An imprint of Melbourne University Publishing Limited
187 Grattan Street, Carlton, Victoria 3053, Australia
mup-info@unimelb.edu.au
www.mup.com.au

First published 2007
Reprinted 2007 (twice), 2008 (twice)
Text © James Morton and Susanna Lobez, 2007
Design and typography © Melbourne University Publishing Ltd, 2007

Text designed by Alice Graphics
Cover designed by Nada Backovic
Typeset in 9/14 pt Lino Letter Roman by Megan Ellis
Printed in Australia by McPherson's Printing Group

National Library of Australia Cataloguing-in-Publication entry:
Morton, James, 1938– .
    Gangland Australia: colonial criminals to the Carlton crew

    Bibliography.
    Includes index.

    ISBN 978 0 522 85273 8.

    1. Organized crime—Australia—History. 2. Gangs— Australia—History.
    3. Mafia—Australia—History. I. Lobez, Susanna. II. Title.

364.1060994

*For Patricia Rose and Alec Masel
and Dock Bateson with love*

Contents

Preface

It was only when I came to Sydney and Melbourne in the 1990s that I realised how seriously the great villains in recent British crime were outpaced by Australian underworld identities. Some of the Sabinis of the 1920s, the Nashes of the 1950s, the Krays and the Richardsons of the 1960s, the Ahmeds of the 1980s—even the feared, if little known, Adams family of the late 1990s—hadn't begun to leave the paddock by comparison with their Antipodean counterparts. The total number of their dead and disappeared victims was probably no more than those of the Darlinghurst Razor Wars of the 1920s and certainly nowhere near the tally of the current Melbourne struggle. Even the gangsters from New York, Chicago and Detroit during the Prohibition years might find themselves outgunned on the other side of the Pacific. The scales fell from my eyes. It was clear that there was a gripping book to be written about criminal gangs in Australia.

How did I ever start writing about crime? For some thirty years—with time out to take up all-in wrestling, run a junk shop and (that last refuge of the derelict) teach English in Paris—I ran a criminal defence practice in London. Although, over the years, I defended some of the biggest names in the game, I had lost heart telling the same old lies for the same old people to the same old magistrates and judges. My original clients were getting old and while their sons were keen to hear, yet again, how their dads had robbed the Clerkenwell bank on election day 1966, their grandchildren weren't so keen to hear of two old codgers cutting up touches. There was also a change in the way legally aided cases were paid and it was not for the better. My bank manager and I sold my practice to two lawyers, one of whom died literally on his desk after a trip to Las Vegas—financed by me, since he defaulted on the quarterly instalment. The last I heard of the other man was about ten years ago when he escaped from a prison in France. The bank manager kept the proceeds and I looked around for something to do.

I had already tried my hand at writing. I had reviewed films for ten years for a variety of magazines, had written a column on antiques for *Diners Club* magazine for just about as long, and had been the gambling correspondent for a girlie magazine where I subsequently stood in as the wine writer and, when the horoscopist failed to come up with his column, had been the divinatory Joan the Wad for a couple of months.

Many of my older and semi-retired clients were sorry to see me shut the doors and they kept in touch. The last thing a defending lawyer wants to know is the truth, but now I began to ask, 'What really happened?' They were happy to tell me, and out of their recollections and some research came my 1992 book *Gangland*, which was a look at London gangs from the start of the twentieth century.

It attracted a bit of attention. On publication I had some trouble with a London family who were not happy with my description of them, but just as that was sorted out I had a message on my answering machine. Would I ring a Mr Francis Fraser?

I knew exactly who he was. I had defended him in the Parkhurst Riot trial of 1969. He is a sort of cross between Neddy Smith and Chopper Read. He was known as the 'Mad Dentist' partly because he had been certified insane three times and partly because he was reputed to have pulled out the teeth of his victims with a pair of pliers. He had been acquitted of murder in a 1965 shooting but had been sentenced to a total of twenty years, every day of which he served as he lost more and more remission for tipping buckets of urine over prison screws, throwing food in their faces and, if they upset him (and he wasn't in a straitjacket at the time), attacking governors. Early in his life he had tried to hang the governor of one prison and he had certainly managed to hang the man's dog.

He had been happy with his defence when he'd been found not guilty of incitement to murder, but had I somehow offended him in the book? He was the last person I wanted to talk to, but he wasn't the type to go away and there was nothing to do but return his call.

'I've got your book,' he said with no preliminaries when I phoned back. 'I didn't buy it. I had it nicked. I'm writing my story and I want you to do it for me.' My agent didn't want me to do it; my family advised against; but it was, in Godfather terms, an offer I couldn't refuse. The book was a great success and, like Chopper Read, Fraser has gone on to appear in films, television commercials and cabaret, even at literary festivals, and together we have written another four books. Meanwhile I had written a history of the gangs of Britain and then, in 1998, *Gangland International*, which taught me far more about the Australian annals of crime than just Squizzy Taylor, the Shark Arm case and the Pyjama Girl mystery.

It was at this point that I met Susanna Lobez for the second time. We had previously met at a conference in Melbourne when I was editing a law magazine and she was hosting *The Law Report* on ABC Radio. She had been an actress, playing numerous lawyer roles, then retrained and worked as a barrister before turning to broadcasting. We got on well and over the years had kept in touch.

We met yet again in 2004. By this time Susanna had pulled together all her career strands as the host of *Law Matters* on ABC Televisioon and I was steeped in Australian gang crime but realised that the book I wanted to write about it was something I could not do on my own. Who was going to read a history of Australian crime by a largely absentee Pom? Who better, then, to have as a writing partner than an Australian journalist and barrister? Susanna thought it was a good idea and put in the pitch to Melbourne University Publishing, and so *Gangland Australia* was conceived.

* * *

In the years before his death the American journalist and playwright Ben Hecht, who wrote *The Front Page*, was working on a biography of the Californian mobster Mickey Cohen. He wrote, in what would have been the foreword, that he had made a major anthropological discovery:

> The criminal has no hates or fears—except very personal ones. He is possibly the only human left in the world who looks lovingly on society. He does not hanker to fight it, reform it or even rationalise it. He wants only to rob it. He admires it as a hungry man might admire a roast pig with an apple in its mouth.
>
> I was pleased to find this out, for I have read much to the contrary. Society does not, as sociologists and other tony intellectuals maintain, create the criminal. Bad housing, bad companions, bad government etc., have little to do with why there are killers, robbers and outlaws.

The criminal has no relation to society to speak of. He is part of man's soul, not his institutions.

He is an old one. A thousand preachers, summer boys' camps, plus a congress of psychiatrists can barely dent even a minor criminal. As for the major criminal, he cannot be touched at all by society because he operates on a different time level. He is the pre-social part of us—the ape that spurned the collar.

The criminal at the time of his lawlessness is one of the few happy or contented men to be found among us … While he remains a criminal he is as free of conscience pangs as the most right-doing of bookkeepers. He eats well, sleeps well, lives well, and his only disadvantage is that he may die ahead of his time from an enemy bullet, the gas chamber or electric chair.

On the evidence, I agree with Hecht.

This book is about organised crime and the professional criminals who have recklessly cut a swathe through Australia since the early 1800s. It is concerned with crime for gain pure and simple and so specifically excludes political crimes such as the explosion on the coastal steamer *Aramac* in July 1893 or the sabotage and incendiarism carried out by the Industrial Workers of the World in Sydney in 1916 as part of a campaign to secure the release of their leader Tom Barker who had been imprisoned for sedition. The so-called IWW 12 were convicted on what might be described as thin evidence and sentenced to long jail terms, before a Royal Commission in 1920 reconsidered the case and overturned the convictions. Nor will this book look at the fighting Aboriginal gangs such as the Judas Priests and the Evil Warriors in Port Keats whose activities derived rather from hopelessness and internecine rivalry rather than being for gain. Profit, not ideology, is the keyword throughout.

Because the book has its roots in urban crime we have decided to omit the exploits of the early bolters and bushrangers which are such a part of Australia's colonial history. For many years, indeed until the discovery of gold, the gangs formed by these fugitives from the appalling conditions under which the transported convicts served their sentences were for survival rather than for out and out profit. They formed the basis of rural criminality, trying to stay out of prison and the clutches of the soldiers and police, rather than laying the foundations of criminal empires.

This book is an account of murder, robbery, standover, prostitution, drugs, great escapes, revenge, betrayal, a little—but not much—loyalty, corrupt police, lawyers, doctors and politicians. Indeed everything which makes life in the underworld so worthwhile. At the end there is an account of the current state of play and the players who are still left in the game, those who have been sent off the field and, in some cases, those who have been buried under the grandstands or in a mine shaft. There is some corner of a foreign state that is forever Sydney or Melbourne or Perth or Adelaide or Brisbane, let alone Hobart or Darwin or Canberra.

As the weeks and months and years roll by there will undoubtedly be cases solved, defendants convicted or acquitted, appeals allowed and dismissed, gagging orders lifted. We will endeavour to record these in any future edition.

Any informal history of this nature is bound to be selective, particularly in the field of armed robbery and drug smuggling, where some former and current participants will, perhaps rightly, believe that their efforts were financially or technically superior to the ones we have recorded. We can only apologise to them. If they, or their friends, care to send details of their exploits we will carefully consider them for inclusion in the future. Nor has it always been possible to trace what has happened to many of the older players. Again, if readers are able to help we would be greatly obliged. It will be a great service in developing this mirror image of society.

Our thanks are due first and foremost to Dock Bateson and then in strictly alphabetical order to Jeremy Beadle, J.P. Bean, Aileen Berry, Ann Brooke, Andrew Carstairs, Nick Cowdery QC, Paul Delianis, David Drake, Richard Evans, Brian Hansen, Ian Hollingworth, Prue Innes, Barbara Levy, Maitland Lincoln, Ray Lopez, Maggie Mandelert, Sandra Masel, Sally Moss, Sybil Nolan, Russell Robinson, John Silvester, Adrian Tame, Edda Tasiemka and Geoff Wilkinson. Also the staff of the British Library; the Newspaper Library, Colindale; the Mitchell Library, Sydney; the National Archives, Kew, England; the Office of Police Integrity, Victoria; the Public Record Office, Victoria; the State Library of Victoria; the State Library of Western Australia; State Records New South Wales; and many other people on both sides of the criminal fence who have asked that they not be named. Any errors are ours alone.

James Morton
June 2007

Part I

Early Days

1

When Governor Arthur Phillip and his reluctant passengers reached the Antipodean coast on 26 January 1788, anyone foolish enough to think that transportation was a way of eradicating crime was swiftly disabused. Although many of those transported were politicals and general riff-raff, there were some high-class English criminals among them. It is hardly surprising, therefore, that from the early years Sydney had a ready-made criminal class. Since neither prison nor any other method of punishment, let alone transportation, necessarily prevents recidivism, its members swung into operation almost on landing. On 11 February the first convict court was held and two men were charged with stealing. On 27 February nine were charged with theft and a seventeen year old was sentenced to be hanged. Nor after forty years had behaviour improved. In 1829 fifty-two were hanged, the most in any single year.

From the beginning, the sale of goods in Sydney by visiting trade ships provided an opportunity for forgers to make both coins and notes. In 1796 a number of convicts were charged with passing a forged ten guinea note bearing the Commissary's name. One of them, James McCarthy, was sentenced to death. To avoid the death penalty one man dobbed in Jemima Robley, the wife of a Sydney blacksmith, as a major receiver. In turn she named George Milton and her husband John as robbers and they were duly hanged. Milton had previously been convicted in Australia and had been sentenced at the Old Bailey in December 1790; John Robley at Middlesex Sessions a year earlier.

Joseph Samuels was 'The Man They Could Not Hang' in early Sydney. Transported for seven years, the former Londoner was now convicted of the murder of Constable Joseph Luker (who was investigating the robbery of the considerable sum of twenty-four guineas from a prostitute, Mary Breeze) and sentenced to death. Samuels admitted the robbery but denied killing the officer. His hanging was a splendid spectacle. The first rope snapped, a second unravelled and a third broke. Suspecting 'divine intervention', the authorities called it a day and Samuels was granted a reprieve. On 24 September 1803 the *Sydney Gazette* thought: 'A Reprieve was announced ... and if Mercy be a fault, it is the dearest attribute of God and surely in Heaven it may find extenuation!' Samuels did not really benefit. A short while after, he and some companions stole a boat and drowned in an escape attempt.

Perhaps the first organised crime worthy of the name in Sydney, still effectively one enormous prison, came with the 1828 Bank of Australia robbery. The census taken that year showed that, of the population of 36 598, some 15 728 were convicts. Executions took place, on average, every ten days and for those who escaped the hangman there were prison settlements at Port Macquarie, Moreton Bay, Port Arthur and the dreaded Norfolk Island.

The Bank of Australia, founded in 1826 on George Street, and standing between a private home and a public house, was regarded as socially superior to the Bank of New South Wales, which had already been in existence for a decade. The plotters were James Dingle, who had obtained his Certificate of Freedom the previous year; George Farrell, who in July 1826 had been charged with robbing a man and had received the relatively lenient sentence of working in irons for three months; and Thomas Turner, a cleanskin, but who in October 1827 had been acquitted of receiving a quantity of soap. A great benefit was that Turner had worked on the construction of the bank's premises. Tools for the dig to the vaults were supplied by the former London safebreaker William Blackstone, known as 'Sudden Solomon', who worked for a blacksmith.

The team decided the digging should be done on Saturday nights and it began on 30 August. Turner, who as a former construction worker on the bank would have been a prime suspect, withdrew after the first night's work but it was agreed that, as he had provided details of the premises, he should still receive a share in the proceeds. A man named Clayton or Creighton, alias Walford, was recruited in his place.

Around 11 a.m. on 15 September the remaining trio removed the cornerstone nearest the street and the smallest of them, Farrell, went in and brought out two boxes. They returned on the Sunday night and the result was probably beyond the team's wildest dreams. By the time they emptied the vault they had taken a total of 14 500 pounds. They also destroyed the bank's ledgers. A reward of 100 pounds was posted, then upped to 120 pounds and, when neither produced a response, the governor, Sir Ralph Darling, offered an absolute pardon and a free passage to England to the man or woman who provided information.

As bank robbers have found over the centuries it is the disposal of the notes that is sometimes the hardest part of the work. There was no way that passing a fifty pound note, of which 100 had been taken, would not attract attention. Anything over five pounds would cause serious problems. Similarly, bills could not be paid with handfuls of silver and there were 8000 shillings and 1200 sixpences in the haul. And, just as so many other robbers have done in their time, they used a receiver, Thomas Woodward, who had lost his ticket of leave the previous July for leaving his wife and living with another woman.

Woodward's terms were not onerous. He was given 1133 pounds and told Blackstone that he would pay back 1000 pounds in smaller denominations once he had obtained them. Yet again, as many have found to their cost, receivers are not always reliable. The pair went to the Bank of New South Wales. Woodward told Blackstone to wait outside, then disappeared through a side door never to return.

Some months later Blackstone tried to rob a gambling den in Macquarie Street and was shot and wounded by a policeman who saw the raid. His colleague on the robbery was killed and Blackstone was sentenced to death, a penalty that was commuted to life imprisonment. He was sent to Norfolk Island which, unsurprisingly, he disliked and in 1831 he decided to dob in his mates from the Bank of Australia job, something which might mean his freedom and return to England. Blackstone did not tell the whole story and Clayton was not arrested. Dingle and Farrell received a very lenient ten years apiece and the cheating Woodward received fourteen years.

Blackstone did not learn from his experiences. Shortly before he was due to be shipped back to England he was caught stealing from a shop and received another life sentence. In 1839 he was sent to Cockatoo Island from where he was released in December the following year.

Four years later his body was found in a swamp at Woolloomooloo. The Bank of Australia never recovered its money or its status and folded in 1843. All in all it is a most cautionary tale.

One of the earliest planned urban armed robberies was that of the cargo of the *Nelson* in 1852, then at anchor in Hobson's Bay, Melbourne, being loaded for London. Part of the cargo was 8000 ounces of gold packed in some twenty-three boxes. The leaders of the team were James Duncan, James Morgan and John James who had worked together robbing diggers in the Black Forest region.

In the early hours of 2 April, they rowed out to the *Nelson* in two boats stolen from a local hotel owner. The gold was loaded and the crew and passengers were nailed up in the storeroom where they remained until a stevedore found them the next morning. With a reward of 750 pounds on offer for the trio, they were brought in within three weeks. In May 1852 they received fifteen years on road gangs, the first three to be in irons.

Bushrangers occasionally ventured into town. For two and a half hours during the afternoon of 16 October 1852 four mounted and armed men repeatedly bailed up every individual 'who came up on foot or horseback or in a vehicle' on St Kilda Road. At sundown they galloped off into the bush towards South Yarra. John Flanigan and Thomas Williams were arrested in Flinders Lane three days later. They had already committed another robbery at Aitken's Gap that day. Both received thirty years and Williams was later hanged for his part in the murder of the prison inspector John Price at the Gellibrand Quarries in 1854. Flanigan, who gave evidence at Williams's trial, had early release in 1862. Robberies of miners in the Victorian goldfields were almost two a penny but a rather more sophisticated one took place one Saturday afternoon in October 1854 when Henry Garrett, Henry Marriott, Thomas Quinn and John Boulton took 14300 pounds in gold and money from the Bank of Victoria on Bakery Hill in Ballarat. The expanding town, where imported coffee and preserves, saddles and perfume were now on sale, was in ferment over the imposition of 'taxation without representation' which would lead two months later to the pivotal rebellion at the Eureka Stockade. The week of the robbery two hotels had been set on fire and the robbers picked their time well. Quinn was the cockatoo, Marriott stood just inside the doors and Garrett and Boulton held up the tellers. It was over in minutes.

Marriott hid out in the town. Quinn and Boulton went to Geelong and then Melbourne, where they sold their gold to the London Chartered Bank. Garrett went straight to Melbourne and sailed for England. It was Boulton whose crass action caused their downfall. Using the stolen banknotes he tried to purchase a banker's draft for 1450 pounds from the bank they had robbed. He and Quinn, who was with him, were arrested and Quinn dobbed in Marriott. All three received ten years. Garrett was traced to London and arrested. Back in Australia he also received ten years. On his release in 1861 he went to New Zealand to continue his life of crime.

* * *

From the earliest days of European settlement, when there were six males for every female (including Aboriginal women), the authorities wished to prevent men committing rape and buggery. By the early 1800s, with insufficient numbers of women in Britain found guilty of transportable offences to balance the genders, the bar was lowered and women were soon transported for much less serious offences than their male counterparts. In 1797 the Second Fleet ship the *Lady Julian* set off for Sydney Bay Penal Colony carrying 240 women sentenced mostly for petty crimes. Twelve per cent of these women convicts were prostitutes before leaving Britain and many of the rest soon joined the ranks to obtain food, accommodation and some sort of security. Thus, just as the Europeans are credited with exporting syphilis to the New World, so the English exported prostitution to Australia.

In 1831 came Tasmania's first sex scandal. Jane Torr had been transported for minor offences in Exeter in 1830. The next year she became embroiled in a prostitution ring operating from the Launceston Colonial Hospital where Dr Spence had allowed part of the hospital to be used as a brothel, under the ostensible management of John Ayton, the overseer. Ayton resigned to avoid facing charges but a subsequent inquiry found the women's ward was regularly used as his bawdy house. One witness told the inquiry about a bunch of Chinese men who had been taken into the ward one by one where 'they stopped about ten minutes each'. The wash-up was that Spence was suspended from the hospital and demoted for his 'misconduct'. Poor Jane Torr was sentenced to six months at the Female Factory in Hobart—not for any prostitution-related offence but for being too often absent from her master.

Ten years later Henry Keck was appointed the first governor of the newly built Darlinghurst prison. So far as he was concerned it was a commercially successful appointment. He hired out the female prisoners as prostitutes and the most talented male prisoners as musicians. Prisoners were allowed out at night to go fishing and he sold their catch. He was dismissed, a rich man, in 1847.

By the 1860s the criminal class in Melbourne was said to be around 4000 out of a population of 140 000. The lanes at the end of Bourke Street, where Charley Wright's Coliseum Music Hall was thought to be the 'rendez-vous of thieves and the lowest-priced prostitutes in town', were dangerous. When night fell, criminals stalked the bars and the vestibule of the Theatre Royal. One bar where prostitutes could be found for a modest charge was known as the Saddling Paddock. Higher class girls worked Collins Street. Both ends of Little Bourke Street, where garrotters lurked, were decidedly unsafe and thieves prowled both the town and the suburbs. Bella Wright's was the 'lowest brothel in Melbourne'.

Naturally there was also sex to be bought at the highest level. When in 1867 the 22-year-old Prince Alfred, Duke of Edinburgh, arrived in Melbourne, Captain Frederick Standish, the dilettante Chief of Police, took him to Sarah Fraser's very high-class and tastefully decorated brothel in Stephen Street. When Standish ushered in the son of the Queen, Mother Fraser must have thought she had died and gone to Madam Heaven.

Fraser was succeeded as the madam of the city's brothels by the German-born Caroline Baum, known as 'Madame Brussels'. By 1874 she was running a brothel in Little Lonsdale Street, an occupation she maintained for the next three decades. She was then described as a 'magnificent pink, white and golden maned animal'. Her second and probably bigamous husband was the German Jacob Pohl and she may have had a child by the composer and critic Alfred Plumpton. The evangelist Henry Varley angrily wrote of her walking on Collins Street with a girl under twenty who had a white feather (signifying virginity) in her hat. By 1876 Baum's seven roomed house at 32–36 Lonsdale Street was well furnished with marble bathrooms, the carpets were 'like meadow-grass' and guests could pay ten to twelve pounds per day without wine or girls for board and lodgings. At the other end of the tariff, parliamentary visitors had a key to a door opening off Little Lonsdale Street.

Early one morning in October 1891 after the House had risen, the parliamentary mace—five foot of silver gilt and weighing 217 ounces—disappeared. Legend was that it had gone to Madame Brussels' but when a board of inquiry into the disappearance sat some sixteen months later it specifically named as the beneficiary the equally popular Boccaccio House, also in Lonsdale Street and run by Miss Annie Wilson. The brothel had one of Melbourne's first telephones installed for the benefit of a member of parliament who lived there. In 1891 one of the first call-girl networks in the world operated from the brothels catering for the businessmen and parliamentarians who did not wish to roll up unannounced. Now the houses booked appointments for their favourite girls to be available, the reverse of the present system of outcalls for girls, which seems to have developed in the 1930s in the United States.

Towards the end of her illustrious career, Madame Brussels suffered at the hands of the new moralists of the era. In August 1898 she was brought before the courts with her Lonsdale Street neighbours Maude Miller and May Baker. The three were tried for 'occupying premises frequented by persons without lawful means of support', a forerunner of the consorting laws of the twentieth century. The charges came courtesy of the Wesleyan Methodists, and the police must have felt between a rock and a hard place. They were obliged to pursue the complaints of the wowsers and to prosecute. But then, once under oath, they had to concede that the 'houses were well conducted'. Dismissing the charges against the trio, Chief Magistrate McEacharn, who also happened to be Mayor, made his feelings on the subject very clear: 'Do you think that Melbourne would be improved if a large street like this were filled with Syrians, Hindus and Chinese?' Madame Brussels' brothel closed in 1907 and, ill with chronic pancreatitis and diabetes, she died the next year.

While Sydney might not have had the palatial premises of some of Melbourne's brothels, prostitutes were also hard at work there. A pupil of the late Professor John Woolley, conducting a rudimentary survey in 1873, found that prostitutes were mainly:

> women who have been in a state of menial servitude; and who from
> the love of idleness and dress, together with the misfortune of good
> looks, in some instances, have mostly from inclination resorted to
> prostitution for a livelihood … girls were corrupted by idle and

frivolous habits encouraged or contracted on board ship when not subjected to the most careful supervision.

His research showed that two or three girls would take a house together in Woolloomooloo or live in a boarding house run by retired whores. Prostitutes mainly worked at the Prince of Wales Theatre before it was burnt down, at Belmore markets on Saturday nights, the Domain Gardens on Sunday afternoons and George Street on Sunday nights. Some were as young as twelve; many were diseased. Elizabeth Street provided an easy escape across the racecourse after they had robbed their clients. He also found there was a certain amount of homosexual prostitution with a degree of cross-dressing. Many of the city's cabmen worked with the prostitutes.

In Queensland major centres of prostitution in the 1880s included Mackay, Cairns and Thursday Island. The Queensland constabulary had their own methods of dealing with and benefiting from prostitution. If a pimp or madam wished to avoid charges, the answer was simple: pay the police to look the other way.

In the 1880s brothel keeping per se was not illegal and the police used brothel owners and staff as a source of information on the clients. New South Wales was late to implement prostitution-specific laws. Only in 1908 was the Police Offences (Amendment) Act passed. This criminalised soliciting, living on the earnings of prostitution, brothel keeping and leasing premises for the purposes of prostitution. There were still problems in securing convictions against brothel keepers because of the difficulties in supplying evidence of ownership and, ironically, the legislative changes made the free-wheeling trade of prostitution an industry in which the girls were controlled by organised crime. Now many prostitutes were forced into houses owned by criminal networks. In Sydney throughout the 1920s and 1930s prostitution was inexorably linked with the sly-grog and cocaine traders.

In Western Australia the official line on prostitution was summed up by Attorney General Walter James in 1902 when the Police Offences (Amendment) Act was debated in parliament:

it would be undesirable to entirely suppress it, even if we had the power to do so ... On the other hand I do not believe in its being carried on in an open, flagrant and almost insulting manner. I believe it should be kept in restraint.

This public policy of 'restraint' meant brothels were tolerated in districts like Roe Street, Perth, and in remote gold settlements like Kalgoorlie where gold rush in the 1890s attracted diggers and fortune seekers from all over the world. Some dug the gold from the ground and some from the pockets of lucky prospectors. Sly-grog merchants, professional gamblers and prostitutes, many of whom were Japanese, all set up shop around Kalgoorlie. And so, from the turn of the century, crime syndicates throughout Australia 'fought for the control of brothels and street prostitution, bought off rival groups of police and politicians and linked drugs … gambling and vice into the three perennial pillars of an illegal economy.'

* * *

Up until the 1860s, thieves stole haphazardly in Melbourne—from the back of wagons, unlocked houses and yards. Then things began to crystallise. Now there were the magsmen or confidence tricksters and the three card trick merchants. There were also coiners and rather more organised burglars. John Christie, probably the best of the Melbourne detectives of the time, joined the force in 1867 at the age of twenty-one, by walking in off the street with a character reference. Within a matter of months his arrest record far surpassed those of other officers.

In the late 1860s there was a series of silk robberies, which for a time went unsolved despite a 250 pound reward. Then, with information received, Christie arrested a Thomas Griffiths living at 56 Stanley Street, West Melbourne, who had robbed the firm of Clarke and Adams at Elizabeth and Collins streets. Griffiths' operation was a family business. He used one of his sons to break in with him and his wife disposed of the goods, selling door to door in Toorak. In January 1869 he received eleven years. Mrs Griffiths, who turned against her husband, later opened a small hospital in Carlton.

Penalties for those caught were indeed severe. John Moore and Thomas Bourke, notorious garrotters who worked Little Bourke Street, each received ten years in 1870. Twenty years later the authorities were still keen to show that violence would be severely punished. On 11 May 1888 at the Collingwood Court, Thomas Donoghue, John Smith and Henry Towerson received twelve months' hard labour after being convicted of being suspected persons. They were then hauled off to the Central Criminal Court for bag snatching and the robbery of a watch, and after pleading guilty, received a further fifteen years' hard labour and fifteen lashes to go with it.

By the 1880s in Sydney clear divisions had been established in the hierarchy of crime. Amateur opportunistic thieves such as domestic servants used pawnbrokers as the preferred method of disposing of stolen goods. Provided the pawnbroker kept a set of books, and not too many fenced items were recorded in them, there was a measure of a defence if he was charged with receiving and, of course, the stolen goods pawned were never redeemed. The professional thief went to a professional fence whose shop would have a sign 'Gold and Silver Bought' or 'Wardrobes Purchased'. In the back room there would be a crucible maintained at white heat. One observer noted: 'People go into that room as freely as if it was a public house parlour and empty their pockets of gold and silver, jewellery and plate into their separate crucibles where they are speedily reduced to ingots.' Watches were sent abroad.

By the early 1880s Sydney had an estimated 288 000 inhabitants and 3167 public houses. Eleven o'clock closing was introduced in 1882 but all night drinking continued in brothels, cafés and oyster shops. At a time when two pounds a week was considered a living wage, so-called brandy was sold at four shillings and sixpence a gallon, real brandy at the same amount per bottle (four shillings and sixpence being almost a quarter of a pound). Many pubs had 'private bars' rented by girls from landlords at between three and ten pounds per week. The 1887 Commission of Inquiry found that there were some ninety-seven of these dotted throughout the city. But the private bar was by no means confined to Sydney. A correspondent in the *Adelaide Advertiser* in 1884 regretted:

> the fearful injury wrought young men, especially clerks, by the seductive influence of young and exquisitely dressed barmaids in the saloons and back bars of several Adelaide hotels. These girls are generally of Melbourne or Sydney extraction ... The girls whose attractions are heightened by artificial means dispensed liquors and toyed with the youthful gommeaux.

One illegal trade that flourished at this time—fuelled by prostitutes, barmaids and servant girls—was baby-farming. In the 1880s un-registered births and the high rates of infant death concealed this lucrative traffic in infant lives. Apart from *coitus interruptus*, abortion was the main form of birth control among working-class women and it was followed by infanticide and baby-farming—the practice of paying a carer to look after an unwanted infant while little was asked as to what would happen to the child. Just as the Thames in London was awash with infant bodies, so were Sydney Harbour and the Yarra River. One Melbourne doctor estimated that half the post-mortems he performed indicated wilful child destruction. In Sydney hundreds of dead and unidentified babies were found in public places and taken to morgues in the 1880s and 1890s.

Most convicted baby-farmers paid fines. But one, John Makin, was executed in 1893. He and his wife Sara, probably the brains behind the enterprise, answered adoption advertisements and took several babies at a time for lump sums followed by regular payments. They included the son of Amber Murray whose body was identified by its clothing. Makin had killed and buried him immediately on receipt in June 1892. He had then cruelly strung Amber Murray and others along, with stories of why they could not visit their children. Much of the evidence against the Makins was that of their daughter Clarrie. Both were sentenced to death but Sara Makin was reprieved and served fourteen years. Before his execution Makin is said to have remarked, 'That's what a man gets for obliging people.'

In marvellous Melbourne, infanticide was prevalent both in the city and in the suburbs and on 5 September 1893 *The Argus*, which had been campaigning against trafficking in babies, reported a 'shocking discovery in Brunswick'. A man working in his garden in Moreland Road dug up the body of a three-month-old child. Its skull had been fractured.

The following year two more bodies were dug up and later Frances Knorr stood trial for their murders. She was the wife of a waiter who had deserted her after which she took up with an Edward Thompson. In prison she wrote a letter telling Thompson how to suborn a witness and how, if she received a long sentence, he was to look after her two children. At her trial she tried to put the blame on Thompson and also a man named Wilson, who she said brought a child to her for burial. He was a complete invention.

Mrs Knorr sang 'Safe in the Arms of Jesus' followed by 'Abide with Me' on her way to the scaffold. But there were suggestions that she had been so liberally dosed with brandy that she was drunk. With her death and that of Makin came the end of the deliberate killing of children by baby-farmers.

Just to what extent the police were benefiting from the abortion racket is not entirely clear. The Birthrate Commission of 1903 was told there was evidence that the police were failing to prosecute but this was explained by the difficulty in obtaining compelling evidence. It may be that they were turning a blind eye in sympathy with the unfortunate women. In turn the police blamed the medical profession for providing suspect death certificates and shielding other abortionists. One doctor, Thomas Sheridan, was convicted of abortion in New South Wales and served ten years. He clearly learned nothing for, on his release, he killed the first patient he aborted. This time he was hanged.

* * *

Just as the American ethnic street gangs of today broadly divide themselves into supporters of either the Crips or the Bloods, in the early 1870s the Sydney 'pushes', as the gangs were known, divided on religious lines. The Rocks Push (then under the leadership of Sandy Ross), the Gibbs Street Mob and the Glebe Island Boys all broadly supported the Oranges or Protestants. The Greens or Catholics were led by Larry Foley.

The pushes lived on a steady diet of theft, assaults and rolling sailors, using their girls as decoys as well as prostitutes. When the whalers and grain carriers left harbour the pushes passed the time by attacking anyone foolish enough to stray into the Rocks and by fighting among themselves.

In March 1871 Larry Foley challenged the heavier, older and taller Ross for supremacy of the Rocks Push. Foley had come under the tutelage of Black Perry or 'Perry the Black', a Canadian prize fighter who had some success in the London prize-ring before being transported in 1846 for passing false banknotes. With good behaviour, Perry had earned his ticket of leave and defeated George Hough in a hundred-pounds-a-side match. In 1858 he defeated both Bob McLaren and Tom Curran and then, finding no new challengers, gave lessons for a living at Bay Street, Glebe, and taught Foley the skills of boxing as opposed to fighting.

The fight lasted for some two hours forty minutes before it was broken up in the seventy-first round by the police. One account has it that Ross recognised at the time that he was badly beaten and handed the leadership to Foley. Another is that Ross's backer was dissatisfied and there was a two-hundred-pounds-a-side rematch which Foley won handily in twenty-eight minutes. There is, however, agreement that Foley became leader of the Rocks Push, with Ross as his first lieutenant. By some accounts he tried to stop the practice of living off immoral earnings but he failed and, now sponsored by local sportsmen, left the Rocks Push to become Australia's last and probably greatest bare-knuckle champion.

Over the next twenty years other pushes came and went. The Waterloo Push thoroughly disgraced itself over the gang rape of a serving girl, sixteen-year-old Mary Jane Hicks in 1886. The unfortunate girl was first molested by a cab driver, Charles Sweetman, who later was sentenced to a flogging and fourteen years' hard labour, then, as she escaped from him, she was chased and attacked by up to a dozen members of the Push. Eleven youths were charged and two, George Duffy and Joe Martin, accepted that they had intercourse, claiming it was with the girl's consent. Hicks and a Bill Stanley, who went to her help, identified eight of the eleven and, after a bitter trial before the unpopular Mr Justice Windeyer, nine (including Duffy and Martin) were found guilty.

After a series of appeals and petitions, five were reprieved and four youths were hanged in a botched execution at Darlinghurst Gaol in January 1887. The hangman had miscalculated the length of rope required and only Duffy died instantly. The seventeen-year-old Joe Martin strangled for ten minutes before he died.

In Melbourne in 1880 the city was in the grip of, if not a crime wave, at least hooliganism, with the Hoddle Street Lairies, including the notorious brothers John and Edward Peddy, taking over hotels and raiding bakeries where they would drink and eat for free.

After an uneventful decade, in 1892 there was an alarming if temporary increase in domestic burglaries in both the city and suburbs of Melbourne, with thieves entering houses by the front window and leisurely proceeding to search various rooms for valuables. They turned up the gas in the drawing room, ate cake, helped themselves to wine and entertained themselves with card games.

By the mid-1890s a series of private bills were brought before the New South Wales parliament designed to curb prostitution and larrikinism and to allow burglars to be flogged. In February 1894 two Victorian burglars, Charles Montgomery and Thomas Williams, were captured after failing to blow a safe at the Union Steamship Company in Bridge Street, Sydney. When challenged by officers, Montgomery, wielding a three foot iron jemmy, fractured the skull of Constable Frederick Bowden and broke the arm of another constable. He then threatened to shoot a third if he chased him. Reinforcements came from the Water Police Station and, after a struggle, Montgomery was captured. Williams surrendered quietly. Both were sentenced to death, with the jury recommending mercy for Williams. For Montgomery, who had already served a six year sentence in the dreaded Pentridge, there was no hope. Despite a petition signed by 25 000 people, including Bowden, there was none for Williams either. They were both hanged on 31 May. It was this incident that led to the arming of the New South Wales police.

On 19 January 1903 Constable Samuel Long surprised burglars at the Royal Hotel in Auburn, Sydney, and was shot in the head. Two men were chased by Theodore Trautwein, the licensee, but they reached a sulky and drove off. At Stanmore, Police Constable Mason saw them driving without a light, the horse soaked in sweat. The job had been on offer from Henry Jones who told safebreaker Alfred Jackson, in a conversation in Bathurst prison, that 'only fools and horses work' and he wanted a man 'who understood the game and was not afraid to shoot'. He spoke well of his other men. Digby Grand would 'stop at nothing' and Snowy Woolford was a 'thorough cocktail'. Sensibly Jackson declined the job. Grand may have stopped at nothing but it did not stop him shooting off his mouth, telling a butcher Joseph Gallagher that he was tired of getting 'stuff' and wanted to go for the 'ready gilt', meaning he wanted money. At the time of the murder he was already on trial for shop breaking and a big boot robbery.

Woolford, the lookout, cracked first, weeping and running away from Long's funeral at which a police band was playing. He was heard by a servant who told another girl who told the hotel owner. Woolford admitted getting an impression in soap of the key to the hotel safe. Grand was arrested on 24 January and Jones was later arrested at 33 Ada Street in Surry Hills. Woolford was allowed to turn Queen's Evidence and at the committal proceedings gave it well. By the time of the trial, however, he had been sent to a mental reception house at

Darlinghurst and was claiming he had been made to give false evidence against Jones and Grand.

He was in a complete state of breakdown by the time the trial opened in April, and the first jury was discharged in the hope that he would recover. At the second trial Woolford was no better and Grand, whose demeanour had been described as that of an amused spectator rather than an accused principal, smiled and gestured to the public gallery. Both men gave alibi evidence and the jury returned guilty verdicts but with a recommendation for mercy. Grand never lost his composure, echoing Ned Kelly when he told Judge Rogers:

> I have to tell you to your face that you have tried this case more like a Crown Prosecutor than a Judge. There was a Judge in this State named Windeyer. Where did he die? Away from friends and relatives where I hope you will die. I shall meet you before our God, and then you will know whether I am guilty or not.

Rubbing it in, Rogers commented: 'I am afraid the principle enunciated by Jones, that it is only fools and horses that work, has had too much weight with both of you.'

They were both hanged in July 1903. Jones's neck was broken but Grand strangled to death. A subsequent medical report assured readers that he had immediately been rendered unconscious and suffered no pain.

* * *

The Sydney robber and standover man John 'Chow' Hayes was, in the years between and after the two world wars, to become a dominant figure. He had started his career in the old Sydney gangs of the early twentieth century. In his authorised biography, he sets out the territories occupied by the various pushes of that century. The Surry Hills Mob, also known as the Ann Street Mob, ran the territory from the railway to Darlinghurst and back to Surry Hills; the Loo Mob came from Woolloomooloo; the Glebe Mob from around Bay Street, Glebe; the Newtown Mob from around the railway station in Newtown. The last were profitably employed by Joe Taylor, at that time managing The Hub theatre and who later became the king of the two-up schools, who would use them as bouncers for unruly patrons. Their great rivals were the Redfern Mob, who controlled an area off Cleveland Street. Hayes himself belonged to the Railway Gang which controlled a part of central Sydney from Grace Brothers, the department store on Broadway, up George Street to the Town Hall. The Railway Gang specialised in shoplifting and while one set would distract shop assistants, others would throw toys and sporting equipment from the first floor window to their friends outside.

It is easy to see how youth gang members can progress to crime proper. If the Newtown boys found they could be offered money to protect a theatre, then it was a short step to go to another cinema or theatre and demand money to protect it. In the days of the two-up ring there had to be people to keep the crowds under control. There would be opportunities to ensure that a successful punter was protected on his way home or to rob him, and to point the winning punter in the direction of a prostitute, the sly-grog shop or both so as to complete the afternoon's entertainment; to lend money at exorbitant rates to a loser or at least to collect the interest on behalf of the lender.

At one two-up school of the 1890s in Melbourne two boxers were kept gloved up so that, in the event of a raid, they could take over the ring and thwart the police. In 1892 there were said to be fifty-five major gambling shops. Formal two-up in Sydney began in 1910 with a school called Thommo's owned by a none too successful boxer George Guest, who fought as Joe Thomas and then opened what would become his legendary game in Surry Hills. By the beginning of World War II, Joe Taylor, perhaps the best known of all the owners, was employing a full-time staff of forty. These included ring keepers, bouncers, doormen, clerks, cashiers and cockatoos or look-out men. During the war single bets of a thousand pounds were quite usual and, just as in the 1920s New York café society flocked to Harlem, so, for Sydney society, would a night out end at Thommo's. 'There were no colour, religious or political barriers between this rowdy classless assemblage of doctors, stockbrokers, graziers, public servants, jockeys, labourers, bookmakers, plumbers, butchers, pimps and criminals either on bail, remand or released.'

Relations with the police were amicable: raids were pre-arranged and a line of down-and-outs would be recruited at two pounds each to be arrested. On the other hand, every Monday morning a plain-clothes officer would arrive with a briefcase for the weekly payout. It was

Joe Taylor, a hugely popular man and a fearless gambler, who would later give a major drug dealer of the 1970s, Nick Paltos, his start in life.

Over the years the street gangs of Sydney underwent a steady transformation to become profitable organisations and by the time World War I broke out many of the fighting pushes had died away. Gone were the Plunkett Street Woolloomooloo Push and the Rocks Push. The last outpost seems to have been in Surry Hills, where the Forty Thieves and the Big Seven still hung on. Lately they had been used by politicians to break up rivals' meetings and to protect their own. Now even their days were numbered. In particular Samuel 'Jewey' Freeman, who once ran the Riley Street Gang and who lived in Surry Hills, was regarded as being quite capable of dealing with rival gangs on his own. And if he could not, then there was Ernest 'Shiner' Ryan, whose criminal career dated from 1901, to help him. Sharing Freeman's bed and, from time to time, that of Ryan, was Kate Leigh, a diminutive woman of vitriolic temper who would go on to carve out a career for herself in the Darlinghurst Razor Wars a decade later.

In fact, the Melbourne pushes survived much longer than the Sydney ones. At the turn of the century there were the Bouverie Forty, the Stephen Street Push, the Flying Angels in South Melbourne, the Woolpacks and the Fitzroy Checkers. In 1919, instead of going to the Melbourne Cup, a group of Collingwood bootmakers known as Little Campbells Push turned on their old rivals, the Roses from Rose and Brunswick streets. Two Campbells, Porky Flynn and Dodger Smith, shot and killed one of their fleeing rivals. In October 1927, on the weekend that gang leaders Squizzy Taylor and John Cutmore were shot in Melbourne, Richard Dunstan of the Hawk Eyes Push had been at war with the Chefs.

It was in the spring of 1914 that Jewey Freeman, Ryan and Leigh planned one of New South Wales's most famous crimes to that date: the Eveleigh Railway Workshops robbery—an attack on their factory in Wilson Street, Redfern.

It was executed on 10 June, four days after Freeman had shot a night watchman, Michael McHale, in the face during a robbery at the Paddington Post Office in Oxford Street. Now two Eveleigh employees arrived on a horse and cart at the factory, bringing the payroll, which totalled slightly more than 3300 pounds. They unloaded the first chest of money and, as they were taking the second tray, Ryan drove up with

Freeman in the passenger seat of an old grey car. Freeman put a gun to the head of one employee, Norman Twiss, and threatened to blow his brains out. The second chest was loaded onto the car and away the pair drove. The *Herald* on 11 June was both enchanted and able to use the robbery as a stick with which to beat the administration:

> The Eveleigh hold-up is surely unique of its kind in Australia. For audacity of conception and cool effrontery of execution it could hardly have been surpassed [but had there been a policeman about, the robbers may have been apprehended]. We commend to the Government's notice the increase of the police force.

Unfortunately for Freeman and Ryan the number of the car had been taken. Even more unfortunately they had not bothered to steal one; they had used one belonging to Arthur Tatham from Castlereagh who had duly reported it stolen and, when interviewed by the police, seemed to know far too much about things. The man in charge of the payroll also told the police that Twiss had been unusually cool. Indeed it seemed almost as if he had expected the attack. Then Freeman was grassed up. He intended to go to Melbourne but delayed too long and on 24 June the police arrested him as he was boarding the Melbourne Express. Although he claimed that he had been at the races on the day of the robbery he was charged.

All of which left Shiner Ryan very much on his own. For the moment it went well enough. He stayed in Sydney, sending his share to his friend Sam Falkiner in Melbourne, but then things began to unravel. First, Falkiner decamped to Tasmania with the takings. Then Ryan went to Victoria and, finding Falkiner had left, told a girlfriend. She, with reward money ringing in her ears, went to the police.

Ryan was surrounded in a house in Albert Park and a sum of 600 pounds was found in a glass jar stuffed into the chimney. It was all that was ever recovered. Ryan was returned to Sydney where he was charged along with Freeman, Twiss and Tatham. The quartet went on trial at the Central Criminal Court, Darlinghurst, in September that year, with mixed results. Twiss was acquitted and Tatham received a mere three months as an accessory.

Ryan's defence was hopeless. The reason he had left Sydney was that he had seen a drawing in the paper of one of the robbers which resembled him and, thinking of his criminal record, knew no one would believe him. Totally unable to explain away the money in the chimney, the evidence of the girl and the fact that he had admitted to the crime on his arrest, he was right. He received ten years and tried to slash his wrists on his first day in Parramatta.

Jewey Freeman's alibi changed slightly, principally because the races were not run in the morning. Now he had been in bed with Kate Leigh. She was called to give evidence and confirmed that it was correct. In fact, they had gone ice-skating together at the Exhibition rink and then gone back to Frog Hollow, Surry Hills where they had stayed in bliss for two days.

Again the papers was taken in. How, *The Herald* wondered, could a woman admit publicly her own lack of virtue if she was not telling the truth? But the jury believed neither her nor Freeman. He received ten years to be followed immediately by a life sentence for shooting McHale in the post office robbery.

It was not the first time Leigh had been found guilty of perjury. Born in 1887 in Dubbo, one of thirteen children of a horse trainer, she was badly mistreated and, found wandering on the streets at the age of ten, was sent to the Parramatta Industrial School where she remained for four years. In 1901 she was released and went to Melbourne where she was promptly sentenced to fourteen days for vagrancy. On her release she became a waitress and in May 1902 she married a small time thief and illegal bookmaker Jack Leigh. That year she received five years when she and Jack were convicted of trying to rob their landlord. She ran the defence that they were so poor that she had been working off the rent in bed with the man. The beating had been because Leigh was enraged at the landlord for taking advantage of Kate. Now, for assisting Freeman, she received seven years.

From John Wren to Squizzy Taylor

2

At 3.30 on the morning of 6 January 1906 a bomb—a stone ginger beer bottle stuffed with powder—was thrown through the front window of the home of Sergeant David O'Donnell in Nicholson Street, Fitzroy. Known as 'Big O'Donnell', he had been leading the police campaign against the gaming clubs run by John Wren, then on his way to becoming one of the state's most powerful men for the next thirty years. O'Donnell— regarded as a man who, 'if he cannot help a man in misfortune never unnecessarily oppressed him'—said he had expected his windows to be broken but never to be the subject of a bomb attack.

It was just one example of the ruthlessness with which Wren drove to the top. He was born the third son of Irish immigrants at Collingwood in 1871. In 1889 his elder brother, Arthur, was sentenced to death for rape. The penalty was commuted but he received a flogging and served a long and hard sentence before returning to work for his younger brother. John Wren began his working life at the age of twelve in a wood yard and he augmented his wages circulating betting cards and as a small-time moneylender. According to his version he launched his Johnston Street totalisator with big wins on the horses, first on Carbine in the 1890 Melbourne Cup and then on other lesser races.

In 1903 he founded the illegal City Tattersall's Club and from then on conducted a long and, for some years, successful war with the police and authorities. At its height it brought him an amazing 20000 pounds a year and Wren took great care to nurse the neighbourhood with donations to the Catholic Church and the needy. But on the debit side there had been the fixing of the 1901 Austral Wheel bicycle race, in which the other riders were bribed to ensure that the ageing Plugger Martin won. There were also rumours that Wren had fixed the 1904 Caulfield Cup, netting 50 000 pounds with Murmur's win.

In the first years of the twentieth century, to keep his tote up and running, Wren's men literally fought the police, led by the courageous and incorruptible Sergeant David O'Donnell. In 1903 the police 'occupied' the tote for a nine week period beginning on the eve of the Melbourne Cup before they were finally evicted. The next year Detective Johnson, recognised as an undercover officer who had been spying on the tote, was attacked and badly beaten as he stepped from a tram-car in Sydney Road.

Cases against gaming clubs could also be tricked out by Wren's solicitor and adviser, the redoubtable David Gaunson. At the time O'Donnell was bombed, a summons against the Metropolitan Club in Bourke Street had been running for two years with no end in sight. The demise of Wren's tote, through the efforts of Methodist reformers William Henry Judkins and his brother George Alfred, was not long in coming. A wisp of a man, described alliteratively in *Truth* as 'a gospel-grinding gammoning ghoul', William had a florid style in the pulpit and attacked gambling, prize fights, racing, drinking, dancing and even barmaids.

In May 1906 he turned his attention to Sir Samuel Gillott whom, as chief secretary in the administration, Judkins held responsible for illegal off-course gambling, claiming it was prima facie evidence of collusion between the administration and the police. Now Victorian Premier Sir Thomas Bent, knighted a year or so later, instructed Gillott to promote a bill that would effectively outlaw off-course gaming.

On 29 November John Norton, the very often drunken editor of *Truth*, wrote an open letter alleging that Gillott had been financing Madame Brussels since 1877. Three days later Judkins disclosed that Sir Samuel held the mortgage on her brothel at 36 Lonsdale Street. Pleading ill-health, Gillott resigned from office and returned to England where he remained for a year.

But Wren was not financially troubled by the loss of his tote to Bent's Lotteries, Gaming and Betting Act; he was already a millionaire and now had many other business interests. Although Wren went from financial success to financial success, there was always the smell of corruption about him. In 1930 a conservative state government inquiry found that because proprietary racing in Queensland was controlled by Wren it was inherently corrupt. A keen supporter of the Collingwood Football Club he suffered a heart attack after the Premiership, having pushed his way through the crowd to stand behind Collingwood's goalposts for the last quarter. He was eighty-three when he died on 26 October 1953.

His obituary in *The Age* describes him as being 'beloved by the poor of Collingwood'. He may have enabled the working classes to bet like their richer neighbours and in later life been a great contributor to charity, but with his fixed horse, running, trotting, cycling and greyhound races and boxing and wrestling matches, he robbed them blind.

* * *

The *Australian Dictionary of Biography* is confident that, 'There is no evidence that Wren had associations with the murderous tout "Squizzy" Taylor.' Many would not be so sure and the communist Frank Hardy, in *Power Without Glory*, his roman à clef of the Australian underworld of the time, specifically links his character John West, a thinly disguised portrait of Wren, to the equally thinly disguised Taylor character, Snoopy Tanner.

It is curious how some of the more undesirable villains—Al Capone and the Kray twins spring to mind—garner the greatest admiration from the public. Melbourne's Leslie 'Squizzy' Taylor—self-promoter, coward, murderer, pimp and grass (not necessarily in that order)—was another. Joseph Leslie Theodore Taylor, alias Leslie Grout, alias David Donoghue, sometimes known as 'The Turk', was born on 29 June 1888 in the coastal town of Brighton, nine miles south of Melbourne. His father was a coachbuilder and the family moved to the city in the Depression years of the 1890s. Small enough to be apprenticed as a jockey to the trainer Bobby Lewis, Taylor rode at the Richmond racetrack but his opportunities dried up as he was considered too crooked even for those days. Some say more charitably that—even though at the time of his death he was still under nine stone—he had had weight troubles.

By the end of the century Taylor had been sent to a boys' home, and by his late teens he was a member of the Bourke Street Rats, who controlled crime at the top end of Bourke Street, in those days a home for variety theatres, clubs, pubs, Chinese cafés and third-rate hotels. Later he was taken on tour as an apprentice shoplifter and pickpocket.

In 1906 Taylor was convicted of assault, serving a week, and in January 1907 he tried to steal a gold breast pin in Ballarat. He went straight to the station but was taken off the 3.15 to Melbourne when it stopped in Castlemaine. This time the fine was two pounds. He was in Bendigo the same year, charged with possessing housebreaking implements and given twelve months reduced on appeal to a discharge. He was then fined ten pounds or three months after stealing ten shillings from the till at the Cherry Tree Hotel in Richmond. When he gave the magistrate some lip, the offer of the ten pounds was withdrawn.

In January 1908 he received two years' imprisonment for a pick-pocketing at Burrumbeet Racecourse near Ballarat. Sentencing him, the judge, Sir Joseph Hood, remarked that Taylor was now a confirmed criminal, but in fact this was his one and only conviction of any substance. Over the years, with a mixture of false alibis, bribed and threatened witnesses, on charges of murder, harbouring, robbery and assault, he would almost always avoid conviction.

By August 1910, and well out of his apprenticeship, Taylor was indulging in a spot of blackmail, something to which he turned his hand throughout his life. His first recorded victim was an abortionist. When she did not pay him sufficient money he reported her to the police. She received five years and was discharged a broken woman in December 1913. By then he was a thoroughly vicious standover man. If a potential victim heard 'Squizzy Taylor has sent for a twenty' then twenty pounds was handed over without protest—at least an audible one.

With a series of girls (including the long-serving Dolly Grey; Lena Carr; and Mollie Jarvie, known as the 'Decoy Duck'), he worked what was known as the ginger game. Once the male victim had been taken to a hotel room and the 'Duck' or another girl was down to her underwear, in burst one of Taylor's team as the irate husband, brother or uncle. A variant of the game was that, once the target was in bed, a jimmer or lurker would emerge from a cupboard and steal the punter's wallet. He and another man would then bang on the door and the girl would advise the man to leave by another door or window. They rarely returned for their wallets. Even at this relatively early stage of his career Taylor had learned that he need not be at risk at the actual sharp end of the crime to earn the money. A schemer and putter-up, he almost literally made the bullets for someone else to fire.

Taylor was moving into bigger (if not always better) things and he was suspected of, but never charged with, the murder in January 1913 of a commercial traveller, Arthur Trotter, who was robbed of 215 pounds in the bedroom of his home at 405 George Street, Fitzroy. Trotter had been followed when he returned late one evening and clearly there was inside information. The robbers knew Trotter brought money home with him and also where the light switches were in the rooms. Bravely Trotter swung a punch at his attacker but, with Taylor hanging back, Harold 'Bush' Thompson shot him in the face. The police identified the fingerprint of Thompson on a window sill. The development of the science, begun in Europe and South America in the late nineteenth century, was still by no means perfect. Somehow the print, initially identified against one taken in Adelaide, did not tally with one taken while Thompson was awaiting trial. Thompson's girlfriend Flossie provided an alibi and the widowed Mrs Trotter was no longer so confident in her identification. After four hours' retirement, the jury acquitted Thompson.

In 1914 Taylor was in hiding in Adelaide, where he had moved with Dolly Grey, at that time his temporary de facto. She was living off the kindness of John Conlon and handing the money from him over to Taylor. Eventually Conlon twigged what was happening and began to threaten Dolly. She promptly applied to have him bound over. It was a question of the gang's all here because in cross-examination she admitted that both of Taylor's henchmen, Snowy Cutmore and stocky Henry Stokes, had visited her at her Adelaide Street address, then not one of the better parts of the city. 'She lives in a locality that is not select; but even persons living in localities of that kind are entitled to the protection of the court,' her lawyer W. A. Rollison told the court. (Many might have thought that those in the worst addresses needed the most protection.) Conlon was bound over in the sum of 100 pounds and ordered to pay costs of four pounds.

It is not clear whether Taylor was present at the shooting of Constable David McGrath, at the Melbourne Trades Hall in 1915, but he was certainly involved in the aftermath. On 1 October John Jackson, Richard Buckley and Alexander Ward burgled the Trades Hall, stealing thirty pounds from the safe. In a bungled police raid a passage light was switched on, leaving Constable McGrath exposed. Twenty-six shots were fired and McGrath was killed. Jackson, who claimed he had fired in self defence, was convicted at the first trial and hanged; but, with Taylor's interference, two juries disagreed over Ward, and also Buckley whose defence was that he had merely fired in the air as a warning. Finally on the third trial they were convicted of committing a felony and Ward and Buckley received five and six years' hard labour respectively. After his release Buckley became a Taylor stalwart.

There is no doubt, however, that on 29 February 1916 Taylor and another of his gang, John Williamson, hired a taxi driver, William Patrick Harries, for a drive in the country on which they took false number plates, suitcases and spectacles as a disguise. The intention was to rob an employee of a bank in Bulleen. It seems that Harries would not go along with their plan and, for his lack of co-operation, was shot. That morning his body was found inside his cab covered with a blanket. There was a partly dug grave nearby, and false moustaches, dungarees, spirit gum and glasses were found not much further away at a waterhole. There were good descriptions of the two men by three witnesses.

Nothing was too big or too small for Taylor. Within days he and Williamson were arrested at Flemington Racecourse for 'being without means'. Now, with Taylor in custody, witnesses to the murder came forward and it was a short step to a charge.

At the trial in April, the three witnesses who had seen the pair with Harries by the waterhole and in the taxi were in retreat and failed to make the necessary identification. Taylor had managed to get at them and he also produced an alibi. He was, however, temporarily inconvenienced when he was found guilty on the vagrancy charge and sentenced to twelve months' imprisonment. Within months of his release he was convicted of a warehouse break-in and received thirty days.

Another member of Taylor's team was Angus Murray, born Henry James Donnelly in Adelaide in 1882. By the time he was twenty-one Murray had not only burgled the home of the Chief Justice, Sir Samuel Way, but he had also robbed the State Governor at Government House, collecting seven years' hard labour. He escaped from the fearsome Yatala Stockade prison and was not recaptured for a year. His success as an escaper was not reflected in his intelligence, for after a number of successful burglaries he boasted to the newspapers, giving details of how he had executed the jobs, something which simply led to a further sentence. He does, however, seem to have had some good points. While in prison in Fremantle he met up with Robert David Bennett, who was serving a life sentence and had received nine lashes of the cat for the rape of a young girl whom he had infected with venereal disease. Bennett continually maintained his innocence and on his release Murray paid to have his claim investigated and also left money with the Salvation Army to pay his fare to join him in Melbourne where in 1916 he had teamed up with Taylor.

In September the next year Murray, Bennett and Taylor robbed the Middle Park Branch of the ES&A Bank. Murray was to go into the bank, Bennett was to be the getaway driver and Taylor took the role of observer and organiser. In theory it was an easy raid but while Murray was rifling the safe a messenger from another bank arrived, knocked and, getting no reply, looked through the letterbox. The next day the police caught Murray and Bennett in the local post office in the process of posting 380 pounds to Sydney. In October they each received fifteen years with hard labour. Naturally Taylor was never charged. Bennett served most of his term but Murray's confidence in him was sadly misplaced. After his release Bennett was hanged in September 1932 for the rape of a four-year-old girl.

* * *

By the end of the Great War, Australia had instituted licensing arrangements which would provide a source of income for organised crime for the next sixty years. To prevent excessive drinking, hotels were closed at 6 p.m. and in consequence what was known as the sly-grog market opened up. Taylor was able to organise protection for the grog shops and supply them with stolen liquor.

Now he was expanding his organisation. In July 1918 diamond rings worth 2000 pounds disappeared from Kilpatricks, a leading Melbourne jeweller's. In a simple but efficient diversion an accomplice returned a ring to the shop, bought something more expensive, handed a banknote which required change and left with a companion who snatched a tray of jewellery. When the assistant returned with the change he found himself padlocked in the shop. This time Matthew Daley and Snowy Cutmore were Taylor's partners in the raid and, in keeping with his double dealing, he arranged that Daley should be the fall-guy. He was sent to a Henry Collins in Sydney to sell some of the jewellery and the police were informed. Word was sent to Cutmore that Daley had been betrayed and, instead of trying to sell his own share, Cutmore gave it to a friend who returned with it to Melbourne.

By the time the trial took place it turned out that Collins was in fact none other than Taylor's henchman Henry Stokes, now a prosecution witness. Stokes, a one-time horse dealer and bookmaker living in Mary Street, Richmond, is described as bulldog-faced and short, with iron-grey hair. He began life as a store clerk before becoming a clerk in a two-up school. By World War I he had progressed to running the biggest of these schools in Melbourne, eventually taking the game from backyard gambling sheds to somewhere society would go when out slumming. After the Kilpatrick raid Stokes and Taylor were certainly long-time loose associates, if not formal partners, with Taylor providing protection for Stokes's gambling in return for an investment in his own grog shops.

Daley, however, was unexpectedly found not guilty and Stokes and Taylor were attacked as they left the court. There is a story that both were tried in an unofficial underworld court and themselves acquitted.

What followed became known as the Fitzroy Vendetta, a feud that lasted over two years from 1918. It began when Taylor employed his brothel-keeping girlfriend, Dolly Grey, who ran a house in Little Lonsdale Street, to spy on the organisation of 'Long' Harry Slater.

After his first conviction in 1910 for larceny from the person, for which he received eighteen months, Slater had gone to the United States where, under the name of Henning Campbell, he beat a vagrancy charge before being convicted of burglary and deported. Now Slater was setting himself up as a serious rival to, and nuisance for, Stokes and Taylor. They wished to find out how the land lay and Dolly was deputed to make the reconnaissance.

Unfortunately for her (and indeed almost everyone else), Dolly the spy, overcome by drink, fell asleep in Ted's, in Little Napier Street, Fitzroy, owned by the former boxer and now two-up school proprietor Ted Whiting. When she awoke she found she had been stripped of her furs and jewellery and left half-naked on the sofa. Taylor and Henry Stokes now took on the Slater operation in a protracted war. Within a matter of weeks five of those thought to be responsible had been either shot or beaten.

In February 1919 Ted Whiting was shot six times in the head at his home in Webb Street and the next day his house was fired on. Amazingly he survived. Taylor then attempted to organise a peace, travelling to Fitzroy to do so. He failed when, on 6 May, during the negotiations, a passer-by, Francis Counsel, was shot in the neck.

Two days later, Slater and Frederick Thorpe were charged with the attempted murder of one Albert Lewis and had been committed for trial charged with the attempted murder of a Constable Cooper. There had been a series of police raids that week and Whiting was charged with keeping a house frequented by reputed thieves.

On 12 May, Stokes shot Slater at Little Collins Street near the corner of Royal Lane. Asked his name, he swore at the officers and said 'Get me some brandy.' Slater was arrested and Taylor turned up to try (unsuccessfully at first) to get bail for him. A month later Slater was out of hospital and on 17 June, in a truculent mood, refused to say anything about the shooting. For his troubles he was remanded in custody. By July he had been acquitted of shooting at Constable Cooper and his memory of events had improved slightly. He could recall fighting and being shot but not by whom.

In July 1921 Stokes and Albert McDonald shot at Ted Whiting in George Street, Fitzroy. This time he rather unsportingly went to the police. The pair were charged with attempted murder and McDonald with shooting at a police officer. Most of it blew over. Whiting had had a chance to think things over and could make no proper identification. The charge of shooting at a police officer was dropped and all that was left was possessing a firearm without authority.

Defended by T. C. Brennan, Stokes said he had never carried a revolver since the Slater affair, but he was found guilty by the magistrate. McDonald, a decorated digger who had received the Croix de Guerre, was given one month's suspended sentence. In September 1921 Stokes received six months. Slater left for Sydney and for the next few years Squizzy Taylor was the apparent new king of the Melbourne underworld. The likelihood is that the true mastermind was the far more intelligent Stokes, always happy to sit away from the spotlight.

* * *

Taylor, described as having a dark complexion and piercing eyes, dressed fashionably, usually wearing a bowler hat and an enormous diamond tiepin and carrying a silver-topped walking cane. It was thought that he was also now involved in the cocaine trade. But this did not mean he devoted all his time to it. In June 1921 he was caught in a warehouse next to a pile of fur coats. His initial explanation was that he had simply walked in off the street, later elaborated to being chased into the shop by a rival, Louis 'The Count' Stirling, who generally worked as a commission agent and at the 'shoddy drop'. Why The Count had chased him to the third floor and left him beside a pile of fur coats was never satisfactorily explained.

Taylor was charged with breaking and entering and, bailed to appear in August at General Sessions, he promptly absconded his 300 pounds' bail. For a year, he continued his career as safebreaker, thief and robber of successful gamblers. In a style reminiscent of that more famous rogue Ned Kelly, he also found time to write to the papers and when the Melbourne *Herald* asked in an article where he was, he replied, 'I cannot understand what all this bull is about.' Other letters said he would surrender when he had completed some outstanding business and would be pleased to take whatever punishment was coming to him. For a time Taylor became a folk hero. During his year on the run he only left Melbourne to go to the seaside at Frankston, moving about the city in disguise, sometimes as a schoolboy.

In May 1920 he had married a waitress, Irene Lorna Kelly, at the Congregational Church, Fitzroy. He and Lorna first lived at a boarding house in Epsom Road, close to Flemington Racecourse, then he paid 1100 pounds for a house in Station Street, Caulfield, within spitting distance of the Caulfield Racecourse. They had two children—a son Leslie; and a daughter June, who died aged seven months—but the marriage did not last, partly because he was still involved with Mollie Jarvie and Dolly Grey but particularly because he took up with a Miss Ida Pender whom he had met at the St Kilda Palais de Danse and by whom he later had a daughter, Gloria. At the time she met Taylor, Pender was working on the hosiery counter at Myer's. Lorna petitioned for divorce in February 1924 and Detective James Bruce gave evidence that when he had seen Taylor and Ida and asked him about his marriage the reply had been, 'Oh, Lorna is a fair-weather friend. I'm going to stick with Ida.' He had paid the estranged Lorna three pounds a week until before Christmas. Now she asked for a pound more but, as her lawyer freely admitted, no one knew exactly what Taylor had in the way of capital or income.

As for Ida Pender (known as 'Jazz Baby' or 'Babe'), the *Victoria Police Gazette* of 30 March 1922 described her as: 'Sixteen and a half years, 5'4" in height, medium build and active appearance, bobbed, brown hair and "shapely legs", "fond of jazzing and skating".' Perhaps the pictures of her do not do her justice because they make her look somewhat stout. A lively dresser, she could sometimes be seen wearing a silk top hat in the street. In a curious way Taylor seems to have been her Pygmalion. After a short time with him, out went the quirky dresses and with them her rough speech.

In March 1922 she was arrested for breaking into Rita Moore's shop in Flinders Street and stealing a georgette frock, five sponge cloth frocks and a number of blouses valued altogether at 221 pounds. It was, however, merely a police ruse to question her about Taylor. She remained staunch, laughing at the questions, until she was finally bailed with two sureties of 100 pounds. Four days later the charge was withdrawn.

When Taylor finally decided to surrender on 21 September 1922 he made sure he was dressed in his best and had notified the newspapers of his appearance at Russell Street Police Station. He was once more released on a personal bond, backed by Richard Loughnan, organiser of the Builders' Labourers Federation, and gave interviews saying that he had surrendered because his mother was ill and his friends were being continually pestered by the police.

While on bail he attended a race meeting at Caulfield and was promptly warned off. In another example of his spite and bravado, at 4 a.m. on 21 October, the night before the prestigious Caulfield Cup, he torched the Members Stand at the track, causing 9000 pounds worth of damage. Despite rewards totalling 1000 pounds and a free pardon to any accomplice who grassed, no charges were brought against him.

When Taylor was eventually tried for the fur warehouse offence he was acquitted and now he moved into big-time robberies—including one of 2750 pounds from the Victorian Railways payroll—in which the planning was done by Stokes, and Taylor was occasionally the getaway driver.

Some of the press and the public may have idolised him but Taylor was not wholly popular with his peers. Apart from anything else, he was now recognised as a dobber. Shortly after he had been re-bailed he was shot in the leg. He was also unpopular with the authorities. A racing film, *In Emergency Colours*, in which he was due to star as a jockey and of which several episodes were actually shot, was banned in Victoria as not being in the public interest. It was eventually released in Brisbane in 1925. The wife of Sir Arthur Stanley, former Governor of Victoria, had the mistaken idea that she could reform him. They met at the Menzies Hotel, as arranged by a social worker. He promised to mend his ways and later presented her with a silver jewel box inscribed 'To one who understands, from one misunderstood.'

Any gang has to have a tame doctor to patch up wounds that there is no need for the police to know of, and Squizzy Taylor had the services of Dr Shirley Francis, whose son became a barrister and parliamentarian. Taylor had a holiday home between Ferntree Gully and Upwey and from time to time Dr Francis, who lived nearby, would be called on for his services. Taylor was apparently a good payer—always in cash—polite and, contrary to the opinion that he was a rat and an informer, Francis thought him brave and indeed rather admired him.

* * *

Although Taylor lived for a number of years after the 1923 robbery of the Commercial Bank, it marked the beginning of the end of his reign. In October, Angus Murray and long-time stalwart Richard Buckley, working on a plan devised by Taylor, robbed Thomas Berriman as he left the bank at Glenferrie Station, Hawthorn, carrying a briefcase containing 1851 pounds. Things went disastrously wrong.

Taylor had long been thinking of an escape for Murray, still serving his sentence for the Middle Park bank. On 24 August 1923 Murray made his break. A rope with a hook as well as a fretsaw and money had been smuggled into the prison and he cut through the bars to his cell and hooked the rope to the outside wall. Although he touched an alarm wire, he managed to get away; and, carrying a travelling rug and a small brown case, he was off to a safe house. The police thought he would return to Melbourne and roadblocks were set up, but instead he remained at Geelong for a week before he was driven to the city.

Murray had been at large for less than two months when he and the lame Buckley robbed Berriman as he followed his usual Monday routine, taking a bag of notes to Glenferrie Station, something he had done at 11 a.m. for the previous six weeks. The plan was simple. Berriman would be attacked as he walked up the ramp to the platform. The bag, together with any gun he was carrying, would be snatched and Murray and Buckley would jump into the waiting car. The driver was to be Taylor but, when it came to it, he preferred to skulk outside the police headquarters in Russell Street, so setting up a cast iron alibi.

Buckley, now sixty years old and with a long record of violence, was on parole at the time of the robbery. Over the years he had regularly been placed in solitary confinement, and for one earlier robbery—of which he claimed to be innocent—he had received the lash. He walked with a limp, something he blamed on a beating by the police. It seems as if the pair had planned a simple snatch because, as Berriman came down the ramp, Buckley asked him if he could carry his bag and Berriman replied, 'No thank you, old man, I can carry it myself.'

When Buckley tried to take his bag, the brave if foolish Berriman refused to hand it over and was promptly shot. Murray helped Buckley as he limped along to the getaway car, from time to time turning and waving his revolver at pursuers. Two days after the robbery two women telephoned the police to say they had seen men burning a briefcase in a yard in Barkly Street, St Kilda. In the early hours of 11 October police broke through the front and back doors of the five roomed detached cottage. Taylor was in bed with Ida Pender and when the police called out, 'Hands up', Murray replied, 'They are up.' Of Buckley there was no trace.

Berriman had been taken to a private hospital, where he died on the morning of 21 October 1923. As he lay in bed he positively identified photographs of Buckley as the gunman and Murray as being with him. The coroner returned a verdict of wilful murder against both and, perhaps somewhat speculatively, a charge of accessory before the fact against Taylor.

The trial was scheduled for November but Murray wanted an adjournment to February. The police were happy because they thought it would give them more time to catch Buckley. But they feared Taylor would use the delay as grounds for bail, which he might put to good use. They were right. In November 1924 Taylor was granted bail with two sureties of 500 pounds and went to live at the Queensland Hotel, Bourke Street.

Taylor did at least have the courtesy to try to assist his former employee. Once more he attempted to have Murray rescued, first in October 1923 and, when that failed, again in January 1924. This time a warder, who was to be bribed with an offer of 250 pounds and seven pounds per week pension if he should be dismissed, told the police. They, in turn, seized a car outside the prison, arrested the four men in it, including Taylor's brother Thomas, and confiscated a rope ladder.

There were, however, suggestions that Taylor was not being wholly altruistic in his efforts to free Murray; it was thought he might crack and divulge details of the Melbourne underworld. *Truth* newspaper thought that, all in all, it was rather fortunate for Murray that the escape attempt had failed.

The trial was a foregone conclusion. On 22 February 1924, after a retirement of an hour and a half, the jury returned a verdict of murder and Murray was sentenced to death. His appeal was heard before the full court on 6 March. 'When death's wings fluttered over gloom of Criminal Court,' said *Truth* when it had previewed the trial. Now the wings flapped in earnest. Meanwhile the evidence—as opposed to suspicion—against Taylor was very thin indeed, relying on the fact that the pair had stayed in his home. On 3 March the charge was withdrawn.

Taylor, along with anti-hanging groups, tried to organise a reprieve for Murray and a petition signed by some 70000 people was presented. A march was organised and Taylor drove in an open car graciously receiving the tributes of the crowd who respectfully doffed their caps. He was with Ida Pender and their baby. *Truth* reported that he provided his handkerchief to be used as a nappy.

It all did Murray no good. Despite petitions and a last ditch attempt to show that he had a child who was a 'congenital idiot' and that his father, his uncle and an aunt had all committed suicide, the authorities did not believe this added up to his being of unsound mind. He behaved as well in the death cell as he had done on the outside, writing to the man—certainly not Taylor—who had financed his appeal and apologising for presuming on him. When he broke his dentures the prison doctor Clarence Godfrey offered to make him a replacement as a matter of urgency but, according to *Truth* or legend, Murray declined, saying, 'Doctor, do you really think it worthwhile?'

The thought of Murray in the death cell had not stopped the underworld continuing its daily or nightly business. Shootings continued apace. Archibald Fletcher was found shot in Exhibition Street in the early hours of the morning on 10 March, and ten days later another Taylor associate, Albert McDonald, also known as 'Kohman', was shot by a policeman. Taken to hospital, he went to the lavatory and promptly escaped through a window.

Murray was hanged in April 1924 in the Melbourne Gaol. He is reported to have said from the scaffold, 'Never in my life have I done anything to justify the penalty passed on me. I have tried to forgive those who have acted against me and I hope those I have injured will forgive me.' Australian criminals of those days tended to be reported as making similar speeches at their executions. When the noose was put over his head he is said to have added, 'Pull it tight.' Another version, said to have been obtained from the lips of the hangman himself, is that the words were 'Carry on, Dig, not too tight.' The hangman, who had served in the First AIF and now worked as an engineer, was apparently paid ten pounds. It was a good day for him. He received an extra seven shillings for a flogging that he carried out in the afternoon. His regular job paid two pounds nine shillings a week.

Outside, a mixed crowd of recalcitrants presented a surly front to the police (foot and mounted), curious bystanders and abolitionists who sang hymns. 'As a distant clock chimed out the tenth hour an enfeebled old man led the gathering in the Lord's Prayer,' observed *The Age*. *Truth* was thoroughly sanctimonious:

> In the Great Beyond there is a whole army of men who have gone forth from the earth through the gibbet and the gallows. Angus Murray will not lack for company of this land.

Now it thought he had been game:

> So he died
> Give him his due
> Poor, wretched, wayward, careless dangerous
> criminal Angus Murray knew how to die.

In June 1924 all four men, along with Taylor (who was defended by the great lawyer T. C. Brennan), were acquitted of conspiracy to spring Murray. Taylor gave a virtuoso defence claiming he was being hounded by the police: 'I receive no credit for my good deeds to say nothing of the charitable institutions I have assisted and the woman I tried to save recently and the Soldier Boys I got jobs for.'

Murray would be the last criminal to be hanged in Melbourne Gaol—unless Buckley could be found quickly. He was not. There had already been suggestions that Buckley was in permanent smoke and, if he was not, in theory it should have been easy to spot him for he was covered in tattoos—a cross on his right forearm, a dancing girl with wreath on his lower inside right arm, a woman's head on his inside right upper arm, a coat of arms was on his inside left lower arm and a vase of flowers on the inside upper left. But he must have kept his sleeves down. Over the years there were reported sightings of him in the United States, in Europe and in other states of Australia. One story had him dying in London under the name of Henry Freeman, an early alias.

In fact Buckley never travelled very far. When he was arrested in 1930 he had been living in Richmond and then Collingwood, before moving to Bowen Street, Ascot Vale, with his granddaughter, Pat, taking occasional exercise at night dressed as a woman. There have been stories that he was supported by John Wren over the years but there seems to be little if any foundation to these rumours. There was now a Labor government in office and Buckley's death sentence was commuted to one of life imprisonment. He was released in 1946 suffering from gout and not expected to survive more than a few months. He surprised everyone and died aged eighty-nine on 15 September 1953.

* * *

Murray or no Murray, life had to go on, as did the weekly round of thefts and robberies. And Taylor was just as tricky as before. In June he, along with his brother Tom, Charles 'Prat-in' Allsop and a man named Davis, held up the players in a card game at a barber's shop in Glenhuntly, stealing cash and jewellery. One of the players, the racehorse trainer Charlie Caylock, recognised Allsop and arrests followed. Then came a series of delicate negotiations. Some of the players wanted the return of the jewellery, which had sentimental value. Caylock declined the 100 pounds he was offered not to go through with the identification and it was arranged, at a meeting between him and Taylor, that the jewellery would be returned if he watered down his evidence. The trial was duly stopped but Taylor never returned the jewellery, saying that Ida Pender had become rather attached to it. Charlie Caylock was wrongly named in a newspaper as a defendant and received 800 pounds in libel damages. The error was repeated in a number of other papers and in turn he sued them.

After the hanging of Murray, Taylor lost much of his power in the underworld. A month later he killed a woman in a hit-and-run accident on St Kilda Road. He was acquitted of intimidating the witnesses but later served six months for harbouring Murray. There were also stories that he had been kidnapping young girls and injecting them with cocaine before turning them out to deal the drug on his behalf.

While Taylor was serving his six months, Ida went out dancing with a young bookmaker back at St Kilda's Palais de Danse. On his release Taylor turned the liaison to his advantage by blackmailing the man. In 1925 he tried to buy Gorry's, a tobacconist and hairdresser's, but the deal fell through when it was discovered who the purchaser would be. It was thought he had continued to be a police informer and now there were also rivals for his empire and for control of the burgeoning and lucrative cocaine trade. He was almost certainly involved in the abduction of one young woman, who was returned to her family a week later in a dazed state after she had been injected with drugs. There were also burglaries, one target being a jewellery shop in Inkerman Street, at which a young girl was shot, and another being the Brighton Yacht Club, which was done over twice.

In June 1927 another of Taylor's henchmen, Norman Bruhn, was shot dead in Sydney and then, in late October, Snowy Cutmore, now Taylor's rival, returned to Melbourne, ostensibly to pick up a horse. One evening Cutmore, who was known to be violent in drink (it was said he had once branded a girl with a hot iron), was imbibing heavily at a brothel in St Kilda which was under the temporary protection of Taylor. Cutmore smashed the premises and, pulling a young girl out of bed, stripped her naked before turning her onto the street. It was not something that Taylor, even in decline, could allow to go unpunished. The pair met at Richmond Racecourse on 26 October where there were high words and in the afternoon Cutmore was warned off the course for life.

Things escalated the next afternoon. As far as can be pieced together from the very mixed statements by witnesses, Taylor and two men took a cab, driven by John Hall, outside the Melbourne Hospital. From there they toured the hotels in Carlton—'getting Dutch courage', suggested Cutmore's uncle, Frank McLaughlin—until at six o'clock they told the driver to stop in Barkly Street, Fitzroy, near Cutmore's house. In the house was Mrs Bridget Cutmore senior, her son John, a tenant John 'Scotty' King (who sensibly told the police he was in bed asleep) and Cutmore (who was also in bed, said to be suffering from a sudden attack of bronchitis and influenza).

Describing the scene of the shooting, *Truth* was at its most lyrical, anxious to show its readers that the mothers of even top standover men did not live in palaces:

A wan light, even on the brightest day, filters through the rickety window to light the room where the death duel took place …

A tiny room, crowded with furniture, its pale pink walls showing dingy and grotesque … its furniture cheap and tawdry … family photographs, cheap fantastic vases, and ornaments litter the mantelpiece while, on a small table in the corner, old musty books jostle each other.

Taylor walked in and shot Cutmore who, with a pistol under the sheets, returned the fire. Between them they fired fourteen times. Cutmore died on the bed, shot through the right lung. Mrs Cutmore ran into the room and was shot in the shoulder. Taylor then staggered out to be taken to St Vincent's Hospital. One man travelled in the cab with him until, at the corner of Brunswick and Johnston streets, he told the driver, 'Here, you do the rest on your own' and jumped out. Taylor, like so many of the Melbourne underworld before and after him, died at St Vincent's.

When reporters from *Truth* went to see Cutmore's widow, there was Taylor's old enemy Henry Slater, back from his Sydney exile, lounging 'moodily about the house'. Cutmore's widow was quick to let it be known that the first wreath had come from the parents of the late Norman Bruhn—which, she said, showed they did not believe her husband had anything to do with his recent shooting.

There are several theories about the details of the shoot-out at Cutmore's home. One is that Cutmore was killed by Sydney criminals over the death of Bruhn; fortuitously Taylor happened to be there and was killed at the same time. Another is that somehow Cutmore shot Taylor first and then was shot by Taylor's companion. If this version is correct it was almost certainly set up by Henry Stokes who by now realised that Taylor was an untrustworthy little monster who might turn on him at any given moment. In any event, Bridget Cutmore was unable to help the police apart from saying she had heard a quarrel. A further complication to the official version is that several Eibar 'Destroyer' .32 calibre bullets of the type which killed Taylor were found under a picket fence some 200 yards from the house. The second man with Taylor had run out of the back of the house, thrown away Cutmore's gun and then told a Dr McCutcheon of Rathdowne Street that he was needed. Taylor's gun was found on him at the hospital.

There is a third theory: that Cutmore's mother, seeing Taylor shoot Cutmore, took a gun and killed him. It shows the gossip and rumour which surrounded the killing. It could also have been Leslie Walkerden.

In the days before Squizzy Taylor's funeral some of the surviving Bruhn brothers had stood outside the Bookmakers' Club soliciting donations. 'I've put you down for 50 pounds,' said one of them to Charlie Caylock, at which Caylock spat 'I'll give you 50 pounds for a kick at his coffin.' Taylor's funeral from 18 Darlington Parade on Richmond Hill was watched by a crowd of thousands. His funeral service took place at St James's Congregational Church, Fitzroy, and he was buried at Brighton Cemetery. Some were not prepared to condemn Taylor out of hand. 'He was a criminal admittedly but he had a very soft-hearted streak, too,' said one local, Ruby Kane. Taylor's brain was reputedly sent for examination where, according to *Smith's Weekly* of 3 November 1927, it showed the same kink as that of Kaiser Wilhelm II.

Ida Pender was twenty-two years old when Taylor died. Always a keen dancer, she returned to be a regular at the St Kilda Palais de Danse. Later she met and married the dancer Mickey Powell but the marriage ended in divorce.

One of the highest profile Melbourne crime families of their time, the Bruhns, were forever in and out of difficulties during this period. In January 1929 Mona Ryan was shot in Nicholson Street, North Carlton. She told the police she had been walking with her landlady Mrs Agnes Genoa, née Bruhn, about 5 p.m. when Genoa heard what she thought was a car backfire. Mona Ryan stumbled but said nothing. They went back to the house where she collapsed, wounded, on the floor. Roy Bruhn, then twenty-four, was charged and alleged to have admitted the shooting.

Of course the real story was quite different. She had not been shot in the street. Ryan and Bruhn had been in her room when they quarrelled and he shot her. At the trial she maintained there had been three men whom she had just met in a hotel and she did not know which one had shot her. On 19 April, Bruhn was triumphantly acquitted and the unfortunate Ryan received a month's imprisonment for contempt of court. In October 1930 Roy Bruhn was shot in the chest in Melbourne. Again it was never clear what had brought this about but in all probability the circumstance was a dispute over the proceeds of a robbery the previous week. Bruhn's first words to the police were, 'I've got it. I'll take it with me.' Later he said he had heard a noise at the back of the house and had been shot as he went to investigate. Since the gun had been pressed against his chest, leaving powder burns, the police said they were not pursuing that particular line of inquiry. Bruhn survived.

That year another of the Bruhn brothers, William George, along with George Lees and George Ferguson, was charged with possessing gelignite. In the early hours of 4 December 1930 they jumped from a goods train travelling from Geelong to Ballarat but a waiting car had been disabled by the police.

* * *

Whether or not Henry Stokes had arranged the shooting of Squizzy Taylor, he now assumed the mantle of undisputed king of the Victorian underworld, a position he would hold for nearly forty years. Naturally enough there were some hiccups.

In December 1928 the premises of one of his main rivals, the Greek Club in Lonsdale Street, was blown up and sentences of up to fifteen years were handed out. The evidence against Timothy O'Connell, Norman McIver and Francis Delaney was not that strong. They were seen together around 9.40 p.m. when the club was bombed. McIver then left them and reappeared with a parcel for O'Connell. They again separated and O'Connell and a man thought to be Delaney were seen to run out of the club shortly before the explosion. Their appeals were heard by the full court, one of whose members had been the trial judge. One judge thought the evidence against McIver was insufficient but he was out-voted by his colleagues. Convictions and sentences were upheld.

In July 1929 Stokes was charged with conspiring to pervert the course of justice over the case. It was alleged he had conspired with a Madge Vaughan to produce perjured evidence in the appeals of the three men. Stokes was put on trial with Norman McIver and Squizzy's brother Thomas Taylor, and Vaughan gave evidence that Stokes had met her in Lonsdale Street and afterwards she had gone to a flat in East Melbourne. Stokes had let her in and she had had a discussion with Taylor and Norman McIver which would have cleared the men of the Greek Club bombing. She was not believed.

Madge Vaughan reappeared shortly afterwards, this time when she brought an action for libel against the magazine *Smith's Weekly*. The paper had claimed she was one of the most notorious women of the Melbourne underworld. Her associate, Snowy Jenkins, was said to be in smoke and she had taken up with the French boxer Fernand Quendroux who had served time for robbery and assault in Queensland. *Smith's Weekly* also claimed something she denied: that she was a licensed 'public woman' in Brisbane.

In January 1932 Stokes was shot but, declining police assistance, said he would take care of matters himself. In 1935 he put together an audacious robbery from the Commonwealth Bank at Ballarat. Stokes approached a young constable, Rex Byrne, with the proposition that he would receive 10000 pounds—10 per cent of the estimated take—if he arranged that neither he nor any other officer was near the bank on the night when Stokes and his partners broke in. Byrne reported the matter to his superiors and Stokes and his crew just managed to avoid being caught red-handed. They escaped, dumping the oxy-acetylene cutters near Melton, and high-tailed it back to Melbourne where they were arrested. Stokes was charged with conspiracy and received four years.

The great turnaround in his fortunes came after he had completed his sentence. In 1938, he promoted Australia's first illegal casino. It must be a matter of speculation which bank financed the enterprise but it was based on the American concept of the floating casino. The *Alvina*, originally a gift from Edward, Prince of Wales, to the courtesan Lily Langtry—complete with hand-carved oak panels and deep pile carpets—sailed nightly around Port Phillip Bay. In December 1938 Stokes was fined 150 pounds after a raid by the gaming squad and from then on the *Alvina* had a marked deck, so to speak.

Stokes had an immediate solution. The next year he opened his first baccarat club, the Ace of Clubs, on the first floor of 2–7 Elizabeth Street near Flinders Street. The entrance to the building was a small, blue-painted iron gate. Up two flights of stairs, the club was a heavily carpeted room with eight dummy tables with cards scattered on them, in case of a raid, and the baccarat table itself. There could be up to 150 fashionably dressed men and women in the club at any time.

There was naturally competition but once again Stokes showed his business acumen. Instead of waging war, Stokes engineered an amalgamation with his rivals. From then on the profits were enormous. The weekly take was more than $60 000 in today's money.

Exports

3

The earliest of the travelling Australian criminals—escapees and ticket of leave men—arrived in San Francisco in the mid-1800s, shortly after the discovery of gold. They soon colonised the waterfront, ironically known as Sydney Town. Collectively they were referred to as the Sydney Ducks and when a particularly unattractive robbery was committed it was said 'the Sydney Ducks are cackling on the pond'. Once installed they turned—returned is perhaps a better word—their hands to traditional forms of crime, many of which had seen them transported in the first place. Robbery and prostitution flourished, with the Ducks' women selling themselves for an ounce or two of gold and setting up the unsuspecting punters to be robbed. One of the Ducks' better tricks was to start a fire: with the prevailing north-east winds, it would sweep through the city and they would then loot shops in the aftermath. Because of the direction of the wind, Sydney Town was left unaffected. It was a stunt pulled six times within two years between December 1849 and June 1851.

The Sydney Ducks finally broke up when two of them, Samuel Whittaker and Robert McKenzie, were arrested for arson and robbery and were hanged by the Vigilance Committee—established to bring law and order to what was an increasingly violent city—in August 1851. The remaining Ducks either left for Sacramento and an easier life or ran their dance halls, saloons and brothels with rather more propriety.

High-class confidence tricksters have been a prime Australian export over the years. Generally, though, in the century after the Sydney Ducks, they travelled as individuals, if necessary teaming up with other Australians or home-based criminals when they arrived. An early expatriate conman who worked the London scene was William Charles 'Bludger Bill' Warren. He had been convicted of false pretences at Sydney Quarter Sessions in February 1901. In England he pulled off a variety of confidence tricks, including taking money to bet on horse racing. He would promptly disappear with the cash and, when found, would either say quite correctly the horse had lost or, if it had won, plead a defence under the Gaming Acts which made gambling debts irrecoverable at law. In 1912, posing as Mr Fairie, owner of the Ascot Gold Cup winner Aleppo, he cleared 12000 pounds.

The end of this particular trick came in 1921 when a bookmaker was awarded 15000 pounds against Warren on the grounds that he had fraudulently obtained the money. A great number of other actions were pending and when his Australian friends Robert Bradshaw (known as Matthew Biggar), Charles McNally and Alfred Dean were arrested over a game of Anzac Poker, Warren decamped. Between them McNally and Dean were said to have cleared over 90000 pounds in crooked card games and racecourse swindles. They each received five years at the Central Criminal Court.

Warren prudently went to Brussels and then France, setting up on the Riviera. Before he left, there had been a number of other coups in London, including the defrauding of a Jamaican plantation owner. He had also set up home with a confidence trickster named Dora, posing as his wife; the pair obtained loans from moneylenders and had been buying goods on extended credit. There was also the ginger game and crooked poker to be played. Left behind in England, Dora received eighteen months' imprisonment.

In early 1923 two Australians were arrested in Paris after relieving an American of 4000 francs. Warren drove from Monte Carlo to Paris to try to assist them and was promptly arrested at the Porte d'Orléans, suspected of being the head of a gang of international swindlers. He claimed mistaken identity but an Englishman was brought to Paris and picked him out as having swindled him out of 23000 pounds over a race at Longchamps. When he was arrested Warren was said to have a staggering 800000 pounds in cash and jewellery hidden in his Rolls-Royce. He received five years.

Another gang of London-based confidence tricksters of the time was led by two Australians, Patrick O'Riley (known as 'Australian Paddy') and his second lieutenant Walter Macdonald (known as 'Australian Mac'). Macdonald earned his first conviction in England at the age of twenty-six and, by the time he joined O'Riley in 1901, he had seven more convictions in Australia. With these two as bait were the girls 'Blonde Alice' — often said to be the notorious 'Chicago May' Sharpe but really 'Blonde Alice' Smith who had been working the rackets for many years — and Clara Whiteley, 'The Woman with the Diamond Eyes'. In 1921 the gang planned the theft at Dover Station of the dressing case of the heiress Ruby Wertheimer. They expected to clear 50 000 pounds in jewellery but they abandoned her case when they found it contained only 260 pounds. This led to Macdonald's arrest for card sharping for which he received nine months.

Daniel John Mulaney was yet another Australian conman and putter-up working London in the first years of the twentieth century. It was said no one looked less like a conman than he did, with his kiss curl of straw coloured hair, bulbous pock-marked nose and waddling gait. In 1908, along with two other Australians, he planned not only to steal the Ascot Gold Cup but also two others at the Ascot race meeting. He was thwarted when, absolutely out of the blue, another man walked up to the cup, removed it from its pedestal and carried it away. The next year Mulaney was sentenced to five years for distributing the proceeds resulting from a jewel theft at the Café Monaco in Regent Street. Other long sentences followed and he received four years at the Old Bailey in November 1923. A broken man, he died of cancer in a Marylebone hospital shortly after World War II. He was well regarded by his fellows, including the English criminal Val Davis who wrote of him:

> In fifty years of profligate living he had committed no hurt on a defenceless person or robbed those who could ill afford the loss. He was a friend to all beggars, buskers and impecunious crooks. To him 'honour among thieves' was a ritual — faithfully observed in his half-century of ill-going.

Undoubtedly, one of the most talented of the Australian criminals in England after World War I was James or George William McCraig, or Enwright, known as 'The Human Fly' when he worked in the United States and 'The Wizard of the West End' in London. It was his ability to scale the highest and most inaccessible of buildings which earned him his nickname. In 1925 McCraig won a bet by climbing the façade of the Home Office. 'The absolute king of his craft' thought the Sunday newspaper *Empire News*.

McCraig was born in Tasmania, supposedly the son of a wealthy cattle dealer, and worked as a jockey before going to the United States in 1919 where he was arrested in May that year. He came to England and received nine months' imprisonment at Marlborough Street Police Court after an attempted burglary of a jeweller's shop in Piccadilly Circus. On his release he returned to New York where he worked as a stuntman. After another arrest in California he escaped from San Quentin and it was back to England.

The noted English cat burglar Ruby Sparks worked with and thought a great deal of him, saying:

> there's one thing Australians such as Georgie McCraig and Cockneys like me share—we can be proper villains but almost never do you find an Australian nor a Cockney playing ponce or gigolo—they're as rare as Jewish sailors.

In June 1924 the pair managed to steal the fabulous jewel collection of the Wehrner family from their house in London's Piccadilly. The problem for them was that the police immediately circulated a detailed list of the stolen jewellery and it became impossible to fence. An arrangement was made between McCraig, the police and the insurers that he would return the jewellery in exchange for immunity and a share of the reward money. According to Sparks, the Human Fly was nevertheless well satisfied with his work.

The money did not last long and the following June a housemaid found McCraig asleep on the sofa in a house in Clarendon Place. When she questioned him he replied that he had been invited in by a lady. The housemaid went to make enquiries and McCraig threw himself out of the window. Falling ten metres, he broke his right leg and four toes. In hospital a friend brought him in clothes, boots and a stick, and out he limped. He was caught at Croydon Airport as he was about to board a plane for Paris. Perhaps unexpectedly he was found not guilty at his trial in September 1925. He was almost immediately re-arrested and found guilty of an attempted burglary at Grosvenor Hotel, Victoria, but his luck held. In October that year the Court of Appeal quashed his three year sentence.

In February 1926 he was sentenced to nine months as an incorrigible rogue after being seen on the fire escape of the Hyde Park Hotel.

He ran away but this time was caught. 'There is no building he would not tackle,' said Detective Sergeant Baker admiringly. McCraig's career was now downhill and he was sentenced to two months' hard labour in April 1928. Given bail pending an appeal, he again promptly disappeared. 'To America,' said the police. Not really. He was found in London on 11 May. This time his appeal was dismissed. Three years later he turned up with the Americans James Hynes—who claimed he had been the bodyguard of 'Little Augie' Orgen in the Prohibition Wars in the United States—and Harry Kleintz in Newcastle in north-east England where in June 1928 they all received five years after being found burgling a jeweller's.

The Human Fly was still working in the mid-1930s when he was dobbed in before he burgled Sir Richard Meller's home in Mitcham, Surrey. In January 1936, under the name George Enwright and described as 'a master criminal', he received a three year sentence at the Central Criminal Court. In May 1939 McCraig, then aged forty-five, received another four years for receiving two suitcases.

* * *

Another Australian who worked in England shortly after World War I was Denny Delaney who specialised in smash and grab raids. Before he went to England he had served sentences in Australia, the United States and South Africa. Now he introduced a relay system of getaway cars in a robbery and of using women as 'spotters' and 'stalls'—the former reconnoitred the premises and the latter diverted the assistants. A charming man who had his women associates billing and cooing over him—he tended to call them 'Sweetie-Pie' and 'Ducksy-Wucksy'—he worked out of Soho with the London criminal Reggie Roberts. One of his more spectacular robberies was a wage snatch at Euston Station and a second was when he organised a raid on a furrier's in the West End. Part of the proceeds was a dressmaker's dummy which, at a crucial moment in the chase, was thrown into the path of the police car. The driver naturally did not wish to run over what appeared to be a naked woman and swerved to avoid the body, so giving Roberts and Delaney time to escape.

Billy Hill, a prominent London gang leader of the 1930s, also worked with an Australian pickpocket Norman Smith, known as 'Codmouth', whose hand he accidentally slashed. Smith took things badly, saying,

'I'm doomed, I'm doomed. I'll never be able to buzz another pocket.' It is good to be able to record that although it apparently took him some time to recover physically and psychologically, Smith continued his successful career.

In 1935 Scotland Yard published its *Illustrated Circular of Confidence Tricksters and Expert Criminals*. Of the 152 men listed—there were no women—fifty-seven were Australian-born. It was a trend that began after World War I. Among them was Thomas Bourke, who received three months with hard labour at Marylebone Police Court on 27 June 1929 for obtaining 200 pounds. Then, working with another Australian, James Casey, he immediately moved on to greater things, obtaining 15 000 pounds in a stocks and shares swindle on 5 May 1930, originating it in Lugano, Switzerland, and carrying it on to Paris. The victim is reported to have had a heart attack and died.

Of the 216 men listed in the updated 1947 version of the Scotland Yard circular, no less than sixty-eight were Australian-born. One of them, Harry Willis (known as 'The Tiger'), a man with ten aliases whose general role was as a businessman, had already headed home to Melbourne. He had last appeared at Bow Street, charged with supplying false particulars for a passport and was fined. Born in 1894 he had three more convictions in England and one in France to go with his five in Australia.

In July 1947 another on the list, a man named James Coates, was shot four times from behind in a children's playground at the corner of Union Street and Punt Road, Windsor, in Melbourne. Coates was a man who never forgot a grudge or remembered a favour and *Truth* judged him the most hated man in the far-flung Commonwealth. Information on his assailant was not forthcoming.

Horses were of interest to Coates. In his heyday he had owned the racehorse Polly Speck on which he wagered huge sums both in New South Wales (where he won) and in Victoria (where he lost it all). He was later warned off. Christened James Mann when he was born in Perth in 1901, he often went by the name of Mark Foy (rhyming slang for boy). He had claimed he was only a Mark Foy when he was caught by a steward rifling a cabin on a liner and the name stuck. In the early 1930s he attended a London school of deportment and manners.

In 1933 Coates had returned to Australia with some 70 000 pounds, the proceeds of two swindles, one involving Sir Michael Watson whom he had relieved of some 30 000 pounds in Paris in 1932. With Coates back in Australia, Frank Lyon, head of the Melbourne Consorting Squad, intended to make life difficult for him. He quite correctly believed that the cigar-smoking, smooth-talking Coates was involved in race fixing and warned him to stay away from the tracks. Coates took legal advice from Raymond Dunn, the barrister son of a police officer, telling him he had finished his life of crime and wanted to make a clean start. Dunn appealed to the Chief Commissioner of Police, Thomas Blamey, who overrode the objections of his experienced officer and decided Coates should be allowed to 'have a run'. It was a major misjudgement.

Back in London in March 1939 a Bow Street magistrate declined to order Coates's extradition to Switzerland where, in the name of Agnew, he and another man had relieved a Prince Jean Sapicha of some 13 000 pounds. The case turned on identification and Coates produced a statement from a businessman that, at the relevant time, he had been at the Melbourne Cup meeting. As was pointed out by his barrister, the colourful John Maude, even with a magic carpet he could not have been in Switzerland—if of course the alibi was genuine. Coates went to the United States from where Scotland Yard tried and failed to have him extradited. He returned to Sydney in 1940 where he was promptly arrested, but yet another extradition attempt failed.

In March 1935 a number of Australian smugglers had been caught after a thirty mile chase from the Belgian border through northern France during which the police fired on the men's armoured petrol tank. Those arrested in the French chase, which ended when the car smashed into a customs barrier at Condé-sur-L'Escaut, included one Bludger Warren. He was first acquitted at Bethune, then convicted at Avesnes and finally his five year sentence was quashed after representations by, of all people, the British Foreign Office.

The very talented Australian conman, the one-legged Robert Bradshaw, also known as Matthew Biggar and nicknamed 'Algy', was first charged in London in 1914 and two more convictions followed swiftly, but in 1916 he applied to join the Royal Air Force. Asked to give his occupation he replied 'Professional Crook' and was promptly rejected. He joined the army and it was then that he lost his leg, which was amputated above the knee. From 1920 he acquired a number of convictions and in January 1921 he was living in Mayfair using his flat for crooked card games. In his heyday he would pose as a wealthy grazier from Queensland and one of his best coups had been when he took a South African, Daniel de Wet, for 9900 pounds in 1935. However, two long jail sentences took the starch out of him and he was destitute by the time of his death in England in 1948.

* * *

After the war Australian conmen still worked in Britain, particularly at the time of the 1951 Festival and the coronation of Queen Elizabeth II in 1953, but it was not until the 1970s that teams of Australian shoplifters descended on Europe. Known as the Kangaroo Gang, they were in fact a loosely connected group numbering over fifty who would work in teams of five or six and would help out other teams when they were needed and it suited them. It was an ever changing personnel. Recruits would be sent over with their return fares paid and money in pocket to join a team and go back if and when things became hot. By the early 1970s they were said to have netted more than 2.5 million pounds in Europe. Travellers' cheques were another of the specialities of the Kangaroos and at the beginning of 1974 they cleared 450 000 pounds from mailbags at Heathrow, working with crooked aircraft loaders. It was, however, a mere fraction of what they made.

From time to time they would work with English criminals but these were often used simply as drivers. One London criminal of the period remembers:

> I used to drink with one of them, Snowy, but he was in a different league from me. He was at the TCs [travellers' cheques] and made thousands at it. He got one English fellow, Terry, to drive him around, drove him to Europe. What he didn't know was the man was a wrong 'un, a grass. He got Snowy eight years at the Bailey.

The London receiver Stan Davies, once associated with the Kray twins, recalls the teams:

> I used to buy from them. They were hotter than anybody in the 60s and 70s. They were the best. The stuff they pulled was incredible. They did business all over Europe—Belgium, Holland, Switzerland. One time I was phoned from Switzerland and flew over to Geneva the same day. They showed me what they'd done. One man who was about six foot three had gone on his back into the window and taken out two trays of rings. And this was in broad daylight, mind. I flew straight to Montreal with the stuff to get rid of it.

A London police officer who dealt with them remembers:

> It was impossible to know who they actually were. They had any number of false passports and they liked London because you could get the morning flight out to Geneva and be back home for tea. One team had its eyes on a 40 000 pound diamond on display there. I don't know how many times they went to look at it but for a long time they couldn't work out how to get it. It became a challenge but they got it in the end.

This must have been the jewellery theft Davies mentions because the officer recalls: 'We had Davies detained in Montreal and stripped down to his pants but the diamond had gone off the plane with someone else.'

One of the Kangaroos' more audacious crimes was to steal a chimpanzee from Harrods Zoo at the request of a prospective buyer who did not wish to pay what he considered an exorbitant price. The animal was put in a pram and pushed out of the shop.

Among the best of the Kangaroos was Richard Jeakins, who was found to have an absolute treasure trove of more than 1100 stolen items, including a William Blake painting, two icons, forty cashmere sweaters, two colour televisions and two stereo hi-fi units in his Kensington flat. Unfortunately he seems to have forgotten the cardinal rule of shoplifting— always steal for other people—and was caught stealing cleaning materials for himself from the London store Bourne & Hollingsworth. On 3 October 1978 he received three years' imprisonment.

Police officers of the era remember the Kangaroos with something approaching admiration. They were generally regarded as non-violent, pleasant to deal with, talkative—'Until you realised they'd told you nothing at all about the future. It was always the past'—and extremely talented. One London Criminal Investigation Department officer recalls: 'Their M.O. was that five or so would go into a shop and create a kerfuffle and then sometimes a [put up] drunk would come in off the street, take out his cock and start to piss on the counter. While the assistant was distracted they'd rifle the place.'

The Melburnian Graham 'The Munster' Kinniburgh was a fringe member of the Kangaroos who went on to greater things. Some of the others, such as Jack 'The Fibber' Warren, metamorphosed into the Grandfather Gang which imported hashish in the early 1990s through Hervey Bay, some 150 kilometres north of Brisbane. Warren had started his criminal career in 1938 with a conviction for riding on the outside of a tramcar but he advanced far beyond that modest beginning. When in the 1980s Warren was caught in Paris shoplifting from a large department store the painter and docker Brian Kane approached a Melbourne barrister for advice about what could be done from Australia. 'He just said, "Jesus. The wheels have come off." I said it was essential that character evidence was provided and a priest was sent over by them. In the end they came out quite light.'

Warren's career as a drug importer came to an end when the Grandfathers' fourth shipment of hashish was intercepted and he received a four year sentence, with only one to be served because of his ill-health. By then the gang was thought to have imported more than $225 million. Some $4 million sat in a bank in Amsterdam for years until the widow of Warren, who died in Queensland in 2002, claimed it. She lost her action.

Another Kangaroo, Neville Biber, who served a sentence for theft in Manchester, went into drugs and at the time of his death in 1983 was dealing in bulk heroin as well as running a carpet fraud. Over the years he acquired convictions for theft, receiving and consorting and was an associate of the celebrated Arthur 'Neddy' Smith. Investigators from the Corporate Affairs Commission interviewed Biber at length in December 1982 and were planning to see him again, but a few weeks later, on 18 January, Biber was found dead in his Sydney office, apparently having suffered a heart attack. He was forty-nine and had been treated for circulatory problems caused by obesity. He was buried without an autopsy the next day.

One story that circulated after his death was that a loaded pistol had been held at his head until his heart gave out. If true, it would certainly have been in Kangaroo style. For despite their non-violent reputation as far as the public was concerned, the Kangaroos could be extremely unpleasant towards their own. Another London officer recalls: 'On the surface they were a very likeable bunch, but they were evil bastards who murdered a lot of their own. You'd think they were loveable scamps and then you'd realise how dangerous they really were.' And yet another:

If they thought one of their team was informing it was the end of him or her. In London two people died. I was talking to one the night before he died of a drug overdose. It was put down that he committed suicide but it was a case of forcible feeding. The other was said to have gassed himself.

Even when they were arrested English prisons could not always hold them. When Michael Duncan, who may well have been Brian O'Callaghan under another name, was remanded in custody in December 1969 over a 13 000 pound jewel theft, his English cell mate David Wayne Griffiths was on remand for a minor offence. A surety giving a false name and address arrived at the prison to bail Griffiths out and Duncan changed clothes with him, was given 28 pence for his bus fare home and promptly disappeared. The unfortunate Griffiths received three years for his part in the escape.

There were suggestions that some of the Kangaroos metamorphosed into the Magnetic Drill Gang—Kinniburgh was a particularly talented safebreaker—which carried out a series of raids in New South Wales over a two year period in the latter half of the 1970s. Of the fourteen robberies credited to them, one that stood out was a $1.7 million heist from a country bank at Murwillumbah, on the Queensland–New South Wales border, in November 1978. The team used an electro-magnetic drill stand which was clamped onto the safe enabling them to drill within five millimetres of the locking mechanism.

In the late 1990s there were signs that the Grandfather Gang had resurrected itself in Queensland. That, or someone had studied their tactics and was copying those of the old Kangaroos. The aim was to obtain the attention of security workers when they delivered currency to offices in high-rise buildings while other members of the team raided the vans. The diversionary tactics included fiddling with lift buttons and the staff being chatted up by good-looking girls, something which led the police to think fathers and daughters were working together. During a raid in Cairns in April 1996, the team was chased by other security staff and threw away the stolen satchels. These were then picked up by the female members, including Rosa Salvucci, the de facto wife of fifty-year-old Steven Levidis, who was eventually persuaded to give evidence against him. He had been sentenced in France in 1980 following a big jewel theft in Paris. Now members of the gang lived on his luxury yacht while they were casing the TNT courier van in Cairns from which they took $200 000 in foreign currency. In 2001 Levidis had his five year sentence confirmed but the Court of Appeal declined to increase it as requested by the prosecution.

Between the Wars

4

By the mid-1920s there were four dominant figures in the Sydney underworld. In sharp contrast to the situation in England and the United States, where females usually had subservient roles—providing alibis, arranging for bail, minding stolen goods—two of these figures were women.

One was the redoubtable Kate Leigh, who had by now served her sentence for providing a false alibi for Jewey Freeman in the Eveleigh robbery. Even before she went away she was establishing herself as a madam when girls of her age were usually simply working in brothels. On her release from Long Bay in 1919, Leigh found her true vocation, opening a series of sly-grog shops in Surry Hills and a string of houses in East Sydney. Additionally there was money to be made from receiving, cocaine dealing and, with the help of her male friends, the standover. She was an enthusiastic recruiter of good-looking working-class women, promising them that jewellery, furs, clothes and a good time were now at their fingertips and telling them: 'It's a nasty world, so it's best to enjoy it while you can.'

In contrast with Kate Leigh, Matilda 'Tilly' Mary Twiss Devine was sometimes described as 'usually good tempered', but others say differently. Born in 1900 in Camberwell, a working-class district in South London, she had acquired a number of convictions for prostitution before she married James (Jim) Devine, then a small-time racecourse racketeer and thief serving with the AIF, on 12 August 1917. Tilly Devine came to Australia at the end of the war on a 'bride ship' and worked in a factory before once again taking to the streets. She and Leigh were said to be charging six shillings a turn, which would produce a very respectable sum when the average weekly wage was three pounds (sixty shillings).

Devine's first brothel was in Palmer Street, East Sydney, from which she rented rooms to girls at two pounds a shift. Often the girls were from the country and were recruited from the Crown Street Women's Hospital. Within five years she owned eighteen houses and the press had dubbed her 'Queen of the Night'. By 1923 she had racked up sixty-seven assorted minor convictions.

Devine and Leigh could not stand each other, using the newspaper *Truth* as their forum for attack on a regular basis. When in June 1930 Leigh called Devine the 'worst woman in Sydney' her rival, at the time exiled in London, replied asking the newspaper to 'keep my name out of papers in any connection with Kate Lee's as I don't wish to know her class'. For a time Leigh and Devine physically fought over the same patch, with Leigh, giving weight to her rival, often prevailing because of her ability to take and give a good punch.

When the pair finally left the streets themselves and set up as full-time madams, they had differing lifestyles. Devine lived in some comfort in a red brick house in Torrington Road, Maroubra, with crystal glassware and a dinner service while Kate Leigh lived, so to speak, on the premises in Riley Street, East Sydney, where she celebrated every Christmas by throwing a great children's street party complete with plenty of stolen presents. There was method in her generosity. The children's fathers thought Kate was 'all right' and so might well visit her girls or work with her. Tilly Devine also had her generous side. When the standover man Siddy Kelly was charged with attempted murder she held a fund-raising dance for him at the Maccabean Hall in Darlinghurst.

In October 1931 Kate Leigh was involved in a curious case. While she was working in the laundry at Long Bay she had befriended Catherine Ikin who was accused of murdering her husband. Mrs Ikin was duly acquitted and left the court in something of a tug of war between Leigh and the Salvation Army, both of whom it seems wanted to take her home. In this case the flesh won and off she went in Kate's smart car. It was only a matter of days before Kate Leigh was in court charged with robbing and stabbing Mrs Ikin for her pension money.

The case was dismissed, with the magistrate saying he did not believe the complainant; Kate had gone to the expense of getting herself

King's Counsel. Of course, as the city's top brothel keepers she and Tilly Devine could afford such a luxury; but what is amazing is that, time and again, these men and women were not defended by mere solicitors or young barristers. The proceeds of crime were such that they could pull up the money to obtain the services of King's Counsel even at the lower courts, and they were prepared to do so.

The third of the Sydney quartet was Phil 'The Jew' Jeffs, born in Riga, Latvia. Like Devine, Jeffs grew up on the streets of London. He worked a passage on a tramp steamer and spent time in South Africa before he jumped ship in Sydney in 1912 and worked at the Coogee Bay Hotel as a boot boy until he was sacked for stealing from the guests.

He was acquitted of killing a woman in a motor car accident. Then came an allegation of rape, which, at the time, was a capital offence. On the face of it Ada Maddocks, mother of two, was snatched off Bayswater Road, Darlinghurst, in March 1928 while on her way home to her babies after she had been visiting a friend. Taken to a flat, she was repeatedly raped—and subjected to other shameful indecencies which the papers could not name—by at least five men including Jeffs and Herbert Wilson, a hulking man otherwise known as 'Budgee' Travers. The newspapers were in uproar. How can any decent woman feel safe in the face of 'perverted satyrs'? 'Compared with this, Mount Rennie is a poor parallel', and so on. The men immediately claimed that what had happened was with her consent and that, in criminal slang, she had agreed to 'pull the train'.

The public and papers were excluded from the committal proceedings but then gradually a very different picture emerged, although not necessarily one that did any credit to the men. First, Ada Maddocks had taken out a summons against her husband for threatening her with a razor and accusing her of being a loose woman. Then her uncle gave evidence that, whenever he met her, he had given her money because she was almost destitute. When she gave evidence of the rape it was clear she was still quarrelling with her unemployed husband and she admitted she had not eaten for twenty-four hours before the incident. The jury did not believe her story, accepting the men's defence that she had consented. Jeffs and the others were acquitted in triumph. Her accusation seems to have come from her fear of her husband finding out how she had come by some money and particularly because Wilson refused to pay her.

By this time Jeffs was involved in mugging and in procuring women. He had a number of girls working for him in the Kings Cross area, was adroit at the ginger game and was aligned to the cocaine trade. Regarded as one of the hardest razor men working in Sydney, he was intelligent and self-taught; some thought him to be the most capable criminal of his generation.

The fourth, if rather less permanent, fixture in the Sydney underworld was the major Melbourne standover man Norman Bruhn, who worked as a labourer on the wharves. Ugly, bad-tempered, a beater of women, a thief and a pimp, Bruhn was one of Squizzy Taylor's top men and he looms large in the story of Australia's gangland murders. Until he left Melbourne in 1926 he had been a standover man preying on people carrying on illegal enterprises. His record ran the gamut of offences—larceny, vagrancy, cruelty to a horse, shop and house breaking and indecent exposure. In July 1926 he had tried to blackmail a woman in South Yarra to the tune of 100 pounds and when she refused to pay he extracted the money at gunpoint. She took out a warrant and Bruhn moved with his wife and children to Sydney. Another version of the reason for his flight was that it was over a man he had shot and feared might die.

In his supporting cast was George Wallace, known as 'The Midnight Raper' because of the way he stood over prostitutes. Apart from forcing the girls to have sex, Wallace, an ex-wrestler and an adroit pickpocket, would bet his male victims that he could guess their weight and, as he lifted them up, would steal their wallets. During his life he appeared in court 140 times. Also acting as enforcers were Lancelot McGregor 'Sailor the Slasher' Saidler, John 'Snowy' Cutmore, and the albino Frank 'Razor Jack' Hayes.

In the relatively short time he was in Sydney, Bruhn took up with the gorgeous Nellie Cameron, described as a 'redhead with a ripe figure and provocative china blue eyes'. Softly spoken and never raucous but with a flaming temper, she had Bruhn as her lover and pimp, allowing him a percentage of her earnings, said to be a remarkable one pound a time for sex. One of the many women dubbed a Black Widow, Cameron began life as a prostitute in the Surry Hills and Woolloomooloo districts. Also known in the press as 'The Kiss of Death Girl', from time to time she commuted to work in Queensland. Admiringly described as 'a filly who could easily run at Randwick', for a time she also taught dancing at Professor Bolot's Academy in Oxford Street around the corner from Sargents' pie factory. With Bruhn she turned ten tricks a day, seven days a week. Even if she only took ten shillings per trick, at thirty-five pounds a week her income was thirty-two pounds more than the average wage. Asked what she saw in the disagreeable Bruhn, she is said to have replied, 'When I wake up in the morning I like to look down on someone lower than myself.'

On the evening of his death in June 1927 Bruhn was in a sly-grog shop in Charlotte Lane, Darlinghurst, with racehorse trainer Robert Miller, demanding drink. When he was refused service he threatened to shoot-up the place. It was a street in which girls sat on their doorsteps or in armchairs in the doorways asking, 'Are you coming in, love?' But this was a night with a sea mist and all the girls were indoors when, outside the shop, two men brushed Miller aside saying, 'You're not in this' and shot Bruhn five times. Understandably Miller was unable to make any positive identification. 'I didn't know who these men were and if I did, I would not dare to tell you,' he answered when questioned. There was speculation that the killing involved the cocaine trade. Either that or Bruhn had fallen foul of some heavy Sydney identities over the proceeds of a robbery.

At this time John 'Snowy' Cutmore was regarded as a leader of the Safe Prosecution Gang—so called because they only attacked people they knew would not prosecute them. He was thought to have been with Bruhn's killer who was suggested to be one Frank Green. Not so, said Cutmore's defenders, who claimed that Cutmore had given up his life of crime and was now going straight. As an example of this change of heart he had, they said, worked for the Sydney Council and for a racehorse trainer, even buying a couple of trotting ponies. This view was not shared by Squizzy Taylor, nor indeed by the Russell Street police. Nor did it stop Cutmore, a few days before he died, pulling a scam in Melbourne by backing a horse that he already knew had won.

The death of Norman Bruhn was followed by a series of shootings and knifings in what came to be known as the Cocaine War. It saw a number of personnel on the move. Razor Jack Hayes went to Germany where he was badly injured in a street fight the next year. George Wallace was in Brisbane when Bruhn was shot and on his return was involved in a losing fight with Tom Kelly in Victoria Street, Darlinghurst. He was hit over the head with a hammer and fled. In July 1928, fuelled

with cocaine, he began a fight in the Plaza Café in King Street where—
after he had thrown a coffee pot at a waitress and slashed the manager,
Harry Murray, with his razor—he was captured and attacked by the
customers. Fined a modest two pounds, and a further three pounds
towards the Plaza's damages, Wallace left Sydney.

That left the small, pale and thoroughly difficult Lancelot Saidler,
who must have suffered from his first name in his youth. For the next
three years he continued to stand over bars and clubs in Glebe and
Elizabeth streets near the Central Railway, until in September 1930 he
demanded five shillings' protection from Ernie Good who ran a wine
bar. Good refused; Saidler threw a glass of wine in his face and, taking
out his razor, threatened to carve him up. According to one witness,
he said, 'I'll slice off your smeller with this little beauty.' Good took
out a pistol and shot him where he stood. Some stories do have happy
endings. Charged with manslaughter, Good was acquitted.

Just as Mrs Bruhn could not comprehend that her husband was
a gangster, nor could Lallie Saidler. She thought 'The Slasher', whom
she had married at fifteen, 'wonderful', telling reporters how he kept
cats and pulled the noses of Chinese children until they squealed with
delight.

There was not only prostitution and sly-grog from which to make
money. From the 1920s cocaine, opium and morphine were just as
important to Squizzy Taylor and his Sydney rivals as the control of the
sly-grog shops. Top grade opium from Hong Kong came in through
Queensland, while lesser quality Dutch opium from Java came via
Rottnest and Fremantle. This was an easy route; once the drugs were
in Rottnest there was no customs enquiry of the boats that went to and
fro. By the middle of the 1920s, however, because of the increasingly
jaded palates of the users and the wild swings in quality, Dutch opium
was falling out of favour.

The first king of the Sydney drug trade was Charles Passmore, who
functioned from before World War I, selling drugs mainly to prostitutes.
In May 1923 he was fined a mere fifty pounds, despite being excoriated
in court by Sergeant Tom O'Brian:

> This man is the representative of all things evil. He is lord and master
> of a dope combine and has waxed fat and flourishing through the
> agency of his hopeless clients. You can see him any evening about
> 11 o'clock standing at the corner of Woolcott and Craigend Streets,

Darlinghurst, and its environs, handing out the deadly contents of an innocent looking package—cocaine—to scores of addicts.

Passmore was rather more fortunate than Melbourne's Henry McEwan, who, the year before, received six months for selling cocaine at two shillings a packet to prostitutes. A number of women had been found in a stupefied condition and, true to form, the Chinese had at first been suspected.

The next down in Sydney was Harry 'Jewey' Newman, described as the king of Sydney dope traffickers, who bought cocaine from doctors and dentists, cut it with boracic acid and sold it in the Haymarket. He would go the rounds of the surgeries, often accompanied by his children, then break the purchases down into five shilling bags for sale to prostitutes and their clients.

When the prostitute Mary Edwards was raided in Pelican Street, Surry Hills, in 1925, the police found thirty packets of cocaine. She told them she had them from Newman but, for the next four years, despite constant raids on his runners—including Rose Steele, 'Botany May' Smith (or Lee) who once threw a hot flat iron at a policewoman, and Lilian Sproule who was known as the 'Human Vulture'—Newman himself remained untouched.

His downfall came in February 1929, when he tried to bribe Sergeant Tom Wickham, then half of the Drugs Squad, telling him: 'I'm taking over Bobbie Carr's fish shop in Goulburn Street, and if I had you fellows with me I could corner the cocaine market, and we could make a packet out of it. These fucking women must have snow you know.' Wickham declined and from then Newman's days on the outside were numbered in single figures. On 23 February the police raided his shop and found eighteen packets of cocaine hidden in a drainpipe. Even then he was only sentenced to nine months' hard labour and given a small fine. However, the conviction represented a breakthrough.

One drug smuggler of the period was Reginald William Lloyd Holmes, a man with seemingly impeccable social and business connections who owned land at McMahon's Point, across the harbour from central Sydney. For no very apparent reason he gave a former boxer, Jim Smith, a contract to erect a block of flats on the land. This was all the more peculiar because, whatever talents Smith may have had as a fighter or billiard marker, he had no experience whatsoever in the building trade. The likelihood is that Smith was standing over Holmes and his grip tightened because the McMahon's Point scheme was a rort: Smith went bankrupt and creditors were defrauded. However, Holmes continued to finance Smith and set him up with the grandly named Rozelle Athletic Club—in fact a billiards hall. He also gave Smith a more or less free hand skippering his speedboat.

It was a time when smugglers usually just took the contraband off the ships at the wharves, but Holmes used his boat *Pathfinder* to outrun customs officials as he picked up packages dumped overboard in Sydney Harbour or on the coast. Much of the contraband was cocaine—then, as now, the drug of choice among the bright young things of Sydney and elsewhere. It was a lucrative but highly competitive game, with fights between rival gangs. There were stories that Holmes's gang intended to kidnap the head of a rival organisation and indeed he had once lured a man onto his boat and then fired shots into the water to indicate what would happen if he did not co-operate.

It all began to unravel when, on Anzac Day 1935, Jim Smith's arm, identifiable by the tattoos it bore, was regurgitated by a captured shark in Coogee Baths. One Patrick Brady was arrested for Smith's murder and police hoped that Holmes would give evidence. But on 11 June Holmes was found shot dead in his car at a known courting spot in Hickson Road, Dawes' Point. Without evidence from Holmes, the case against Brady withered and died. On 10 September he was acquitted on the direction of the Chief Justice. Nor was the prosecution any more successful in the cases of two men, John Patrick Strong and Albert Stannard, who were accused of the murder of Holmes. The evidence was again weak—a flimsy identification and fingerprints found on the dashboard of Holmes's car— and the pair were acquitted shortly before Christmas.

In his analysis of the case, author Alex Castles suggests that Smith, not only a blackmailer but also a police informer, was shot and killed by another criminal, Edward Frederick 'Eddie' Weyman, who Smith had been threatening. Castles also suggests that Holmes, who was heavily insured, hired men to kill him—suicide would have voided his life policies.

On 23 December 1928 the crusading *Truth* claimed, in good old tub-thumping prose, that Darlinghurst was the centre of crime in Sydney: 'Razorhurst, Gunhurst, Bottlehurst, Dopehurst ... a plague spot where the spawn of the gutter grow and fatten on official apathy.' Underworld czars ruled over: 'bottle-men (thieves who bludgeoned their victims, usually from behind with a bottle), dope pedlars, razor slashers, sneak thieves, confidence men, women of ill repute, pickpockets, burglars, spielers, gunmen and every brand of racecourse parasite.'

Underworld shootings continued happily, with no one ever able to say who was responsible. In the autumn of 1928 there were no fewer than twenty, and in most of the cases the victims refused to co-operate with the police. In January 1929 a William McKay, accounting for a wound in his chest, said that he had carried a gun and accidentally shot himself when he put his hand in his pocket. No gun could be found and McKay explained he had thrown it away the moment it went off.

The first major trouble in Sydney since the death of Norman Bruhn and the dismantling of his team came two years later—in the form of a half hour pitched battle in Eaton Avenue, Normanhurst, fought by around twenty men. It occurred because Phil Jeffs had been discovered cutting cocaine with an unacceptable level of boracic acid. Sensibly he left the scene of the action and returned home where, around 4 a.m., he was shot in the shoulder after a break-in. He crawled out of the house and was found by a milkman to whom he called rather piteously, 'Milkie, take me to hospital.'

Jeffs was indeed taken to hospital, where the 'dying' depositions that he gave were at pains to deny that he was the head of an international gang. He survived and Ernest James Taylor was charged with his attempted murder but Jeffs gave evidence that he was not the man. So far as Jeffs was concerned peace was temporarily restored.

* * *

The war between Tilly Devine and Kate Leigh for the control of prostitution in East Sydney seems to have begun at precisely 7.30 p.m. on 17 July 1929. It had been simmering for a couple of days—since James Devine was fined fifty pounds on 15 July for possessing illegal ammunition when gun cartridges were found in a settee at their Long Bay address. He claimed that, ten weeks earlier at Newtown, he had been robbed of a diamond stick pin and ten pounds, and the gun was for his protection.

In the yard of the courthouse a ring of men formed while Tilly Devine rolled on the ground fighting with another woman, Vera Lewis, both later being described as fashionably dressed. When the police broke it up and hauled the pair into court Lewis was fined three pounds and Tilly Devine, who was said to have been trying to bite her opponent's finger, was remanded. 'She seemed to think I was responsible for her husband being fined,' complained Lewis.

In the early evening of 17 July, Frank Green, a major activist in prostitution and illegal betting who was thought to have shot standover man Norman Bruhn two years before, met George 'Gunman' Gaffney from the Leigh camp in Nicholson Street, Woolloomooloo. Green, who was accompanied by one Sidney McDonald, received a good kicking from Gaffney and headed for the casualty ward. Three hours later McDonald met Jim and Tilly Devine, with whom Green was living, and told them what had happened. They took a taxi and returned to Torrington Road, Maroubra, where Green, who had discharged himself from hospital and taken a tram, arrived a little before midnight. Also on their way to Torrington Road in a taxi were Gaffney and Kate Leigh's long-time bodyguard, Walter Tomlinson.

Shortly after midnight Jim Devine heard someone trying to climb the fence and shouted a warning from the balcony. His revolver had been forfeited by the courts and because he feared trouble he had borrowed a .303 from a friend. As Gaffney announced he had plenty of friends with him, yelling, 'I'm out for the blood of you, you bastard', Devine shot him in the chest. He also shot Walter Tomlinson, smashing his arm. 'Plenty of friends' seems to have been something of an exaggeration. A third man escaped in a taxi shortly before the police arrived and Gaffney died on the pavement soon afterwards. As he died Gaffney refused to say who had shot him and in turn Devine refused to prosecute Tomlinson for the home invasion. Devine was, nevertheless, charged with the unlawful killing of Gaffney.

Three months after the party thrown for Devine's acquittal on the grounds of self-defence, Frank Green was out for revenge. On 9 November, and admittedly by mistake, he killed a Leigh soldier, Bernard Dalton, as Dalton left Sharland's Hotel in William Street, Woolloomooloo. Green and Sidney McDonald went into hiding and Tomlinson, his arm now healed, drove Kate Leigh in her Studebaker to Dalton's spectacular funeral.

Five months later Tomlinson, forgetting his place in life and possibly thinking he had had enough, picked out Green on an identification parade. It naturally only served to cause more ill feeling. On the tram to Long Bay jail, Green was heard to remark, 'The bastard picked me today. It's a pity I didn't get him as well as Dalton while I was at it.' Amazingly Tomlinson went through with his evidence and for his pains was knocked about by Sidney McDonald during the luncheon adjournment of Green's trial. McDonald received twelve months and Green was acquitted.

Then, in the middle of March, three months after Green's arrest, Leigh's house at 104 Riley Street, East Sydney, was attacked by a gang of men looking for the Judas, Tomlinson. One, Jacky Craig, managed to reach the bedroom and damaged the furniture before the police arrived to evict them. Next day Kate Leigh, now described as a shopkeeper, bought a pea-rifle and fifty cartridges. She was well advised to have done so; on 27 March there was another attack. Giving evidence at the subsequent inquest Kate said that she warned she had a gun and would shoot but the men, including the Prendergast brothers John (known as 'Snowy' because of his cocaine habit) and Joseph, demanded that she give up Tomlinson. She shot John Prendergast in the stomach after he threw a brick at her. When the police were called Prendergast is said to have told Leigh, 'Shoot me, you ****. I am dying.' The following month Leigh was acquitted by the coroner of Prendergast's killing. Later she would say, 'I've never stopped saying a prayer of repose for the blackguard's soul.'

But by now, with the press on their heels, the politicians had acted and the New South Wales *Vagrancy (Amendment) Act 1929* was passed, providing penalties for those consorting with reputed thieves, prostitutes and those with no known means of support—that is, with each other. In 1930 sixty-eight men and women were charged under the 'consorting clause', and nearly double that the next year. Tilly Devine was charged in January 1930 with consorting with prostitutes which, since she employed them, was hardly surprising. She negotiated a settlement that if she was not tried, she would agree to leave Sydney for two years. She sailed for England the next month, leaving Jim Devine, half the man his wife was, to look after the shops.

The arrangement was not a success. In her absence Jim hired what might euphemistically be called a housekeeper, an arrangement which did not meet with Tilly Devine's approval on her return well inside her exile time. On 9 January 1931 he arrived home with the housekeeper and Tilly was enraged. A shot was fired. At me, said Tilly; in the air to pacify her, said Devine. A week was sufficient for everyone to see sense and she withdrew the charge.

Worse, however, was to follow. In March 1931 Jim Devine was badly slashed and, in the convoluted way in which the underworld conducts its alignments and re-alignments, he now fell out with Frank Green. Devine does not seem to have had a great deal of luck with his diamond stick pins: Green now turned up at Torrington Road on the evening of 16 June and robbed Devine of another at gunpoint.

Devine seized a gun and ran after Green as he was getting into a waiting taxi. He fired at him and missed, killing the driver, Frederick Moffitt. Devine had been using soft nosed high velocity ammunition and the shot tore out the unfortunate man's lungs. Devine, now described as a fruiterer, was charged and, once more, he was acquitted. Once more Tilly Devine threw a lavish party for her husband but, in truth, her empire was in trouble.

For once, Devine decided to give evidence against Green, who was having a bad time of things. First he was committed for trial on the charge of stealing the stick pin and then, in October 1931, he was found shot in the stomach at the rear of St Vincent's Hospital. He was carried inside the hospital by a young man and woman who promptly and sensibly disappeared. (Coincidentally, Bruhn's former girlfriend, the redhead Nellie Cameron, was also in St Vincent's, shot in the chest.) On 30 October a young man of good character, Charles Brame, recently arrived from Victoria, was arrested at what was described as a musical evening in a Darlinghurst flat. On 25 February 1932 Brame was committed for trial for attempting to murder Green, but the charges were later dropped.

* * *

It was not all Devine/Leigh, though. In April 1930 a wharf labourer, Walter Williamson, and the standover man and greyhound trainer, Charles Bourke (known also as Edward Brown and MacRogers), were taken to hospital together, where Williamson later died. On the previous Christmas Eve Bourke had been shot in the face. Although the coroner was brought in to take a statement, Williamson refused to disclose who had shot him, while Bourke denied knowing Williamson altogether. The police were convinced that both men had been cornered together and been shot as they tried to run away.

Later that year Bourke went to Queensland, probably to avoid consorting charges under the new legislation and also to conduct a little piece or two of business there. On 30 December he was charged with shooting a police officer at Breakfast Creek. Court stories are rarely the whole truth and Bourke's case was that he had badly beaten a man named Ross in a fight and the next day heard that reprisals were to be taken against him. That was why he armed himself and no doubt why Clive Crowley and George Brown, as well as Jack Morris, were also there backing him up. There was a quarrel in the Breakfast Creek Hotel that day and Sergeant Francis Fahey, an off-duty officer who heard someone say 'He's got a gun', went to investigate. Brown tried to hold Fahey back while Bourke ran into the street. Fahey shook off Brown and followed him, so Bourke shot him above the left knee.

The prosecution alleged Bourke had been living with a brothel keeper, a known cocaine transporter, which is what the quarrel may really have been about. On 12 March 1931 the Chief Justice Sir James Blair, who had been in a testy mood the last couple of days, rowing with the Crown Prosecutor when he declined to call evidence in a previous case, sentenced Bourke to five years' hard labour: 'You say you carried the pistol to protect yourself from other undesirables. I intend to put you where you will be safe from them for a long while.'

A few months later, bookmaker George Cooper was shot when three men, Jack Finnie, John Hogan and Phonsie Cune, raided a sly-grog shop party in Thurlow Street, Redfern, apparently demanding bottles of beer. The place was well known to the police and had been a hang-out for Victor Hoare, a well-known bank hold-up man. When a fight broke out Cooper was accidentally shot near the heart. He was taken to hospital but naturally refused to say anything. At the time he was too weak to have the bullet removed and he died two days later. Although everyone knew everyone else involved, the police claimed it was not part of the racecourse wars, in which standover men were demanding money from bookmakers, who in turn were hiring other standover men to protect them. In May, Finnie, who in his younger days could have been a bantamweight contender, appeared in court charged with Cooper's murder. For once Finnie does seem to have been trying to be a restraining influence and happily he was acquitted. A guest at the party had been the ubiquitous Nellie Cameron, but it is not known who she came with.

An interesting little case in which Finnie stood on the periphery was that of the November 1935 killing of boxer Leslie Tickner, one of two men who fought as Darkie Sullivan. He was found shot in the back of the head in his rooms where he ran a sly-grog shop and a safe house for guns deposited by Finnie and his friends. Blanche Elizabeth Peterson, one of his girlfriends, was arrested and after nine hours made a confession that she had picked up a gun he had on the table and, while fooling around, accidentally shot him. She left the house and threw the gun away. It was never found.

At her trial she completely changed her story, admitting she had said she had shot Tickner accidentally but denying it was true. She had, she said, been home alone on the evening when he was shot. Perhaps to everyone's surprise, shortly before Christmas the jury acquitted her in less than two hours.

Still in Sydney, over the years Kate Leigh had been in constant trouble. In 1929 she served a four month sentence under the consorting law after a raid on one of her brothels, at 25 Kippax Street, Surry Hills. The following year she was raided again and this time cocaine was discovered at her East Sydney home. On 1 February 1931 *Truth* now claimed 'she had held the dope game in a grip that was as tight as that of any Midas'. Leigh was sentenced to twelve months' imprisonment and fined 250 pounds which, at the option of the court, could be converted into a further twelve months. Her appeal was dismissed and she was dragged screaming from the dock. She had more fortune shortly before Christmas 1931 when she was acquitted of the attempted murder of Joseph McNamara, who had been shot in the groin; but he was another who did the decent thing and failed to identify her.

Meanwhile the bookmaker Frederick Dangar, described as Leigh's right-hand man, received twelve months after he attempted to purchase fifteen grams of cocaine without a prescription from a North Sydney chemist. His defence was that he wanted it for a horse. He was given a 250 pound fine or twelve months' imprisonment.

Leigh did not serve the extra twelve months for her drugs conviction. She used her influence with a Labor alderman to persuade the courts that payment of the fine was sufficient punishment, but for the moment her empire was also on the wane. In March 1932 her daughter Eileen agreed to exile for three years from New South Wales to avoid a prison sentence and in January 1933 Leigh herself agreed to a five year rustication at least 200 miles from Sydney after being found in possession of stolen goods.

Deprived of Tilly Devine's guiding hand, Frank Green's career declined. He had achieved his pinnacle in 1930 when he was regarded as Sydney's top gunman. Now he spent the next five years of his life either in hiding, in prison, or locked in battle with another top standover man, Guido Calletti, for the favours of the delectable Nellie Cameron. After Norman Bruhn's death, Ernest Connelly, also known as Hardy, took up with Nellie only to be shot by Calletti in Womerah Avenue, Darlinghurst, in February 1929 after what was described as a 'wild night party'. His dying deposition was taken but Connelly declined to help the police. Calletti's home, also in Womerah Avenue, was searched and five live bullets and an empty cartridge case were found, but no charges were preferred.

Connelly was replaced in Nellie's affections by Alan Pulley, who was later fatally shot in Glebe by Florrie Riley, a Redfern blonde. He came from New Zealand and was a noted housebreaker as well as a feared standover man. Always expensively dressed except when he was working, he had been drinking in the Town and Country Hotel in St Peters on 6 March 1937 when he went to stand over an SP joint run by Florrie and her sister Elsie O'Halloran. He came into the backyard while a race from Randwick was being broadcast and demanded three pounds from the women. Florrie Riley said he was too late and that they had paid out to other standover men. The women then went into the house and shut the back door. If they thought that was the end of the matter, they were wrong because Pulley leapt in through a window. O'Halloran grabbed the chocolate tin where they kept their money while Pulley tried to snatch it from her. Riley ran upstairs to get a gun. As Pulley and her sister were fighting she shot him twice. Pulley fell down and asked, 'What have you done to me? I can't get up.' At first he thought she had stabbed him with a pencil, but in fact both bullets lodged in his spine. Six days later he died doing the right thing—not blaming the women.

Then came the Green–Calletti–Cameron triangle, the stuff of which whole television soap series could be made. By the time of his death Guido Calletti had appeared in the courts nearly sixty times, in three states. A major standover man in Woolloomooloo whose career began at the age of nine when he was ruled to be an uncontrollable child, he was charged in February 1929 with an attempted murder and, after his acquittal, racked up a quick two years for assault with intent to rob. By 1934 he had joined the line of gangsters who sought to draw attention to themselves by bringing libel actions. He was awarded a farthing against *Truth* over an allegation that he had married Nellie to avoid charges under the consorting laws and the story goes that he framed the penny stamp he was sent as his winnings. One street fight with Green over Nellie was said to have lasted three quarters of an hour and ended with honours even and the clothes of both men in tatters.

Nellie Cameron's love life apart, all the Devine/Leigh shootings left the retiring and very smart Phil Jeffs on top of the pile to became one of the great sly-grog dealers in the city. In the 1930s he had a half share in the appropriately named 50-50 Club, a sly-grog shop on the corner of William and Forbes when, tired of constant raids by the police, his partner upped and left. Jeffs was now the de facto owner and made of sterner stuff. He transformed the large hall—now with a piano and, more importantly, a string of prostitutes—into one of the best-known drinking rooms in the city. It had all the scams of a near beer joint, with the girls drinking water and the customers paying for their 'gin'. The girls themselves were not charged admission but paid five shillings every time they left with a customer. Frank Green, although in decline, was hired to calm the more rowdy element. Above the club there were apartments for the prostitutes to whom the leading and lesser lights were steered. The men were drugged and photographed in compromising positions but the negatives were always available for purchase to avoid family embarrassment.

Jeffs was another who kept out of the limelight. When in April 1933 the 50-50 Club was raided, Harold 'Snowy' Billington took the rap. Jeffs was there for his protection, he said. This was rather contradicted by the evidence that it was Jeffs who took control during the raid, telling the staff to say nothing and reminding them that the cash receipts were for food and not liquor. The police generously described him as a 'former' gunman.

Curiously this robber and pimp acquired a certain measure of social respectability. Perhaps more importantly he acquired a defender in the form of Anthony Alexander Alam, a member of the state parliament. In 1936 *Truth* named Alam as the part owner of Graham's on Hunter Street, where he could be found on a regular basis. This time Harold

Wilkinson Vaughan was Jeffs's floor manager. Alam sued the paper for 10000 pounds but the case was settled for a derisory five pounds.

Jeffs also opened a classier establishment, the 400 Club in Phillip Street, Darlinghurst, which for a time he owned in partnership with the doctor–abortionist Reginald Stuart-Jones. Their relationship came to an abrupt end in 1937, with the good doctor being slipped a Mickey Finn, thrown out of the club and barred further entry. In December the previous year Jeffs had fought off an action by the black singer Nellie Smalls, who claimed she was not being paid her agreed wages. Jeffs's defence was that since she was there to sell sly-grog, her contract was illegal. She (or possibly he, since it was another line of defence that Nellie was a man) abandoned the action.

Jeffs had organised his contacts in the police force so well that, by 1936, it was tacitly accepted that his 400 club was almost immune from prosecution. Almost but not quite. When the club was raided in March 1938 the thirty or so upper-class patrons were reported as saying they had found the whole experience and their ride in the police van to be rather exciting. And there was Alam in the state parliament denouncing these bully-boy tactics. After all, the club was run on the most respectable lines—why, the Governor's wife could go in unattended. As crime writer Alfred McCoy points out: 'It was indicative of Jeffs' influence that the major address-in-reply to the Governor's speech should be a passionate defence of the city's leading criminal and that not a word of objection should be raised.'

Once cocaine had temporarily disappeared from the streets of Sydney the standover men had to turn their hands to some other occupation and again their chosen victims were the SP bookmakers. In 1936 a war which lasted two years broke out. On one side were ranged the standover men and on the other the equally violent men employed as guards by SP bookmakers in Darlinghurst, East Sydney and Surry Hills. In September 1937 George Jeremiah Lynch was shot dead in the Tophatter's Cabaret at Kings Cross where he had gone with Nigger Reeves and Fatty Sweetman. Lynch's killer was suspected to have been Tommy de Valle but he provided an alibi and *Truth* used the killing as another cosh with which to beat the unpopular Police Commissioner William McKay.

Clarrie Thomas had been one of the youngest men to serve in World War I but after his discharge he became a standover man. In 1937 he and

Jack Finnie went to stand over the Ginger Jar Club, which later became the Ziegfeld Club. The bouncer, Richard Reilly, took a gun, followed them up Castlereagh Street and fatally shot Thomas. He was acquitted on a plea of self-defence.

Even when there was no gang war as such going on, the underworld's casualty rate was still high. At a time when guns were carried on a regular basis, quarrels over women and perceived insults, not to mention business troubles, ended not with a slap but a bullet. In his memoirs notorious criminal Chow Hayes recalled that among his Sydney friends who died early in life were Barney Dalton, an SP bookmaker shot at the Tradesman's Arms in Palmer Street; Henry 'Sap' Johnson, a shoplifter and thief who was kicked to death in Surry Hills; and Cecil Charles 'Hoppy' Gardiner, shot while trying to stand over Paddy Roach's two-up game at Erskineville. In February 1938 thief and standover man Harold Robert Tarlington was shot twice in the stomach by Myles Henry 'Face' McKeon after a house was wrecked in St Peters. Two nights later George Baker, known as Jack, was shot and killed. He had been convicted of selling sly grog the day before while Nigger Fox was stabbed on the porch of his sly-grog shop in Alexandria.

It is unfair to blame the police if they often failed to obtain evidence sufficient to charge, let alone to convict, anyone. Even those shot at point blank range sometimes professed not to have noticed they had been wounded. But occasionally there were chinks in the armour. When Charlie Madden and his assistant John Earver went to tax the Waterloo bookmaker Samuel Young they found him unco-operative. As a result Madden pinned the bookmaker's hand to the window sill with a knife. Young was fortunate. His cockatoo pulled out the knife and stabbed Madden. Incredibly Young was not prepared to leave things as they were and he went to the police.

Until then Madden had been fortunate. He had been acquitted three times of shooting with intent to kill when his victims either declined to give evidence or could not be sure that he had been their attacker. Now Young was prepared to go through with it and Madden received ten years' imprisonment.

Bookmaker Jack Keane was not as fortunate as Young. In August 1938 Jack Finnie and Norman 'Mickey' McDonald, another whose speciality was standing over SP bookmakers, were shot as they visited a former colleague in Mascot. McDonald was hit in the chest and Finnie in the neck but, amazingly, both men survived. Once at the Royal South Sydney Hospital, the pair indicated to the police that the identity of whoever shot them was their business and theirs alone. One early morning four weeks after the double shooting, Jack Keane's body was found near the house where Finnie and McDonald had been shot. His crime had been to tell the police the identity of the gunman. His penalty was three bullets in his head.

Two years earlier Finnie and McDonald had fallen out. In September 1936, in an argument over money, Finnie shot his friend near the greyhound track at St Peters. Surprisingly McDonald identified him and Finnie stood trial. He was acquitted after telling the jury that he had fired in self defence when McDonald had threatened him with a gun. Clearly they had patched up their quarrel by this time.

For a standover man Mickey McDonald was wholly unreliable. In 1944 he was at it again, admitting he knew dozens of gunmen but maintaining he had never carried a gun himself and gigging on Colin Campbell whom he accused of demanding money with menaces. He had been clean, he said, for eight years and denied he was operating as an SP bookmaker. This time the dispute was over a two pound bet. Not guilty.

What very different behaviour from that of another standover man, William McCarthy, who in 1944 was shot four times in a two-up school and survived. Seven years later he needed fifty-three stitches following an attack in Wilmot Street, Sydney. On neither occasion could he identify his attackers.

* * *

There were robberies as well as standover tactics. The Mudgee train robbery took place at about 11 p.m. on 8 April 1930 when two masked and armed men entered the brake van after the train left Emu Plains on Sydney's outer west and held up the guards. The thieves jumped off just before the train, travelling at about 30 miles per hour, entered the tunnel on the Glenbrook side of Sydney, taking with them 4600 pounds' worth of bullion and another 13000 pounds in cheques. At first it was suspected that American criminals were involved and for a time it was suggested that the D'Autremont brothers, who in 1923 had robbed a train in Oregon, had been responsible. This was always highly improbable, even given lax prison security for, at the time, the brothers were serving sentences of life imprisonment in the United States. But, when it came to it, it was good old Australian planning.

In May the next year the Canberra mail train was robbed at Queanbeyan and this time 10000 pounds were stolen. It was a very different affair. The Commonwealth Bank had sent the money to Canberra in a mailbag. The train stopped at Queanbeyan at 4.15 a.m., when the bag and other sacks were unloaded and left on the platform for transfer. When the train reached Canberra it was found that the Commonwealth sack no longer contained the cash but was packed with telephone directories. The bag, minus the money, was found in the Queanbeyan River.

The very talented robber Harold Joseph Ryan was charged with both of the train thefts on 30 April and James Caffrey and Arthur Collins were charged with receiving from the Canberra mail theft and also with a well planned and executed robbery of jeweller Samuel Cohen. Everyone was given bail and Ryan made the most of this unexpected opportunity and absconded. The papers thought he would soon give himself up but he did not do so for another four years. Meanwhile on 4 October 1931 *Truth* wrote, 'His sad-eyed mother, grey with years and care waits in a little home in Iris-street.' Over the years there were various sightings of him in and around Sydney and on one occasion he gave a statement to the press that he had absconded because the police had 'smoked' his principal witness away. Ryan did not reappear until June 1935, when he surrendered himself and optimistically thought he might have bail again. Not surprisingly, this cut no ice.

Much of the Crown's evidence regarding the Canberra robbery came from an informer named Percy Jacobs, who gave detailed evidence of Ryan's pre-planning. At crunch time, crucially, Jacobs denied he personally had been involved although Ryan had promised him 1000 pounds. This produced from Judge Curlewis the outburst 'Why you were to get 1000 pounds I do not know. You did nothing to earn it', to which he added, 'I do not know if the jury will convict on this man's evidence alone.' In fact, Jacobs was supported by a George Morris (known, because of his size, as 'The Ambling Alp'—in a reference to the boxer Primo Carnera), who had driven Ryan and his friend Collins from the Mudgee robbery and had buried the cash on his farm. Morris claimed that Ryan had been standing over him because of a conviction some eight years previously and, if it came out, he would lose his job as postmaster. There was clearly more to Morris than was apparent at first glance. Yes, he knew a man Jenkins but, no, he had never shot him nor had he placed a bomb in his car. He also knew Alexander McIver and Francis Delaney, convicted of bombing the Greek Club in Melbourne in 1928.

Ryan's counsel, mixing his metaphors, made a splendid attack on the evidence: 'The rotten house the Crown has built, you would not hang a dog on.' And the jury declined to do so.

On 8 October, with T. S. Crawford appearing once more for the prosecution, Ryan went on trial for the Mudgee robbery. This time Arthur Collins, who had done amazingly well for himself in plea bargaining—a bind over for the Mudgee robbery and an order to leave the state for his part in the attack on Cohen—was there to put his old friend away. Morris was again on hand to give evidence that he had collected Ryan and Collins after they had made their way from the track and had taken them back to his farm where the money had been buried to be collected by Ryan later. Collins was there reluctantly, demanding that he be given assurances he would not be prosecuted before he said a word. By the end of his evidence he was being treated as a hostile witness.

Ryan, making a statement from the dock (which meant he could not be cross-examined), claimed that Morris and Collins were lying and trying to put their crimes on him to save themselves. Invited to account for his wealth he ingeniously did so. His savings in the name of George Brown had been put together years earlier and were used for betting purposes; those in the name of Thompson were used to give to his mother. Thompson had kindly allowed him to use his name. He also called alibi evidence that he had gone to the funeral of a taxi driver—the same Thompson—and he had been at the widow's home with two other drivers on the night of the robbery. After deliberating for twelve hours the jury announced they could not agree and a retrial was ordered. Collins clearly thought he had had enough and failed to appear to give evidence. In December 1935 after a retirement by the jury of rather less than an hour, Joseph Harold Ryan was finally acquitted of the Mudgee train robbery.

The robbery had something of a tragic aftermath. In April 1932 a young courting couple, Frank Wilkinson and Dorothy Denzil, both of irreproachable character, were murdered in horrifying circumstances by the career criminal William Cyril Moxley. Denzil was raped and made to watch as Moxley killed her boyfriend before she was shot and mutilated. Moxley was caught sixteen days after the double killing. It was then that the crusading newspaper *Smith's Weekly* was tricked by an ex-police constable into printing that Wilkinson had been the driver of the getaway car in the Mudgee train hold-up and labelled him a pimp and blackmailer who was the victim of a gangland execution. *Truth*, as well as other newspapers, attacked *Smith's* but the paper took a statutory declaration from the constable and reprinted his unfounded allegations. On 31 July *Truth* came up with a letter from Moxley, which it published, headed 'Clears dead man's name'.

It was not until 13 August that *Smith's* finally admitted it had published a story which was 'Wicked Beyond Belief'. The public, however, did not forgive it and the grave error substantially contributed to the decline of the paper.

* * *

In April 1932 the Irish-born Hughie Martin was convicted of the attempted snatch of a bullion bag in Coles Arcade in Melbourne's Flinders Lane. A Constable Derham was escorting a cashier when he was attacked by six men and shot in the arm. Martin had arrived in Australia in 1929 on a false passport but apparently without any convictions in Ireland. He worked hold-ups in Sydney, including a bus on which a policeman was a passenger. In late 1931 he moved to Melbourne.

Martin was sentenced to twenty years and fifteen lashes and the appeal, in which he said that his co-defendant Harold Williams was not involved, was dismissed. He was also the man behind numerous armed hold-ups on service stations, a suburban bank and a pawnbroker or two.

At his trial for the robbery of a Richmond pawnbroker of the sum of 769 pounds Martin declined to name his colleagues, saying it was a matter of honour. When he decided to rob a Clifton Hill service station with a colleague, he ambushed the car of a doctor and offered the driver the choice of being driven to the country and tied up or being in the car on the robbery. The doctor chose the former. He then offered the doctor a drink or a smoke and when he said he wanted both, Martin took a pound from the doctor's pocket and bought him both at the next hotel. The doctor was tied to a bush and a handkerchief was left to mark the spot. Martin then rang the man's home to say where he and his car could be found. He claimed he gave his colleague on the robbery a pound to post back to the doctor.

After the Coles failure Martin went to Sydney and then returned to Melbourne to try to hold up the police van and so release his colleagues. The police had mounted a secure operation and he failed. He planned to return to Sydney in his baby Austin and hold up the Strathfield service station but he was in the process of filling the car when he was pointed out by an informer and arrested.

At the end of April, Martin was sentenced again, making a total of fifty-five years' imprisonment, but the sentences were concurrent and he was due to serve only twenty. He was released in the spring of 1947.

* * *

Roy Bruhn was still in and out of the Melbourne courts. In November 1937 a man, John Demsey, was shot three times, his dead body buried in a shallow grave near Bendigo and his lorry load of wool stolen. Bruhn and three others were arrested and the trial was eagerly anticipated. There were no eyewitnesses and the Crown called more than 100 others in an effort to prove guilt by circumstantial evidence. Bruhn ran an alibi that he had been sleeping at his mother's home in Coronet Street, Flemington, not far from the abattoir. He had told her, 'Mum, I'm going to take on the vealers.' In March the trial judge directed the jury to acquit the four men, adding that this did not necessarily mean they were not guilty, simply there was not sufficient evidence to convict. Bruhn was immediately rearrested and charged with having stolen rails and side tip trucks to the value of 470 pounds.

Meanwhile, in Sydney, shortly before the war, Guido Calletti was shot twice in the stomach in August 1939. His practice had been to stand over standover men, in his case the Brougham Street mob, who collected from bookmakers. He would isolate members and deal with them. He had already survived several shootings and soon he began to boast of his invulnerability. On the day of his death he had been to his grandmother's funeral, taking the opportunity to stop and have a drink with his friend 'Pretty' Dulcie Markham—described by Sydney's *Daily Mirror* as having seen 'more violence and death than any other woman in Australia's history'.

Calletti decided he would gatecrash a birthday party being held that evening in Brougham Street for a nurse who knew some of the crowd. He went with Markham and at first all was well. But then Calletti began to drink and boast of how he would deal with his hosts. In an ensuing fight he was outnumbered and, as he went for his gun, the lights went out, his arm was turned, two shots were heard, and indeed the lights went out for Calletti, who lay dying in the arms of Dulcie Markham. When the police arrived, he told them he did not know who shot him—and he may have been right.

The funeral was spectacular, even by gangland standards of the period. Five thousand people were said to have either filed past his body as it lay at the Reliance Funeral Chapel in Darlinghurst or to have attended the service, many simply checking out for themselves that he was indeed dead. There were 200 wreaths at the funeral at the Catholic chapel at Rookwood cemetery, including one from Nellie Cameron who, working interstate at the time, did not make the journey back, instead sending a four foot high floral cross. Dulcie Markham wept bitterly at the graveside.

The police thought the birthday girl might solve the killing for them. Promised immunity from prosecution as an accessory, she gave the names of those who had been at her party and in August two men, Robert Branch and George Allen, were arrested. The nurse was now tucked away safely in a boarding house in Moss Vale and the proprietor was told to report any suspicious behaviour to the police. It would not have been suspicious when the girl's 'sister' visited her, had the sister not been Nellie Cameron back from work in Queensland to help out.

The trial went badly wrong for the prosecution. The nurse was now convinced she had made a mistake and that Allen and Branch were not the men responsible. She was just as convinced that Nellie Cameron had not been to see her. It was probably a tactical error to call Nellie Cameron for she was no help either; she could not remember a single thing. Amnesia may have struck but she had realised which side her bread was now buttered on and, of course, Frank Green was still there to offer a comforting shoulder.

In all, eight of Dulcie Markham's lovers died from either the gun or the knife. On her death *The Sydney Morning Herald* wrote rather charmingly, if inaccurately, that she had never been a prostitute; rather, she had been a gangster's moll. A girl with the looks and poise of a model, from a respectable family, she was working the Kings Cross area before she was sixteen. In the late autumn of 1931 a standover man, Cecil William 'Scotchy' McCormack, wooed the eighteen-year-old Dulcie away from another youth, Alfred Dillon, whose mother ran what was euphemistically called a 'residential' in George Street. With McCormack promptly sentenced to six months for associating with criminals—he ran a fruit stall with Guido Calletti—Dillon reasserted his charm. By 13 May, a fortnight after his release, McCormack had reclaimed his 'property' and that evening Dillon stabbed him in the heart. For no very good reason except that he had been with Dillon, Matthew Foley was charged with him. The magistrate refused to commit him for trial but Dillon was sentenced to thirteen years for manslaughter. For a time Dulcie, when going about her duties, wore a black wig as a mark of respect.

The next of her lovers to go was Arthur 'The Egg' Taplin, shot in a bar in Swanston Street, Melbourne. A Sydney standover man, Taplin took over as Dulcie Markham's pimp when she was working in a Melbourne brothel. On 15 December 1937 Taplin was in the Cosmopolitan Hotel with two friends when they began to stand over a hairdresser, persuading him to buy them drinks. When Taplin threatened the man, smashing a beer glass on his head, he drew a gun and shot Taplin, who died a week later. The hairdresser, who pleaded self-defence, was later acquitted.

In 1936 Dulcie married a mobster, Frank Bowen, but the relationship did not last. He was shot dead in Kings Cross in 1940.

In the winter of that year she took a trip to Melbourne with the up and coming Frederick James 'Paddles' (because of the size of his feet) or 'Big Doll' Anderson—not living with him, just staying at the same house in Fitzroy Street, Fitzroy, she told a court in Brisbane in June 1944. On that visit Anderson was perhaps fortunate to escape a long prison sentence. Anderson, described by journalist Tom Prior as 'the most unpretentious of men', had already served a two year sentence for assault and was later regarded as one of the principal Sydney villains. Now he was alleged to have shot and killed John Charles Abrahams in June 1940 outside a nightclub. Abrahams and Anderson had been with James 'Red' Maloney, of the then-well-known Maloney family from Fitzroy. Anderson left the group and Abrahams was shot as he left a club some time later. A woman identified Anderson but later downgraded her evidence, claiming she was no longer sure. One of the problems for the prosecution was that they could not show any motive for the killing. Anderson produced an alibi in the form of a taxi driver whom he had treated to a steak and egg meal at a diner in Bourke Street and the jury took only a short time to acquit him.

Outside court Anderson promised his barrister a present on each anniversary of the acquittal and indicated that this was the last time he would be associating in unlikely company. It was not to be. Four months later he appeared in court in Sydney on a charge of consorting with criminals in William Street, for which he received a month. He was acquitted of standing over a bookmaker and fined for assaults on two police officers and obtaining a motor licence and registration documents by false pretences. From then on his career would be onwards and upwards.

In 1939 Melbourne had a higher crime rate, per capita, than London. Its record for violent robberies was, noted *The Sydney Morning Herald* a trifle smugly on 1 May that year, the worst in Australia. And the situation had certainly shown few signs of improvement in the ensuing five years. This was, more or less, the picture of major crime that prevailed just before war broke out and the screen changed completely.

The War Years

5

War is a good time for criminals. In his memoirs, Frankie Fraser, the London villain and friend of the Kray twins, whose career spanned half a century, thought that war made criminals out of everyone:

> The war organised criminals ... Before the war thieving was safes, jewellery, furs. Now a whole new world opened up. There was so much money and stuff about—cigarettes, sugar, clothes, petrol coupons, clothing coupons, anything. It was a thieves' paradise. I was a thief. Everyone was a thief.
>
> Before the war some people wouldn't grass on you, but they wouldn't take part in villainy. In criminal terms they was honest, but now everyone was crooked. Mums, they'd want to buy extra eggs for their children and a bit of extra meat ... Everyone was involved. It was wonderful.

While Australia did not suffer the looting that followed the bombing of London or the rationing that so damaged Britain, it did have soldiers—visiting soldiers, deserting soldiers, soldiers on leave ... all to be catered for and, particularly in the case of visiting soldiers, there for the plucking.

When the first seven vessels containing 2100 American troops arrived in Sydney in 1941 an estimated crowd of half a million greeted their arrival with streamers, confetti and petals. When US troops arrived in Brisbane it was thought a quarter of a million people were there to welcome them. And among those who gave the men the greatest welcome was the underworld.

As the war progressed, American troops arrived in their tens of thousands, causing a wholesale boom in sly-grog shops, gambling and prostitution at all levels. There were pregnancies to be terminated and venereal diseases to be cured. There was the opportunity to work variations of the ginger game and the even greater opportunity to steal from drunken clients.

The Americans were sold cigarettes rolled with cabbage leaves, and cold tea and tobacco water passed off as beer and whisky; and they were overcharged by the girls and mugged by their pimps. American soldiers would dash madly about Brisbane whenever they heard of a pub in the suburbs that would be selling beer for an hour or so. North of Brisbane, the Yanks had to provide their own glasses, and a beer bottle with its neck removed was known as a Lady Blamey, either because she suggested this as a form of glass or because of its resemblance to her shape. From time to time the soldiers appear to have struck back. On 6 February 1943 at around 9.30 p.m. taxi-driver Francis Phelan was found shot dead half a mile from his abandoned taxi in Melbourne. He had been involved in sly-grog as well as running American soldiers to brothels in Prahran and it was thought that he had been trying to stand over them. A cap belonging to a sergeant was found near the taxi. Its owner explained that there had been a good deal of pilfering in the barracks and his cap had been stolen. The matter was taken no further.

Business expanded to fill the opportunities available; and now, to add to all the other ongoing enterprises, a new market developed in forgery and blackmarketeering—making available not only papers for deserting troops but also items that were rationed.

Before, and in the early part of the war, furs from Canada were favoured smuggled goods along with silks from Japan and China; silk stockings from the United States, England and Europe; and miniature radio sets from various countries. Since the duty on furs was 70 per cent and on stockings and perfume between 50 and 60 per cent, the potential profits for the underworld were enormous. Before National Security Regulations stopped people from boarding ships, two or three women would visit 'a friend' on board and come off wearing furs and several sets of underwear. Some would come off re-dressed from head to foot. Asian seamen donned ladies' underwear as they left the boat and the profits were substantial: silk stockings, once on the black market at seven shillings and sixpence a pair, now fetched two pounds ten shillings.

In Sydney in July 1940 the Empire Club, a sly-grog shop on George Street, was closed by the authorities. It reopened in September and within the month the proprietor, Maltese-born Anthony Pisani, was sentenced to six months' hard labour and fined 100 pounds for selling beer without a licence. Pisani had previously been convicted of selling liquor without a licence in March 1939 at the Foreigner's Club in Oxford Street and had convictions for sly-grog selling dating back to 1929. What was really up the nose of the authorities was that it was a hangout for black servicemen and white girls, many of whom were drunk. In September 1940 a magistrate called it 'One of the worst conducted clubs in Sydney'.

Two years later, in October 1942, Phil Jeffs's 400 Club was shut down and from then on he lived off his substantial investments at Ettalong, where he had built a library consisting mainly of philosophical works and where he surrounded himself with these as well as a series of good-looking women.

But no sooner had one club closed its doors than another opened, very often on the same premises. Some were ritzier and longer lasting than others and some established their owners as kings of the nightclub and underworld scene. In Sydney's Kings Cross, Abe Saffron, the nephew of Mr Justice Isaacs, followed his uncle into a career which involved many appearances in court, albeit as plaintiff and defendant rather than as advocate and judge.

The small, dapper Abraham Gilbert Saffron was one of five children of a draper in Annandale, Sydney. Saffron's mother wanted him to be a doctor but he had a taste for business, begun by selling cigarettes to players at his father's poker games. Educated at Fort Street High School, whose other alumni included the New South Wales Premier Neville Wran and Paddles Anderson, Saffron left at the age of fifteen and began work in his father's shop. In 1938 he acquired his first gaming conviction and the next year he was sentenced to six months' hard labour, suspended provided he joined the armed forces. Presumably because of his connections, over the years there were few prosecutions and those that were brought mostly failed, or convictions were overturned on appeal. In perhaps the most celebrated of them, in 1956 he was acquitted of 'scandalous conduct' involving four girls, feather dusters and oysters.

Saffron's clubs, often owned in partnership with Hilton G. Kincaid, included the Roosevelt Club at 32 Orwell Street, described by Mr Justice

Maxwell, who ordered its closure in 1943, as 'the most notorious and disreputable nightclub in the city'. Saffron moved north to Newcastle where he obtained a bookmaker's licence from the less than demanding Newcastle Jockey Club and also took a licence on the Newcastle Hotel.

Some old friends were more fortunate. In Melbourne in July 1940 Henry Stokes had all the money that had been confiscated in a raid on the Caulfield Sporting Club returned to him when charges that he had the care and management of a common gaming house were dismissed. The social club, said Raymond Dunn, Stokes's lawyer, had 'many and varied legitimate activities' and was 'a heavy contributor to the Australian Comforts Fund and charitable appeals'.

Sadly, other old friends did not see out the war. Henry Slater did not even last the first year. Since his run-in with Stokes twenty years earlier, Slater had become something of a peripatetic villain gravitating between Sydney and Adelaide, living by theft and the standover of SP bookmakers. He had had his share of fortune however. After three trials, he had been acquitted of the murder of Peter Monaghan in Surry Hills.

Now, in a somewhat low-key end for one of Sydney's senior standover men, Slater was shot at La Perouse near the Yarra Bay shanty town after he had left his home to catch a tram. The shooter pumped two bullets into him and then rode away on a bicycle. At the inquest into his death the coroner was told that Slater had been shot by a poulterer, Christopher Ransome, who had said as he stood by the body, 'You won't worry me or anyone else again.' Ransome had allegedly shot him because Slater had been calling him a pervert. By the time of the inquest Ransome had been committed to an insane asylum. Appearances are deceptive, though, and not everyone was convinced by the official account.

Another survivor of the Razor Wars went down around the same time. In July 1940 the 39-year-old William Smiley (sometimes Smillie), gunman and razorman, was found in a lane off Butt Street, Surry Hills, lying next to a dead cat. In 1928 at the height of the wars he had received five years for slashing. In 1935 he had slashed a man at a party and had himself been shot through both feet a few days later.

The next year, when he was found in Elizabeth Street shot in the thigh, he refused to help the police, saying, 'If I had the Town Hall clock in my pocket, I wouldn't tell you the time.' Now John McIvor and George Dempsey were charged with his murder. It would seem that Smiley had shot Dempsey in the past and was standing over him. They were acquitted.

As World War II went on, the demand for after hours drinking establishments increased. They had, of course, maintained a regular trade before the war but now there was much more money around to meet the increased prices. Breweries were required to provide beer for the troops and for four years from March 1942 a quota system was imposed. The importation of Scotch whisky was also prohibited from the beginning of the war and both beer rationing and this ban created a ready black market. In 1943 the licensee of the Wentworth Hotel in Sydney was charged with selling whisky at a price ranging between four and six pounds a bottle, yielding him an overall annual profit in the region of 30 000 pounds.

In March that year Kate Leigh, still protesting at having her name linked with Tilly Devine—'I am respectable and won't be insulted'—received six months for selling beer to a policeman. In October the same year, in what was described as her 'positively farewell appearance' in the courts—for six months anyway—Tilly Devine retired to Long Bay when Judge McGhie dismissed her appeal against two convictions of being the owner of a house frequented by reputed thieves. The same week she was fined ten pounds on a language charge for using words 'not found in Webster'.

There was also the opportunity for a certain amount of freelance pimping. In August 1943, 46-year-old Westbrook Walter Turnbull, described as an invalid pensioner, and his younger brother, the 43-year-old John Alexander, pleaded not guilty to charges of procuring girls for the purposes of prostitution. The girls, whom they had met at the Ziegfeld Club, were paid three pounds per customer, half of which went to the brothers. Two months later, found guilty, the Turnbulls each received three years and three months' imprisonment.

Considerable attention was paid to morals, with clergymen in disguise investigating Sydney nightclubs, hotel lounges and dark doorways. In November 1943 the President of the New South Wales Temperance Alliance claimed that the police were prevented from cleaning up Sydney because the state government was controlled by liquor traffickers.

During the war racing was reduced to one afternoon a week but this did nothing to curtail gambling; more money was waged on a

Saturday afternoon, the SP business still boomed and operators still paid for protection—if they complained they could expect visits from heavies. Bets of 1000 pounds by Americans in Thommo's Two-up School were not uncommon. Telephone mechanics installed gadgets to kill a telephone in the event of a police raid and two well-known Sydney standover men were battling for control of the whole business of standing over SP bookmakers. When the prime minister, John Curtin, asked for a telephone call to be put through one Saturday afternoon to discuss the situation in Japan he was told there were sixty bookmakers ahead of him in the queue for connection.

In Melbourne touts were handing out cards inviting servicemen to clubs run by Italians in and around Russell Street. 'Near beer' joints (sellers of soft drinks as beer or champagne) sold a mixture of lemonade, raspberry and a smell of gin. Charges for an evening's drinking could run from five to fifteen pounds a night. Now girls were being set up in flats along St Kilda Road.

Substantial rents of four pounds a week were being offered to landlords in Fitzroy Street, St Kilda, when thirty shillings was the going rate, with the view to establishing a brothel area in the street. Landlords who declined were warned of the possibility of the premises being damaged or being reported to the health authorities, which might lead to costly repairs.

Meanwhile, in Brisbane, vice did a roaring trade as never before. With the volume of custom it is said the prostitutes were literally red hot and more recruits were needed. In September 1942 a message was sent to Thommo's, and Sydney criminals arranged for a train load of girls to go to work in Queensland. It is generally accepted that John Curtin gave the train a high priority clearance.

With sly-grog, doctored spirits, prostitution and taxi drivers cheating and robbing servicemen on leave, there was work and money for everyone. American servicemen roamed the town looking for re-creation and the town roamed looking for the soldiers. There was a special area for black American servicemen between Victoria Bridge and the old South Brisbane Town Hall.

'Pretty' Dulcie Markham was another to return to the pickings of the Gold Coast, where she was known as Dulcie Williams and where, along with her new de facto Arthur Williams, she was charged in January 1944 with vagrancy. She claimed that she had been living with Williams for some six years, subject to interludes with Caletti, Anderson and so on; that, when they came to Brisbane, Williams had 600 pounds and he gave her money for the rent and groceries; and no, she was not working in that way; and no, she did not know the money came from sly-grog; but yes, she was known as Tosca de Marquis and Tosca de Marine, but what had that got to do with things? Case dismissed.

In Sydney there was a special brothel, the Tradesman's Arms Hotel in Palmer Street, for the black servicemen. Lilian Armfield, one of the first policewomen in Sydney, wrote in her memoirs: 'We found it necessary to not only turn a blind eye, but to give tacit approval, to the existence of a brothel which catered exclusively to American Negro Servicemen.' This was putting it a little delicately. The military police were employed keeping the queues in the street in order and moving along, as if the patrons were buying tickets to the cinema.

Just as there were queues outside brothels in Sydney so there were in other cities. In Townsville there were long queues outside houses in the Ford Street area and prostitutes worked out of doors, night and day, in the harbourside park, charging between one and two pounds. Townsville had its own brothel for the black troops, situated at Stuart. The madam was said to have two large automatic pistols which she strapped to her waist and a leather money bag hung around her neck. When the situation demanded it she would fire the pistols in the air to restore order.

Also shameful to the white folk was that some women went with the black servicemen voluntarily. Worse, some of them were married women. When the Booker T. Washington club was formed for black servicemen in Sydney, there were not enough working girls to entertain the members. A screening test was established to check all women who wished to become members and they were required to provide their particulars and a photograph. Policewoman Lilian Armfield commented: 'It was like a knife through the heart when we found that one Sydney girl, only twelve years old, was in the bed of a Negro serviceman.' In January 1944 *Truth* was seriously unhappy: 'Not much has been said, outside the courts, of the spreading depravity involving our white women and visiting colored men.'

In Perth, Roe Street was still the brothel centre and venereal disease was rife in Fremantle. One madam, asked her occupation by the Manpower Inquiry, replied, 'Essential service; madam of a brothel' and heard no more.

* * *

By the end of the war the various players who would establish themselves as the kings of crime in Sydney and Melbourne over the next twenty years had begun to emerge. Some, of course, did not last that length of time. One such star was the cold-eyed Leslie 'Scotland Yard' Walkerden (not because of his regrettable tendency to dob in his rivals but because of his predilection for pulp crime paperbacks). During the war he was employed by the baccarat club owner Frank Regan, who needed help standing up to the predatory James Coates and Robert James 'Pretty Boy' Walker. By now Walkerden was in his late twenties and, although he had been in and out of the courts since the age of fifteen and was known as Australia's first 'two gun' man, he had never been found with a gun. It was thought that any gun was carried for him in a woman's handbag—either by his wife or by one of his girlfriends, who included the legendary Dulcie Markham. Regan hired him at the bargain rate of five pounds after he had been swindled by Coates and then beaten up by him and Walker near the Ritz Hotel in St Kilda.

In July 1943 a waitress, Pearl Lilian Oliver, was shot in the back and had her skull fractured as she tried to run away from a boarding house on Brunswick Street, Fitzroy, where wharf labourer Joe Fanesi and an Allied sailor Peter Croft had been shot. The case was argued on the basis that there had been a blue because Harold William Sydney Porter Nugent, a standover man who served three years for robbery in 1939, had been paying her unwanted attention. But it was more a question of establishing a pecking order. A so-called domestic matter usually called for less punishment than one involving a standover. Nugent was acquitted of Oliver's murder but in April 1944 he was sentenced to three years for unlawfully and maliciously wounding Fanesi, a one-time light-heavyweight boxer from Western Australia.

Pretty Boy Walker was another who commuted between Sydney and Melbourne. In the 1930s Walker had been questioned over a number of murders, including the shooting of Jerry Lynch in the Top Hat Club in Sydney. He was also suspected of two other murders, but the worst thing on his record was a sentence of two and a half years for the theft of a tray of jewellery in Lismore. Released in 1939 and regarded as courteous, charming and cold blooded in equal parts, he moved to Melbourne at the outbreak of war as a gun for hire and debt enforcer commanding high fees.

In 1941 he opened his own baccarat school in a one bedroom flat in Grey Street, East Melbourne, reckoning on profits of 100 pounds a night. One of his partners included the treacherous James Coates who was crooked enough to cheat his own school, which was regularly raided by the police on the dob-in of Henry Stokes and lasted only five months. Walker returned to the standover and was shot by Walkerden in the thigh after he had approached a club run by Frank Regan. Some weeks later he was shot once more by Walkerden near the old Melbourne Hospital. Walker dragged himself up the steps and, amazingly, survived. He had clothes smuggled into the hospital and went back to Sydney. On his return to Melbourne he was once more set up to be killed by Walkerden in what he thought was to be a meeting of reconciliation in Lonsdale Street. Instead, in a taxi-cab chase through Swanston, Burke and Russell streets, Walkerden opened fire in Little Collins, hitting the taxi in which Walker was travelling. Two of the bullets ricocheted into the wall of the King's Hotel. Walker had the cab driver take him to Spencer Street Station and once more padded back to Sydney.

From there he took a job as a kitchen porter on the *Queen Mary*, which was being used as a troop ship. It would not be until 1953 that he returned to Australia, went to Adelaide and then ventured one final time to Melbourne.

Another whose star was rising towards the end of the war was Freddie 'The Frog' Harrison, a close friend of Nugent. During his career Harrison faced fifty-four charges and was rarely convicted. During the war he joined the navy and deserted, apparently not because he did not wish to fight but because he could not stand the cramped conditions on the troop ship HMAS *Lonsdale*. He served a ninety day sentence and back in Melbourne he became an enforcer for a sly-grogger who operated at the notorious Peanut Farm Betting Stand in St Kilda.

He shot a seaman in an argument in a Flinders Street baccarat school but no charges were brought. The turning point in his career occurred just after the war when the baccarat bosses of Melbourne selected him as their standover man and enforcer to see off a number of small time operators who were pestering them. It was something at which he excelled. He received twenty pounds a week plus tips and would escort winning punters home. This was a time when two-up schools would close their doors for half an hour after winners left to give them a sporting chance of reaching safety.

Now Harrison began to gather a nucleus of men—including Nugent as well as one Jack Eric Twist and the one time boxer, the beetle-browed Norman Bradshaw (known as 'The Chauffeur' because he was usually the driver and backup man for Harrison on his shootings). Along with Joey Turner they would come to be regarded as the principal standover men and, therefore, kings of crime in Melbourne in the late 1940s and 1950s.

* * *

On 29 March 1944 an old friend from the Canberra train robbery, George Morris, was shot to death and his body, with twelve bullet wounds, was found in his car near a block of flats in High Street, Miller's Point, Sydney, almost directly above the spot where Reginald Holmes had been shot in the Shark Arm case a decade earlier. Six of the shots had been fired into his head. A man had apparently telephoned him and asked him to be at Miller's Point at 9 p.m. It was thought he had been killed in a dispute over proceeds of crime rather than as revenge for some of his earlier misdeeds. At the time, Morris was on bail, having been committed for trial on a charge of stealing a safe containing about 2500 pounds in jewellery, coins and cash.

A man who had been on the fringes of the underworld in the 1930s and who emerged as a leading figure during the war was the very dubious Dr Reginald Stuart-Jones. Born in London as plain Jones, he had arrived in Australia with his parents at the age of nine. A fine sportsman, he played for Sydney University at cricket, football, tennis, athletics and rifle shooting. Once he graduated he returned to England where he married his first wife Sheena, heiress to a chain of cinemas. He returned to Sydney where he set up practice in Macquarie Street as a gynaecologist and later lived in a mock Moroccan mansion in Bellevue Hill that had its own shooting gallery in the old fashioned sense.

There appears to have been a louche streak in him for his constant companions were criminals. He carried a revolver, which he liked to fire into the ceilings of bars in Surry Hills, and in 1939 he was arrested for drunken driving. For a time he held interests in several nightclubs of varying degrees of quality. At the one end was the Lido at Bondi Beach and at the better end, certainly financially, was the 400 Club in Phillip Street, which he owned with Phil Jeffs until they fell out in 1937.

An interest in a nightclub or two can provide an endless stream of patients for an abortionist and in this aspect of his career he went into partnership with the former bouncer Richard Reilly, the man who in 1937 had shot Clarrie Thomas. With the proceeds Stuart-Jones became a great racing man, owning, quite successfully, thoroughbreds, trotters and greyhounds.

His decline began when he appeared before the courts charged with 'unlawfully using an instrument for a certain purpose' in 1944. When the police raided the second floor of 229 Macquarie Street they found Stuart-Jones gowned up, preparing to operate on a girl who had paid his secretary forty pounds. He was duly acquitted.

That year he married his second wife, Mary Kathleen Ryan, having divorced Sheena in 1936. His second marriage was not a happy one either, more so when he found her in a flat in Leichhardt wearing the pyjamas of the welterweight Cliffie Thompson who boxed as Cliffie Thomas. He sued for divorce but before the decree was made absolute they were together again.

Then came one of the stranger episodes in Stuart-Jones's fairly extraordinary career. Just before midnight on 31 October 1944 he was kidnapped from outside his house in Bellevue Hill. He was asked by two criminals he knew to look at a man they had in their car. When he reached it there was his wife's lover Cliffie Thompson, along with a man he didn't know, Alexander 'Scotty' Jowett. He was taken at gunpoint to Maroubra and told he would be shot and his body thrown over the cliffs. Indeed, just after midnight Jowett shot Stuart-Jones in the chest, hitting him in the lung. The doctor then, amazingly, seems to have talked his captors into dropping him off at the Vassilia Private Hospital in Randwick. He survived.

The resulting trial was all the press and public could reasonably hope for. There were details of Stuart-Jones's drink, drug and abortion dealing. There was the story of Cliffie Thompson's love for Stuart-Jones's wife and Thompson's wife's love for Jowett.

* * *

Still in Sydney, it was towards the end of the war that a figure emerged in black market circles who in later years would have a devastating effect on crime and politicians alike. The 35-year-old Richard Gabriel Reilly, now euphemistically described as an electrician and still a friend of the good doctor, was supplementing his income as a standover man by running a forged clothing coupon ring from Roslyn Road, Elizabeth Bay. When it was broken up and nine people were arrested in February 1945 the police seized 250 clothing coupons and Reilly's wallet. It held 632 pounds—approximately two years' wages for a working electrician. He had built up a substantial operation collecting forged, stolen and otherwise illegally obtained coupons and selling them on to retailers. It was only part of his expanding empire.

Then in June that year came the death of Henry Stokes, survivor of the Squizzy Taylor era and dictator of the biggest of Melbourne's gambling rackets. Appropriately he died in a gaming club; lurching away from a table, he slumped in a chair and was dead within half an hour. Rather less than forty people attended his funeral and what became of his huge fortune was never clear. On the face of things, he died leaving only some 15 000 pounds. The state declared baccarat illegal in July but in another example of how crime flourishes through prohibition, by August there was a rash of small 'bloodhouses'.

Stokes was survived for only a few months by Phil Jeffs who had been persuaded out of retirement by the 1944 Sydney baccarat boom to organise clubs with standover man and racehorse trainer Siddy Kelly and the young up-and-coming gambler Perce Galea. When Jeffs died in October that year it was suggested that the cause was the lingering effects of bullet wounds from the 1929 war.

Siddy Kelly was another veteran of the Razor Wars who in Melbourne in 1934 had been sentenced to the lash and five years' imprisonment for slashing one John Penfold while others held him down. In 1928 Kelly had slashed Betty Carslake, for which Gordon Barr, the husband of Diamond Dolly, took the blame and received five years. In August 1928 Dolly took the trouble to travel to Melbourne to the Richmond Pony races to tell the stewards that Kelly, who was running a horse there, had put a battery in the saddle. Kelly, an assistant and the appropriately named jockey John Hook were all warned off for life.

Now Kelly emerged from the shadows to establish himself as one of the great crime bosses of this, and indeed many another, period until his death in 1948. With his 100-pounds-a-night profits from Chemin-de-fer, or Boxer as it was known, Kelly played at The Shirt Factory in Darlinghurst. From an early stage he was able to secure the assistance of the police, and his clubs were rarely prosecuted. Apart from raids early in 1944 there seem to have been none until an abortive one in 1947 when there was a tip-off and all the police discovered was a game of gin rummy. When Kelly became ill in 1947 he employed Joe 'The Pig' Sinclair, whom he brought from Melbourne to run his games and it was the pair of them who again employed Perce Galea. When Kelly died in 1948 it was rumoured that he had left 30 000 pounds buried in Centennial Park where he lived. The park was promptly invaded by treasure hunters who dug up tracts without success.

By the end of 1944 there was a good clear-up rate in Sydney for murders generally, with only sixteen killings (down from thirty-two in 1940), and the authorities were quietly congratulating themselves on keeping crime under control. In 1944 there had been a total of forty murders in New South Wales; sixteen murderers committed suicide and only two cases remained unsolved by the end of the year. One was the murder of George Morris. Although an arrest had been made the Crown refused to file a bill because of an alibi supplied by the principal suspect. The police, if not the press, nevertheless regarded it as solved. The second was that of 28-year-old Joyce Pattison of Bourke Street, found dead on the bank of a lake. She and another woman had gone there with two black Allied servicemen.

However, other crimes of violence had risen to a high peak in Sydney. Black servicemen were regarded as responsible for many of the affrays and servicemen generally were still victims of robberies when they were taken by prostitutes to rooms and then mugged.

Despite all this, the authorities believed there was a general falling off in crime, which they attributed to a variety of reasons. First was the absence of thousands of potential criminals serving in the armed forces. Then there was the efficiency of the military police and the increased discipline to which young men were subject. Thirdly, the criminals left behind were moving into the lucrative black market and unemployment had disappeared.

The black market bit was certainly right. The black market in cigarettes and liquor was now regarded by the underworld as more profitable than robberies. When a shortage of cigarettes followed the exodus of American servicemen, the prices rocketed. There was a black market in vegetables and there were premiums on potatoes, carrots and onions as well as on car tyres, often taken from vehicles stolen for the purpose. In nine months in 1944 more than a million smuggled cigarettes were seized. The contraband also included silk stockings and women's underwear hidden in boiler tubes, coal bunkers, false bottoms of cabin lockers and lifeboats. There was also a revolving market in liquor, with whisky bought at three to five pounds and sold in battle areas at up to twenty pounds. The profit was then invested in cigarettes bought at three shillings and fourpence a carton and resold at up to thirty shillings, which was again reinvested in liquor. At the end of the war there was a black market in homemade cigarette papers and one enterprising outfit began manufacturing toilet paper soaked in starch. The trade broke down when a newspaper kindly published the recipe.

It was now that opium began to arrive in ten and twelve pound lots. By the end of the war it came generally from India and was smuggled in the heart of packs of butter, inside sausage skins and in the carcasses of sheep. Cooks took the drug from their ships in kerosene tins purporting to contain dripping.

* * *

The police may have had great success clearing up the run-of-the-mill murders but what they could not clear up were the gangland murders and the weekly shootings. They may have known full well who was responsible, but proving it was a wholly different thing. Witnesses were there to be threatened and bribed by the friends of the suspect. Even on the rare occasions when a man was seen almost literally standing over a corpse with a smoking gun and there was a witness prepared to say so, then, as now, juries were happy to find self-defence.

One reason for the proliferation of gun crime in the period was the number of thefts from the army. As a result a .38 could be purchased for twenty-five pounds, Birettas and Lügers for thirty pounds and ammunition was five pounds for 100 rounds. Every criminal—from the bosses of a baccarat game to (much more dangerously) the back lane sneak thief—carried a gun. By 1947 prices had fallen. A .38 or a Biretta then cost ten pounds and a Lüger five pounds more.

The year 1945 started with a remarkable claim by Vice Squad Inspector Thompson that 'Sydney is freer of vice and illegal gambling than any other city of its size in the world.' In 1944, 851 women were charged with vagrancy in the city compared with 885 the previous year. An explanation for this might, however, have been that 258 women had been arrested in the suburbs, compared with 100 in 1943. There were 6225 arrests of men and 336 of women under the Gaming Act and arrests under the consorting laws ran at 100 a week.

The next month a major theft took place when 800000 butter coupons representing half a week's rations for every man, woman and child were stolen from the office of the Rationing Commission in George Street. It was thought to have been the work of an interstate gang operating in both Melbourne and Sydney.

When it came to it, 1945 was something of a vintage year for gangland murders and deaths, both in Sydney and Melbourne. The first to go had actually been on New Year's Eve 1944 when Chow Hayes shot and killed Eddie Weyman in Sydney. There had been bad blood between them after Weyman kept 1200 pounds for himself in a deal over stolen cigarettes. Later Hayes stole 3800 pounds from Weyman's safebox, which was kept in the cistern of his outside lavatory, but he still did not regard this as adequate compensation. On Christmas Eve, Hayes met Weyman in the London Hotel and demanded repayment of the 1200 pounds. Weyman promised it but that afternoon Hayes shot him at his home, hitting him in the shoulder. When he was released from hospital he repaid the money but, according to Hayes, Weyman would not shake hands and had been saying that he would back him up.

On New Year's Eve, Donny 'The Duck' Day threw a party at the Paddington Town Hall but Weyman went to another in Newtown and then home to Surry Hills. Hayes had put in an appearance at the Day party and then was driven to Weyman's home, where he shot him before returning to the Town Hall. Hayes later wrote in his biography: 'I fired and hit him five times with the .38. The last I saw of him he fell down alongside the bed. I knew he was badly wounded and I thought he was dead—but he wasn't ...'

He wasn't quite. He managed to crawl to his porch where he died. Hayes was acquitted after witnesses said he had been at the Day party all night. His costs were paid for him by his old friend Kate Leigh.

The Duck did not last the month. In the early hours of 29 January a woman telephoned Darlinghurst Police Station to say the black-marketeer, who had recently purchased a car from Stuart-Jones, had been shot in a house at the corner of Crown and Foveaux streets. By the time the police arrived they found that, indeed, he had a bullet hole through his cheeks and nose and two wounds in his chest. Earlier there had been a fight in the house when a man was kicked in the groin. Two stolen revolvers were found.

Day was another who had been a jockey but had been disqualified for life. At the time of his death he was on bail for unlawful possession of tyres and was appealing his conviction. He was also awaiting trial on a charge of conspiracy over black market liquor. Three women, including Renée Day, and a 27-year-old salesman Keith Kitchener Hull were arrested and charged with murder. Hull was acquitted after telling the jury that he had fired in self-defence. Stuart-Jones's wife took the opportunity to drive another nail into the good doctor's reputation, telling the press in some detail just how close he and The Duck had been as friends and just what they had got up to together.

The day The Duck died Jones's attacker, Cliffie Thompson, was shot at Long Bay jail. A warder heard a shot at around 1 p.m. and there was Thompson with a chest wound. He would not say how the gun came to be in his cell but it had probably been smuggled at the instigation of Jowett. Both men were convicted of the attack on Stuart-Jones and sentenced to death, later commuted to life imprisonment. In the end they each served a relatively short period.

Before that, on 9 January, Cyril Norman, also known as Thomas Couldrey, held up a gunsmith's in King Street, Sydney. He invited the manager Maurice Hannigan to show him some guns. Norman loaded one and shot him dead before he escaped with a total of six guns, ammunition and 164 pounds in cash. For a time the police thought that Hannigan's killer was Stephen Henry Cunningham, who shot himself after a siege with the police when they went to arrest him over an assault; but they were wrong.

The next day Norman returned to his more usual trade of stealing passengers' luggage at the city's stations. It would be his undoing. He picked up two suitcases at Woolloomooloo and found they contained American army officer uniforms. He had them altered and, now posing as an American, went to the country town of Blayney in the Central Tablelands where he booked a room in the Exchange Hotel. He was caught on 12 January by pure mischance. While he was showering a maid looked in his room and saw the guns on the bed. She reported this to the manager who said not to worry as they belonged to an American officer; but nevertheless she told the police.

Constable Eric Bailey and another officer went to investigate and at first they were convinced by the story Norman told them. They said, however, they would take him to the station to check out the story.

Norman panicked and ran. Bailey tackled him and cuffed him to his own wrist but, as he did so, Norman shot him. Bailey collapsed on Norman, pinning him to the ground. When reinforcements arrived Bailey was sitting on the kerb. 'He has shot me, don't let him get away,' he told the officers. 'I had a go. I didn't squib it.' Then he died. Norman was sentenced to death but reprieved.

Joe Taylor, the proprietor of Thommo's Two-up School, was more fortunate than Constable Bailey. In February 1945 at Hawkesbury Races he quarrelled with and fought the bludger and drug addict Joe Prendergast, brother of John who had been shot dead fifteen years earlier by Kate Leigh. The evening after the quarrel Prendergast shot Taylor as he was standing in Reservoir Street outside his school. It seems that Taylor would not allow revenge to be taken because he feared that if Prendergast was murdered the police would use it as an excuse to close The Game. In fact, to divert attention from his school, the report was that Taylor had been shot at his home by an unidentified man. True to tradition he refused to identify Prendergast, who prudently absented himself in Melbourne for some years.

Tilly Devine's last major criminal case came later that month. The previous year she had been acquitted of threatening a butcher with his own knife—she claimed he had sold her bad meat. Now, on 18 February, she was charged with shooting Eric Parson with intent to murder him. She said he had been shot on the street while she was in bed. Four days later, when he failed to recognise her as his assailant, she was acquitted and, amazingly, the pair were soon married. The papers described her as a 'plump thin-lipped blonde with marble-hard features and an expensive perm'.

At the end of the war it was all change in the Melbourne hierarchy as well. After the death of Henry Stokes the baccarat world was up for grabs and one who wanted a slice of the action was the gunman Leslie Walkerden. Strictly speaking, he was Frank Regan's man but he also worked for Stokes for twenty-five pounds a week, increased over time to 250 pounds, at the Ace of Clubs where he checked out the punters and also acted as a late night chauffeur. On one occasion he found he had a flat tyre. At first he thought it was a puncture but then he realised the tyre had been deliberately let down. Those with him thought this was a sign that Walkerden was becoming vulnerable but he would have nothing of it, claiming he had a gun in the boot to deal with trouble.

He was wrong. Early in September 1945 Norman Bradshaw and Freddie Harrison, working for a man known as 'The Old Greek', began harassing customers outside Stokes's casino and Walkerden, leading Stokes's troops, administered a bad beating to them. Two nights later, on 11 September at about 2.30 a.m. when he left a baccarat school in Waltham Street, Richmond, he found another tyre on his black Buick had been let down and this time, as he changed it, he was shot. One arm was almost severed and his stomach was torn out. He still managed to stagger to the house of his friend George De Sanctis, calling out to another friend George Newman, who had been with him in the club, that he had been shot. Walkerden survived until he was taken to St Vincent's Hospital, where he declined to talk to the dubious detective Frederick 'Blue' Adam, also known as 'Thumper'. Walkerden told him 'Don't waste your time on this. I will fix it my own way.' He lived through the night, dying at eight o'clock the next morning.

During the inquest on her husband, Walkerden's wife Gladys sat composedly reading a racing paper. Walkerden's blonde girlfriend, who was never named (for her own protection) but was Dulcie Markham, maintained that she did not know Walkerden was associated with baccarat games. His killer was never named but there was little doubt in the underworld that Freddie Harrison, with an assist from Norman Bradshaw, was responsible. That did not in any way stop them shifting the blame onto John Gilligan, James Coates and Bob Brewster.

By the end of World War II a new group had established itself as the top standover men in Melbourne. In alphabetical order they were Norman Bradshaw, Harold Nugent, Joe Turner and Jack Eric Twist. But at first the undoubted leader of the pack was Freddie 'The Frog' Harrison.

After the War Was Over

6

With the war over, life in the Australian underworld continued in much the same way as before, with a number of outstanding debts being cancelled. One of the earliest came in March 1946 when Myles Henry 'Face' McKeon, the pre-war killer of Chow Hayes's friend Harold Tarlington, was found dead in Rose Street, Sydney. McKeon was shot as he drove along the street, and his car crashed. He was said to have had more enemies than friends but there were sixteen cars at Rookwood Cemetery for his funeral.

Raymond Emmett Bollard, Thomas Esmond 'Ezzie' Bollard and Harry Wyndham were arrested on suspicion of murder but by the time the trial was heard at the end of June the prosecution's case was in ribbons. The only witness was 72-year-old Edward Atkin, more or less a derelict known as 'Okey Doke', who had around eighty convictions, including robbery with violence. He told their committal hearing that he had seen the men drinking together in the Darlington Hotel and they had all gone off in McKeon's car. Unfortunately he had written to the men in Long Bay saying he was sorry he had told lies at the earlier proceedings. They were all acquitted on the direction of the trial judge.

One man who was among the most dangerous of his time, and who has perhaps never received sufficient recognition for his exploits over a thirty year period, is William 'Joey' Hollebone. In October 1935, aged nineteen, he was sentenced to ten years' imprisonment for the manslaughter of Leslie Archibald Hobson in King Street in the Sydney suburb of Newtown. Hobson had come out of a newsagent's to find Hollebone, along with James Charters and Edward Smith, about to steal a man's bicycle. In the ensuing fight Hobson was knocked to the ground and the trio kicked him to death. It was a case, said the judge, that came close to murder.

It was while he was in Parramatta jail that Hollebone teamed up with Chow Hayes in a partnership that would last until his death. After their respective releases Hayes and Hollebone became minders at Joe Taylor's two-up school but in 1946 Hollebone was sent to prison for possessing an unlicensed pistol and while he was inside Alfie Dawes went to his home and took all his clothes. When Hollebone's wife Hazel complained, he hit her.

On his release, on 29 August Hollebone undertook a short but lethal shooting spree in Mary Street, Waterloo, killing nineteen-year-old Marjorie Nurse and Alfred Dawes junior and wounding four others. The level at which they lived can be gauged by the fact that, after the shootings, Mrs Elizabeth Dawes had no sheets to cover the corpses. The police borrowed three from her neighbour and later Mrs Dawes quite properly washed and ironed them and quite improperly popped them at Grace's Pawn Shop in Chippendale. Hollebone gave himself up the day after the shooting but, with confusion over identification, he was acquitted. Some years later he put a cut requiring nearly forty stitches in his wife's face.

Stuffy Melbourne was now really rather proud that Sydney had worse violence than the Victorian capital. *The Argus* believed the lower crime rate to be because of Melbourne's more open layout and particularly because disputes tended to be settled 'by comparatively peaceful means, using fists, knuckle-dusters and small cordial bottles rather than the decisive but noisy firearm'.

Within a year the Melbourne press would be sadly disabused; 1947 was something of an open season, with Freddie Harrison standing over the confidence trickster and general bad egg James Coates, shot four times from behind in a children's playground at the corner of Union Street and Punt Road, Windsor. On his return from England and Europe, Coates had turned his attention to baccarat and tried to take over Henry Stokes's school. He did not succeed and before his death Stokes appointed two men to look after his clubs. The pair fell out and Coates openly supported a man who was later seriously injured in a shooting. In addition to his other disagreeable habits, Coates was regarded as a grass and a man who took pains to revenge himself on those who slighted him. The week before his death he was badly beaten up in Elizabeth Street and ran into a shop crying, 'Will no one help me?' No one did.

On 19 July 1947 Coates left his heavily barricaded flat in Windsor to 'buy a paper' from a shop a mile from his home. Somehow he acquired a car and then noticed he was being followed. A high-speed chase ensued and Coates, realising he was in the slower car, abandoned it and began to run. His body was found the next day near a baccarat club he used. He had been shot four times. Although there appeared to be numerous potential independent witnesses, no one was ever charged with the hit. Coates was buried at Melbourne General Cemetery, Carlton.

One witness spoke of the killer wearing a smart coat and it was generally accepted that Freddie 'The Frog' Harrison had carried out the hit for a fee of 600 pounds. The always well-dressed Harrison was in smoke at the time and that might have allowed him to get close to the deeply unpopular man.

The reason for Harrison's absence was a shooting one evening in June 1947. It was another outbreak in the baccarat club wars. John Francis Gilligan and an innocent bystander were shot near Fink's building in Elizabeth Street where Henry Stokes had once run a baccarat game and which still housed a card club. The immediate reason for the shooting was that the previous night Gilligan had set fire to a car belonging to George Henry Newman—then a cleanskin with poor taste in associates who had found the dying Leslie 'Scotland Yard' Walkerden. Harrison disappeared after the shooting.

Now Newman effectively called Gilligan out and a meeting was arranged in Elizabeth Street. Gilligan, a man with convictions dating back to 1924, survived the shooting and maintained that high words had been exchanged and, as he was walking away, he was shot in the back. Bob Brewster, who was with him, called out to the crowd, 'Kick him [Newman] to pieces, he shot my mate.' That was when Harrison, who had been there with Newman, promptly disappeared.

Newman was charged with attempted murder and when he stood trial he told the court that, in the quarrel, Gilligan had said, 'I should have done you when I done Scotland' and told him to get out of the state. Newman said he had only carried a gun because of his fear of Gilligan, and the night he shot him, Newman thought he himself was going to be killed. The judge took the view that while Gilligan was 'a worthless person', this did not entitle Newman to shoot him if Gilligan was unarmed. He got two years.

Over the years Gilligan, who sometimes described himself as an industrial chemist, had further troubles with Harrison and with Norman Bradshaw, mainly over control of gambling. In the summer of 1949, with Bradshaw in his usual role as driver, Harrison opened fire on Gilligan and Bob Brewster, now described as a miner but really a high-class forger, when they were in a taxi in St Kilda.

Then things took a more serious turn. On 6 February 1950, with Bradshaw at the wheel of a grey Holden, Harrison opened fire on Gilligan and Brewster with a machine gun. Gilligan was hit in the right arm. Eight bullets hit the gates of the Melbourne Cricket Ground. The police were mobilised and the next day the Holden was found with its windscreen smashed by shotgun fire. Harrison and Bradshaw were duly rounded up and charged. Initially Brewster was prepared to say that he recognised the pair as they opened fire but Gilligan, loyal to the cause, would not. The committal proceedings began on Friday 17 February but there was no Brewster. He surfaced the following week, saying he had received threats that his house would be bombed if he did give evidence. Harrison and Bradshaw were duly acquitted after Harrison called an alibi to say he had been with his aunt. It was back to court again for the St Kilda shooting and once more they were acquitted.

Back in 1947, in late November, another standover man, Mally Appleby, had been found shot in the head outside Footscray's Railway Hotel after he had been at the Pakenham races. His girlfriend, Dulcie Johnson, who had met him when he was a boarder at her mother's home, claimed that Appleby knew it was indeed open season on him as well. He was said to have been involved in beer trafficking, something she denied. He clearly had a number of enemies; in February 1945 Harry Hinge had been charged with wounding with intent to murder him but was acquitted when Appleby refused to give evidence. Appleby had killed Ernest Jones in a fight in July 1946 and was himself acquitted later that year. Three men were charged over Appleby's death but the charges were later withdrawn at the inquest.

Meanwhile, in Sydney, the long-time standover man Jack Finnie was still around and in due course he was shot by Chow Hayes over a rort that involved substituting cabbage leaves for cigarette papers and a policeman who wanted his money back when he discovered the trick.

Finnie went to see Hayes on the officer's behalf and was promptly shot in the shoulder. He went to a private doctor to be patched up and the matter was never officially reported.

Down south, the Melburnians Harold Nugent and Joey Turner were alive and well, feasting on pickings great and small. Nappy Ollington, one of the uncrowned kings of the post-war two-up games in Melbourne, recalls them well:

> When my game in Elizabeth Street got big I remember I had a visit from the standover men Harold Nugent and Joe Turner. My cousin Kevin had been a very good boxer and I said, 'He won't cop.' Joey Turner said, 'Kevin wouldn't want a tin of jam [a bomb] through the window'. Kevin said, 'All I can tell you is don't miss. That's the only warning I'm giving you.'

Joseph Patrick 'Joey' Turner, usually described as a painter and docker but sometimes a miner, was a man with a finger in many pies. The journalist Tom Prior, meeting him for the first time, described him as wearing 'a well cut grey suit, smart yellow overcoat, cream sharkskin shirt, grey tie, hat and shiny black shoes'. He had a diamond in a front tooth and piercing blue eyes. When his friend, professional gambler Jimmy Jenkins, was robbed of 7000 pounds at gunpoint at the Victorian Club the gunman was later found shot through the buttocks in the urinal of the Post Office Tavern in Elizabeth Street. Like Twist, Turner was someone who could be used by the real world to do its dirty work. When Prior and other journalists at the *Truth* were having problems with another identity, Turner was brought in to explain the facts of life to him.

* * *

Around this time, some of the pre-war figures began to slip away from power and indeed life itself. One of these was George Wallace, The Midnight Raper, who had left Sydney shortly after Norman Bruhn was shot. Over the years Wallace had been in numerous fights and had convictions in Brisbane, Melbourne and Perth. Finally, in November 1948, he was stabbed to death with a butcher's knife outside the European Club in Perth. He died in hospital a fortnight later, suffering from hepatitis aggravated by the wound. He had been in Perth for four months trying to sell suit lengths and living in the Grand Central Hostel. He had apparently been attempting to rob a miner, Leonard Levy. At the time of his death he was wanted in both New South Wales and Victoria.

In 1949 Dr Stuart-Jones divorced Mary Kathleen and an Adelaide beauty queen, Adeline Morick, became his third wife. Life was, however, becoming increasingly difficult for him. After losing a tax case, in which he had run the usual and almost invariably unsuccessful defence that his wealth had been acquired through gambling, he was obliged to sell Casa Grande. For some time he had been suspected of being involved in horse doping and race fixing and in 1958 he was disqualified by the Queensland Turf Club after his horse, Kingperion, had run oddly at Bundamba Racecourse. He turned to managing a middle-of-the-road boxer, Norman Valentine Gobert, whom he also employed as a driver. After Gobert went to work for Sammy Lee's 417 Club, in theory Stuart-Jones again employed Richard Reilly, of whom he was clearly in some awe—or perhaps Reilly employed Stuart-Jones. There were suggestions that Reilly simply relieved Stuart-Jones of any substantial sums of money he carried with him and the doctor could or would do nothing about it. In December 1960 he received another tax bill, this time for 186 000 pounds and again he claimed his wealth was from betting. Six months later, in June 1961, Stuart-Jones died suddenly in Coogee following a heart attack. After his death Richard Reilly went into partnership with the confidence trickster Ivan Markovics in an abortion clinic in Bellevue Hill. Markovics also ran a scam arranging that, for a substantial fee, suitable people (including the gambler Perce Galea) could become Knights of Malta.

In the middle of August 1947 Dulcie Markham, still in Melbourne after the death of 'Scotland Yard', had been charged along with Edwin Martin—with whom she was now involved—with having conspired to murder Valma Hull. On 31 July Dulcie and Martin had gone to a boarding house demanding to see Hull. But who was she? None other than the wife of Keith Hull, acquitted the previous year of the murder of Donald 'The Duck' Day in Sydney. On 27 July, Keith Hull had been shot and wounded in the cabin of his truck at St Kilda. On 4 August, George Barrett and Edwin's brother Charles were charged with the shooting. It was all sorted out to everyone's advantage. Charges against Dulcie and Edwin Martin were dropped and Barrett and Charles Martin were duly acquitted in September.

By 1948 Tilly Devine had become something of a grande dame. Over the years she had more or less patched up her quarrels with Kate Leigh but her temper could still be roused. In November 1951, despite advice, she returned to Victoria for the Melbourne Cup and was promptly arrested on an outstanding consorting charge. She served five weeks before being released on the grounds of ill-health, suffering from cancer.

Then, thirty years after the Eveleigh robbery, Shiner Ryan returned to the life of Kate Leigh. Over the years Ryan had become something of a celebrity, not because of his robberies (for which he was usually caught) but because of his ability to escape. By the outbreak of World War II, Ryan was fifty-four years old and had racked up what the newspapers saw as an Australian record of sentences totalling forty-three years. In 1947 he and Kate Leigh began corresponding and he sent her a painting he had done; it showed Christ holding a black lamb named Shiner outside Fremantle Gaol. On his release he went to Sydney, where Leigh, along with the press, met his plane and their engagement was announced shortly after. They were married in Fremantle in January 1950—he in a fawn double-breasted suit and green fedora and she in a delphinium blue gown with silver beading, a black veil, white gloves and white nylons. Were they two old villains who had found happiness? Hardly. They returned to Sydney where Ryan pined for Western Australia. He stuck it out for three weeks and was off. Some little time later Leigh tried to claim three pounds a week maintenance from him. Ryan resisted, saying he would rather go to prison, where he would at least get treatment for his asthma. When he died in 1954 she said he was a brilliant man, the planner of the Eveleigh hold-up—which in retrospect doesn't seem to have been too brilliant—and someone who could open any lock with a wire coat-hanger. She also placed a little poem in the Sydney papers, a forerunner of the tributes that would one day be paid to dead Melbourne gangsters:

> Shiner, we cannot clasp our hands sweetheart
> Thy face I cannot see
> But let this token tell
> I still remember thee.

Both Kate Leigh and Tilly Devine were finally brought to earth by their failure to file proper tax returns and Leigh was made bankrupt shortly before she died in February 1964. Devine survived her tax battles although she claimed to have been ruined by them. Lawyers still in practice today can remember her, ravaged but dressed in furs and finery, going shopping at the local supermarket almost up until her death. Like so many of her kind she was thought to have taken to religion. The 'Queen of Woolloomooloo' died in hospital in Concord, Sydney, on 24 November 1970. She left a little over $11 000 to be divided between her adopted son John Eric Parsons and a niece and nephew in London. It is said that when a toast to her memory was proposed in a bar in Kings Cross no one could be bothered to lift their glasses.

* * *

Sometimes Sydney identities, possibly finding New South Wales a little warm for them, thought they might go to Melbourne and stand over the bookmakers there. Very often they found out to their cost that it was not the gravy train they had thought. One man who discovered this the hard way was the 106 kilogram 'Big' (and sometimes 'Tiny') Percy Charles Neville. Neville had had a long and successful criminal career, beginning in 1928 when he received probation for stealing and then running the gamut of crime through malicious damage, breaking and entering, demanding with menaces and breaching national security regulations. It peaked with the acquittal of the murder of his partner in crime, Francis John Allard.

On 10 June 1948 the body of Allard, who claimed he was a wharf labourer but was a standover man and a confidence trickster, was found in a storm water canal at Huntley Street, Alexandria. He had first appeared in court at the age of eleven. Immediately before his death he had been working as a card sharp on trains. About 9 p.m. the previous evening, according to witnesses, he had literally been lifted off the main street in Lidcombe and bundled into a car, which was driven away with his legs hanging out of the window. A post-mortem showed he had at least twenty-five small wounds in the head and on one hand, suggesting he had been prodded with a heavy instrument, most likely a hammer. In the early hours of Saturday 12 June the police forced a car to the side of the road in Camden and Neville was arrested and charged with Allard's murder.

At his trial in September, Neville made a statement from the dock saying he knew Allard only slightly, had certainly not killed him and had been playing cards with friends at Kings Cross that night. The jury failed to agree, as they did at the retrial in December. No further evidence was offered.

In the autumn of 1951 Neville was dividing his time between Sydney and Melbourne. There were reports he had been shot at in a gambling den in Little Lonsdale Street and had returned to Sydney where he picked up a vagrancy charge. He again returned to Melbourne and, moments after he arrived and booked into the New Treasury Hotel on the corner of Bourke and Spring streets, he received a rousting from the detective Bluey Adam and was promptly charged with possessing illegal firearms in the form of a Lüger and a .38.

On the night of 9 April 1951 he went to stand over a baccarat game run by Lou the Lombard on the corner of Elizabeth Street and Flinders Lane. Help was clearly needed and Norman Bradshaw was telephoned at his home in St Kilda. Along with another man Neville left the game shortly before midnight and was in Flinders Lane when a car with someone in the front passenger's seat came down the street the wrong way. Neville's antennae were working and he pulled out his Castelli revolver. But they were not working sufficiently fast, for before he could fire, the passenger shot him in the shoulder and lungs. Neville fell, picked himself up and ran across Elizabeth Street, where his companion put him in a taxi cab to be taken to the Royal Melbourne Hospital where he died. Curiously, had he not run he might have survived but his injuries were exacerbated by the energy he expended getting to the cab.

Once again it was a question of witnesses. Certainly no one in the club had seen anything; the man who left with Neville was never found, nor was the driver of the car. That left a soldier and his girlfriend who had been courting in a doorway. Initially they identified Bradshaw as the shooter, placing him as firing while standing in Flinders Lane. He was acquitted on 10 July 1951 after the trial judge Mr Justice Barry told the jury that in his opinion the case for the Crown was not sufficient for them to return a guilty verdict. Later Bradshaw told the journalist Alan Dower that he had indeed fired the shots, but from inside the car. The identity of the man who left the club with Neville and put him in the taxi was never known but Bradshaw's driver was undoubtedly Leslie Eugene 'Lair' Brown, who had been acquitted of the killing of a waitress, Pearl Oliver, some years earlier. Bradshaw was said to have killed Neville himself to show that he was not merely Freddie Harrison's chauffeur.

* * *

The career of Chow Hayes as one of Sydney's top standover men effectively ended on 29 May 1951 with the shooting of another hardman and film extra William John 'Bobby' Lee in the Ziegfeld Club in King Street before an audience of hundreds. The quarrel which led to Lee's death had begun some months before over a complex misunderstanding in arranging bail for two other criminals, Seppi Allen and Johnny Flanagan. Under the pretext that Allen and Flanagan were trying to stand over Thommo's two-up game, Lee and a number of ex-boxers gave them a bad beating. Hayes decided to involve himself and after he had quarrelled with Lee in the London Hotel, he knocked him down and gave him a good kicking.

On the evening of 1 May 1951 Lee waited outside Hayes's home in Thomas Street, Ultimo, and watched him, his wife and daughter leave the house to go to see the film *Annie Get Your Gun*. Lee had been drinking and thought the male with the two women was Hayes's son. Hayes's nephew, Danny Simmons, once a promising boxer, had remained in the house and Lee, compounding his error, shot him twice in the back of the head, believing it was Hayes. Hayes and his long standing mate Joey Hollebone now began a search of Sydney for Lee. On 29 May they learned through Jackie Hodder that Lee would be eating in the Ziegfeld Club later that evening with Hodder's brother Walter.

Hayes and the ultra-violent Hollebone went to the club with their wives. Hayes was all for killing Lee on the dance floor but the more prudent Hollebone wanted them to wait until he went outside. Eventually Hayes went to Lee's table and sat down. Lee asked if bygones could be bygones and Hayes pretended to go along with things until Hollebone came over and began to quarrel with him over the beating given to Allen and Flanagan. Hayes then wanted to go outside but Lee thought there was safety in public. He was wrong. Hayes shot him twice in the chest and then three times more. Hayes and Hollebone grabbed their wives and ran from the club. Hayes threw the gun off the Harbour Bridge but instead of falling into the water it landed on a grass patch, where it was found the next morning.

His loyal wife Topsy went to the police with her solicitor and made a statement saying she had seen the shooting but it was not Hayes who had done it. The unfortunate Walter Hodder was charged with Lee's murder and given bail in the sum of 400 pounds. In short order Topsy Hayes and Hazel Hollebone were also charged. They were initially remanded in custody, but after four days Joe Taylor put up the necessary 1000 pounds' bail.

Now the police began a manhunt for the missing Hayes and Hollebone. After a week Hayes returned home to Thomas Street, theorising that this would be the last place the police would look for him. It was not until 10 July that Hollebone was found hiding under a bed above Bronze Monsetti's fish shop. Hayes lasted only three days longer before the detective Ray Kelly, along with other officers, arrested him at his home.

Now began a bitterly contested series of trials, with Kelly claiming that Hayes had made a confession and the gunman maintaining that Kelly had verballed him. The inquest in October was well attended, with Kate Leigh prominent in the public gallery. During the adjournments she kept up a running commentary about the iniquity of the police in general and, on one occasion, took the opportunity to slip a bottle into Hayes's pocket. It was promptly confiscated. Then Walter Hodder's wife Betty told the coroner she saw Hayes holding a gun between his legs just before Lee was shot. As soon as she completed her evidence the coroner ruled there was no case against her husband and, on 28 August, said there was nothing to connect the Hollebones with Lee's death either.

Later Hollebone did his part to confuse things, introducing a 'blond stranger' into the evidence, saying that he had seen Lee knock the man out in the club's lavatory and had also seen the man holding a gun shortly before the boxer was shot. The police were not convinced. They could, they said, account for the whereabouts of everybody who had been in the club. More or less everyone had been asked to try to pick Hayes out of a line-up and without exception had failed to do so.

The crucial evidence against Hayes was that of the very dubious detective Ray Kelly who claimed that Hayes had said, 'What else could I do? There were a lot of people there, and they saw me shoot him. I think I was entitled to shoot him ... I got in first ... The police didn't catch anyone for shooting Simmons, so I decided to do things my own way.' The coroner returned a verdict that Lee had been shot by Hayes and his wife. She was granted bail and a separate trial.

The trial proper began on 26 November 1951 with Simon Isaacs KC appearing for Hayes. Mrs Hodder, her husband now safely outside the dock, hedged her evidence saying she had not seen the gun in Hayes's hand. There were frequent and bitter clashes between Isaacs and Kelly, with the barrister alleging that the officer was known as 'Verbal' Kelly, something he denied.

Hayes made a speech from the dock saying he was at Lee's table talking to him when the shots were fired by a man standing beside him. He called Hollebone as a witness. Hollebone denied he knew how guns worked and there was enough confusion for the jury to disagree after a five hour deliberation. That left Hayes facing a retrial and Topsy Hayes still awaiting her first.

The retrial came in March the next year, with George Amsberg replacing Isaacs as Hayes's barrister. Again much of the trial focused on Kelly's evidence. There was also a newspaper reporter who said he had called at the Hayeses' house three days before the shooting of Simmons. Hayes had shown him a gun saying, 'And that's what I'll use.' Again the jury could not reach a verdict and the Crown announced there would be a third trial. This was most unusual. The only time it had happened in recent years was in 1950 when, on the third round, the radio announcer John Brian Kerr was convicted of the murder of a girl on a beach in Melbourne.

Now the judge was Mr Justice McClemens who banned the use of nicknames, saying it resulted in the 'oblique glorification of crime'. This did not stop Amsberg suggesting Kelly was known as 'Verbal'. In reply the detective said the name had been made up not by criminals but by Isaacs. There was no evidence from Betty Hodder but McClemens summed up against Hayes and the jury was out only an hour before convicting him. Hayes said he hadn't expected anything else after the summing up and that he hoped Kelly would 'die of cancer of the tongue'. It was one of the many cases worldwide in which the defendant is guilty but the evidence has been embroidered to secure a conviction.

Hayes did not appeal and the case against his wife for aiding and abetting him was heard in June 1952. In less than an hour, at the close of the prosecution case, the judge ruled there was no evidence to go to the jury. Hayes was sentenced to death and reprieved. He was released in July 1967. It was suggested he was suffering from cancer and had only a matter of months to live. The prognosis was wrong. Later he admitted that, as everybody knew full well, he had indeed shot Lee. In October 1970 Hayes received a further five years for smashing a glass in the face of one Gerald Hutchinson in the Prince Alfred Club opposite the Royal Prince Alfred Hospital. Hutchinson lost an eye as a result of the attack.

* * *

In March 1952 Nellie Cameron was shot in the spine at her flat in Darlinghurst. A man was charged but she refused to identify her alleged attacker, claiming she had been shot by a stranger who had emerged from the shadows. The man was discharged and they left court arm in arm. In the operating theatre she was found to have a number of healed bullet wounds. She gassed herself in November the next year after apparently being told she was suffering from inoperable cancer generated by the old wounds. She was forty-one. Earlier she had adopted the seven-year-old daughter of a neighbour and had brought her up conscientiously. After her death the *Sun-Herald* wrote of her that she had nerve, could be trusted with secrets, had 'exceptional sex appeal' and 'was completely loyal to the criminal scale of values'.

Something of a Victorian counterpart to her, Tasmanian-born Jean Beaumont, who once earned 300 pounds a week on the Melbourne streets, died in January 1958. In 1945 she had been acquitted of murdering James Varney, who had lived off her earnings. Over the years he had broken more or less every bone in her face and body. On 17 June that year she walked into the Windsor Police Station at about 1 a.m. to say she had shot him in self-defence when he was about to give her another beating. She went into steady decline in the 1950s and in 1952 she was slashed by two women in St Kilda Road and had eight stitches in her face. In the years before her death, her looks gone with the scar of the razor slashing and with a lung disease, she had lived penniless and in squalor in a house in Pakington Street, St Kilda. Known as the most beautiful of streetwalkers of her time, she had chewed ten-pound notes in her heyday. In the better days of her relationship with Varney they gave lavish underworld parties at their flat in Raleigh Street, Windsor, with guests required to leave knives, razors and knuckledusters on the hall table.

* * *

While Pretty Boy Walker was abroad on the *Queen Mary* for most of the 1940s, his wife Rita had taken up with a Melbourne bully and standover man, Tom Fogarty. It appears that, in March 1953, Walker, back in Melbourne, was in Barkly Street, St Kilda, on other business when he heard a woman call out and realised it was Rita. She was fleeing from Fogarty, who was threatening to kill her. Walker, armed with a shotgun, shot Fogarty in the stomach and when he cried out 'Help me ...' Walker said he would and did so by firing again. He was arrested in South Yarra two days later.

In 1954 he was sent to Pentridge prison to begin his life sentence. He seems to have had friends on both the inside and the outside because he had a constant supply of both cigarettes and alcohol. Then in May that year he managed to get hold of a gun and decided to execute criminals whom he considered to be scum. They included William John O'Meally, who had killed a policeman, George Howell, in Caulfield in 1952. One morning Walker reported sick and that afternoon he went to the office of the chief warder, produced his gun and demanded that three other prisoners be brought to the division and locked in their cells. Later he returned to his own cell and instead killed himself. He left behind long and detailed notes of his career. One Melbourne gangland death that had gone unsolved for twenty years was that of James John, a standover man at a two-up school, who, as he walked in Exhibition Gardens, was shot five times by a man who leapt out of a car. It was not until Walker's death that diary entries confirmed it was he who had shot John.

Meanwhile, in May 1952, Margaret Clement, a fairly wealthy socialite living as a recluse on an 800 hectare property Tullaree, in Gippsland, disappeared. Shortly before, she had sold the land for the ridiculously low sum of 16 000 pounds to the former 1930s Footscray player Stanley Livingstone and his wife. Twenty-six years later some human bones, a spade, a shawl and some coins were found in the Venus Bay district and two years later an inquest was held. Much of the evidence was that of witnesses who said that Livingstone's wife Esmai had told them her husband admitted forcing Margaret Clement to sign the documents at gunpoint and had then killed her; according to reports Norman Bradshaw and Freddie Harrison had been given 500 pounds to dispose of the body. The former *Truth* journalist Brian Hansen thought they would have actually killed her (not merely buried her) for that sort of money. Livingstone founded his wealth on the sale of that property and died in Queensland when he had a heart attack fighting a bushfire. Although Esmai Livingstone survived him, she refused to confirm or deny whether her husband had been responsible for Margaret Clement's death.

In town meanwhile, after the Gilligan shooting, Harrison had divided up the city and took north of the Yarra as his territory. There may have been peace and quiet within his boundaries but he preyed on the others. For some years, one or more of Bradshaw, Twist and Harrison were hardly ever out of court. At the time of his death, Bradshaw had appeared on at least one charge a year, with one exception, for the past twenty-one years. He may have had old world courtesy but he was ruthless. On one occasion he poured petrol on a woman's back and set fire to it.

In July 1952 Harrison acquired his first conviction for violence after he stood over a stall holder at the Eastern Beach Carnival in Geelong in the January. The next year Harrison and Twist were acquitted of stealing a gold bar and Twist was alleged to have stood over Leonard Flynn and shot his de facto wife, Nancy Lowe. This led to all sorts of complications. First, Flynn went to the solicitor Frank Galbally to say it was he who had shot his wife accidentally. Then in court she said that neither he nor Twist had shot her; it had been a man standing at the gate when she answered the door. It ended in the usual way, with an acquittal. For each conviction in those days, there were usually half a dozen acquittals.

However, William Thomas McNamara, 'Tommy the Trotter', was not so fortunate. He had been organising a compulsory collection for Twist's defence fund. By mischance he had settled on members and staff of the Albanian Club as contributors; they took his pistol away from him and whipped him with it. He was taken to hospital where the police charged him. While all this was going on Twist and Harrison were accused of standing over the Cedar Club. Then, in November, Twist was also accused of standing over the Bohemian Club and later that month he had nine appeals adjourned. This time he received five years, quashed on appeal. And so it went on.

By the summer of 1958, there were rumours that all was not well in the triumvirate, principally with difficulties between Harrison and Jack Twist, and inevitably there was a falling out at the top. At the beginning of February, Harrison, Twist and Harold Nugent went with other friends on a pig shooting expedition to Bangaroo Station on the Broken Hill side of Oxley. On 3 February, Nugent appeared at Baranald Hospital with much of his right hand missing and pellet wounds in his stomach. The clear inference was that his hand was shot while he was protecting his abdomen. Not so, said Nugent. His gun had accidentally gone off as he was getting out of the car to shoot a kangaroo. He was given a blood transfusion and transferred to Royal Melbourne Hospital.

Then, at 4.40 p.m. on 6 February, Freddie 'The Frog' Harrison was publicly executed with a shotgun blast to the neck at 13 South Wharf. Although the wharf was crowded at the time, no one, not even one man who was spattered with blood, saw anything. Harrison had been returning a trailer borrowed a few days previously when the gunman walked up to him, said 'This is yours, Fred' and shot him in the head with a 12-gauge shotgun. Witnesses said Harrison gave an upwards jerk and then collapsed in the gutter. A nearby police officer noticed a youth running away from the wharf clutching something under his cardigan. He searched him and found a box of 12-gauge cartridges. There were twenty-two in the box of twenty-five and the boy had two more in his pocket. The shells contained the same number four shot that killed Harrison.

Harrison's wife Beryl, who had been in a state of collapse since the shooting, did not attend the funeral, instead sending a three foot high cross of red roses. Jack Twist sent a wreath. Apart from Norman Bradshaw, few of Harrison's friends attended. The wounded Nugent was still in hospital. Of the eleven cars travelling to the crematorium three were occupied by reporters and photographers.

It was thought times had become hard and Harrison died owing money on his rented flat and being in arrears with payments on his car and television. Within days it was clear that Twist was the new czar and there seemed to be a marked reluctance among Harrison's friends to do anything about avenging his death. Bradshaw in particular made no move. One suggested reason is that he had been the butt of Harrison's remarks for so long and he was not altogether displeased at the way things had turned out. A South Melbourne bookmaker offered 50–1 against the conviction of Harrison's killer but never had to pay out. Both the press and police were convinced Twist was the gunman—indeed *Truth* ran the headline 'New Twist to Harrison murder'—but no charges were ever brought. The young boy stopped with the cartridges was the stepson of Nugent. His name was Charles Joseph Wootton.

Now, for the time being, Twist and Bradshaw, aided by Joe Turner and Nugent, were in control of things. Twist was a former amateur heavyweight champion of Victoria and lawyers were not above using him on occasions. Lawyer Frank Galbally recounted how, when a conman was threatening another barrister over a lost case, he said the man should be sent to see Twist. At the time Twist was in Galbally's chambers on a conference and Galbally introduced the conman to him and left the room. Almost immediately there were cries of 'Don't hurt me' but as Galbally went to re-open the door the conman was knocked to the carpet and helped to the exit.

They did not always have things entirely their own way. In 1960 Twist, Turner and Nugent (who was said to be making 250 pounds a week in standover money on his own account) were challenged by Terance Clyde Sheehan. Collecting a debt he owed, they shot up his St Kilda flat only to find this did not faze him in the least. In return Sheehan and a friend allegedly shot up Nugent's flat on no fewer than three occasions. The last time, it was sprayed with some twenty bullets. He was acquitted of conspiracy to demand money with menaces—he had allegedly asked Nugent for 200 pounds to go to Sydney—but was found guilty of discharging a firearm in a public place.

One man whom Twist, Bradshaw and the others considered with something approaching respect was Horatio Raymond Morris, first convicted in 1932, who continued his life in crime until his death in 1973. In July 1946 he was charged with the murders of Ernest F. 'Ikey' Dew and William Sheargold. Dew and Sheargold disappeared some time after 21 June and their bodies were found in a river near Geelong on 14 July. Dew had been shot in the eye and there was some medical evidence that he had been disembowelled, possibly to help his body to sink. Sheargold had been shot behind the ear. The police theory was that they were killed over a dispute involving illegal liquor. At the end of the month both Morris and his friend Edward Carr, at whose house the killing was said to have taken place, were arrested. The inquest in September did not go well. Sherrie Morris repeatedly refused to give evidence against her husband and was jailed for contempt. The medical evidence was not strong. It was thought the bodies had been in the water for a fortnight and the contents of their stomachs could not be analysed. Morris told the police he had been drunkenly sleeping and, when going to the kitchen where he heard noises, had been attacked by Sheargold. He had picked up a pea rifle, seemingly an essential accessory in every home in those days, and shot Sheargold in the leg in self-defence. That was all he was going to say. There was some evidence that Morris had driven a lorry away that night, singing as he went. The coroner, commenting that both

Morris and Carr knew a good deal more than they were saying, returned an open verdict. When it came to it, Morris faced a trial on his own in October, charged only with wounding Sheargold.

In 1952 he received ten years for manslaughter after a killing in Carlton. Then in 1971 he was shot in the leg outside his home in Orr Street, Carlton. Two years later, after he went out to celebrate his thirty-ninth wedding anniversary, he was arrested for being drunk and died in the South Melbourne Police Station. Despite the fact that he was by then an alcoholic and losing his sight he was still working, standing over South Melbourne SP bookmakers.

As the years went by Twist and Bradshaw drifted apart and in 1954 Bradshaw served fifteen months in Brisbane for fraud. He was not popular among either inmates or staff and on one occasion was badly beaten by his fellow prisoners. He later served two years in Pentridge for demanding money with menaces from a Melbourne businessman. On his release he married and there are claims that he went straight. He certainly had a car repossession business in Richmond but there may well have been something under the surface. It is likely he was trafficking in firearms—that, or planning to take part in an armed hold-up because, in the spring of 1961, guns were found in a security box in the strongroom of the Commercial Bank of Australia in Swan Street, Richmond, and not just any guns. They included a .45 Colt, a .9 mm Lüger automatic and two 8½ inch barrel Mauser automatics. The owner of the box was Richard Ross Le Gallien who earlier in the year had been convicted of possessing rifles and automatic shotguns. Bradshaw was Le Gallien's car repossessor.

The police learned that on Friday 13 October 1961, Le Gallien, Bradshaw and two other men were due to fly from Moorabbin to Balranald, New South Wales, and it was planned that a raid would take place on their Proctor aircraft before the plane took off. However, on the Thursday one of the other two men was sent to prison and the flight, and with it the raid, was cancelled.

There was never another chance for the police to find out exactly what the situation was. On Sunday 15 October, shortly before 5 p.m., the Proctor took off and within minutes crashed in the sea about three-quarters of a mile off Mornington. Moments before the crash the plane had done a loop. On board were Le Gallien, a Kenneth George Napier, Bradshaw and his twenty-year-old friend Gail Connolly who owned a ladies' hairdressing business. Water skiers went out to the wreckage and that night the bodies of Bradshaw and Gail Connolly were retrieved. Le Gallien's body was never recovered. Bradshaw's funeral at New Cheltenham cemetery was attended by nearly 300 people. At the inquest the following year the coroner said he was satisfied Le Gallien had been the pilot. There was evidence the men had been drinking at Bradshaw's home earlier in the day. On 6 May the coroner was quite unable to say whether the deaths were accidental or otherwise.

Over the years a variety of reasons have been offered for the crash. A struggle during or after take-off, engine failure, sabotage, drink and drugs, a genuine accident … all have been canvassed. Nor could retribution for some of Bradshaw's previous bad behaviour be ruled out, but no evidence was found to support foul play.

Despite Bradshaw's apparent earlier retirement, his death sparked a war for control of the baccarat games and the prostitutes of St Kilda. In November 1961 the Snowball Gang from Sydney arrived with the intention of running the area. In turn they were countered by another partnership from Sydney and Adelaide and the prostitutes ran for cover, turning to old established Italian interests for protection. A series of heavy police raids followed and those not arrested left Melbourne to return to Sydney or travel to Queensland. With Joey Turner in prison, all of this left Jack Eric Twist in sole charge.

Back in Sydney the old players from the 1920s and 1930s were decaying or dying, sometimes both. 'Lair' Brown was one of the dying. Over the years this relic from the Darlinghurst Razor Wars had run up nearly fifty appearances in the courts of New South Wales, Victoria and Queensland, charged under a variety of names with a variety of offences including assault and robbery, possession of explosives, housebreaking and bribery. Now, on 1 August 1962, he was shot at Seven Hills, Sydney, and died ten days later in Parramatta Hospital.

Frank Green, who had fought Guido Caletti for so long and hard over the favours of Nellie Cameron, was decaying before dying. He had female breasts tattooed on the outside of his right arm, was going bald by his fifties and was reduced to working as a cockatoo for a Woolloomooloo SP betting shop on a Saturday while doing house painting during the week. He was now living with, and abusing, Beatrice 'Bobbie' Haggett, a saleswoman in a city department store, and he had acquired a disconcerting tendency to pawn anything within reach. In

October 1965 Haggett left him and he took up with a prostitute. In turn she left and in early April 1966 Haggett succumbed once more to his blandishments and returned. He continued to be violent towards her. On 26 April he was squabbling with her while she was cutting up liverwurst with a 12-inch knife. A struggle developed and the knife went into Green just above the heart. She ran to a hospital for help but by the time that help arrived he was dead. An autopsy showed there were eight old bullets in his body. Apparently he used to say you had to be unlucky to be killed by a bullet. Haggett was later acquitted.

Twist finally went down for standing over a restaurant in St Kilda. Afterwards the police banned him from Melbourne and the suburbs and he settled permanently at Port Albert, in Gippsland, south-east of Melbourne. With permission he returned to the city from time to time before he died of cancer in July 1988. But by then control of major crime in Melbourne had long passed almost exclusively into the hands of members of the Painters' and Dockers' Union.

Part II

Italian and Other Connections

7

On 11 February 1930, Domenico Belle was stabbed to death in broad daylight at Newtown railway station in Sydney. He had been with another Italian who went up the stairs to catch a train as Belle, blood gushing from his chest, staggered towards the ticket office. Did this mean the Black Hand organisation was now established in Australia? Yes, said police and prosecutors. No, say historians; there was no such thing.

Most of the initial immigrant Italian population of the pre-war era arrived in the 1920s and totalled well over 40 000 by the end of the decade. The historian and author Richard Evans regards the suggestion of early organised Italian crime in Australia as an overrated concept. He believes that, at a time when the White Australia policy was an article of faith, the local population was bigoted and hostile towards a conspicuously male dominated society in which few were married and most were law-abiding.

Although there were plenty of individual Black Handers in Australia in the early part of the twentieth century it was never a formal organisation such as the Mafia or the Camorra; rather, it was a linked number of individuals who extorted money from their fellow Italians. Nor, in fact, was it an organisation worldwide. The only two known instances of any sort of formal Black Hand organisations are of a Spanish self-help society which had died out by the 1900s and a Serbian-led secret society designed to obtain dominance over Bosnia. In the non-political sense, the Black Hand originated in Sicily and Italy as early as the 1750s, then spread to the United States in the 1890s and to Australia in the first quarter of the twentieth century.

The method of extortion was simple. The victim would receive a letter or a note to say that, if a sum of money was not paid, a business or livestock would be destroyed or the recipient or a family member would be kidnapped or killed. The note would contain instructions on the method and place of payment and would be signed with the imprint of a black hand and decorated with symbols such as the skull and crossbones, a smoking gun, a bomb about to explode. It was a very effective way of obtaining money from a largely illiterate populace already suspicious of the police.

Perhaps the earliest exponent in Australia was the Milanese Vincenzo Dagostino, who came to Brisbane in 1928 and began to put together a gang numbering half a dozen or so which extorted money from the Italian families working in the cane fields. Non-payment resulted in having their farm animals killed and their water poisoned. Nevertheless there seem to have been factional squabbles even before then. There was also anti-immigrant behaviour.

In 1925 the Italian Club in Innisfail was bombed, leaving two dead. Then, on 27 October 1927, a group of Italians was blown up as they waited for the train at Morawa, a wheat belt town 360 kilometres north of Perth. Ciresano Giuseppe had his leg crushed and four others were badly injured. The main station building was destroyed.

The Morawa bombing was a culmination of events. There was anti-immigrant feeling, fuelled by the fact that migrants were very often more hardworking than the itinerant labourer. They were more likely to stay and finish a job than their Australian counterparts, who would work for two or three days clearing land and then take a 'draw' from their employers and disappear into town. The Italians took the new contracts and this caused resentment. There was also some evidence that George Hearn, who was accused of the bombing, was standing over them for beer money and had also been trying to take 10 per cent of their wages under the pretext of finding them work. He was also resentful because he thought that the station master at Morawa had allowed the Italians to stay in some huts by the lines and had refused some Australians the same privilege. Hearn bought fifty plugs of gelignite and blew up the station. Asked to explain, he said he had mislaid a plug and had lit a match to look for it in the dark.

Dagostino's first recorded victim to be killed was Alfio (or Nicky) Patane, who, after paying increasing demands, was ordered to mortgage his farm. When he refused, first his horses were poisoned and then, in August 1928, he was shot at his home. He died without naming his killers. His widow Marie de Salvo remarried but she was again unfortunate in her choice of husbands. Her second, Venerando, was killed on 5 June 1934.

The killing of Domenico Belle was never solved. Belle was established to be a member of an Italian secret society. As he left home on the day of his death he told his wife he was going to see a barber, Giuseppe Mammone, who owed him fifteen pounds. It was almost certainly Giuseppe Mammone who had been with him. A document headed 'The Life of Joseph Mammone', found in his barber's shop, purported to show he had been sentenced to death in Buffalo, New York, for murder but this had been commuted to two years' imprisonment. There was also a letter which began 'I greet you with a sting ...' Now he had been told to collect funds for a companion who had been killed. Questioned by the police, he denied that he and Belle were leaders of the Camorra. The coroner returned a verdict that Belle had been murdered by a person unknown. He added that he thought it highly desirable that there be an arrangement whereby Mammone could be returned to Italy. He was sure Signor Mussolini would deport any known Australian criminal and there should be some reciprocal arrangement. Mammone was never charged.

In early December that year, fifty-two Italian migrants were refused leave to enter Australia and the Royal Mail liner *Orford*, which was carrying them, was ordered to return to Italy. Nine escaped from the vessel and disappeared after it docked in Melbourne.

On 26 January 1931 Giuseppe La Spinsa was killed at his home cum workplace, a fruit shop at the corner of King and Fitzroy streets, Sydney. In the middle of the night a man appeared, demanded money and shot him. La Spinsa had served two years in 1918 for shooting with intent to kill Donati Rafti, and another sentence in 1928 when he was imprisoned for running a coining plant from his fruit shop. The police found that, almost without exception, the Italian community was hostile towards them in their investigations. That same month Ignazio Gatti was found lying by his motorbike. He had been returning from a farm where his wife was working when he was shot in the groin, apparently in a dispute over money.

One girl who worked for Dagostino was the very beautiful Jean Morris, said to be the daughter of an Italian opera singer. Known, because of the knife she carried, as 'Stiletto Jean', she was sexually involved with both Dagostino and the white slaver Francesco Femio, who had arrived in Australia in 1927. Femio bought New South Wales women for between fifty and 400 pounds and they were literally shipped to Townsville and Cairns to work—one boatload contained over seventy women. He was Morris's most regular lover.

It was not, of course, only the Italians who worked prostitutes in the cane fields. From the 1890s there were steamers running between Marseilles and the French convict settlements in New Caledonia. Girls offered non-existent jobs as housemaids or companions to elderly ladies were trapped and sent to work as prostitutes in the goldfields. As these became unprofitable the girls drifted to Perth and Fremantle from where the lucky ones, who had kept some of their money, went home. One girl who arrived in the 1920s with eighteen pounds had some 500 pounds when she was deported two years later. In October 1927 a French syndicate ran an upmarket syndicate in Perth importing immigrants and (worse, thought *Truth* newspaper) sending Australian girls to Java and Singapore. The case is interesting because it appears to be the first use of a professional bondsman in Western Australia. Until then friends and relatives had put up bail money. A language test was applied to foreigners who had not lived for three years in Australia. Intended, in theory, to keep out Asians it was occasionally used against pimps such as the Frenchman Eugène Perrière in November 1927.

The Corsican Salvatore Bua and others such as Saveur Teboul also worked girls in the cane fields, requiring them to send back to them in Sydney not only the money they earned but also a detailed account of their clients and the amount of money they had spent. In 1929 Bua was arrested and deported. Another French pimp set up blinds as a film director—he had previously worked in Brisbane posing as a doctor and portrait painter—and yet another offered treatment for venereal diseases.

In Perth, prostitution was run north of the railway line by what *Truth* described as 'Jugo-Slavs who have come to this land without their women, but with a desire for women to ease the hard lot of their lives'. They also had their fair share of the sly-grog market. *Truth* was always keen to expose sin to its readers or the other way around. White slavers had 'slicked back' hair and, worse, 'satin pyjamas'. They smoked 'only the best cigars'. Once, searching for sin in Perth, the reporters found a four girl brothel where one was doing some embroidery and another was reading Tolstoy. The two others were smoking cheap cigarettes. 'We know they were cheap because we gave them to them,' they wrote. Undeterred by the lack of rampant vice, the paper reported it would continue to expose things where necessary.

At the time of her death the 22-year-old Jean Morris had worked the streets of Cairns, Innisfail and Ingham and was renting a cottage in Lower Main Street, Ayr, for five pounds a week. On 4 October 1932 one or more people stabbed her thirty-two times. Her body was found the next morning by a man who came to read the electricity meter. Dagostino and Femio were interviewed and produced alibis. A third Italian sailed from Townsville back to Italy and was arrested on his arrival in Naples. It is thought he either hanged himself in his cell or was killed by other inmates. The writer Bob Bottom suggests that Morris knew too much about Dagostino's affairs and it was he who ordered her death. He also records that the police identified her as the missing Sydney girl Philomena Morgan. This identification seems unlikely to be correct. Morgan could charitably be described as plain, while the photographs of Morris show a most striking woman. The next month Dagostino appeared in court charged with inducing a taxi driver to withhold evidence against two other Italians.

In November that year Antonio Cavalto pleaded not guilty to threatening to blow up the Ingham shop of Giuseppe Zavattori unless he was paid 250 pounds. His defence was that it was a prank arising from stories that there was a Black Hand gang in Ingham. The prosecutor told the court that it was no joke and the police had evidence of the existence of the Camorra in the town. The jury found him guilty after an hour and he was sentenced to eighteen months' hard labour.

In 1933 Detective Ricci was shot from behind in his car and in September that year Crown Prosecutor Jack Quinn was bombed in Sussex Street, Townsville. A 10 metre fuse was used to set off a device which destroyed his house. In February 1934 cane worker Giovanni Iacona was sent a Black Hand letter by Nicolo Mamone, Giuseppe Betti and Giuseppe Parisi, who re-enforced their request by cutting off his ear. Reprisal was swift. As soon as he was released from an Innisfail hospital on 6 March, Iacona took a taxi to the cane barracks and shot Mamone dead. Rather harshly, he received life imprisonment. For their part in the blackmail Parisi and Betti received seven years apiece.

Later they were all transferred to Italy and imprisoned in Lipari before being sent to the Penal Battalion to fight in the Abyssinian war. One version of their demise is that Iacona and Betti were killed in battle. Another is that one or the other of them was beaten to death in an uprising in Parina while Betti was finally executed as a communist spy in World War II.

That year, on 1 September, a girl's body was found on waste land near Albury, New South Wales, by a farmer bringing a bull back home from market. It was wrapped in the pyjamas that led to the name 'The Pyjama Girl'. The body was so disfigured that it appeared at first to have been scalped. In fact, it turned out that the girl had been shot and the body set on fire. There were difficulties in establishing identity through dental records because a bullet was lodged in her jaw. She was thought to be English and had distinctive ears, in that they had no lobes. A Jeanette Rutledge claimed the body as that of her illegitimate daughter, Philomena Morgan, but Rutledge had something of a mental history and her claims were not accepted. The body was placed in a formalin tank at Sydney University where, for the next ten years or so, desultory identification parades were held.

Meanwhile Mrs Rutledge was stepping up her campaign to have the body identified as that of her daughter and a totally eccentric Dr Palmer Benbow more or less gave up his practice to try to establish her claim.

In 1944, following pressure from lawyers urged on by Palmer-Benbow, a further inquest was arranged and, almost on its eve, Antonio Agostini, an Italian journalist then working as a cloakroom attendant in the fashionable Sydney restaurant Romano's, was arrested. He had been interviewed following the disappearance of his wife Linda, a former cinema usherette, some ten years earlier. Then he had been shown photographs and said the body was not that of his wife. Now he made a confession. The body was taken out of its tank, and make-up and a hair-do were applied, and this time seven people identified it as that of Linda Agostini.

The inquest was devoted to an attack on the identification, with Agostini's representatives trying to prove the body to be that of Philomena Morgan. The eyes of the body, which might have helped in the identification, had been removed and suddenly disappeared during the hearing. Agostini's confession really did not stand up. Why had he driven so far to dispose of the body when, many miles nearer, there was a lake said to be bottomless? There were also suggestions that he was in trouble with the Camorra and was not displeased to be out of the way. However, the coroner's jury found that the body was that of Linda Agostini and he was committed for trial.

Now, once more, Agostini changed his story. Yes, the body was that of his wife, shot and killed accidentally in a quarrel after which he panicked. Despite an intervention by Palmer Benbow, who tried to reopen the whole identification question, the jury returned what the judge, Mr Justice Lower, described as a merciful verdict of manslaughter. Agostini was given six years and when asked what he wished to have done with the body replied that he did not mind as it was not that of his wife.

The body was buried in grave 8341 in Preston Cemetery, Sydney, at the State's expense in July 1944 and Agostini was deported on the liner *Strathnaver* to Italy on 22 August 1948 on the completion of his sentence. He told the authorities he would probably live with relatives in Genoa. Right to the time of sailing he continued to deny his involvement with The Pyjama Girl.

There are some grounds for thinking the body was indeed that of Philomena Morgan, killed by the son of a Sydney detective. This would account for the enthusiasm the police had for proving the corpse to be that of Linda Agostini. In any event, neither she nor Philomena Morgan was ever seen alive again.

* * *

Meanwhile, back in North Queensland, the Black Hand continued its activities. Pina Bacchietta died in October 1934 when her home in Ingham was bombed after her husband refused to submit to blackmail demands. The next year Domenico Scarcella was murdered at Stone River in North Queensland. On 8 June 1935 he had received a letter which effectively was a demand for 250 pounds. The money was supposed to be put under a tramline bridge on his property. On the night of his death, when he went to let the horses out at about 9 p.m., his wife Francesca heard three shots and a cry for help. Scarcella's brother Vincent, who had once lived in Ingham, had earlier been sentenced to sixteen years in Italy for a shooting. Soon Italian homesteads were surrounded by wire fences with bell systems; gadgets on doors were in place, along with guard dogs.

About 8.30 p.m. on 13 December 1936 the slaver Francisco Femio was shot and killed in his bed at the cane barracks at Stone River near Ingham owned by two Italians, Rotondo and Lamotta. When Sicilians were questioned after his death they thought three more lives would be forfeit. 'Somatime mebbe next year. Thisa time bomb—and pouf,' one is said to have told a reporter. If one of them did say this, they were correct. The 35-year-old Dagostino was seriously injured in Brisbane in the early hours of the morning of 14 January 1938 when a pipe bomb exploded outside the bakery owned by another Italian, Di Prima, where he worked in the off season. Di Prima's four-year-old son slept through the explosion. At first it was thought Dagostino would survive, but he died the next day in the Ingham Hospital, refusing to talk to police. Two officers and a solitary man attended his funeral. One report has him saying before he died, 'Mamma Mia, why they do this to me?' Another is that, when asked by the police who had done this, he replied, 'Everybody good friends with me.'

The possibility is that a Sydney criminal was brought to Queensland to do the job on both him and Femio but crime writer John Harvey suggests both may have been killed by one or more Italians imported for the occasions. Much as they struck fear into the large Italian population in Queensland, Femio and Dagostino had not dared to tangle with the senior crime figures in Sydney and Melbourne such as Guido Calletti. The first of the modern *Mafioso* killings in Melbourne was probably the death of forty-year-old Giuseppe 'Fat Joe' Versace at a Fitzroy apartment house in October 1945. He had been stabbed a total of ninety-one times. He had allegedly been pestering 22-year-old Dorothy Dunn, the sister of the woman with whom Versace lived. Michele Scriva, Domenico Demarte and Domenico Pezzimenti went to speak to Versace on the subject and fighting broke out. Versace, a known standover man, carried a fully loaded automatic but he had no opportunity to draw it. Pezzimenti agreed that he had stabbed Versace eight or nine times because he had a gun but no one ever explained to the jury how the victim received the other eighty-plus wounds. The trial judge directed that Scriva and Demarte should be discharged and the next day the jury acquitted Pezzimenti. Despite the evidence that the fight was over a girl, the more likely view was that it was over control of Italian interests at the Queen Victoria Market.

In July 1950 Michele Scriva was charged with another murder, this time of a former veteran of the Sixth Division of the AIF, Frederick John Duffy, who was stabbed to death after he tried to help a man Scriva was attacking. Scriva's daughter had been hit by the man's car in Peel Street, North Melbourne. This time Scriva was condemned to death but, as was the usual practice, he was reprieved and served ten years of the commuted life sentence. His friend Antonio Romeo, who was with him, received a twelve year sentence for attempted murder. The previous year Giovanni Cirillo, believed to be a member of the *L'Onorata Società*, the Honoured Society, had been deported after being convicted of the stabbing of Ilario and Domenico Roccisano at their home in Mildura.

Truth took a close interest in the activities of the Society and on 7 April 1951 had an investigator on hand to say:

> The activities of this society must sound like fairy stories to Australians who have never experienced such victimisation. Most Australians could never calculate the terror and horror this band of scum produced among the Southern Italians in this country.
>
> The State and Commonwealth Governments must take actions now against the dreaded Society. Already it has secured a stranglehold on a fear-stricken Italian community.

Domenico Italiano, known as 'The Pope' and regarded as a modern Godfather of Victoria, died peacefully in West Melbourne on 13 December 1962. Italiano was seen as the head of *L'Onorata Società* which then effectively controlled the Queen Victoria Market. To obtain work there it was desirable to be Italian, particularly Calabrian. Shortly after Italiano's death came that of his right-hand man Antonio Barbara, a short squat man known as 'The Toad' who had served five years for manslaughter in 1936 when he killed a woman near the market.

Their deaths served to spark a power struggle over who would control and extort money from the decent stallholders who worked in the market. At first it seemed the transition of power had gone smoothly. Into the breach stepped the very well respected Vincenzo Muratore and Domenico Demarte, who had been acquitted of the killing of Versace. Their accession was, however, challenged by a former standover man from Calabria, Vincenzo Angilletta, who had a market garden in Kew and saw the opportunity to transform the operation into something resembling the Mafia, leaning not only on the Italian community. His suggestions were rejected, and foolhardily he turned his back on Demarte and the market, declaring he would no longer sell his fruit and vegetables to the Society wholesalers. Asked to reconsider, he refused and was stabbed for his pains. He still refused to conform and was kidnapped and taken to Woodend where he was stripped and smeared with excrement as a final warning.

He still would not co-operate and went against all known rules, selling his market garden to a Greek family. Now he set up his own Society, *La Bastarda*, in opposition to Demarte and there must have been some displeasure with the top brass of *L'Onorata*, for he quickly picked up 300 members. Angilletta was clearly at risk. He was shot in the early hours of 4 April 1963 outside his home in Chapman Street, Northcote, with two barrels fired from a *lupara*, the sawn-off shotgun favoured first by Calabrian shepherds and later by the *Mafiosi*.

Six months later 'The Market Wars', as they became known, began. First, Demarte was shot in the back and seriously injured on 26 November 1963 as he left his North Melbourne home for market. The shootings continued after the New Year and on 13 January 1964 Antonio Monaco of Braeside, survived after he was shot in the shoulder and chest as he also prepared to go to market. It was not clear whether this was part of the power struggle or a domestic dispute.

However, the death three days later of Vincenzo Muratore certainly was part of the struggle. He was killed at 2.30 a.m. as he left his home in Hampton, again on his way to the market. The shootings of Demarte and Muratore were thought to have been in revenge for the death of Angilletta. Michele Scriva was a pallbearer at the funerals of both Domenico 'The Pope' Italiano and Vincenzo Muratore.

Domenico Cirillo was the next victim, shot and wounded on 6 February, again in the early hours of the morning, as he left his home in Moonee Ponds. Once again, the factors behind the attack were thought to have been a combination of domestic and financial rather than to do with the power struggle.

On 23 January, Jack Matthews, then Chief of the Homicide Squad, had led a raid on the Victoria Market, halting every truck and lorry. The resulting searches produced a haul of weapons including daggers and flick knives as well as twelve shotguns, five rifles, two pistols and fifty-three detonators. Later that year, market worker Francesco de Masi disappeared. His blood-stained car was found but there was never a sighting of him again. It was thought a contract killer had been imported from Italy.

Following the Demarte and Muratore shootings, the Victorian government brought in a Mafia investigator from the United States, John T. Cusack, who reported that there was indeed a Mafia-style operation dealing in extortion, prostitution, counterfeiting, gambling, smuggling, guns and office breaking. He believed that, if left uncontrolled, in twenty-five years the Society would have branched into all facets of organised crime and legitimate business.

Even then, there was a generally dismissive attitude by some of the press and by the government of what was seen at best as clearly fledgling and, at worst, fairly well structured, home-grown organised crime in the Italian community rather than any worldwide operation. Indeed this is a view that has persisted.

Unsurprisingly the Society was not pleased with the unwanted publicity and investigation into its affairs, and its saviour was Liborio Benvenuto, then in his mid-fifties and originally from Calabria. Fearing a full-scale war, he negotiated a peace between the warring parties and took over the Society's leadership.

It was a situation that lasted for twenty years until, on 10 May 1983, his Toyota Landcruiser was blown up at the Melbourne Wholesale Fruit and Vegetable Market in Footscray Road. Gelignite had been strapped under the car. No one was injured but it was regarded as a sign that another power struggle might be about to break out. More trouble came nearly a year later when, on 6 May 1984, the mutilated bodies of Rocco Medici and his brother-in-law Giuseppe Furina were found weighted down in the Murrumbidgee River near Griffith. One had an ear cut off and both had apparently been tortured. It was never quite clear whether this was a revenge attack or the elimination of top brass prior to an attempted putsch. On 19 June the next year, Giuseppe Sofra was shot in the legs in his Springvale Road shop which actually belonged to Antonio Madafferi. This might have been related to a greengrocers' price cutting war or to serve as a warning to Madafferi.

However, not all attacks and murders of the period were market-related. On 18 July 1985, Dominic Marafiote disappeared from his home in Mildura and it was not until two years later that his body was found buried under a chicken coop. In fact he had been killed by the sociopath Alistair Farquhar 'Sandy' MacRae, who was thought to have killed up to twenty-five people. On the pretext of a drug deal, MacRae had apparently lured Marafiote to his home, where he stabbed him. MacRae then drove to Adelaide and killed Marafiote's elderly parents, Carmelo and Rosa, for the money he expected to find on Carmelo. He was disappointed; later it was found sewn into Rosa's clothing.

Market-related trouble became much more serious in 1988. First, Liborio Benvenuto died of natural causes in June. There had been discussions about his successor. Benvenuto's son, Francesco ('Frank'), was not favoured and it was thought that his son-in-law Alfonso Muratore, who had married Benvenuto's daughter Angela, was perhaps too inexperienced to take the reins just yet. Insurance broker and money launderer Giuseppe 'Joe' Arena, regarded as 'The Friendly Godfather', had been in discussion with Benvenuto as his possible successor but things changed dramatically within weeks when he was himself shot and killed in his own backyard in August 1988.

Now Alfonso Muratore took control but things did not work out either domestically or business-wise. In August 1992 he was killed by a shotgun blast to the head outside his home. After his succession he had left Angela for another woman, Karen Mansfield, and his wife's family was not impressed. He had also been talking to retailers such as Coles Myer about price fixing by market identities. It was suggested that the Honoured Society had organised a ring so that payment was made to a preferred supplier. Muratore had been saying that better and cheaper produce could be obtained by avoiding the ring. He had known he was at risk for some time and had with him a bodyguard who was shot in the legs to immobilise him.

At the inquest on Muratore, Ms Mansfield told the coroner that Frank Benvenuto, who had taken over his brother-in-law's stall when he left Angela, had hired someone to kill her lover. Joe Quadara denied he was the man named, claiming it was a relative. But when it came to it, it was Quadara rather than the relative who was killed, shot with a handgun as he sat in his V8 Holden Commodore outside the Toorak Safeway store in Malvern Road in May 1999. For a time after Muratore's death, Frank Benvenuto took to using one of the notorious Pettingill crime family, Victor Peirce, as a bodyguard. Later, as things became even more blurred, he employed Alphonse Gangitano, who would in time be known as the 'King of Lygon Street'.

In the afternoon on Monday 8 May 2000, Frank Benvenuto was found shot dead in his car in Dalgetty Road, Beaumaris. It was parked away from the kerb and the door was open. His sister, saying the family would forgive his killer but not forget the killing 'because that's what my brother would do', described him as a 'good hard-working Christian who loved his family'. According to Victor Peirce's wife Wendy, Benvenuto was shot by Melbourne identity Andrew 'Benji' Veniamin because Benvenuto had ordered the killing of another identity. It seems that, as Benvenuto lay dying, he called Peirce on his mobile telephone but was only able to groan. Some $64000 had been left in the boot of Benvenuto's car. Peirce and Veniamin later met in Port Melbourne and agreed there would be no backup or payback for Benvenuto.

Out of the mainstream of the Melbourne gang wars, fifty-year-old Domenico Italiano, an alleged *Mafioso* and grandson of the old Domenico, died on 25 June 2005, hours after being granted a retrial on charges of blackmail and false pretences. In 2002 he had served a sentence for rigging the Youth Motor Sport Foundation raffles. Granted bail, Italiano had taken the opportunity to have too much recreation and not sufficient rest. He purchased a quantity of Viagra and, after a night with a former girlfriend, 'his heart packed in', a source told the newspapers. Italiano had been suspected of hiring Philip Lander, also known as Matthews, to make and plant the bomb in the 1998 murder of mechanic and businessman John Furlan, killed on his way to work when his Subaru Liberty blew up near his Coburg home. It was thought that Furlan had discovered the raffle rigging and had been killed to ensure his silence. Lander, however, had died on 23 July 2004. Italiano's funeral at St Mary's Star of the Sea, West Melbourne, included a mass and the traditional rendering of 'My Way'.

* * *

Not until the Costigan Inquiry into the Painters' and Dockers' Union in Melbourne had it become apparent just what progress the Mafia had already made. The 1970s were also the decade when drug trafficking began in earnest and when much of the marijuana sold was home-grown. It also led to the disappearance on 15 July 1977 of the anti-drugs campaigner Donald Mackay.

The first real signs of production came in 1972 when two farmers, originally from the Calabrian region, were prosecuted for producing around a quarter of a million dollars' worth of marijuana and fined $250 and $500 respectively. Much had been made of their previous unblemished records and that they had been led astray. In fact Rocco Barbaro and Giuseppe Scarfo were related by marriage to Antonio Sergi, a vineyard owner, six of whose brothers-in-law were investigated in the 1979 Woodward Royal Commission into Drug Trafficking.

A year after the convictions Barbara Mackay, a Griffith housewife, wrote to the local newspaper complaining about the disparity in sentencing between the Italians and three youths fined $1800 and sent to prison for smoking the weed. She now handed the matter over to her husband, Donald, the local leader of the Liberal Party. Largely by-passing the local police, Mackay contacted the Sydney Drugs Squad, and raids followed. In Coleambally in November 1975, drugs with an estimated street value of several millions of dollars were seized. Antonio Sergi's brother-in-law, Francesco, was one of five Calabrians arrested along with Luigi Pochu and Pasquale Agresta, the business associate of Robert Trimbole, the Sydney businessman who laundered some of the profits through his wholesale fruiterers. On 5 March another raid, this time at Mount Diversion, seized a not dissimilar amount. In both cases it became common gossip that Mackay was the informant. He had not, however, contented himself with giving specific information but waged a campaign against what he saw as too lax laws on cultivating marijuana.

In June 1977 Trimbole contacted Gianfranco Tizzone, an old friend from his days working in the amusement arcade business, and a chain of introductions resulted in robber and former painter and docker James Frederick Bazley reportedly asking for $10 000 for the hit. In the 1970s Bazley had bought a gun from a George Joseph and now Joseph contacted him saying that the Family was looking for a hitman. Since his career on the wharves, in February 1975 Bazley had been foiled when fleeing from a raid on another bank, this time in Gardiner, by a one-legged butcher. He was granted bail over police objections and promptly absconded.

On 11 July 1977 Bazley, giving his name as Ray Adams, contacted Mackay and suggested a meeting outside the Flag Inn in Jerilderie, 140 kilometres south of Griffith. Four days later Mackay telephoned his wife saying he would be home around 7 p.m. and went to the Griffith Hotel for a drink. He left the pub at 6.20 p.m. and was never seen again. His wife reported him missing at 8 p.m. His car was found still in the hotel car park and there were bloodstains and spent cartridges on the ground.

The newspapers were swift to campaign for an inquiry and it seems that local residents took action themselves. Antonio Sergi complained that shots had been fired at his home and his winery had been bombed. In the face of complaints that the murder inquiry was being hampered by corruption, on 5 August the New South Wales government appointed a Royal Commission to be headed by Mr Justice Woodward.

Woodward finally reported that the marijuana industry in eastern Australia had been organised between 1974 and 1977 exclusively by a group of Calabrians in Griffith with distribution markets in Sydney and Melbourne. Profits were laundered through legitimate businesses. He believed that *L'Onorata* was led by Sergi and Trimbole, the former of whom he believed to have amassed assets of $2 million from the profits. He found it highly probable that the group had been responsible for the killing of Mackay. He did not think there was any connection between the marijuana and heroin trades. He also believed that organised crime was controlled by a Mr Big with a hierarchical structure.

For most of the 1960s, Robert Trimbole lived with his wife and four children in Griffith next to the Pool garage where he repaired cars and sold petrol. It did not pay and on 1 November 1968 he was declared bankrupt, with a deficiency of $10 986.63.

Trimbole was by no means the first or last to benefit from a bankruptcy. From then his life was an upwardly mobile one. In 1972 he opened the Texan Tavern, a licensed restaurant, followed by the Texan Butchery. Both were sold to Sergi in 1973 and Trimbole and his family opened a supermarket in Casula, Sydney. He kept faith in his home town where he owned the Pant Ranch. The Woodward Royal Commission also found him to be an active member of the Mr Asia organisation. It had already reported in November 1979 that Trimbole was 'in all probability ... the practical leader of the organisation growing illegal marijuana crops in Griffith, New South Wales'.

Trimbole fled the country on the advice of his doctor, the drug dealing Greek-born Nick Paltos, who would go on to be a seminal figure in Australian organised crime. He left on 7 May 1981 on a Pan-Am flight to Europe via the United States. He never returned.

Bazley was not arrested until 1980, when the police finally caught up with him as he was driving a stolen car. He had changed his hairstyle and had an operation on his nose but he was identified through his fingerprints. In February 1982 he received nine years with a minimum sentence of six and a half years for an armed robbery. It was while he was serving that sentence that he was charged with the Mackay murder as well as those of Douglas and Isabel Wilson, players in the heroin ring that came to be known as Mr Asia.

It was Gianfranco Tizzone who cracked. He had come to Australia in 1955 and worked for Tom Ericksen as a debt collector before becoming the Melbourne distributor of the Griffith connection, moving around 200 kilograms of marijuana a week. Tizzone wanted to move higher in the echelons of the Italian Mafia and spoke to Trimbole about his ability to have people killed. Trimbole took him at his word that he could find someone to kill Mackay. According to the story he told the police and the court, he went to George Joseph, a Fitzroy gun dealer, who contacted Bazley.

On 31 March 1982, Tizzone was driving a gold Mercedes moving a marijuana crop from near Canberra to Melbourne, when he was pulled over by the police on the Hume Highway. When he found he could not bribe his way out of the problem and faced a lengthy sentence, he decided to turn informer, becoming known as 'The Songbird'. In October 1984 he pleaded guilty to conspiracy to murder Mackay and Isabel and Douglas Wilson and received five years' imprisonment. The next month he was back in court giving evidence against Bazley.

In 1986, Bazley was convicted of conspiracy to murder Mackay and the murders of the Wilsons and was sentenced to life imprisonment for the latter, along with a further four years for another armed robbery. He has always maintained his innocence. In March 2000, then aged 74, he was given day release from the medium security Loddon prison near Castlemaine and in early 2001 he was released, returning to his wife in Brunswick. He declined to reply to reporters' questions concerning the whereabouts of Mackay's body. When he was later interviewed by journalist Tom Prior, he claimed he had been set up by George Joseph, a man he did not like, and suggested, with some credibility, that the corrupt former police officer Fred Krahe had actually done the killings.

It was not until 25 October 1984 that Trimbole was arrested in Ireland on suspicion of possessing a firearm. He was then living under the name Michael Hanbury of Westport, Co Mayo. Efforts were made to seek his compulsory return to Australia but the Irish courts ruled he had been illegally arrested in preparation for the extradition attempt, which did no great credit to either the Australian or the Irish governments.

Adrian Neale, the London solicitor who represented Robert Trimbole in Europe and went to Ireland to assist in the defence of the extradition proceedings, remembers:

> When he was released by the Irish court he literally walked out onto the street. He had no idea whether he was going to be killed by the Mafia. We went to a hotel—the middle of three on the Lansdowne Road. There was no way he could get out of the country on normal transport so I rang a friend of mine in British Airways and we found a guy who would take him out on a Lear Jet the next day. The pilot had contacts and I didn't wish to know where he had gone.

In fact he went to Spain, where he died on 13 May 1987 near Benidorm. Neale is convinced Trimbole was killed—sprayed with a gas which caused him to suffer a heart attack. Curiously, on 5 July 1985, *The Canberra Times* reported his death on a boat in the Mediterranean the previous month and that he was buried at his birthplace of Plati.

Tizzone was released on parole in February 1986 and fled to Italy, leaving a tax bill of $1 million. George Joseph received a five year sentence.

The fallout over Robert Trimbole continued. His long-time friend, 49-year-old one-time racehorse trainer, Reginald 'Mick' O'Brien had long been expecting his gangland execution and it came at 5.15 a.m. on 13 January 1992. O'Brien was shot dead through the screen door of a granny flat in Onslow Street, Granville; one shot went through his arm and into his chest and the second into his abdomen.

On 8 May 1981, the day Trimbole left Australia for the final time, he and O'Brien had pulled off a coup at Hawkesbury Racecourse when Species, backed from 33–1 down to 8–1, won the Provincial Stakes netting an estimated $300 000. Until Trimbole's death O'Brien stayed in contact with him, and it was thought he was linked to an attempt to smuggle some of Trimbole's estimated $20 million back into Australia. Certainly he had seen Trimbole in the village of Alfaz de Pi in Spain shortly before his death and he wept copiously enough at the drug dealer's funeral.

In Trimbole's absence O'Brien started a steady decline, beginning to drink at five in the morning. His nerve went when he was interviewed by Australian customs officers while on his way to visit Trimbole, then in Italy. And he cracked completely when he was detained by Italian officials. It was then that he looked for Superintendent Bruce Provost and became an informer for the Federal Police.

O'Brien's problem was that he began to play both sides of the fence. He was now suffering from eye disease and shamelessly dobbed in a friend who had taken him to the Pasteur Clinic in France in search of a cure. In May 1989 he became involved in an unauthorised importation of 1.6 tonnes of hashish worth $25 million. He was arrested and now became an informer for the National Crime Authority (NCA), giving evidence against the men with him and alleging that he had been lured into the drug deal by another undercover NCA informer. Using the name Travis McGee he claimed he was an 'unwilling witness'. His evidence was thin and hopelessly unreliable. In May 1991 he was released by the NCA and his protection terminated. At the time, protected witnesses were given a twenty-four hour bodyguard or a new identity and relocated interstate or overseas. They would also be given a new driver's licence and Medicare card. Without help he was effectively a dead man walking.

In 1992 Bruno Romero was arrested after 2000 marijuana plants were found at his home in Lismore, New South Wales. Now it was thought that three men controlled Mildura. In 1993 Marco Medici, allegedly a fruit grower but in effect a king pin in the Mildura Mafia cell, was shot in the back of the head at his small fruit block at Red Cliffs on the outskirts of Mildura. In 1984 it was his cousin Rocco Francesco Medici and another man Giuseppe Furina who had floated to the head of the Murrumbidgee River near Griffith.

Nor was it only alleged identities who died in the area. It seems that seventeen-year-old Robby Joe Coulter saw a drug deal going down in the town and was promptly murdered. He was found in the Murray River on 3 January 1989, his hands and feet bound and chained and his body weighted with construction bricks. To the surprise of some, the coroner returned an open verdict.

But still some senior officers remain to be convinced about the Mafia. Appearing on the television program *George Negus Tonight* on 30 August 2004, Superintendent Jack Matthews went on record as saying: 'Well, I never have [conceded] and still do not concede that the Mafia exist in Victoria or Australia, but I still don't overlook the possibility and I'm not shutting that entirely from my mind.'

In 2006 the respectable Costa family, the Geelong based vegetable and fruit wholesalers, told of the decades of extortions by the Calabrian Mafia operating in Victoria. In 1996 FBI agents travelled to Australia to warn police that local Mafia gangs were linked with the United States Mafia. It has also been alleged that for forty years before his death in April 2005, former immigration minister in the Whitlam Labor government Al Grassby was at the beck and call of the Griffith Mafia.

Some Painters and Dockers

8

In March 1980 *The Bulletin*, then owned by Kerry Packer, published a series of articles by journalist David Richards. They were based on interviews with Billy 'The Texan' Longley—so-called because he wore a Stetson and carried a Colt .45—then in Pentridge prison serving a sentence for the murder of Pat Shannon whose real name, said Longley, was Bowie. It led to an investigation into the activities of members of the long established Federated Ship Painters' and Dockers' Union, which ranged far and wide into aspects of organised crime in and out of the union.

The surprise is that it was so long in coming. Throughout the first half of the 1970s members of the union fought a long and bloody, and generally unhindered, battle for control, with shootings, bombings, arson attacks and disappearances in which officials, rank and file members and innocent bystanders (including at least one child) went down.

The Painters' and Dockers' Union had a difficult history. In the 1950s there had been inter-union troubles on the wharves with the communist members who were stopping ships being built. After some conflict it was agreed they would keep to the public sector, leaving the more lucrative private sector to the general membership. Troubles in the union were not confined to Melbourne; there were also killings in disputes in Sydney, Perth and Brisbane. It was, however, the Melbourne branch that attracted the most, mainly unwelcome, publicity.

One of the bonuses offered by the union was that false identities were readily available to its members. This had a number of benefits. Criminals were more easily able to stay on the run and in work, and false claims for unemployment benefits and multiple claims for workers' compensation could be made. 'If you didn't have a criminal record you didn't make it', recalls a lawyer whose father had been on the wharves. 'If you were a registered painter and docker you had a legitimate income and so a good defence against a consorting charge. It did not matter if you were in a hotel with other criminals. That was simply where you were picked up for work.'

There was ghosting—the process whereby fifteen men would unload a ship and the owners were charged for sixty. The proceeds would then be divided among the executive; being a wharfie also provided a good alibi. There you were recorded as being on a particular shift.

All but two of the Victorian branch senior members in the early 1970s had at some time or another used aliases and one of its secretaries, Jack 'Puttynose' Nicholls, used at least four. The New South Wales branch was just as keen on name-changing. On 3 February 1975 it was recorded at a meeting of the branch executive committee that forty-three members, of whom twenty-two adopted Italian-style aliases, changed their names.

Serious troubles in the Melbourne branch of the union erupted in 1970 after the secretary, Jimmy Donegan, who had supported Frank Hardy in the libel action brought by John Wren, died of liver disease. It was said that, to keep some sort of order, he used to make committee members put their guns in the safe before meetings. At the time of his death it was estimated that 70 per cent of the top 100 criminals in Victoria had links with the Painters and Dockers. After his death a bitter, bloody struggle broke out for control of the union. On one side was Pat Shannon, appointed caretaker after the death of Donegan and wanting to be re-elected secretary; Longley, who wanted to be president and did not oppose Shannon for secretary but wanted Burt Aspel as vice president and James Frederick Bazley, known as 'Machine Gun' because of his rapid speech, as the quaintly named 'vigilance officer'. On paper Bazley's early career did not really suggest he was suitable for the job. In 1947 he was convicted of carrying an unregistered pistol while working as a bouncer at an illegal baccarat game in Lonsdale Street. Just before Christmas 1964 he was convicted of a robbery of $2970 from a bank in Collingwood. He escaped twice and was released in 1969. On reflection, perhaps he was indeed suitable. Former detective Paul Delianis recalls:

James Bazley was not a lucky crook. On one occasion he locked the bank door shortly before closing time and when he went to leave with the loot he found a crowd outside complaining it had shut early. Another time, after he'd herded the staff into the strong room, he took off his mask and was caught on a security camera.

In 1969 Longley had been charged with receiving part of the proceeds of the $580000 robbery of Mayne-Nickless in Sydney and Donegan had died before he, too, could be arrested. Longley was acquitted. He had already been acquitted, after a retrial, of the manslaughter of his first wife, Patricia. He had also been charged in association with the shooting in the Rose and Crown in Port Melbourne in the mid-1960s. Once again he was acquitted.

Three months after the Mayne-Nickless robbery a gang of Dockers robbed the security company MSS in a precisely planned raid. It was an inside job with information provided by Charles Raymer who had worked for the company for six weeks. On 4 June 1970 an MSS van was stolen from Camberwell. Inside was a set of about 100 keys. On 10 June the East Melbourne Police Station was broken into and a cap and a coat were stolen. At 2 a.m. the next morning the security guard at MSS answered a call on the intercom only to find it was a couple of police officers returning the stolen keys. He buzzed them in. The one in plain clothes said he was a detective. In fact he was Joey Turner. As the guard was picking up the bundle of keys a gun was shoved in his face. He was pushed to the ground and tied up, a pillow case was put over his head and he was told that he would be killed if he did not co-operate. The two men then cut open the wire cage protecting the pay-roll money and made off with $289233.

The MSS robbery was solved because the robbers did not know how to get rid of the loot. Turner was caught because of a pile of wet $2 bills. He had left them in a trouser pocket and his wife had washed them. He tried to iron them but they were still damp when he bought a kangaroo skin rug in the souvenir store in the old Southern Cross Hotel. When the shop assistant took them to the bank the cashier became suspicious and checked the serial numbers.

The trial ran intermittently for a period of years. The first was aborted after a juror said she had been approached. The second collapsed when a juror took time off to go to a concert in Sydney. The third never started because Turner failed to appear. When retrieved, he received a two year sentence for breach of bail. In the fourth trial the jury disagreed and finally, on 22 October 1973, Turner and five others were convicted. Turner received twelve years with no minimum, the judge uttering the traditional words, 'You played for high stakes, you lost. The game is forfeit.'

The year after the robbery another high profile case involved a Docker. Neil Collingburn was a new breed of criminal, 'far removed from the old dockers whose hands would cover half a table'. He wore 'beautiful suits and had impeccable manners', recalls one barrister. He was also a most talented warehouseman and safebreaker. He died after a fight with police officers Carl Stillman and Brian Murphy (the latter known as 'Skull' because, like the wrestler of the period, he had shaved his head). Collingburn had been wrongly arrested over a set of golf clubs which turned out to be his own. The two officers, charged with manslaughter, were acquitted at their trial after telling the jury that he had attacked them in the charge room. It was said the underworld put a $2000 contract on the officers but it was not taken up.

By the time Turner was sentenced what was to be a decade of violence had begun during the 1971 Painters' and Dockers' Union election campaign. At the end of November, Robert Crotty, a Longley supporter, was involved in a fight behind a South Melbourne hotel. As he went to shake hands afterwards he was hit with a brick and then kicked and beaten. He was left with brain damage until his death seven years later. Witnesses told the police he had fallen over and hurt himself.

Retribution was swift. One of his supposed attackers, Alfred 'The Ferret' Nelson, disappeared three days before the election. He had been snatched from under the shower at his home in Langridge Street, Collingwood. His body was thought to have been left in his car in the Yarra River off No. 21 South Wharf. Certainly the car was there but when it was pulled out there was no Ferret. One suggestion is that he was buried under tons of freshly poured concrete being used to construct a ramp, but no one checked. Another suggestion on offer was that The Ferret's body had been burned in an incinerator only 55 metres from the Lorimer Street offices and yet another that he was placed in the bilge tank of a Hong Kong freighter or dumped at sea. It was thought he had fallen out with Joey Turner when part of Turner's $60000 share of the MSS robbery went missing.

On 10 December, the morning of the elections, the ballot boxes at the Williamstown Naval Dockyard, the car of Pat Shannon's driver and the Port Melbourne union offices were all machine-gunned. Longley had his men outside the Williamstown wharf helping their men inside. He thought he had won the vote but later discovered that, early in the morning, Shannon's men had arrived and stuffed one of the ballot boxes while holding observers at gunpoint. When a rival group appeared a gun battle followed, with over fifty shots being fired into one car. The returning officer, Paul Cullen, resigned—at pistol point, it was said. The next day the car of Doug Sproule, a Shannon supporter who had a conviction for the attempted murder of a police officer, was found burned out. He suggested to police that it might have self-combusted.

What was amazing was that the union members operated in a complete vacuum. There was no report of the battle in the next day's *Age* and it was not until 14 December that even a mention was made of any of the shootings. More post-election press space was devoted to a war between youth gangs known as the Devil's Raiders from Williamstown and Altona's Borrack Boys. They caused havoc in North Altona by randomly shooting at cars and shop windows.

The day after the election another Longley supporter was shot in the face and died. Again it is not wholly clear whether this was strictly union rivalry because Desmond St Bernard 'The Dog' Costello was also thought to have been a receiver of the proceeds of the Mayne-Nickless raid as well as being one of the abductors of Nelson. But it is the way to bet. Costello was another noted hardman who, ten years earlier, had been acquitted of the murder of another standover man, Osmond 'Hoppy' Kelly, found shot dead in a lounge chair at his Fitzroy home. Costello had also been a member of one of the top international shoplifting gangs. Costello's body was found in December 1971 dumped in a ditch at Clifton Hill by the site of the new Eastern Freeway. One arm was shattered and part of a hand blown away suggesting he had been trying to protect his face. He was due to stand trial in the February for factory breaking. It was thought there were three killers. A young man was arrested shortly afterwards in Gippsland but no charges were brought over the murder. The story goes that, before Costello died, he asked for a last cigarette and was told there was insufficient time.

That month Ian Revell Carroll was arrested on two charges of carrying an unlicensed pistol. Fined $150, he denied he had been riding shotgun for a Painters' and Dockers' Union official.

Over the next fifteen months there were numerous incidents of gunfire between the rival groups and on 20 December 1971 Laurence Richard Chamings, whose brother had been killed in 1970, was wounded in the shoulder and survived for the time being. Jim Bazley managed to survive two attacks. The first came in May 1972 when he was hit in the thigh and shoulder as he stood outside his North Carlton home. The second was in the September when he was hit in the head and hand while sitting in his car. Longley's second wife and daughter also survived when, the day after the results announcing the success of Shannon were published, a bomb was thrown at their home.

On 26 September 1972 painter and docker Francis Bayliss was found with four sticks of gelignite as well as a sawn-off shotgun. Questioned, he said he needed them for his own protection, adding: 'You're not silly. You know what's going on.'

Then, shortly after 4 a.m. on 15 December, another union man, Brian Sulley, was shot twice in the head as he walked away from the Painters and Dockers office in Lorimer Street, South Melbourne. He told police that he heard two shots but did not see who fired them.

One Docker who did go down was the old street fighter Johnny Morrison. Known as 'The Face' because of his pimple and boil scars, he was found shotgunned to death and buried in a paddock in Werribee in December 1972. His body was discovered when a farmer saw a hand sticking out of a field of barley. At first the corpse was thought to be that of Ferret Nelson but it was agreed it was too big. No one was ever charged with Morrison's murder.

In May 1972, Shannon had issued a statement reminiscent of the 'we only kill our own' statements made over the years by many of the world's criminals. He said: 'Remember, no stray bullet or bomb has harmed a non-unionist.' Not for long. In April 1973 eleven-year-old Nicholas Kolovrat was killed by a stray bullet in the Moonee Valley Hotel when his father went to to buy him a lemonade. Father and son were unfortunate to be in the place when a gunman came looking for Lawrence Chamings who had just walked in. Chamings fled but was chased and killed as he tried to reach what he thought might be the safety of the lavatories. Barry 'The Bear' Kable was arrested and, as is the nature of these things, was acquitted. He was later attacked in Sydney by three men and suffered a blood clot in the brain.

In fact Shannon did not see out the year. On 17 October, shortly before 10 p.m., he was drinking with another unionist and two local women in the Druids Hotel in South Melbourne when, moments after Gary Harding had checked to see Shannon was there, one Kevin James Taylor shot him with a sawn-off .22 rifle with a silencer added. The Painters' and Dockers' Union membership levied fifty cents a week per man for the next eighteen months for his widow and family. His death was to be the catalyst that would ultimately bring about, albeit a decade later, the deeply controversial and much criticised inquiry by barrister Francis Xavier Costigan.

The week after Shannon was shot, Gary Harding was arrested and confessed, implicating Taylor and also Billy Longley, who he said had offered Taylor $6000 to shoot the secretary. Longley, who has consistently denied his involvement in the killing of his rival, was arrested.

In his interviews with the police Taylor named Longley but when The Texan went on trial in 1975 Taylor said that the contract had been taken out by a man he knew only as Puttynose. However it was Longley's .22 rifle that had been used by Taylor. He had borrowed it saying he wanted to go rabbiting. At Longley's trial Taylor told the court that he would put the blame on Longley 'if things came undone'. And the reason? He did not think Longley would live that long anyway.

Puttynose can only have been Jack Nicholls, later secretary of the union. By now Longley had a $10000 contract out on him and it did him little good. Known in the press as 'The Godfather of Australian Crime' and 'the most dangerous man in Australia', he was sentenced to life imprisonment. Nicholls, who had convictions for robbery and robbery with violence, somewhat uncharitably thought Pentridge or death was the best thing for him. Taylor and Harding went to prison with Longley.

In September that year Gary Harding told two other prisoners in Pentridge that Longley was not the contractor and he was promptly murdered by Taylor for his indiscretion, literally hacked to death in his cell. 'I have never seen stark terror on a man's face until tonight. I will never forget the look until I die,' said the warder who found the body.

In prison Longley was also subjected to a series of attacks, including acid being poured on his blankets while he was asleep. He was protected by Mark 'Chopper' Read but after five years inside he broke the rules of silence and talked to the journalist David Richards:

> The present day executive is there illegally. They are a bunch of criminals. Everything they do stems from the barrel of a gun or the fear of a gun. My being here is the result of the gun. I am kept here by the barrel of a gun. It is evil.

Longley claimed that, in the struggle for union control, between thirty and forty men had been killed in the period 1958 to 1979—fifteen in the years since 1970. He later gave evidence before the Costigan Commission which had opened on 1 October 1980.

Jack 'Puttynose' Nicholls did not. On 16 June 1981, shortly before he was due to give evidence on subpoena, he was found shot through the head in his car on the Hume Highway some 270 kilometres from Melbourne. There was a note in the car:

> To my members and executive, I tried very hard but the rotten Fraser government did not want me to survive. Do not think I have taken the easy way out but the rotten system has cut my life short. I had big ideas for advancement but these were chopped short. Farewell Comrades, Jack Nicholls XX.

While it was not suggested he had been murdered as such, there were thoughts that he and another two men had been given the option of taking their own lives.

The Costigan Inquiry expanded to an extensive examination of how the Dockers had been used in what were called Bottom of the Harbour schemes. It delved into tax evasion costing millions, drug dealing, laundering and the irregularities of the Nugan Hand Bank as well as in the Deputy Crown Solicitor's Office in Perth. Its findings led to the establishment of the NCA. It did not lead to a new trial for Longley. He served thirteen years and on his release he joined with the former detective Brian 'Skull' Murphy in setting up as business mediators. Many thought this was curious because much of the telling evidence against Longley had come from Murphy.

Just as Lennie McPherson and George Freeman were alleged to be the Mr Bigs of Sydney, so was Charlie Wootton alleged to be the Mr Big of Melbourne in the 1980s. The difference between him and the others is that Wootton only occasionally popped his head above the parapet.

He left school at the age of fifteen to work on the wharves and claimed to be a professional gambler. If so, he was very successful because his bank accounts showed transactions of $250 000 in one year.

Wootton, synonymous in the Melbourne underworld with illegal gambling, first came to notice when he failed to appear as a witness to the shooting of Freddie Harrison and later stood staunch against a battery of questions from the police. Six years later, in September 1964, he was shot while taking his dog for a walk. He did not, he said, know his assailant. On 13 March 1972 the home and car of his neighbour, Ronald Hamilton, in Longmore Street, South Melbourne, were shotgunned, mistaken for Wootton's. That autumn he served two months for consorting with sixteen reputed thieves. When Shannon was shot dead in the October, Wootton was one of the union members who paid for a bereavement notice. The next year, in December, he was acquitted of eighteen charges of consorting but the following year he was convicted of a gaming offence and five years later of yet another.

At the Costigan Commission, Billy Longley described him as 'one of the faceless men behind the docks'. He had big interests in both trotting and card clubs, including the Red Aces, the Hungarian and the Zorro—known throughout Melbourne as Charlie's Place—all above shops in Acland Street, St Kilda. In 1980 he was warned off all trotting tracks in Victoria after a search of his home revealed a .22 silencer, five Buddha sticks and a substance used to pep racehorses. He was said to have close links with George Freeman, with drug dealer Murray Riley and with John Doyle, Riley's Hong Kong-based partner.

Overall the years 1974 to 1976 were relatively quiet for the Dockers but in December 1977 there was one attempted murder and the killing of June Thompson, closely associated with the union. First, Victor George Allard was shot on 5 December at the Bayview Hotel, Cecil Street, South Melbourne, where he had been drinking with friends in the afternoon when a man walked in, fired one shot and left. By the time the police arrived his friends had also left. A bullet was later removed from Allard's bowel.

* * *

June Thompson of Coogee, Sydney, was last seen alive by friends outside a Chinese restaurant in Little Bourke Street, Melbourne, on

13 December 1977. She was later found shot in the back of the head. Her body had been dumped under the Bass Strait ferry loading ramp by two men who had posed as Harbor Trust employees. She had come to Melbourne to see friends and had visited the crew of a ship berthed at Webb Dock. It was the sixty-second murder in Victoria that year, equalling the 1961 record. June Thompson was, however, by no means an innocent tourist. In the October she had appeared in the Sydney Federal Court on a charge of imposition following unemployment benefit frauds in the Sydney suburbs. She also had a number of aliases and a criminal record. Unfortunately her friends could not identify the Chinese restaurant in which they had been eating. No one was charged with her murder.

* * *

In 1978 the murder of docker Leslie Kane started a chain of reprisals throughout the Victorian underworld. It followed perhaps the most successful of all Australian robberies, the Great Bookie Robbery, which took place in 1976 at the Victorian Club, 141 Queen Street, Melbourne. Built in 1880, the club was where the Victorian bookmakers would meet to settle up on the first working day after a weekend's racing. Even though security was amazingly informal—three detectives would drop in to see things were all right and invariably they were—over the years the club had been looked at by a number of criminals, including the celebrated robber James 'Jockey' Smith. They had all decided it was just too difficult. The raid was finally devised by Raymond 'Chuck' Bennett when he was serving a sentence in Parkhurst, a high security prison on the Isle of Wight. With his great friend Brian O'Callaghan, both members of the Kangaroo Gang operating throughout Europe robbing jewellers, he was caught following a raid in London.

During a period of home leave in 1975 Bennett took just that and returned to Australia to case the Victorian Club premises before flying back to Parkhurst to complete his sentence. Like Bruce Reynolds, the leader of Britain's Great Train Robbery, he had the brains to organise and the charisma to lead a team. He was regarded by Chopper Read, himself no slouch, as not only being a top gang tactician but also 'one of the Australian underworld's foremost bank robbers'. However, just as there have been few, if any, success stories among the Great Train Robbers so, over the years, there seemed to be a similar jinx on the participants in the bookie robbery.

Bennett, who had acted as a minder for Longley in the waterfront war, put together a team of nine serious professionals and took them out of the city for a period of training away from their wives and girlfriends and the capital's snares and attractions. Bennett had learned from his time in English prisons, and his team copied the raids of London-based Bertie Smalls and his Wembley gang of bank robbers. His team included another painter and docker, Ian Revell Carroll who became the Quarter Master Sergeant, and Anthony Paul McNamara.

When Bennett was satisfied the training had gone well and the team was ready, he chose the day. An armed guard was carrying what would be the increased takings into the club from 116 bookmakers at both the Caulfield and Moonee Valley meetings for the three day Easter weekend's racing. It was to be a quick in and out job. The club was deserted at the weekend and Bennett took his team of six with three back-ups into the premises for a dress rehearsal.

On the Wednesday the money was delivered by armoured car and at midday a man arrived to say he had been called to repair the refrigerator in the second floor bar. At 12.07 he met with at least five accomplices, wearing balaclavas, dustcoats and overalls, in the stairwell. Armed with machine guns they burst into the settling room, tackled the armed guards and ordered the bookmakers to lie on the floor. Telephones were ripped out and bolt cutters were used to open up metal cash boxes filled with more than a hundred calico bags with untraceable notes variously said to total between $1.5 million and $15 million. The gang jammed the lift with the empty security boxes and in only eleven minutes the raid was over and the robbers were gone into the traffic in Queen Street. A reward of $70000 was promptly offered.

The next problem faced by Bennett was the disposal of the money. An earlier successful job had gone wrong when Peter Macari began wildly spending his $500000 takings from the 'Mr Brown–Qantas' hoax. The Great Train Robbers had been trapped largely because of their inability to hide the large sum of cash they stole. The wiser Bennett had already made arrangements for the laundering and some money was invested through a Sydney estate agent. Other money went to Manila and some to Canada.

There was, however, also the danger of other gangs taking an interest, including the Sydney-based Toecutters, led by Kevin Gore and the crooked former police officer Fred Krahe (they were so-named because of their tendency to amputate the toes of criminals to persuade them to part with their ill-gotten gains). It spoke enormously well of the regard in which Bennett was held that the Toecutters decided to leave him alone.

Some of the laundering did not go well. On a visit to a Melbourne solicitor, Bennett's mother collapsed. When the paramedics undressed her they found some $90000 in cash in her clothes. One theory about solving crime is to follow the money. A close friend of Bennett, Norman Leung Lee, who ran a dim sum restaurant, was arrested and appeared in court in the autumn charged with the robbery. The evidence against him was circumstantial. In the month after the robbery he had spent $13000 on extensions to his house and had bought $60000 of dim sum equipment. He was also said to have laundered money through his solicitor's trust account. On 19 August he took $60000 in a plastic bag to his solicitor's, saying he wanted to invest it for a friend. But when he was raided Lee remained as staunch as Bennett had expected. The magistrate ruled that there was no evidence to link the money to the robbery and Lee was discharged. He was the only person ever charged in the case and shortly after his acquittal the squad investigating the robbery was dissolved.

The predatory Toecutters may have decided to leave Bennett alone and the police to abandon their squad. However, the Kane brothers, Les and Brian, also connected to the Painters and Dockers, who led a team of standover men into illegal gambling and casino protection, were his arch-rivals. The Kanes had grown up as children with a mutual dislike of Bennett, who had long believed that they were informers.

In 1971 Leslie Herbert Kane, who had thirteen prior convictions (including five for various forms of assault), pleaded guilty to shooting a police officer in the leg after being asked to leave the Croxton Park Hotel in Northcote. He had been placed on a $5000 bond, leniency which might give some credence to the belief that he was a grass. However, the Attorney-General appealed and in May 1974 the Court of Appeal sentenced him to eighteen months.

After Kane served the sentence he and Bennett had fought in the Royal Oak Hotel in Richmond and Bennett was fortunate not to lose an ear. Unfortunately Les Kane then made threats against Bennett's family and that was probably what sealed his fate. On 17 October 1978 three men went to Les Kane's home in Wantirna and, after pushing him into the bath, shot him with machine guns. His body was never found. It is thought quite possible that he became dim sum.

Bennett, Francis William Mikkelsen—known as 'Vincent'—and Laurence Joseph Pendergast were charged with, and acquitted of, the murder. During the trial, Kane's wife Judith had accurately predicted what might happen when she said, 'There's going to be revenge. Not only from his family, but a lot of other people.' Mikkelsen and Pendergast went straight into hiding but on 12 November 1979 Bennett, charged with a separate armed robbery, had an appearance at Melbourne Magistrates' Court to attend. While he was waiting without handcuffs and with an unarmed guard outside the courtroom, he was shot three times in the chest. He staggered out of the courthouse followed by police and died in St Vincent's Hospital within the hour. It is highly probable that the gunman was Brian Kane, who had refused to accept the not guilty verdict in relation to his brother's death. Another theory is that the killer was Chris Flannery, possibly with an assist from a police officer. This was certainly suggested by the press. At the inquest the coroner found that two named officers were not involved. Many years later one of them claimed that the killer was indeed Brian Kane.

The day after his death Bennett's old mate Brian O'Callaghan from Kangaroo Gang days escaped from a prison van taking him to work at the prison bakery in Long Bay, Sydney. He then published a tribute in the *Herald Sun*.

> No words I speak will say how I feel. I loved you Ray like a brother. Memories of you will be mine to keep. Today and Forever. Much loved friend of Brian O'Callaghan.

With O'Callaghan temporarily on the loose, the press and police predicted immediate trouble and possibly an all-out gang war, but, for the time, it did not materialise. There were, however, further reprisals to come—but not at first—from the Bennett side. Early in the morning of 15 July 1981 Norman McLeod, Mikkelsen's brother-in-law, was shot three times through the window of his car outside his home in Coolaroo by two men armed with shotguns. The police thought that possibly he was killed in mistake for Mikkelsen. In November 1982 a gunman finally caught up with Brian Kane as he was sitting with a woman in the Quarry Hotel in Brunswick. Now Pendergast came out of hiding but he also went missing in August 1985.

Another of the bookie robbers, Ian Carroll, following in the master's footsteps, became one of the great planners of armed robberies. He would leave nothing to chance and team members were supplied not only with weapons but also a medical kit in case of injury. He was killed in an argument in his own backyard in a supposedly safe house in Mount Martha on the Mornington Peninsula in March 1983. Searching the house, police found what they described as a 'huge number' of weapons, including machine guns, along with uniforms from a security firm, some hidden in a false ceiling.

The house had also been used as a safe house for such criminals as the celebrated bank robber and escaper Russell 'Mad Dog' Cox and former South Australian police officer Colin Creed. Cox was later tried for the Carroll murder and acquitted. He and Creed were identified as part of a gang running through Victoria, New South Wales and South Australia that had pulled off nine armed robberies netting them in excess of $1.3 million. Creed, a master of disguise, was captured in Perth in September 1983. He served twelve years of a twenty-one year sentence for assorted robberies. A charge of murder was not proceeded with.

Over the years those suspected of being on the Victorian Club team or in its three-man backup squad were arrested for other jobs and served long sentences. Anthony McNamara died in Collingwood in 1990. He had become a drug addict and it was suspected that he had been given a hot shot. The laundering contact in Manila featured in the Costigan report. Although wealthy and involved in football and trotting horses, he also became involved in drugs and subsequently received eleven years.

As for Norman Lee, he moved quietly to Singapore but the lure of Victoria proved too much. On 28 July 1992 he and Stephen Barci failed to close the doors as a getaway van accelerated during a robbery at the Ansett Air Freight Terminal at Melbourne Airport. Lee was thrown from the van and, armed with a .357, ran after it. An inquest would hear that he appeared to bring up the gun before he was shot by a member of the Police Special Operations Group. A post-mortem showed that Lee had a 70 per cent blockage of his left coronary artery and the chase after the van might well have killed him anyway. It was thought he had returned to Melbourne some time earlier and had since been involved in a number of successful robberies. In September 1993 Barci claimed that the police had deliberately shot him in the back as he tried to escape with Lee. It was not a claim which appealed to the court and he and the getaway driver Stephen Asling received a ten year minimum sentence.

What happened to the money immediately after the bookie robbery? In 1998 Phillip Dunn QC, who had represented Lee, said his client had told him that for a month the money never left the premises. The robbers had rented offices upstairs from the Victorian Club and it was removed at their leisure over the next four to five weeks. 'When you think about it, that's very smart, verging on genius almost,' said Dunn.

The 1984 Costigan report was both bitterly criticised and stoutly defended. One of the most controversial aspects came from leaked extracts in the draft report published in *The National Times*. It implicated a prominent Australian businessman given the name Goanna as being involved in organised crime, including drugs, pornography and murder. Kerry Packer came out to identify himself as Goanna, deny the allegations and denounce Costigan. His counsel, Malcolm Turnbull, condemned the Costigan Commission as an abuse of power and no charges were ever laid. Investigative journalist Paul Barry, author of an unauthorised biography of Packer, later described some of the allegations as 'outrageous'.

In 1987 federal Attorney-General Lionel Bowen formally dismissed all allegations but there was still a question raised over the receipt by Packer of a cash loan of $225000 from a bankrupt businessman in Queensland. Packer had told the commission, 'I wanted it in cash because I like cash. I have a squirrel-like mentality'. For that reason he had been code-named 'Squirrel' in case studies by Costigan but *The National Times* changed the name to Goanna. Ironically, had Packer's own magazine *The Bulletin* not interviewed Longley, there might never have been a commission.

Despite the notoriety of *The National Times'* Goanna story, on Packer's death in early 2006 his family was offered, and accepted, a state funeral for one of the most powerful public figures in post-war Australia. At the funeral, which was televised nationally by Packer's Nine Network, son James publicly denounced Costigan. In turn Costigan replied in the newspapers saying that, as a Royal Commissioner, he simply investigated and neither made allegations nor prosecuted.

The Federated Ship Painters' and Dockers' Union was de-registered in 1993.

The Seventies

9

The sociologist Alfred McCoy observed in 1980:

> No city in the world could rival Sydney's tolerance for organised
> crime ... During the eleven years from 1965 [to] 1976, with the
> Liberal–Country Party in power, the State endured a period of
> political and police corruption unparalleled in its modern history.

It was during this period that the so-called East Coast Milieu began its
inexorable rise, becoming an all powerful loosely linked association of
criminals who gradually expanded their empires and who forged links
with police, politicians and criminals in Australia, the United States and
the Far East. It lasted nearly twenty-five years.

Who were its members? The senior member until his death in
January 1985 was undoubtedly the standover man Paddles Anderson,
who had never kept to the promise he made when he was acquitted of
murder in Melbourne in 1940 to stop mixing with undesirables. Perhaps
it was just a question of how to define 'undesirable'.

Another senior man in the scheme of things was Lennie McPherson.
Born in Balmain in 1921, he did not receive the acclaim he deserved
until Mr Justice Moffitt's 1973 Royal Commission into the infiltration
of organised crime into the clubs of New South Wales. By then he had
been before the courts seventy-three times, the last serious charge
being in 1955 when he received twelve months for possession of an
unlicensed pistol. He left school at the age of twelve and worked as a
driller at Morts Dock, helping to turn out sloops during the war. From
there he drifted into crime, beginning his long career as a standover

man working for Paddles Anderson. By the 1960s he was a man to be feared. In an article in *The Sydney Morning Herald* on 19 November 1994 journalist Malcolm Brown wrote of him:

> McPherson always had that bit extra, a greater degree of cunning, a ruthlessness, to rise above the level of the common crook. As his life went on, others fell behind. McPherson, by whatever means, overcame a very ordinary start in life, at least in the terms of material prosperity.

One example of his ruthlessness came on his crippled mother's seventieth birthday. McPherson was not invited to her party, so when she returned to her flat he went to visit, tore the head off a white rabbit he was carrying and threw both head and body on the floor behind the horrified, one-legged woman.

George David Freeman was another late beginner—one who did not flourish until the mid-1960s. He was born in the poor area of Glebe–Annandale in 1935 and, like Squizzy Taylor, rode out for a racehorse trainer. He was tall for a jockey, standing 174 centimetres. At one time he sported a variety of tattoos, including a heart, a dagger, 'Mother' and 'Maria' on his right arm and a dagger in a scroll on his left. 'True Love' was tattooed on the backs of his fingers.

During his life he racked up nearly fifty convictions, most of which amounted to little more than petty theft, evading train fares and the like. His one serious conviction appears to have been in 1954 when he received three years' hard labour for breaking and entering. His metamorphosis from a workman at the Homebush abattoir to a multi-millionaire businessman without a business came in the early 1960s when he realised that to move out of the stultifying circle of petty offences he needed to forge links with some of the top men of the time.

Now he moved into the company of the likes of McPherson and Stan 'The Man' Smith, born in Balmain in 1936, who had a police record dating back to 1954. Other associates naturally included Abe Saffron who went to the same school as Anderson (only a little later). There was also Karl Bonnette at whose home in Double Bay a Sydney-style Apalachin meeting of the Mafia was held in 1972. Bonnette had a variety of names, including Karl Solomon, Frederick Brock and Graham John Alleman, the last adopted by deed poll to facilitate his entry into the United States. Born in Melbourne in 1935 he was a great traveller who first became known to the police in 1954. Also part of the group was Morgan John Ryan, another who had worked as a jockey in his youth. Born in 1920 he qualified as a solicitor and opened his firm Morgan Ryan and Brock in the early 1950s. Certainly down the ranking was Milan 'Iron Bar Miller' Petricevic, born in 1938 in Croatia, a debt collector and standover man for Paddles Anderson who once volunteered his services (declined) to the authorities to deal with the Vietnam demonstrators.

While criminals in the Italian community often favoured bombs, up until the end of the 1950s killings in traditional non-ethnic crime were, as Alfred McCoy has pointed out, generally face-to-face or back-of-the-head matters. The killing in July 1960 of 59-year-old William Joseph Thompson, who ran a gambling school in Palmer Street, East Sydney, known as the International Club, was a traditional affair. Thompson, supposedly under the protection of Charlie Bourke, was found slumped across the front seat of his car near his home in Macdougall Street, Kensington. He had been shot at close range. It cannot have been a case of robbery because the sum of 1000 pounds was found on him.

Three years later, on 8 July 1963, a marked change came about when Robert Walker, another also known as 'Pretty Boy' and an associate of Thompson, was shot dead in Alison Road, Randwick. Walker was nearly cut in half when two men in a stolen 1960 Holden with false plates drove slowly past him and fired eleven shots—six of which hit him—with an Owen sub-machine gun.

As is usually the case, a number of explanations for the killing were on offer. Walker had been involved with gangs of safebreakers and burglars as well as with controlling prostitutes and it was thought that his death might have resulted from this connection. The theory was eventually discarded in favour of a reprisal for an earlier shooting at Walker's home in May that year of Stan 'The Man' Smith, now described as 'an associate of some of the most vicious criminals in this state'. There had been some sort of row between Smith and Walker, or possibly between one of Smith's friends, Gordon Reilly, and Walker in which Reilly suffered a broken leg. Instead of a simple stand up between them, Smith went to Walker's home with a number of colleagues and was promptly shot in the chest with a .303 rifle. Walker was duly arrested and at first did not apply for bail, for fear of further reprisals. According to the not always wholly reliable murderer Neddy Smith, it was arranged for a girlfriend to tell him that things had been patched up. Walker was given bail and then very prudently went into hiding in Randwick. The girlfriend promptly told his seekers where he was.

According to the evidence of Detective Sergeant Jack McNeil at the inquest on Walker in February 1964, an Italian criminal Carlo Marchini left Australia for Italy four days after the shooting. He had apparently indicated he was not going to return and feared he would suffer reprisals for having warned Walker of the possible visit from Smith and his friends.

The gunman most favoured for Walker's killing was the 29-year-old up-and-coming standover man, the psychopathic Raymond Patrick 'Ducky' O'Connor, who was a most reluctant and unhelpful witness at Walker's inquest. Later he was charged with possessing an unlicensed and loaded .45 pistol. According to Detective Sergeant W. A. Rait, when the raid took place O'Connor said tellingly, 'Who put me in? I bet that bloody McPherson and Stan Smith gave you the drum about me.' The killing was intended to be seen as, and indeed was, an example to lesser members of the underworld that a new force had arrived and was now in charge. It could be said that, in the winter of 1963, the East Coast Milieu was born.

The Walker killing was followed shortly afterwards by the slaying of Charlie Bourke himself. After his conviction for the shootings he carried out in Queensland in 1930, Bourke—club owner, standover man and greyhound trainer—escaped from Boggo Road jail in Brisbane and came to Sydney where the authorities left him. A violent man, he shot a taxi driver who he believed was having an affair with his wife. As the years went by he was acquitted of the attempted murder of Jordan Eastaughiffe in April 1939. Eastaughiffe remained reasonably staunch, claiming the man who had shot him was bigger than Bourke although he was at a loss to explain how he had come to name Bourke in the first place. In turn Bourke refused to talk to the police when he was himself shot in the back in October 1943.

Still standing over Greek clubs, he was finally machine-gunned to death just before midnight one Sunday in February 1964. Up to twenty bullets were fired at him as he took out the front door key to his Norton Street bungalow in Randwick. No charges were ever brought.

In March the following year Chow Hayes's friend Jackie Hodder was killed at a dance at the Waterloo Town Hall. Hodder had been stabbed in a fight on the dance floor but his death had not interfered with the spirit of things. The band played and the guests danced on. Indeed no one saw anything at all, something which mystified the trial judge. Along with Maurice 'Barney' Ryan, Charles 'Chicka' Reeves was charged with the murder but in a most curious plea bargain he pleaded guilty to manslaughter and received three years. In the underworld it was known that the actual killer was Ronald Feeney, a bludger and fraudsman, known as Ronnie Royal, and that Reeves had taken the easier option rather than risk a life sentence for murder.

As far as these problems can be untangled, it seems that Lennie McPherson, now well on the way to being the Mr Big of Sydney, making an appearance at the dance, had egged on Feeney to fight, suggesting that Hodder was telling people Feeney was a police informer (which indeed he was). The older, but more able, streetfighter, Hodder had given him a bad beating but when he turned his back Feeney stabbed him. The charges against Maurice Ryan and his wife, who had also been dragged into the dock, were withdrawn. Feeney, who did admit he was a police informer, died some years later in Boggo Road jail. He had been suffering from cancer.

Throughout the latter half of the 1960s there was a series of gangland contretemps (if not wars) in Sydney with, as usual, a large number of casualties. Highly respected in the underworld, Robert Lawrence 'Jackie' Steele, who had served a seven year sentence for armed robbery and a five for safebreaking, was shot near his home in Woollahra in November 1965. He was not a difficult target. Most nights of the week at about 8 p.m. he tended to walk to the Lord Nelson for a drink. On his way back he was followed by a car with the false plates CIB 1, its passengers wearing hats of a style favoured by the detective branch. Steele thought they were police, after him for money, but in fact the men were sent by Lennie McPherson. Blinded by the headlights, he received up to fifty pellets and bullets. He staggered the 300 metres to his home and climbed two flights of stairs to his flat before he collapsed. More than twenty bullets were extracted but some were not removed because of their position. His wife and daughter went into hiding. When questioned by the police, Steele said he had no idea who was responsible, 'I didn't think I had an enemy in the world.' He had. McPherson was annoyed that Steele was claiming the Number 1 position in Sydney. He was also furious with an article in *Oz* that labelled him as a 'fizz-gig' (an informer). Steele had bought up a number of copies and was circulating them. It was not for nothing that Steele was known as the Iron Man because he survived a second attack when he and two others were badly beaten by a nine man gang in Macleay Street, Potts Point, in October the next year.

The week after the Steele shooting another standover man was in court. The up-and-coming but vicious Graham Leslie Moffitt, who had already served almost four years in Adelaide for robbery, was sent to prison for six months after pleading guilty to possessing two firearms at Annandale in November. He claimed they were for his and his family's protection. He had been badly beaten in Kings Cross by men with iron bars shortly before he bought them. The police said the weapons were not connected to the Steele shooting and he received a six month sentence.

Moffitt had been right to be scared. On 31 March 1966 he was fatally wounded in an explosion while experimenting on the ignition detonator of a stolen 1964 Holden. Given Jackie Steele's noted skill with explosives, Moffitt's death may have been other than self inflicted. In any event it was certainly fortuitous. He had been using excessively forceful debt collecting tactics and had savagely beaten a well-known doctor and his wife. The doctor had complained to the Milieu.

The unofficial, and indeed official, suspect in both the Walker and Bourke cases had been Ducky O'Connor, who died on 26 May 1967 in what were unusual circumstances, even for that period. Shortly after 3 a.m., O'Connor went to the Latin Quarter club on Pitt Street and stood by the table of Lennie McPherson, near which Detective Sergeant M. J. Wild and a colleague were sitting. At around 3.25 a shot was fired but, because at that very moment people were leaving, Wild did not get a clear view of what happened. As soon as he heard the shot he went to McPherson's table and found O'Connor lying on the floor with a bullet in his head. Two pistols were beside him. By then they were clear of prints. Wild asked what had happened and McPherson told him that O'Connor had approached his table, pulled a gun, said 'Here's yours' and, as he was about to fire, one of the men at the table had grabbed his arm. In the struggle, McPherson said, O'Connor 'sort of' shot himself. A woman sitting at a nearby table said she had seen McPherson drop a gun to the floor but as no charges were preferred she must have been unsighted.

At the time of his death the 29-year-old Ducky O'Connor was on bail, charged with the murder of a Melbourne woman. He was also suspected of being involved in a number of underworld deaths in Sydney quite apart from those of Bourke and Walker. During the month he had been acting independently, collecting money at random from prostitutes, club owners and SP bookmakers. He was effectively out of control and was becoming a considerable liability to the Milieu.

Earlier in the year, about 9 p.m. on 15 January, 'Big' Barry Flock was shot five times in the head in the grounds of the Scottish Hospital, Paddington. His body was found the next day in the undergrowth. One bullet had gone through his hand as though he had raised it to protect himself. There were believed to be several gunmen. The male nurse had been running 'massage parlours' in the area and had recently received threatening telephone calls, probably from a group who wished to take over control. He was also thought to have been talking too loudly about the parlours and to have had financial problems. He had told police he was scared and thinking of leaving Sydney. One of his associates was Johnny Regan, known as 'Nano the Magician' because he could make people disappear, and Flock's killers almost certainly included him. Extortionist Ross Christie, who was a partner with Regan in a dress shop opposite one of the massage parlours, disappeared almost immediately after Flock's killing.

By the 1960s Richard Reilly had graduated from his standover and bookkeeping duties with Dr Stuart-Jones and was regarded as one of the most powerful men in Sydney crime. His police and political contacts had ensured that he avoided any prosecution after 1952. Now he controlled two baccarat clubs, the Kellett and the Spade Room. Lavishly furnished but illegal casinos had replaced the earlier, shabbier baccarat schools. Their profits were enormous, even after $15 000 had been paid out monthly to a police bagman. 'I wouldn't be surprised if some police officers in Sydney have shared as much as a million dollars out of graft over the years,' a detective told *The National Times* in 1973. Even at the time of Reilly's killing the profits were rising. He was also a standover man of abortionists and prostitutes.

Reilly's murder—which created the most interest and, ultimately, unrest in the community that year—came a month after O'Connor's death. He was leaving his mistress's flat in Double Bay on 26 June 1967 when he was shot. The killing seems to have been part of a wild takeover bid by John Warren, a baccarat operator, who had been banished from the Kings Cross area by Reilly. Said to have a backer who was never named, his plan was to control gaming by eliminating his rivals—including the formidable Lennie McPherson—one by one.

Although he clearly had grandiose schemes Warren, a man who never grew out of a love of comic books, seems to have been relatively small time. He had been in a youth gang in Annandale with Leonard 'Ray' Brouggy, and progressed via stealing car radios to a theft-to-order business—the items ranged widely from radios to pianos. In 1951 their lock-up store was found to contain 7000 pounds' worth of stolen goods and Warren received four years, Brouggy half that.

By the early 1960s the pair were reunited, with Warren running a small-time baccarat game in William Street. He then moved to Macleay Street and it was then that Reilly ordered him out. Warren transferred his centre of operations to Liverpool and also began a highly successful operation—said to net $2000 a week—with his girlfriend Aileen McGlinn, stealing from poker machines at the South Sydney Junior Leagues Club.

Warren, along with McGlinn and with a 'Joe Smith' who was never named and who became a Crown witness, waited behind a stone wall until Reilly left the flat in Manning Road at 7.30 p.m. and walked to his blue Maserati. Warren had initially planned on torching Reilly's car but changed his plans to a shooting and had undertaken several dry runs. On the appointed day, however, Warren's aim went slightly awry. Intending to hit him in the stomach, he shot Reilly in the throat and chest and the club owner managed to get to his car and drive away along Manning Road and into the hilly New South Head Road where he collapsed. The car rolled back fifty yards and crashed into the window of a dress shop. Within an hour *The Sydney Morning Herald* received a call: 'Tell them that was for O'Connor and there's going to be more.'

An ecstatic Warren went straight to the South Sydney Junior Leagues Club to establish an alibi. The trio celebrated its success with doughnuts and coffee in a local café. 'Smith' received the less than magnificent sum of $500 for driving the getaway car.

Warren was questioned briefly, gave his alibi and was released. Then, on 25 January 1968, the police received an anonymous call from 'Joe Smith' about the reward then on offer. Warren's name was again in the frame. Reilly's girlfriend told the police of a letter addressed to Len McPherson in the old Black Hand style with a picture of a man stabbed in the back and the words, 'We'll get you all little by little.' At the time it was generally thought the sender had been Charles 'Chicka' Reeves.

Reeves had survived a shooting in Brisbane during the 1974 Painters' and Dockers' war. He was not so fortunate when he was shot in the head by Barry McCann as he drove his Ford Falcon stationwagon along Port Kembla Road near the Wollongong golf course in January 1979. His car veered onto a fairway but happily caused no damage to the greens. Reeves had been standing over a casino run by the much under-rated McCann.

Aileen Glynn, the woman Reilly had been visiting when he was killed, told the police of a debt he owed to an elderly Jewish man, Charles Rennerson. When Claude Eldridge, a garage mechanic and gambling operator, was killed in the previous April, Reilly had tried to contact a man named Walker.

And it was James Cyril 'Johnny' Walker and Charles Edward Rennerson who appeared in the dock charged with having conspired with Warren to kill Reilly. They were said to have been paid $12 000 for the death of Reilly and a further $8000 for the killing of Claude Eldridge.

Brought to court with heavy security, 'Joe Smith' gave his evidence with the public excluded. He wrote down and then printed his real name and told the court that Warren had been 'the best friend I ever had'. Warren, he said, had told him that the retired millionaire who had commissioned the killings was doing it as an act of public good. 'He's only having people killed who have killed other people.' 'Smith' had not exactly done well out of the killing of Eldridge either. On this occasion he received $50.

Rennerson and Walker had the case against them dropped when in January 1968 Warren shot and killed his girlfriend, the man he claimed to be her other lover, another person and then himself. Rennerson, a frightened man, refused to leave the Long Bay jail for some time and then went straight into hiding.

But who was the informer 'Joe Smith'? To those capable of working out the simplest of the Da Vinci codes it cannot come as a great surprise that it was none other than Leonard 'Ray' Brouggy. Possibly he had nursed a grievance that he had been relegated to the position of doorman at the Liverpool baccarat club or over the paltry wages he received. His career had not exactly prospered and he became known as 'Chooky Raffles' because he had taken to running a number of chicken raffles in hotels in the 1960s. He had also told the police that he believed that

Warren was involved in the killings of Charles Bourke and Jackie 'Iron Man' Steele who, in 1965, finally died of his injuries from the shooting.

Reilly left behind him a series of black books containing 389 different telephone numbers, including (as might be expected) those of leading criminals and (as perhaps might not be expected) those of politicians, senior police officers and lawyers along with details of money payments. The numbers and notes, regarded as political dynamite, were investigated by the police and the results sent directly to the Premier Bob Askin. The results were never made public and gambling bosses and other identities continued to operate with impunity.

* * *

What had the other leading members of the Milieu been doing during the period? They had been expanding exponentially in Australia and forging links with crime figures in the United States and the Far East. By the mid-1960s George Freeman, according to his autobiography, saw that he was getting nowhere as a petty criminal and determined to change his life. He bought a house with his safebreaking proceeds and in 1963 became an SP bookmaker, working first for 'Melbourne' Mick Bartley. From then on his fortunes changed. By his own account, Freeman was never more than a vastly misunderstood racing identity. *The Sydney Morning Herald* took a slightly different view, regarding him as holding no lower than the Number 3 position in Sydney crime for the twenty years before his death.

In 1965 Freeman was involved in a turf scandal that would rankle him for the remainder of his life. On 5 August he won a very substantial amount—said to be up to $350000—at Canterbury on the horse Mr Digby, named after his guard dog. Two days earlier it had finished down the track at Randwick. At a subsequent inquiry trainer Harry Clarke and jockey Keith Banks were banned for twelve months before being cleared on appeal. Freeman claimed that the horse's improvement was due to a change in the distance and ground.

That year Freeman became involved with Joe Dan Testa, from the Chicago Crime Syndicate, and later visited Las Vegas using a false passport and accompanied not only by his minder, Stan 'The Man' Smith, but also by his physician, Dr Nick Paltos, there to administer to his pneumonia. Just what real intention lay behind the association with Testa, who set up Grants Constructions Pty Ltd with Freeman, is unclear. Richard Hall, in his book *Disorganised Crime*, tends to discount any serious Mafia influence in Australia, pointing out that the development company soon went bust and Testa was not exactly a key player. Perhaps Hall was wrong. Testa was certainly significant enough in the United States to be worth blowing up. Nor does the fact that a company goes bust mean that many have not made a good deal of money out of it. Freeman also moved around Australia and, in the middle 1960s, acquired a conviction for theft and receiving in Perth and later one for possessing explosives.

Lennie McPherson had also had a busy time. In July 1959 George Joseph Hackett was shot in Elswick Street, Leichhardt. He had had an interesting career outside his day job of wharfie. In 1951 he was acquitted of the murder of Albert Flarrity in a case known as the 'Body in the Brisbane River'. There were suggestions that the jury had been got at. A list of potential jurors was found on a well-known criminal in an envelope bearing his name; it had 'To Be Collected' typed on it. He and a solicitor were questioned but no charges were brought. Five years later Hackett was again acquitted, this time of the murder of ex-boxer John William 'Joey' Manners, who was shot in the Australia Hotel at Millers Point. Again there were suggestions that witnesses had been nobbled.

A week before his death Hackett was involved in a stabbing and it was thought his death might have been a reprisal. It seems he had been shot and pushed out of a car. McPherson and his friend William Louis 'Snowy' Rayner were arrested the next day, prompting McPherson to remark, 'I suppose it's over the Hackett shooting last night. It's a funny thing that whenever anyone is shot in Sydney, the first thing they do is run for me.' McPherson ran the successful alibi that he had been visiting his sick mother in hospital and had then been discussing with two friends whether she should undergo an operation. Both men were acquitted.

For McPherson 1960 was a difficult year. First he was involved in one of the many Painters' and Dockers' power struggles and then John Joseph Unwin and another man were charged with attempting to murder him. They were acquitted—as was McPherson, not only of the murder of Hackett but also of the attempted murder of his own wife and driving a car at Unwin with intent to murder.

By the early 1970s much of vice and protection in Sydney was firmly in the hands of Johnny Regan, 'Nano the Magician', who began expanding his territory rapidly in 1973. He took over a string of brothels after contracting the killing of their owner, Eric 'The Monkey' Williams.

Regan's career had followed a slightly different path from the careers of his colleagues. Instead of relying on the help of the likes of Dr Stuart-Jones to avoid conscription, he desperately wanted to join the army but was rejected because of flat feet. By the age of seventeen he was involved in armed robbery, two years later he began work as a bouncer and by 1967 he was running a string of prostitutes. The previous year he had survived a shooting in Sydney by James Finch and when, in 1973, Regan was implicated in a multiple murder after a Brisbane night-club was torched, Finch would be one of the defendants.

The next year Regan started trying to extort money from some of the up-market casinos such as the 33 Club—and, not surprisingly given the volatile state of the market, it may have cost him his life. It was either that or his curious involvement in a quite genuine organisation, the Independent Action Group for a Better Police Force. Regan, taking time off from his everyday standover duties, began making statutory declarations denouncing high-ranking New South Wales police officers.

Among Nano's 'disappeared' were Robert Donnelly who was spirited off the street in 1972. There was also the killing of Ross Christie, which the police sought to attribute to Regan. Another to go was Kevin Gore of the notorious Toecutter gang, who was seen walking with Regan in Darlinghurst in the winter of 1972, but never again after that. Gore's colleague, William Donnelly, had disappeared only a few days before that. He had gone for a drive in Gore's car, which was later found burned out.

By the time of his death Regan was playing both sides, writing letters to the police naming those he claimed were trying to kill him. He had, he said, made known his intentions to close illegal gambling and to stop prostitution. This, said his enemies, was a blind in order to be able to extort more from them. With his other hand he was still busy denouncing police officers. A particularly nasty murder attributed to him was that of Karlos, the three-year-old son of a friend, Helen Scott-Huie, for whom he was babysitting. Regan told the police he had left the child in his car when he went to buy a paper around midnight in

Taylor Square and on his return found him missing. The cognoscenti believed he had killed the child when Karlos began to annoy him.

Someone decided to end it all as Regan walked alone to an appointment in Marrickville after a September picnic in Watsons Bay Park. Three different .38 guns were used and some of the bullets were fired from as little as eight centimetres. The getaway car had also been used a month earlier in the killing of one of Regan's associates, John Edward 'Ratty' Clarke, shot in the Newington Inn in Petersham.

In his memoir *Catch and Kill Your Own*, Neddy Smith attributes the death of Clarke to Regan and that of the Magician to The Team, the major group of players led by George Freeman and Lennie McPherson, acting in retaliation over the death of Clarke. Given his own circumstances, Smith can never be regarded as wholly reliable on these finer points but in *Infamous Australians* Andrew Dettree and his co-authors say Clarke was killed by Regan to gain control of Sydney's inner and western suburbs and because Clarke had been bad-mouthing him. Writer Bob Bottom maintains that Regan's death was specifically in relation to a Marrickville club he wished to protect but which was already under American control. Another theory is that his death was at the hands of the police in the form of Ray Kelly.

* * *

One of the worst mass killings in Australia came in Brisbane when the Whiskey Au Go Go club was firebombed in March 1973 at a time when the Sydney underworld was looking for easier pickings. It had been thought, at the time, that Brisbane was safe from the excesses of organised crime on the basis that a city had to have a population of around 800 000 to support 'quality' criminals. The thinking was wrong. Brisbane had always been something of a holiday home for the East Coast Milieu and Brisbane was a growing city.

In 1969 Donald Smith, a Sydney gunman, ran an unlicensed nightclub, Interlude, at Fortitude Valley. Called 'The Glove' because he wore a lead-lined leather glove, Smith had had a quarrel with another identity, Jackie Clark, and Fred Krahe had arranged with another police officer, Glenn Hallahan, that Smith and his wife Linda should go to Brisbane. The Interlude, frequented by prostitutes, was the hangout of some of the best Brisbane criminals of the time. Smith was later shot dead in a Sydney nightclub and Interlude was later re-opened, as Pinnochio's, by Geraldo Bellino and his brother Antonio.

In the autumn of 1973 the first of two nightclubs to be bombed was Torino's in the Fortitude Valley area. It sustained extensive damage but there were no casualties. There was, said the police, no suggestion of any protection racket. They were wrong: on 8 March 1973 fifteen people died in the fire at the nearby Whiskey Au Go Go club. Shortly after the main band had finished their set, two canisters of petrol were rolled onto the carpeted entrance to the club and set alight with a lighted folder of matches. Immediately afterwards a private detective said he had warned the police of the likelihood of a bombing. The police denied they had ever received such information. It was a question of 'the usual suspects'. The name of Linus Driscoll, 'Jimmy the Pom', was circulated as someone wanted for questioning.

Within a week Barbara McCulkin and her two daughters disappeared. Shortly after that Barbara's husband Billy McCulkin was charged with bombing Torino's, something he denied. The case was dropped when the Director of Public Prosecutions decided there was no prospect of a conviction on the evidence available. Another man, former boxer Ian Hamilton, who was alleged to have been the driver, also disappeared. His body was never found but a Billy Stokes was later convicted of his murder. In November 1973 prostitute Margaret Grace Ward disappeared after leaving a lawyer's office with the de facto wife of Vince O'Dempsey; he was another named as being involved in the Whiskey Au Go Go firebombing but was never charged. Also named were the club owners Geraldo and Antonio Bellino on whose behalf Billy McCulkin was alleged to have carried out the attack. Both denied any involvement and Antonio said the family was blamed for anything that went wrong in the city. Neither was ever charged.

Meanwhile came the arrest of two serious criminals, John Stuart and Richard Finch. Stuart had been convicted in November 1965 of shooting John 'Iron Man' Steele in the power struggle in the Sydney underworld. He was sentenced to five years and while in Long Bay prison was found what was delicately called 'wandering'. He was thought to have been looking for Steele who was in the same prison serving twelve months for carrying an unlicensed firearm. Stuart had his own troubles during that jail sentence. In October 1966 he was stabbed in the stomach and the following March he was stabbed in the back while taking a shower.

In October 1966 Finch had been convicted of wounding with intent to murder following the shooting of John 'Nano the Magician' Regan. After serving most of a seven year sentence he was deported to England. He had kept in touch with Stuart whom he had met in prison and the allegation was that Stuart had re-imported Finch to do the bombing while setting himself up with an alibi. Finch had been staying with the McCulkins.

Allegedly both men made confessions and Finch is said to have named Billy McCulkin as the getaway driver after the Au Go Go fire. The trial was a lengthy affair drawn out by the fact that Stuart took to swallowing twisted paperclips bound with rubber bands. When the rubber rotted the clips uncurled and stuck in his intestines. By the time the jury retired he was undergoing his third operation and was thought to be too ill to attend the hearings. He had already discharged his counsel and the court was regularly reconvened in the hospital.

On 22 October the jury, which had been sequestered for some six weeks, took a bare two hours to find both Stuart and Finch guilty. Neither man accepted his conviction and both staged a series of protests. Stuart sewed his lips together. Finch, denying his confession, claimed to have bitten off a finger to show his indifference to pain, arguing that if he could do such a thing, was he likely to show the remorse the police alleged? In fact the finger had been sliced off for him by a fellow prisoner.

On 17 January 1979 Stuart was found dead in his cell. Aged thirty-nine he had suffered a heart attack. Finch, a good-looking prisoner, became the target of romantically inclined females. In 1986, while still in prison, he married a woman, Cheryl, who suffered from a debilitating disease. This led to belief in his reformation and a campaign was started for his release. Finch was again deported and the pair moved to England, to be greeted by a *Daily Mirror* front page headline: 'Welcome Home Killer'. It was only a few months before his wife returned to Australia. In October 1988 he confessed to the Brisbane-based journalist Dennis Watt, who had campaigned for his release, that he had, in fact, started the fire. He later retracted this confession saying he had only made it for money.

* * *

The authorities had done nothing about the Apalachin meeting of the Mafia held at Karl Bonnette's Double Bay home the year before the bombing, in July 1972, by either 'the boys playing cards' (as described by New South Wales police) or 'a summit meeting of criminal minds' (as described by Mr Justice Moffitt). That the Australian meeting was undisturbed and unremarked by the police was not altogether surprising. The Moffitt Royal Commission into organised crime found that three of the officers in charge of state investigations had deliberately or corruptly attempted to cover up organised crime links with a seemingly legitimate poker machine business, run by the identity Jack Rooklyn.

Born in London in 1918, or perhaps ten years earlier, Jack Rooklyn had gambling interests throughout South-East Asia. During the war he had arranged illegal poker games for US troops and his gaming machine interests were bought out by the allegedly Mafia-related American company Bally for 10 million pounds. He remained as general manager and by 1972 Bally had 20 per cent of all poker machines in New South Wales.

Said to be present at the meeting, and their names noted by an observant police officer, were Bonnette, Saffron, McPherson, Anderson, Freeman, Milan 'Iron Bar' Petricevic, and others including a Labor member of the state parliament who denied that he was there. Confusingly, Bonnette denied that any of them were there.

It would also appear that Stan 'The Man' Smith, who seems not to have fully understood that tape recorders, unless deleted, record for posterity, had been coached in his evidence to Moffitt's Commission. At a meeting at the popular Taiping restaurant in Elizabeth Street, Surry Hills, on 22 June 1976 he was again recorded, this time explaining how it was essential 'to get the game sewn up'. He was referring to the likelihood of licensing gambling and was, naturally, keen to ensure that the licences would be granted to existing, if illegal, operators and not to newcomers.

Following recommendations from Mr Justice Moffitt, a police operation, *Southern Comfort*, began tapping George Freeman's telephones. From the conversations it became clear that by 1976 he was supplying the Chief Stipendiary Magistrate, Murray Farquhar, with a series of almost infallible racing tips. Freeman was now well established in the senior echelons of both the underworld and the police. A decade later Mr Justice Stewart reported that he was involved in SP bookmaking, illegal casinos and the fixing of horse races. He also had improper relationships with three named police officers at inspector and superintendent level. As for the American connection, he was involved with Danny Stein, who had given him a power of attorney on an account at the ANZ bank in Pitt Street. In September the following year it was closed and more than $56 000 was transferred to Stein. Three years later Stein was back in Australia where it was thought he was setting up a network for the importation and distribution of heroin both in Australia and the United States.

It was Murray Farquhar who almost single-handledly put an end to the consorting laws when, in 1969, McPherson was in front of him, pleading guilty to consorting with criminals. According to McPherson's barrister, he had been a motel manager for the past fourteen years and was highly thought of by his employers, earning $40 a week. By then he had a good quality house and what seemed to be an equally good quality lifestyle. Instead of sending McPherson to prison Farquhar fined him $100. It is well known that police forces can develop a collective anomie if they think their efforts are not being rewarded. Gradually, as fewer and fewer charges were brought, the law faded into disuse.

Indeed steps could be, and were, taken against pro-active police officers. In 1977 Tony Lauer, then a sergeant, later commissioner, prepared a report which implicated Freeman in illegal gaming. In turn his allegations were investigated but no criminal charges were brought. For his pains Lauer was exiled to the Blue Mountains.

On 27 July that year it became apparent that Farquhar's relationship with Freeman was seriously unhealthy. Freeman was watched over a two hour period and photographed as he sat in the member's stand at Randwick with Farquhar and Dr Nick Paltos before being evicted by racecourse security. It was an afternoon that would have considerable repercussions for Farquhar and lead to another inquiry, this time conducted by the chief justice, Sir Laurence Street. What was alleged against Farquhar was that, because of the stream of winning racing tips, he had allowed himself to be influenced when he intervened in the trial of the then New South Wales Rugby League executive director Kevin Humphreys, who had pleaded not guilty on 11 August to embezzlement of some $50 000 worth of funds from the Balmain Rugby League club. Despite what was a strong case for the prosecution, properly presented, the stipendiary magistrate, believing that he had instructions from the chief magistrate, dismissed the charges, refusing to commit Humphreys for trial. On 18 October 1983 Humphreys was re-tried on the charges and fined $4000. Within a month of his conviction he was employed as a publicity manager for the Illawarra Turf Club.

What was even worse was the other line of inquiry: that this intervention had indeed been made at the request of the Premier of New South Wales, Neville Wran, from whom Farquhar said he received a telephone call on the morning of the hearing.

At the Street Inquiry, Freeman gave a highly entertaining perform-ance, including a denial, despite a photograph, that he had been in the members stand at Randwick that fateful afternoon and complaining that he had been falsely maligned by journalist Bob Bottom. At the end he took the opportunity to make a plea: 'Who am I to talk to? If I talk to the baddies, I'm in trouble; if I talk to the goodies, they're in trouble ...'

In the end Sir Laurence Street found that Farquhar had influenced the outcome of Humphreys's committal proceedings but that he was not acting at the request of Neville Wran. There had been no such telephone call. The loser in all this was Farquhar. In March 1985, at the age of sixty-six, he was sentenced to four years' imprisonment on a charge of conspiracy to pervert the course of justice. His time in prison was not as difficult as for some errant judges. He was reclassified from A2 to C2 in one day. He was then sent to the Metropolitan Training Centre and later taught prisoners to read and write.

The decade ended dramatically for Freeman. On 25 April 1979 he was shot in the head with a .22 pistol. He had been to dinner with Dr Nick Paltos when a gunman opened fire as he got out of his car at his home at Yowie Bay. In March 1979 Bruce McDonald, Deputy Leader of the Opposition, had asked a question suggesting that Freeman had too much influence in 21 Division. Freeman then tried to meet McDonald at Parliament House and a subsequent motion that his conduct should be deplored was defeated when the Labor Opposition voted against it. One thing that sensible criminals do not do is come to the notice of the public and a theory is that the motive behind the attack was a protective measure by the underworld.

No one was ever charged with the shooting. After he recovered from the attempted murder, Freeman went to Noosa Heads in Queensland with his family. While he was there, on 7 June, John Marcus Miller (or Muller or Milner), a man thought to have been the ill-aimed shooter, was shot to death outside his home in Sydney's Coogee. Miller, who had served sentences for theft and who at the time of his death was working as a doorman at a casino in Kings Cross, was shot through the driver's window as he pulled into his own driveway. Freeman declined to answer questions when interviewed by the police and the coroner indicated there was no evidence to link him with Miller's death. There were suggestions that so far as Miller was concerned it was a family matter.

Freeman married in August 1981. Guests including Paddles Anderson, McPherson and Kevin Humphreys, who would later say on television that he believed he had the right 'to attend a wedding of a friend of mine'. In January 1983 the police had a rare triumph, albeit a minor one, in their contest with Freeman. Meat was thrown over the garden wall of his home at Yowie Bay, so distracting his Rottweiler dogs. The police then managed to gain entry to the house and as a result Freeman was fined $500 for illegal SP betting. It could not exactly be described as a major triumph for the authorities when in April 1985 Freeman was fined the maximum $5000 after pleading guilty to more telephone betting offences.

On 20 March 1990 Freeman suffered a severe asthma attack and died shortly after he was taken to hospital. His funeral was a fine one, attended by the likes of Lennie McPherson and Freeman's solicitor, Christopher Murphy, who had assisted him with his privately published autobiography. Dr Nick Paltos, who couldn't attend, sent a wreath.

The reason for Paltos's absence was that he was in prison. He was born Paltogou on 21 July 1940 of Greek parents and came to Australia in 1947. His father died when he was young. Paltos worked as an apprentice in a metal factory and drove a cab to support his family until he was encouraged by Joe Taylor, of Thommo's Two-up school, to study. He qualified as a doctor in 1968 after being awarded a Commonwealth Scholarship to the University of New South Wales in 1961 and became head of the casualty department at Sydney Hospital. By 1976, his voice was turning up on intercepts of George Freeman. In 1978 he resigned from the hospital and set up practice in Woolloomooloo. Apart from Freeman his distinguished clientele included not only the magnate Kerry Packer, the chief justice and the entertainer Sir Harry Secombe but also Farquhar, the drug dealer Bob Trimbole and Lennie McPherson. The latter combination was his final undoing.

After Trimbole fled to Ireland, Paltos assumed his role as a key figure in the Australian drug trade. 'He thought he resembled Marlon Brando in *The Godfather*,' recalls a police officer. Trimbole may still have made the decisions from abroad but Paltos was his willing lieutenant. By the time Paltos organised his final ruinous shipment in October 1983 the dapper figure pictured at the Randwick races with Freeman had long since blown up into a balloon. He was in debt to solicitor Ross Karp to the tune of $300000, chain smoking and, worst of all, talking too much.

The end for Paltos, Karp and club owner Graeme 'Billy Crocodile' Palmer came with the anchoring, some 80 kilometres out of Darwin, of the 12 metre trawler the *Moray* on 23 February 1984. Some 1400 bags of Lebanese Gold had been unloaded from a mother ship, the *Gulf Frio*, which was then scuttled. Palmer was among the men who met the *Moray* as it sailed to an inlet north of Darwin where its cargo was off-loaded into lorries and driven to Sydney. One of the drivers was Danny Chubb. Stephen Nittes, the Painter and Docker, was used as an enforcer and drug distributor. The ring was broken by the police using surveillance and bugging devices in Operation Lavender. Nittes, who had previously received sixteen years for his part in the Mayne-Nickless robbery, was now sentenced to seven years. On 7 March 1986 Paltos received twenty years for conspiracy to import drugs—alleged by the police to be worth some $40 million. Ross Karp and Palmer each received fourteen years.

Karp, born Karpuouzis in 1948 on Kastellorizon, the same island as Paltos, practised law in Darlinghurst and was the ring's accountant. He refused to give evidence at Paltos's trial and in 1986 he again refused to give evidence in the trial of the police officer Roger Rogerson.

Palmer came from a more traditional background. He is said to have obtained his nickname when, after he had bitten off a man's ear, a police officer asked the victim, 'Who's been fighting with a crocodile, then?' He had been a doorman at gang-owned clubs before opening his own in Parramatta. He then became a casino and greyhound owner, having some success with his dogs.

Freeman's death left Lennie McPherson holding the Mr Big title. He had mostly kept out of the limelight for much of the 1960s and 1970s, surfacing rarely. He was, however, thought to have held kangaroo courts in Parramatta jail in which he passed sentence on those who had offended him or, he believed, had conspired against him. One had been Ducky O'Connor. One rare sighting of McPherson came when, following his hearing at the kangaroo court, O'Connor decided to kill himself at McPherson's table in the Latin Quarter nightclub. Then there was a brief mention of McPherson, for those in the know at any rate, in October 1965 when the satirical magazine *Oz* published a mock top twenty Sydney criminals. Sensibly surnames were not printed and there was no Number 1. But Number 2 was all too recognisable to the cognoscenti: 'A Gladesville resident known as Lennie almost qualifies as a mastermind. He is feared and hated by most. He is a fence and a fizz-gig.' Number 3 in the list was named Perce. At the bottom, sharing Number 20, Kate and Tilly were described as 'retired'. The December issue of the magazine published a sort of retraction: 'rest assured Lennie is not an informer'. The reason for this climbdown may well have had something to do with a visit to the editor by McPherson who, taking him for a drive, showed him the bullet holes in the roof of his car.

In 1973 McPherson was once more before Murray Farquhar, this time charged with being in possession of money extorted from the Pussy Galore nightclub in Kings Cross. Farquhar was not convinced that the $400 found on McPherson had indeed come from the club. He was acquitted.

Small paragraphs in the centre pages of newspapers became page one news when McPherson was summoned before the Moffitt Commission. He claimed he was anxious to appear and, asked how he made his money, he replied, 'I do the best I can.'

Now he was referred to as a 'vicious and powerful criminal'. McPherson was quick to deny the existence of a Mafia in Australia 'but if there is I hope they will soon take over the place so people will know I have nothing to do with them,' said the man who had been kangaroo shooting with Joe Testa.

As the years went by McPherson became more and more recognised as a leading figure in the Sydney underworld. In 1977, on a visit with two others to Manila, he was arrested—because, he maintained, the Australian police had sent an advance warning that he was there to assassinate President Marcos—and he spent three days on death row in Fort Benefacio prison before being released.

The next year he changed his name to avoid unwanted attention. He was now Leonard Murray but his alter ego was short-lived and he soon reverted to his real name. By this time the press was seriously on his tail, as indeed were the politicians. In 1980 the Woodward Royal Commission reported that perhaps McPherson had gone to Manila not to assassinate Marcos but rather to look after his interests there.

The commission suggested that a wanted criminal, Martin Olsen, was his man in Manila, running his bar and looking after his prostitutes. It was also suggested that, during 1975, someone in the company of Danny Stein and George Freeman had been bringing back 'white powder' for McPherson, something he denied.

In 1983 he was involved in yet another major inquiry when Sydney heiress Juanita Nielsen disappeared from a nightclub owned by the legendary Abe Saffron. Now McPherson denied that he had told a federal police officer that the former New South Wales officer Fred Krahe was responsible for the killing.

The disappearance of the beautiful Nielsen remains one of the great unsolved mysteries of Australian crime. Heiress to the Mark Foy department store fortune, she led a somewhat chequered life. Born in 1937, she married a Danish seaman and lived with him in Europe until, on the breakdown of the marriage in 1973, she returned to Australia. She started *Now*, a local newspaper in Kings Cross, taking a strong social line and opposing in particular a project at Victoria Street, Potts Point, where builder Frank Theeman was planning to redevelop much of the street into a four hundred unit block of flats. Nielsen's campaign cost Theeman something in the region of $3 million. Operating a green ban for two years, the Builders Labourers' Federation refused to demolish the existing buildings and when, following government pressure, that ban was relaxed, Nielsen managed to persuade the Water Board Union to refuse to work on the site. Theeman was losing $3000 a day.

On the morning of 4 July 1975, Nielsen visited the Carousel Cabaret, otherwise known as Les Girls, a transvestite club run by Abe Saffron in partnership with James 'Big Jim' McCartney Anderson, known as 'The Overlord'. She went there, in theory, to discuss the inserting of an advertisement into *Now*. She left at 11.30 and was never seen again.

At the thirteen week long inquest her friend John Glebe told the inquest jury that in 1976 he had received a call telling him to back off and that Nielsen's death, which had been a mistake, happened shortly after her abduction. The jury ruled that she was dead but was unable to say when, where or at whose hands she had died. It was at this inquest that Lennie McPherson denied telling a federal officer that Krahe had admitted responsibility. Another name in the frame was the standover man Tim Bristow, who also denied involvement, again putting the blame on Krahe.

Over the years bits and pieces of the story have leaked out, but another opportunity to solve the riddle died with the death of James Anderson from cancer on 15 July 2003. In the 1980s Anderson had been badly burned in a petrol bomb attack and had also been shot and wounded. He had been a police informer, an occupation which carries an inordinate number of risks. In 1988 he saved six sailors during a typhoon and received a bravery award. In 1995 Anderson suffered a heart attack and moved first to the Blue Mountains from where he regularly visited Las Vegas and the Philippines, where he was a welcome visitor. Later he contracted bird flu from feeding rosellas and was taken to hospital where his cancer was diagnosed.

No relation to Paddles, Anderson was born in Glasgow in 1930, joined the Marines at the age of sixteen then worked as a coach driver before becoming a traffic policeman in New Zealand. He could clearly turn his hand to most things because in the late 1950s he came to Sydney as manager of the Hi-Fives, a Maori showband. It was then that he met Abe Saffron, the so-called Mr Sin. Superficially Anderson was a friendly, gregarious man. The journalist Neil Mercer recalled him as saying on parting, 'Remember, mate, every day's a bonus, tahdetah', but those who knew and feared him thought he had a very nasty temper.

In 1970 Anderson encountered the fearsome standover man Donny 'The Glove' Smith in the Venus Room in Orwell Street, Kings Cross. Smith hit Anderson, breaking his jaw, and in turn Anderson shot him three times in the chest and the back as Smith was running away. He claimed self-defence on the basis that Smith was running away to get a gun. His initial charge of murder was reduced to manslaughter and the case was then 'no-billed', a decision which the Parliamentary Joint Committee found 'difficult to understand' except that it was made under the corrupt Askin government where certain criminals held at least a partial control over parts of both the police and the administration.

In the late 1960s, in partnership with Saffron, Anderson owned a number of clubs, strip joints and bars, including the Carousel, the Venus Room, and Les Girls, which he managed. When asked whether the girls were renting rooms above the Venus Room for the purposes of prostitution he replied, 'I don't think they were playing Scrabble.'

Around the time of Nielsen's disappearance, Anderson fell out with Saffron and turned informer for the National Crime Authority, which listed their allegations against the pair as including extortion, arson, bribery, drugs and running prostitutes. He then turned state witness against Saffron who was sentenced to three years for tax evasion.

Anderson had always denied any involvement in Nielsen's disappearance, also naming Fred Krahe as the actual killer. Certainly Krahe had connections. It was he who organised the gangs that terrorised the Victoria Street protesters.

The theory that Anderson was involved in Nielsen's death was based principally on circumstantial evidence and association. His club was the place where she was last seen; he knew the three men convicted of conspiracy to kill her; and he was a close friend of the developer, Frank Theeman, and his son Tim. On 25 May the Theeman family company, FWT Investments, paid $25 000 to Anderson. That September, Anderson was declared bankrupt with debts of over $450 000. He maintained that, acting on behalf of Theeman, he had paid $23 000 of the $25 000 for a club in Bondi Beach but at the Nielsen inquest the club owner denied he had ever received any money from either Anderson or Theeman. Over the years there were rumours that Anderson was blackmailing Theeman and that he had been 'lent' hundreds of thousands of dollars which had, of course, never been repaid.

After Anderson's death two transvestites who were in the club on the morning of Nielsen's visit spoke to reporter Emma Alberici. Then 27 years old, Loretta Crawford was acting as the receptionist. She maintained that Anderson was not in the club that morning but that the meeting was with the barman Shane Martin Simmonds and the night manager Eddie Trigg. Monet King (formerly Marilyn, a cocktail waitress in the club) was the live-in lover of Trigg and she maintained that after the visit there was blood on Trigg's shirt and that Trigg's hand was badly bruised and swollen. Trigg had told King that, if she was asked by the police, she was to confirm that Trigg had hit her. Crawford claimed that she saw Juanita lying on the stairs going down to the storeroom and a third person, not Trigg or Simmonds, was there with a gun. 'The bullet wound was only very, very tiny. It was, like, probably like a cigarette butt, the size of a cigarette butt, but there was, like, maybe a trickle of blood that I saw.'

Theeman did not live long after the killing of Nielsen, dying in 1979. In 1983 Trigg received three years and Simmonds two for their involvement in her disappearance.

McPherson's final court appearance ended in 1992 with a sentence of four years for paying $20 000 to have the former general manager of his nephew's importing company beaten up. There had been a dispute when the man left, taking a substantial client with him—standard business practice but it did not seem that way to McPherson. The beating was organised by strip club owner Kostas Kontorinakis, known as Con Kostas. Kostas was imprisoned but the case against McPherson was endlessly delayed and in the meantime he took the opportunity to ingratiate himself with potential character witnesses by visiting a hostel for down-and-outs. A plea bargain was turned down by the prosecution and it seems that at the trial McPherson feigned illness. Neither the hostel visiting nor the illness benefited him.

McPherson died in the recreation room of Cessnock jail on 28 August 1996. He had been speaking to his wife on the telephone when he collapsed with a heart attack. Aged seventy-five, he was due for parole the following year. At his funeral his daughter Janelle Olive told the congregation, which included many old friends and some relatively new ones (among them nightclub owners Sam and John Ibrahim), that her father had 'chosen a path in life that you or I might not have chosen but at least he was at the very top of his profession.' After 'Abide with Me' was played, so was the traditional gangster hymn, a tape of Sinatra singing 'My Way'. McPherson is interred in a mausoleum at the Field of Mars Cemetery, Ryde. The magnificent tomb—the only one in the cemetery—is said to have cost some $50 000. Perhaps unkindly, it has been said that, 'For once, he's in solitary'.

The always immaculate, hail-fellow-well-met Tim Bristow—model, private detective, casual journalist, intermittent standover man and self-styled friend of Lennie McPherson (who refused to acknowledge the association)—died following a stroke on 10 February 2003. He had been sitting on his verandah in Pittwater. He claimed his divorce practice was the biggest in Australia and that on a good night he would break down eight doors. He was also a major standover man in the building industry. Once he explained the death of a union man who fell off a building as 'You can't help bad luck.' In 1976 he was sentenced to eighteen months for assault and in the 1980s served five years for supplying cannabis. He would also be a witness at the long running inquest into the death of hitman Christopher Flannery. After Bristow's death, an action over the ownership of his property was settled in favour of his mistress.

In September 2005 Karl Bonnette accepted counsel's description of him as a 'retired colourful identity' when denying that he knew anything about the disappearance of the housewife Kerry Whelan in 1997. His memory was now so bad, he said, that he could 'barely remember my way home'. He had, he told the court, never been involved in extortion or kidnapping. Admittedly he had used a couple of false names but this was simply to avoid the unwelcome attentions of ex-wives.

McPherson's passing really left only the reclusive Abe Saffron as the last of the old timers. The golden age of the East Coast Milieu was effectively over. Saffron remained spiky to the end, suing the *Gold Coast Bulletin* over a crossword clue 'Mr Sin (3.7)' and, rather less successfully, John Silvester and Andrew Rule over his entry in their *Tough: 101 Australian Gangsters*. He settled the action on part payment of his lawyers' costs. The sales of the book increased enormously.

Saffron died on 15 September 2006. At his funeral service at a Woollahra synagogue the rabbi spoke of him as 'acknowledged as a man of goodwill' and 'a true Australian icon'. Karl Bonnette, whose memory appeared to have partially recovered, at least so far as his old colleague was concerned, said, 'He was always a gentleman and I don't believe any of the things that were written about him being a criminal.' One of his former employees thought differently, saying, 'He made sure his girls had enough heroin to work and make him a dollar. He always took 60/40. He was a hoon.'

Australia's 'favourite larrikin' of the 1920s— Squizzy Taylor, always a dapper dresser.
(*VICTORIA POLICE GAZETTE*, 30 MARCH 1922)

IN MEMORY OF
JUNE LORRAINE TAYLOR
10. 1. 1921 - AGE 7 MONTHS
ALSO
JOSEPH THEODORE LESLIE
TAYLOR
29. 10. 1927 - AGE 38 YRS.

Squizzy Taylor was buried with his infant daughter.
(COURTESY FRANKIE BATESON)

Above: Police mugshots of Richard Buckley, wanted for the murder of bank employee Thomas Berriman in Melbourne in October 1923. (*Victoria Police Gazette*, 18 October 1923)

Right: The stylish and staunch Ida Pender—Squizzy Taylor's girlfriend whom he met at the St Kilda Palais de Danse. (*Victoria Police Gazette*, 30 March 1922)

The one-legged Matthew Biggar, one of the great Australian conmen who toured Europe in the 1920s. (COURTESY NATIONAL ARCHIVES, UK)

The hated James Coates, shot in 1946 by Freddie Harrison and missed by no one. (COURTESY NATIONAL ARCHIVES, UK)

William 'Bludger Bill' Warren, arrested in Paris in 1925 with an estimated 800 000 pounds in cash and jewellery hidden in his Rolls-Royce. (COURTESY NATIONAL ARCHIVES, UK)

English born Tilly Devine, one
of the leading lights in Sydney's
brothel scene in the 1920s to
1960s. (NEWSPIX)

Abe Saffron, who died in 2006,
was king of the Sydney club
scene for more than fifty years.
(NEWSPIX)

Chow Hayes (right) is
restrained by Detective
Ray Kelly after
threatening journalist
Bill Jenkings immediately
after Hayes's arrest for the
1951 murder of bouncer
and film extra Bobby Lee.
(NEWSPIX)

Left: Fred Krahe (right), c. 1968, the talented if corrupt New South Wales detective who fell foul of prostitute Shirley Brifman. (COURTESY HERALD & WEEKLY TIMES PHOTOGRAPHIC COLLECTION AND STATE LIBRARY OF VICTOIRA)

Below: Lennie McPherson (left) entertains Chicago *Mafioso* Joey Testa (right) and Nick Giordano on a roo shooting expedition in 1969. (NEWSPIX)

James Bazley, c. 1973,
former Painter and Docker,
convicted of the murder
of drug reformer Donald
Mackay and drug dealers
the Wilsons. (Courtesy
Victoria Police Museum and
State Library of Victoira)

Flamboyant Shirley Finn,
Perth's leading madam
before her death, was shot
in her car in June 1975.
(Newspix)

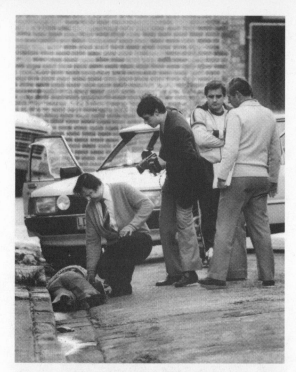

The talented if wayward New South Wales Detective Sergeant Roger Rogerson (far right), inspecting the body of drug dealer Warren Lanfranchi in June 1981.
(NEWSPIX)

Kath Pettingill, matriarch of an infamous crime family.
(NEWSPIX/JAY TOWN)

Zarah Garde-Wilson, who has defended the cream of the Melbourne underworld. (NEWSPIX/TREVOR PINDER)

Alphonse Gangitano, shot dead in 1998, was the leader of the Carlton Crew in Melbourne's underworld. (NEWSPIX/BEN SWINNERTON)

Mick Gatto (right) greets a mourner at Mario Condello's funeral. Condello was gunned down at his Melbourne house in February 2006. (NEWSPIX/CRAIG BORROW)

Two Wars in the Eighties

10

It was not until the Vietnam War, when Sydney was used as a home for servicemen on R&R, that the heroin trade took off in Australia. As late as 1966, with only a handful of known addicts in the country, drug possession and importation were a very low priority for the New South Wales Drug Squad.

It was a police officer who was among the first to take advantage of the vacuum. That year John Wesley Egan masterminded a high grade heroin smuggling ring. He had already begun his criminal career. A fine swimmer, commended for his lifesaving, he was a member of the Police Underwater Diving Squad which was asked by the Customs Department to try to recover some gold ingots thrown overboard by Chinese seamen pre-empting a search. He duly located them but taped a number to a pylon for later personal recovery. After that Egan began smuggling watches, transistors and cameras which, he later claimed, were mainly sold to police officers. An unfortunate sale to a customs official blew the lid off the scheme and five officers resigned. It was then that Egan was introduced to the possibilities of heroin smuggling by a man connected to the Painters and Dockers and he determined to make a million dollars inside three months then quit.

He learned of a potential customer, an ex-CIA agent in New York, borrowed money for home improvements, obtained compassionate leave to attend the funeral of an aunt in California and booked a flight to New York on Qantas with a kilo of almost pure heroin supplied by a contact in Bondi. He made $6000 from the run and now he was up and flying. Four months later he resigned from the Special Branch and began a full-time career organising drug smuggling.

On Egan's first run he wore a special vest that he had made for the purpose and now all his couriers—officers on leave from the New South Wales Police paid $2000 a run—were similarly kitted out, earning the group the name the Corset Gang. Six months later, with twenty couriers operating, he was netting $80000 a week. The couriers were sent to Hong Kong where they collected the drugs, which were then flown to the United States via London, Tokyo and New Delhi.

Egan's downfall came after a tip-off that there was to be a raid. He flew to Hong Kong to tell New Zealander Glenn Reid, in charge of buying from Chinese suppliers, to suspend operations. Unfortunately Reid kept 2 kilograms of heroin and when he was arrested in Honolulu he dobbed in Egan and arranged to set him up. Egan was given and skipped bail, went to England and was arrested in Paris three years later. Extradited to the United States he served just under half of an eight year sentence. Back in Australia, Egan retired to the Gold Coast where in 1978 he was fined $1500 for illegal gambling. As Alfred McCoy points out, the exercise revealed the capacity for corruption within the New South Wales Police. Its tolerance for that corruption paved the way for a level of drug trafficking that would have astounded even Egan.

The first killing linked to the Australian heroin trade seems to have been that of the relatively small-time dealer and user Jan O'Truba. He became addicted at the age of fifteen while at school and in 1971 was arrested after breaking into a pharmacy. On his release he began to deal on at least a semi-professional basis but he was also willing to cheat his customers over the delivery and quality of the drugs. On the day he died he was peddling heroin capsules at $20 each—friends said he had bought an ounce for $450 from a New South Wales detective. On 2 September 1972 his body was found against a tree on an embankment off the Wakehurst Parkway in Oxford Falls. He had been shot in the head three times with a .32 pistol. Despite a $10000 reward no charges were ever brought.

The next death was that of the much higher profile, 24-year-old fashion designer Maria Anne Hisshion, lover of solicitors, models and criminals, who lived in Rose Bay and was a darling of the drug users known as the Windsor Castle Set. On Christmas Eve 1975 Hisshion had dinner with her mother and was never seen alive again. Her body surfaced off North Head two weeks later and was identified through her jewellery. She had been shot in the head with a .32 bullet and tied to an anchor. Her body had almost certainly been dumped from a boat. Ten days later Barry Pyne, an associate of a group of dealers known as the Double Bay Mob, refused to answer any police questions about the suggestion he had borrowed a boat on the night of her disappearance. He was later said to have left Australia. It seems that Hisshion had become involved in the heroin trade reluctantly and wanted out.

After the deaths of O'Truba and Hisshion the killings came thick and fast. On 18 May 1979 the bodies of Douglas and Isabel Wilson were found in a shallow grave in Danny Street, Rye, Victoria. They had both been shot. They were two of the victims of Terrence Clark, otherwise known as Alexander James Sinclair, in his bid to eliminate leakage in his drug importing syndicate. On 9 June 1978 they had been arrested by the Queensland Police in Brisbane and although they were never charged they spent some time providing information on tape about the workings of the Clark organisation. Through a dishonest solicitor's clerk, Brian Alexander, Clark purchased copies of the tapes for $25 000 and that was the end of the Wilsons. They were killed by James Bazley, who had also shot Donald Mackay.

Also among Clark's victims, killed personally by him or ordered killed by him, were Gregory Ollard, Julie Theilman, 'Pommy' Harry Lewis and—the most high profile of them—Christopher Martin 'Marty' Johnstone, a founding member of the so-called 'Mr Asia' syndicate, which imported and exported drugs worldwide.

Lewis, on bail for drugs charges, reported to Customs House at Circular Quay, Sydney, on 21 May 1978. He was never seen again. It was believed he had gone with Clark to Queensland where he was killed within a few days. His remains were found in scrubland near Port Macquarie. Ollard, another heroin dealer who was too keen on his own product, was shot in September 1977. He had refused a buy-out offer from Clark, who then simply eliminated potential opposition. His body was not located until 16 August 1982, when his remains were discovered in Ku-ring-gai Chase National Park near Sydney. Three days earlier the remains of Julie Theilman, his girlfriend and a onetime brothel keeper, were excavated at Mount Victoria in the Blue Mountains. She had been shot in the chest.

Clark was born in New Zealand in November 1944 and began seriously dealing in cannabis at the age of thirty. Johnstone was then his supplier. The next year he bought a boat, the *Catana*, to bring heroin out of South-East Asia and by the end of 1977 he had become a major importer into Sydney with a distribution network across Australia. Johnstone, who was thought to have been the leader of the organisation, was in fact merely an executive officer and a dishonest one at that. For some months he had been skimming up to $100000 to set up his own organisation. He had also fallen out with the syndicate's Singapore supplier Choo Cheng Kui or Jackie Choo.

In 1979 Clark sent Johnstone to London and then on to Scotland under the pretext that there was a deal to be set up in Glasgow. With him on 9 October went Andrew Maher and a James Smith. Maher had already acquired ropes and weights and an axe. At Eccleston Delph, a flooded quarry near Carnforth in Lancashire, Maher asked Johnstone to take over the driving and, as they changed places, shot him twice in the head. Johnstone's hands were cut off and his body was mutilated but Maher failed to remove a pendant with a Chinese 'long-life' symbol. The body was rolled into the water but caught on a ledge. Some five days later it was found by members of a sub-acqua club—at first they thought it was a tailor's dummy—and Johnstone was later identified through the pendant. After a 112 day trial Clark and Maher were convicted at Lancaster Crown Court and sentenced to life imprisonment. During the trial, held in the cavernous and draughty Lancaster Castle, one of the defendants complained he was cold. 'Not nearly as cold as Mr Johnstone,' remarked prosecuting counsel.

Ten years after the deaths of Hisshion and O'Truba there was a full scale drugs war in Sydney and reports that five gangs were struggling for control of both clubs and drugs in Kings Cross. Two gangs were said to be controlled by Chinese, another by Irish union toughs and a fourth by central Europeans. The fifth and most dangerous was controlled by a Melbourne hitman, the baby-faced Christopher 'Mr Rent-a-Kill' Flannery, thought to have been eventually responsible for fourteen shootings.

In 1987 a witness at the inquest on Christopher Flannery gave evidence that the line-up of gangs was slightly different. Roger Ford (a pseudonym, his name having been suppressed by the coroner Greg Glass), the former right-hand man of bookmaker and dealer Barry McCann, claimed that there were three rather than five main gangs operating the heroin trade in Sydney. One was the famous alliance between Neddy Smith and Detective Sergeant Roger Rogerson, another was the Freeman–McPherson combine and the third an assortment of identities including McCann, Tom Domican, Roy Thurgar and Vic Camillieri. Flannery, said Ford, was simply operating as an independent hitman in Sydney, available to the highest bidder.

Just who were all these players? Flannery, born in 1949, was a schoolboy swimming champion, had a tattoo 'Lunchtime' on his stomach with an arrow pointing to his groin and had a very changeable temper. He began his career as a basher and worked upwards. In October 1981 he was acquitted of the February 1980 murder of businessman Roger Wilson whose body was never found, for which he was said to have been paid $35 000. One problem for the prosecution had been the disappearance of a key witness, Debbie Boundy, who has never been seen since. As he left the court Flannery was arrested and charged with another murder, this time of Raymond Locksley, a Sydney massage parlour standover man on 11 May 1979. After a retrial he was acquitted and became a hired hoon for George Freeman.

Career criminal Arthur Stanley 'Neddy' Smith had served a twelve year sentence for a particularly violent rape. On 14 June 1967 he, Robert Arthur Chapman and two other men raped a young mother after they broke into her home. They threatened to kill her young child if she screamed and then to firebomb her place if she reported the matter. Smith was released on parole in March 1975 and in November the next year was arrested by Sergeant Roger Caleb Rogerson and charged with shooting with intent to murder, attempted armed robbery and possession of an unlicensed pistol. Eventually he was acquitted of all charges. It was then that he formed a close association with Rogerson and became his informer. He also took the time to renovate his home, installing security doors and windows, a spotlight and closed circuit television.

Smith had a wide variety of friends, including James White and Neville Biber, two members of the old Kangaroo Gang (White later disappeared and Biber was found dead in suspicious circumstances), Rugby League player Paul Hayward and heroin courier Warren Fellows, as well as a senior clerk in the prison service. As a result of a tap on Smith's telephones in the late 1970s the police learned that he was organising a heroin importation from Thailand. Hayward and Fellows were arrested and convicted there. An acquaintance, William Sinclair, who was a friend of another disgraced ex-policeman, Murray Riley, was acquitted on appeal. Smith himself was arrested on 12 October 1978 in Sydney and charged with conspiracy to import heroin. His brother Teddy Smith was later arrested, pleaded guilty and became a crown witness. It was not a success. Blood or fear was thicker than water; he retracted his evidence and on the second day of the trial the judge directed Neddy Smith's acquittal.

Smith had been returned to prison to serve out the remainder of his rape sentence and there he met the drug dealer Warren Charles Lanfranchi. Smith was released in October 1980 and Lanfranchi two months later. Meanwhile Rogerson had become the blue-eyed boy of the New South Wales Police, following, in almost every way, in the footsteps of Ray Kelly.

First a folk hero and then a folk villain, Roger Rogerson's association with a number of colourful identities would cause immeasurable grief to the New South Wales Police. He joined the force at seventeen in 1958 and the Criminal Investigation Branch four years later. His career has to be set against the background of the conduct of some of his superior officers at the time. He caught the end of the Kelly era and therefore served under both the corrupt Fred Krahe and his protégé Detective Inspector Donald Fergusson.

He became a member of the Armed Robbery Squad in May 1974 and was there when the bank robber and murderer Philip Western was shot and killed in June 1976. The following year Rogerson shot and killed a man trying to hold up a courier from South Sydney Junior Leagues Club taking money to the bank. He was an arresting officer in the high profile Ananda Marga case in June 1978, and in August 1979 he was there when Gordon Thomas, another bank robber, was shot and killed at Rose Bay. In 1980 he received the Peter Mitchell Award for the most outstanding performance in any phase of police duty. By now he was well on his way to what many thought would be a dazzling career, with words such as 'future commissioner' being bandied about. But he was far too close to Neddy Smith for that to happen.

The crucial moment came in June 1981. Lanfranchi was wanted by the police and Smith, acting as honest broker, indicated to Rogerson that the dealer was prepared to pay up to $50 000 to avoid being arrested. Later Rogerson said he had been offered $80 000. Lanfranchi was then living with the prostitute Sallie-Anne Huckstepp and, according to her version of events, he left their home, unarmed and carrying $10 000, to meet Rogerson alone in Dangar Place, Chippendale. Rogerson had discussed the arrest with senior officers and at 2.45 p.m. on 27 June some eighteen officers were in the area, with Rogerson and three others in an adjoining lane. Smith drove Lanfranchi to the meeting where, according to Rogerson, Lanfranchi pulled a gun that had been manufactured around 1900 and which later turned out to be defective. Rogerson shot him twice, once in the neck and once in the heart. The police said that Lanfranchi had no money on him. At the inquest the four man coroner's jury found that Rogerson had shot Lanfranchi while endeavouring to make an arrest but specifically declined to say it was in self-defence. An internal inquiry headed by Superintendent Ronald Ralph, known as 'Click' because he said when he saw a criminal something 'clicked' in his mind, cleared the police of any misconduct. Over the years there were claims by Huckstepp that Smith had set Lanfranchi up.

In early November 1983 Rogerson recruited Christopher Flannery as another informer. By now, however, his career was slumping and it involved the shooting by Flannery of another officer, the honest and talented Michael Patrick Drury, the following year.

After Drury joined the police in June 1972 his rise was rapid. He joined the Drugs Squad in January 1974 and was sent to work under cover. He was part of a team that, in 1975, broke a drugs ring at Colleambly where a whopping 31.46 acres of cannabis plants were being grown. He also won the Peter Mitchell Award.

In 1982 Drury began the infiltration of a heroin ring run by members of the Victorian branch of the Painters' and Dockers' Union. First he contacted a Sydney drug dealer, Robert Richardson (known as Jack), and agreed to buy $110 000 worth of drugs. He was taken to Melbourne to 'buy' the heroin from a connection of Brian Hansen. It was arranged that he would be watched by Victorian police and when he gave a signal they would move in.

At 9 p.m. on 4 March 1982, Hansen took Drury to collect the heroin from a man called Alan Williams outside the Old Melbourne Hotel in Flemington Road. Drury gave the signal but the detectives who came to arrest were spotted and Williams fled in his car with the heroin, which was later found abandoned.

Hansen and Richardson were committed for trial on 6 December that year but Williams was discharged. A bill of indictment was then granted against him but, when the case of the three men came for trial, there was only one present and the trial was adjourned. Williams had absconded and Richardson's body was found on 31 March. He had been shot in the back of the head. When Williams re-appeared the case was further adjourned.

In May, Williams, who like so many criminals had a pathological fear of prison, then arranged with Flannery to murder Drury for a fee of $100 000, of which he claimed Rogerson would receive half. Now efforts were made on behalf of Williams to bribe Drury to change his evidence. Two Victorian detectives told Drury that Rogerson wanted to see him and Drury later told the court that when the meeting took place he was offered a maximum of $25 000 to change his evidence. When he said he could not do that, he realised he was in serious danger.

On 6 June 1984, shortly after 6 p.m., an attempt was made on Drury's life as he was about to wash up after his evening meal at his home in Nerida Street, Chatsworth. He was shot though an open window in the stomach and chest. It was believed he would not survive and he made a dying deposition in which he said that Rogerson had approached him with a bribe. Fortunately, for once, Flannery had had an off day and Drury lived. Later Flannery would say he went to the hospital to try again but could not get past the police guards.

Drury's troubles were not over. He spent eleven weeks in hospital and the week he was released to convalesce, barely able to walk, the police took him to Sydney to be asked if he had shot up Flannery's house straight after he came out of hospital. At the inquest on Flannery in 1996, Drury had to go into the witness box to deny that he had anything to do with the hitman's disappearance.

In November 1984 Rogerson was charged with trying to bribe Drury and the next year in June he was acquitted. But the damage had been done. For the next seven years he was in and out of court. Now in the uniform branch, he was made the subject of anti-corruption surveillance and on 1 July he was photographed when he closed two accounts in false names. The sum involved was over $110 000 and a fake contract was drawn up by Dr Nick Paltos and a businessman, Maurie Nowytarger, to account for the movement of the funds. The next year, in April 1986, Rogerson went on television denying that he had ever taken a bribe and doubted he had ever had so much as a free lunch. On 28 July that year he was dismissed from the police force after seven of nine counts of misconduct were found to be proved against him. He had been suspended for a time during the inquiry but he still interceded in a quarrel between Louis Bayeh and Lennie McPherson, going to a meeting at Bayeh's home to try to help.

In February 1988 Alan Williams was extradited from the Northern Territory, to where he had gone to hide and dry out, charged with conspiracy to murder. Three months later, Williams pleaded guilty and was sentenced to fourteen years' imprisonment. Now he would give evidence against Rogerson on the like charge. At the end of a three week trial the judge warned the jury it would be extremely dangerous to convict Rogerson on Williams' evidence and on 28 November he was acquitted.

Next up was Rogerson's trial over the bank accounts. It was the Crown's case that the money in his account was from illegal sources and part of the evidence against him, strongly challenged, came from a woman who claimed that she had taken a bundle of money to Sydney airport on behalf of the Melbourne drug dealer Dennis Allen, 'Mr Death'. There she had given it to Rogerson in exchange for plastic bags of heroin. He maintained the money came from the sale of a vintage Bentley and successful gambling.

In March 1990 Rogerson, Paltos and Nowytarger were convicted of conspiracy to pervert the course of justice over the bank accounts and Rogerson was sentenced to eight years. Nowytarger received a minimum of four and Paltos, who was serving his drug sentence, another thirty months. On 11 December the Court of Appeal quashed Rogerson's conviction and, in turn, the then Director of Public Prosecutions, Reg Blanch, appealed that decision. Rogerson finally served three years and was released from Berrima jail on 15 December 1995. He was just in time to attend an inquest on Flannery and appear before the Wood Commission into the New South Wales Police. The inquiry had begun the previous December and was by now in full swing as, week by week, ever more amazing revelations were made. Rogerson was not co-operative, saying, 'I don't care about this inquest and I don't care if you find out anything about Flannery at all.'

* * *

Tom Domican, who was born in Ireland in 1943 and had been a bouncer in London, where he served a sentence for breaking and entering, came to Australia in 1968. In July 1980 he was seeking Labor pre-selection for Marrickville Council but he withdrew six weeks later. A fortnight after that, on 14 August, he was charged with conspiracy and forgery. The charges were dismissed on 7 May 1982. Barry McCann had owned a gaming club at 88 Kembla Street, Wollongong, and standover man Roy Thurgar was shot and killed at Randwick in July 1991. Domican's friend Vic Camillieri was more fortunate. He survived a shooting on 3 April 1985 at Kingsgrove.

The body count in this particular war totalled either eight or nine, depending who was counting. Two of the earlier victims were Brett David Hanslow, killed at Neutral Bay on 13 February 1983 and Kevin Arthur Browne who was shot on 28 March that year. The hitman who killed these two drug dealers was thought to be Emil Rusnak acting on the orders of Francis Michael Salvietti, then one of Sydney's biggest heroin suppliers. Rusnak was shot by the police as he interrupted their search of his house at Homebush. He had been suspected of sending a letter bomb to the Kings Cross restaurateur Stephen Novak. In turn Salvietti was executed on 19 March 1985. A Melbourne man was extradited for Salvietti's murder but was acquitted.

The shooting of Drury destabilised the already fragmented situation in the Sydney drug wars. One former detective recalls:

McCann was getting more vicious—no one has ever given him true credit as to how violent he was. After a couple of shootings he let it be known that if the old timers got in the way they would come undone.

As a result George Freeman was on edge and there was a period when he tried to arrange a truce. Messages were sent to McCann on the basis 'enough's enough, it's attracting too much attention'. It was decided to send over a bloke who wasn't so active a player to organise a meeting with him and that man was Chris Flannery. He was seen as fairly neutral. He went unannounced to what was McCann's hotel, the Lansdowne near Sydney University, and asks for McCann. He talks to McCann's wife but he doesn't explain quite who he is. There's a bit of a verbal altercation and out comes her son to support his mother. The end of it is Flannery gives her a crack and breaks her jaw. Of course, all hell broke loose. That was the end of any truce.

Chris Flannery was in a state. He'd infuriated everyone. He'd incited everyone to continue the war by breaking Mrs McCann's jaw. It was time for him to go and pressure was put on George Freeman to step back and not take responsibility for him. There was also the risk of him naming names on the Drury contract.

Among the other casualties was Danny Chubb, killed on 8 November 1984. Chubb, known as 'The Brain', was shot dead at Millers Point as he left his new Jaguar carrying fish and chips for his mother's lunch. He had just completed another successful $2 million heroin collection from a group of Chinese businessmen. (It was big money then but today that amount would rate him little more than the role of bit player.) At one time he had been the working partner of a bookmaker, Michael Sayers, suspected of being the deviser of the Fine Cotton ring-in, then a Sydney-based SP bookmaker and drug supplier to the Kings Cross clientele. They had split up and for a time Chubb worked with Nick Paltos until the good doctor went to prison. After that he worked with Brian McCauley who was later sentenced to nineteen years for drug trafficking. He also had a number of Chinese associates. Before he went to buy the fish and chips he had been drinking with Neddy Smith and his then partner Abo Henry. No charges were ever brought over Chubb's killing but it is generally accepted that the reason for his death was financial. He was thought to have been owed more than $1 million by his distributors. One cheap way of eliminating a debt in the drug world is to eliminate the creditor. Suspects have included Michael Sayers (himself killed on 16 February 1985), Christopher Flannery and Barry McCann, as well as everybody's perennial favourite Neddy Smith, who has flatly denied any involvement.

On 17 August 1984 Frank Hing, one time bus conductor and more lately the $1 million purchaser of the Goulburn Club in Goulburn Street, was attacked in the Empress Coffee Lounge, Kings Cross. Hing had come to Australia in 1973 and was named in parliament as an influential member of the Triads. George Freeman, Branco Balic and Tony Torok were arrested but Freeman was correct in his boastful prediction that no one would identify him and all were duly acquitted. The next year the premises were damaged by fire. They reopened in December as the Wong Sing Kee restaurant and Rose's nightclub.

On 3 January 1985 Stanley Wong was found badly injured at his Maroubra house. He and his wife, along with their maid, had had their throats cut. Wong died but his wife's life was saved by Dr Victor Chang, leader of the heart transplant team at St Vincent's Hospital, who was himself later murdered, in July 1991. Immediately the police said that

Wong had been a 'respected businessman in this area (Chinatown) for a long, long time'. In fact the situation was somewhat different. He was certainly a significant figure in Chinatown but the 'respected businessman' part was more open to question. Born in 1912, he had fled the communist regime in Shanghai and escaped to Hong Kong in the 1940s, sending his five children, including his daughter Tina, to Australia to be educated. Another daughter, Linda, married Michael Luey in 1962 and for a time they used George Freeman as their driver. Wong himself settled permanently in Sydney in 1972. His funeral at St Andrew's Cathedral was attended by two Cabinet ministers and the Police Association president.

On 10 January 1985 Wee Lam Choo, an illegal immigrant, was charged with Wong's murder. Interviewed by police, he claimed that Wong had ordered him to sell 'white powder', meaning morphine, or he would denounce him to the authorities. On 28 February 1986 he received life imprisonment. An eighteen year old who had been with him received fourteen years for assault with intent to rob.

In May 1984 Wong's daughter Tina had been charged with what was then the state's biggest ever heroin importation: some 28 kilograms with a value of $70 million. Charged with her were an Adelaide man and a Bangkok jeweller. Two months after her father's funeral, the magistrate, John Williams, ruled that all three had a case to answer. Tina Wong elected to give evidence at the committal proceedings and the case was adjourned until the next day. Overnight she suffered a cerebral haemorrhage and was taken to hospital in a coma. She never recovered. The next day Williams dismissed the charges against her and on 4 April 1985 awarded her estate some $25 000 costs.

In January 1985 Flannery, his wife and children were sprayed with bullets from an Armalite rifle as they stood outside their home in Arncliffe. Happily no one was hit. Three years later the one-time potential Labor party candidate Tom Domican was charged with the attempted murder and sentenced to fourteen years' imprisonment. In 1992 the conviction was quashed but Domican was not required to stand trial again.

On 16 February 1985 Michael John Sayers, who had been using Chubb as his distributor, was killed. Sayers, a great gambler and now sampling his own product, had ripped Barry McCann off in a drug deal. He was on his way home to Hewlett Street, Bronte, when he was shot with a .22 rifle. A second man then shot him with a .357 Magnum. In 1988 Tom Domican, Vic Camillieri and Kevin Theobald were charged. They were all found not guilty.

In an effort to settle matters down, a meeting was called on 1 April 1985 by Louis Bayeh, the Lebanese sidekick of Lennie McPherson. Present at his home were Flannery, Neddy Smith, Roger Rogerson, McPherson and the corrupt Detective Sergeant Bill Duff. It produced no great result because, on 3 April, Vic Camillieri survived a shooting at Kingsgrove and later that month, on 23 April, Anthony 'Liverpool Tony' Eustace, one of Flannery's close friends, was gunned down, shot in Arncliffe as he sat in his gold Mercedes-Benz. Eustace, also known as 'Spaghetti', operated Tony's Bar and Grill in Double Bay. This time money was thicker than friendship. The killer was said to be Flannery, acting on behalf of George Freeman.

Flannery, a completely loose cannon said to charge $50 000 a job, was the next to go and the circumstances of his disappearance occupied Sydney's courts on and off for the better part of a decade. He was so hated and feared in the underworld that any of six people, including George Freeman and Lennie McPherson, could have been involved in his death. If anything is clear about his disappearance, it is that he was last seen on 9 May 1985 when, according to his wife Kathleen, he told her he was going to visit Freeman at his home at Yowie Bay. One reason for the visit was to pick up new weaponry supplied by McPherson. Flannery had with him a passport and a .38 pistol. It is possible he went to the airport; a taxi driver claimed that he took a very nervous Flannery there that afternoon.

Most of the conflicting theories are that he was killed either by the underworld or by the police; shot by a police officer at the Geelong racetrack; lured to Sydney Harbour and killed with a machine-gun; shot by police at traffic lights; buried at sea; killed at a hide-out in Connaught; buried in Sydney's western suburbs; killed by a biker and fed through a tree-shredder. Then there is a minority Lord Lucan—JFK theory that he was still alive a decade later. One former detective laughs at this:

> There's no real question of Flannery being anything other than dead. He'd have surfaced. Even if he's living in the jungle he'd want to come into a small town and stand over the chook raffles. He went to George's house and he was taken out there. That took the pressure off them.

What is also absolutely clear is that while the heroin war killings did not completely cease with Flannery's disappearance, there was a much greater survival rate among the remaining combatants.

But one who probably did not survive was Flannery's close friend Laurie Prendergast. It is suggested that he and Flannery, who used to alibi each other for the various killings they undertook, botched the shooting of Tom Domican in early 1985. Prendergast disappeared in August that year. Neddy Smith has it that he was lured into a police car and driven away. In any event his wife found his car in the driveway with the driver's door open. In 1990 an inquest returned an open verdict. It was thought he might have faked his disappearance rather than face questioning over a number of murders, but the better view is that members of the Sydney underworld disposed of him when he came seeking revenge for the death of Flannery. After all, as Sydney identity Jackie Steele had found, the underworld was never averse to dressing up as police officers.

One who did survive was Neddy Smith himself. On 2 April 1986 he was run over outside his own hotel, the Iron Duke in Waterloo, managed by an ex-police officer James William Duff. The previous month Duff had been dismissed from the force over allegations of offering a bribe in relation to a drug deal. In 1997 he was jailed for eighteen months for heroin trafficking. He had been found with some $40 000 of the drug and $17 380 in cash.

In the attack outside the hotel Smith sustained broken ribs and a broken leg. An ex-boxer, Terrence Edwin Ball, was charged with his attempted murder and found not guilty. Ball was later shot by Abo Henry in revenge for the attack on his then friend Smith. Smith was now drinking more and more heavily—two bottles of wine at lunchtime and up to thirty glasses of beer a day. On 30 October 1987, after a day's drinking with Rogerson, he stabbed truck driver Ronald Flavell to death in a road-rage incident on Coogee Bay Road. He received life imprisonment.

Another who did not survive was Warren Lanfranchi's girlfriend Sallie-Anne Huckstepp, whose body was found strangled in Busby's Pond at Centennial Lake on 7 February 1986. She came from a Jewish family named Krivoshaw and had been privately educated when, at the age of seventeen, she married Brian Huckstepp and went to Kalgoorlie to work for him in the tin-shed brothels. A number of the usual suspects came in the frame, including Smith, who claimed he had never spoken to her. However, in a conversation with a fellow prisoner, Smith apparently confessed that he had killed her, not because she was a police informer (which she undoubtedly was) but simply because he did not like her lifestyle. He later denied this.

In December 1987 Barry McCann was found dead near a lavatory block in the J. J. Mahoney Reserve, Marrickville. Recently McCann had been importing drugs from Singapore, sending suitcases of drugs back to Australia as unaccompanied baggage which was passed through Customs by a tame officer. McCann's great mistake, according to Neddy Smith, was the grandiose belief that in the middle 1980s he could cut himself into the profits of organised gambling in Sydney, then run by Lennie McPherson, who explained to him the potential dangers of this way of thinking. The fatal mistake came when he began to deal in heroin with George Savvas, a one time Marrickville Council member.

The arrangement, according to the prosecution at Savvas's subsequent trial, had been to sell some 3 kilograms in Melbourne but instead Savvas sold it in Sydney, undercutting McCann's normal distribution price. McCann announced that he would be taking reprisals. On 27 December 1987 McCann went to an evening meeting at the Reserve. He was seen there about nine o'clock by an off-duty detective walking with his wife and dog. Next morning McCann's body was found face down on a bench. He had been shot twenty times in his back and head.

In 1988 Savvas was arrested and charged with McCann's murder. At the trial it was suggested there had been a falling out between the pair not only over price undercutting but also over the apparent disappearance of two valuable suitcases or at least two suitcases with valuable contents. The immediate reason for McCann's death, alleged the prosecution, was that Savvas knew his partner was out to kill him and he needed to get in first. After a ten week trial he was acquitted on the direction of the judge but was later sentenced to twenty-five years' imprisonment for heroin trafficking.

Savvas was a good wake-up call to those who think that prison necessarily has reformatory qualities or is an impediment to further offending. On 7 March 1994 he was sentenced to a further eighteen years after being found to be the mastermind in a conspiracy to import 40 kilograms of cocaine from South America while he was in prison.

Down with him went Constantinos Kapelotis, who had been convicted along with Dr Nick Paltos back in 1984 and this time received a minimum of five years. Another defendant, Alex Nuchimov, believed by some to be the leader of the Russian *Mafiya* in Australia, had escaped in January that year on a visit to a dentist in Bondi.

Another of the alliance, Roy Thurgar, was shot and killed in Randwick. In 1988 he and Domican had been charged with conspiracy to murder a prison official but both were acquitted. On 20 May 1991 Thurgar was shot at point blank range in the throat as he stood waiting for his wife outside their home in Alison Road. Garry Nye, a man with various convictions, including one for armed robbery, was arrested on the word of a police informer, Danny Shakespeare. Shakespeare was a man known to supply false evidence to the police and one entry on his file read, 'He is an extremely convincing liar.' Shakespeare did not convince the jury. Nye was acquitted the following year and a decade later, when dying from cancer, was awarded $1.3 million for malicious prosecution.

The Roy Thurgar case never completely went away and there were suggestions that police might re-open it after the 1998 discovery of a shotgun that was forensically linked to the death of Desmond Anthony Lewis outside his home in Bondi Junction in 1992. It was also linked to two home invasions that took place some years later and to one of the top, if generally underrated, faces of the last thirty years, Robert Douglas 'Bertie' Kidd, whom a prominent Melbourne barrister regarded, along with Graham Kinniburgh, as one of 'the master criminals of the past twenty years'.

Until the end of the 1990s Kidd had only one conviction of any note when in May 1983 he was sentenced to four years' hard labour. Then, in his middle sixties Kidd led what might be called the Great Grandfather Gang and began to be a little careless. In July 1997 a raid on a Manly hotelier's home produced $275 000 in cash and jewellery and two months later a raid on a Sydney motor dealer's home in Burraneer Bay netted another $14 000 worth of jewellery. The next year the shotgun was found at the home of another veteran, Eric Leonard Murray, who was alleged to have been the driver in the raids.

In March 1999 Kidd was sentenced to eleven years for striking with a projectile to prevent lawful arrest and in July 2004, then aged seventy-one, he was jailed for a minimum of twelve years for his part in the home invasions. Murray, two years his senior, was sentenced to three years for possession of the shotgun. Throughout the trial Kidd denied he had ever used the gun.

* * *

In Melbourne a different type of war was being waged. By the end of the 1980s the Melbourne police and the underworld were at each other's throats. Two or three bank robberies were going off every week. Ray Watson, former head of Victoria's Armed Robbery Squad told *The Age* on 26 April 2003: 'Crime was out of control. But we took the view that it was time for the good guys to fly the flag. A number of criminals were shot during their apprehension, and slowly the culture changed.'

In the two year period from 1987 eleven suspects were shot dead by the police. They included, on 25 March 1987, Mark Militano, a member of a group of criminals from the Flemington–Ascot Vale area specialising in armed robberies. He was shot six times by members of the Armed Robbery Squad outside his Kensington flat when they went to question him. One bullet lodged in the back of his neck as he was running away. The coroner found that he had been pointing a gun over his shoulder before he was shot. One member of the team who survived, only to die in prison, was Santo Mercuri, convicted of an armed robbery on 11 July 1988 when $33 000 was stolen and a security guard, Dominik Hefti, was shot. The robbers are alleged to have included Jason and Lewis Moran and Russell 'Mad Dog' Cox. Mercuri, a fitness fanatic feared by other inmates, died following a heart attack in Barwon Prison on 22 July 2000.

In the most celebrated case, Graeme Jensen left a hardware store in Narre Warren in Melbourne's outer east on 11 October 1988 and climbed into his Commodore. He was approached by members of the Victoria Police Armed Robbery Squad who told him not to move. Instead he accelerated. Officers opened fire and Jensen was shot in the back of the head. By the time the car crashed into a power pole Jensen was already dead. At the inquest the evidence was that the police saw Jensen pick up a weapon and they shot to protect themselves. A sawn-off bolt-action shotgun was produced which they said had been found in the car. Jensen's friends and relations would not accept the evidence.

There is no doubt that Jensen, then aged thirty-three and described as something of a ladykiller, was an armed robber by profession. He had convictions from the age of fifteen, when he had robbed a bank and been sent to a detention centre. This had been followed by imprisonment for housebreaking and, at the age of twenty-three, three more charges of armed robbery. He had escaped from custody and robbed another bank. Released in 1987 he had, said the police, resumed his profession. It was over the Hefti killing that the police wished to question Jensen.

Around 4 a.m. on the day after Jensen's death a newsagent, going to open his shop, saw a Holden Commodore parked in Walsh Street, South Yarra. It was empty but the lights were on, the doors open and the windows smashed. He telephoned the police and Constables Steven Tynan and Damian Eyre were sent to investigate. While they were looking at the damage they were attacked. Tynan was shot in the head at almost point blank range and Eyre, who had an instant's notice of the attack and tried to struggle with the gunman, was shot three times. It was the first double killing of police officers since Ned Kelly's gang shot three officers near Mansfield, north-east of Melbourne in 1878.

The police hunt that followed the double shooting was, not unexpectedly, massive, with the Victorian government posting a $200 000 reward. One hundred police were drafted to comb the underworld, and the crime rate dropped. One of the men whose name came into the frame was Jedd Houghton, a known friend of Jensen. He was traced to Bendigo where he was staying in a caravan park with his girlfriend. A listening device that had been planted by police was discovered by Houghton. The police, listening before he dismantled it, realised their cover was blown and moved to arrest him. He was still in the caravan park when the police opened fire and he was hit with two shotgun blasts. He died instantly and his friends believed he had been shot as a reprisal for Walsh Street.

Seventeen-year-old Jason Ryan, an accomplished little thief, named Gary Abdallah as being involved in the Walsh Street shooting. Ryan, a member of the extended and infamous Pettingill family of Melbourne brothel-owning fame, had been convicted of a drug dealing offence and, deciding co-operation was the best way towards daylight, became an informant.

On 22 February, Abdallah went to see the police with his solicitor and was told that it was only rumour against him. Six weeks later, on 9 April, he was killed when police not connected with the Walsh Street inquiry shot him. They said he had threatened them with a firearm. It turned out to be an imitation one and his friends once again refused to accept the official version. Abdallah died after forty days in a coma.

Jason Ryan, it appeared, had been trying to deflect interest from himself but on 31 October the police arrested him, along with two more Pettingill sons, Victor George Peirce and Trevor Pettingill, as well as Ryan's best friend, Anthony Leigh Farrell, and Peter David McEvoy, who lodged with Ryan's mother. The police named Houghton as the sixth man involved in the Walsh Street attack.

Ryan, who became a witness for the Crown, gave the following self-exculpatory version of the killings. The other four had stolen the Commodore, left it in Walsh Street and waited for the police to come. Ryan had not wanted to be part and had stayed behind. When they returned Farrell told Ryan that he was the one who had done the shooting. There was some back-up to the story from Peirce's de facto wife Wendy, who temporarily disappeared into the witness protection program. At first she had stood staunch and gave Victor Peirce a false alibi but in July 1989 she made a thirty page witness statement and asked to go into the scheme, claiming her husband had a pathological hatred of the police.

At the committal proceedings Wendy Peirce gave evidence that on the night of the police murders her husband had left her and the children at a motel, saying, 'Don't worry, I won't be late. I'm going to kill the jacks that knocked Graeme [Jensen]'. The next morning he had told her they were dead.

At a pre-trial hearing in January 1991, Wendy Peirce walked out of the witness protection program and declined to give evidence. Found guilty of perjury in December 1992 she was sentenced to eighteen months' imprisonment with a minimum of nine to be served. For a time she and Victor Peirce lived together again but they eventually split up.

In her absence the case now effectively depended on the evidence of Ryan, whose story became less and less credible as he was questioned and who finally admitted to a string of lies. By the time he came to give evidence he was on his fifth version of events. There were no eyewitnesses or forensic or fingerprint evidence of the men to assist the prosecution. On 26 March 1991, after a retirement of six days, to no one's great surprise the jury returned a verdict of not guilty on all the men. The trial was estimated to have cost $30 million. Later, when a man from a different team was arrested, it became clear that Jensen and his firm had not been involved in the murder of the security guard that had begun the trail of events.

The Pettingill family was one to be reckoned with. Perhaps in terms of international crime they were small fry. But in terms of the carnage that they in general, and that Dennis Bruce Allen in particular, achieved, they were leaders of the field.

The eldest of the former brothel keeper's seven children, Dennis Allen, born in 1951, grew up in West Heidelberg in what was the old Olympic Village. He built a substantial drug trafficking empire, at the same time working as an enforcer, robber, murderer and police informer. As a juvenile he recorded a string of minor convictions and then at the age of nineteen was charged with rape. He was acquitted but convicted of unlawful carnal knowledge and put on a $200 bond to be of good behaviour.

His career took off when, on 17 October 1973, with his younger brother Peter and two others, he went to a girl's flat in Sandringham after being paid $500 to shoot her boss. The girl said she did not know where he was and, for her pains, was raped by Allen. Her young sister was indecently assaulted. A shot was fired through a wall and Peter Allen clubbed the girl's boyfriend with a pistol. It was a pattern of violence which Allen would continue to exhibit for the rest of his life. On this occasion he received ten years and was ordered to serve a minimum of five. He and his brother had separated after the assaults and Peter Allen, who had gone on a shooting spree around Melbourne, received fourteen years. In August 1985 Peter Allen was released after serving twelve years. In 1988 he received a maximum of thirteen years for dealing in heroin and conspiracy to commit armed robbery. In 1994 he received another seven for drug trafficking while in prison. In 2007 it was announced he was to be given a sentence audit.

In fact Dennis Allen served four years and was immediately in trouble on his release in 1978. First, he had his young half-brother Jamie Pettingill to stay for four nights. Unfortunately Jamie was on the run from a young offenders' institution at the time and Allen was charged with harbouring. He was charged separately with possessing a pistol and a rifle and quickly added another gun charge and another of theft. Convicted on the gun charges, he was allowed to remain on bail while he appealed, but he failed to appear at his trial.

Despite the fact that he was supplying guns to Jamie, who was now undertaking a series of betting shop robberies, Allen stayed at large until May 1979, when he was attacked in a hotel in Frankston. He had been telephoned by a girl who said she was in danger. She was right. Shots were fired and Allen was hit over the head with a rifle. He had armed himself with a piece of pipe before he went into the hotel and, as he staggered out, he was arrested. He was successful in pleading self-defence but the gun conviction stood and he was returned to prison for breach of parole.

Released on 2 July 1982, Dennis Allen moved into the drug business in Stephenson Street, Richmond, where his one-eyed mother—whose right eye had been shot out by another woman in a fight—ran a brothel. Kath Pettingill lived in number 106, which she rented, and owned 108, for which she had paid $28 000 and which she used as a massage parlour. Allen lived with his mother, his wife whom he had married while in prison, and their two children. Late in 1982 he was arrested for possession of heroin. Property prices in the neighbourhood were going up and he was obliged to pay $35 000 cash when he bought a house in Chestnut Street just before Christmas. He also started to grow cannabis plants and was arrested for that enterprise in February 1983.

There had been a temporary set back for the family on 16 February 1982 when Jamie took the rap for Dennis over the shooting of a barman two years earlier. Jamie received a remarkably lenient four years for that and two other armed robberies. When he was released his brother employed him as a standover man.

Throughout his life Allen acquired 'brothers'. Greg Pasche was one of them. At the age of thirteen Pasche had met Lex Peirce, one of Kath Pettingill's sons by Billy Peirce, when they were in Turana Boys' Home and used to spend weekend leave with Kath. When she was visiting Peter Allen in Long Bay jail in Sydney she heard Pasche needed $500 for bail, so she paid it and he returned to live with her in Stephenson Street.

Two weeks later, on 27 May 1983, Pasche vanished and did not reappear until the late summer when his decomposing body was found on Mount Dandenong. He had been stabbed so fiercely in the head that the blow had fractured his skull. There was a variety of reasons why he might have been killed. He was drug dealing and debt collecting on behalf of Dennis Allen and also working as a male prostitute.

Shortly after that, another Allen associate, drug addict Victor Gouroff, disappeared. He was last seen on 20 November and his body was never found. Allen was considered to be a prime suspect in his death as well as that of a woman shot in the same year. Gouroff had convictions for armed robbery, theft and possession of firearms and had also met Allen in prison.

At least Allen was not wasting the money he was earning. Before the end of the year he bought another three houses, including 35 and 37 Stephenson Street, from where he would run his drug dealing and do his killings. Once, sent out by his mother to buy dog food, he returned hours later. He had forgotten to buy the meat but had bought another house instead. Accompanied by a minder who was paid $2000 and who paid cash for all the shop purchases, Allen would still try to steal nails from boxes on the hardware store counter.

Building work took place at 106 and 108 so that clients could go into the massage parlour at 108 and order their drugs, which would be passed through from 106. If the brothel was raided in a drug bust, there would be little evidence on the premises. Allen was also acting as an armourer and it was about this time that he became a police informer. It was also about this time that, in a drugged and drunken fit, he shot and killed Wayne Stanhope. Stanhope's van was dumped 70 kilometres out of the city and found the next afternoon. Of the body there was no trace although clothing identified as the victim's was found in a national park. The body may well have been eaten by wild pigs.

Allen had now become involved with Alan Williams, as well as Roger Rogerson and Chris Flannery. At his instigation Roy 'Red Rat' Pollitt killed the wholly innocent council worker Lindsay Simpson, having mistaken him for his brother-in-law Alan Williams, who was owed between $15 000 and $20 000 by Allen for drugs. On 18 September 1984 Simpson was shot outside his home in Cheverton Road, Lower Plenty, as he was about to take the baby stroller from his car. His wife, still in the car, heard her husband say 'You've got the wrong man', and then 'Get down, sucker', before Simpson was shot. Pollitt was sentenced to a minimum of eighteen years. 'I had to shoot the guy because he saw my face,' he said.

In the revealing but not altogether unbiased biography *The Matriarch*, Kath Pettingill maintains that Dennis Allen killed Simpson himself and confessed to her that he had done so. Indeed she gives a different account of the later death of Helga Wagnegg and a number of other killings that others have attributed to her son.

Business was going well. Dennis Allen now had a property company for his house purchases. Then in November 1984 a prostitute named Helga Wagnegg, who had been given a hot shot by Allen, died. She had only recently been released from a sentence for an attempted robbery at another brothel. In his role of informer, Allen told the police that her body could be found in the Yarra River. Police observation and pressure was paying off and by November 1984 Jamie Pettingill had joined Trevor in facing drug dealing charges. Six months later, on the eve of the inquest on Helga Wagnegg, Jamie, again acting on his brother's behalf, bombed the Coroner's Court in Flinders Street. He had panicked and threw the bomb too early, causing only minor damage. Five days later, on 14 May, he died of an overdose. He was twenty-one and, like so many others, had been introduced to the drug in prison. There was speculation, with nothing to back it, that Dennis had given him the fatal overdose. Those who knew Jamie claimed he was frightened of injections and would never inject himself.

Dennis Allen must have been passing high quality information because this violent man, a career criminal, was repeatedly given bail and, on conviction, was being bailed pending appeal. At the time of his death three years later, he was awaiting trial on no less than sixty charges. He had suffered one minor inconvenience on the way. On 21 January he appeared at the County Court in respect of charges of possessing heroin relating back to 1983. Two days later there was a police raid on his home; seven pistols, two shotguns and a silencer were found. Two days after that, Allen just happened to be shot in the leg. He hoped that this ruse would abort the trial but the judge merely adjourned it until Allen was fit. It resumed on 3 June and this time he swallowed a small dose of rat poison. Again the judge retained the jury but Allen had his way when the jury was shown books of photographs, one of which contained a picture of some gelignite, the charge in respect of which had been dropped. A retrial never took place although the case was re-listed for the September.

It was after this that Allen committed the murder for which he is best known—that of Anthony John Kenny, who was a member of the Nomads, a sister chapter of the Hells Angels. Kenny, as befitted any self-respecting renegade biker, had convictions for theft, assault and rape. On his release he was involved in the supply of amphetamines to prostitutes. He was arrested at the home of Roger Biddlestone, a key member of the amphetamine supply group. Then this vice-president of the Nomads committed a mortal sin: he co-operated with the police and was expelled from the chapter. He drifted on the fringes of crime and drugs and was introduced to Dennis Allen with whom he became friendly.

On 7 November 1985 after an afternoon's drinking at the Allen house with his friend Peter Robertson and some others, Kenny was shot. An essential for any killer is to have the ability to dispose of the body quickly and cleanly or else to walk away. Allen lacked talent in this field. After he had killed Helga Wagnegg it was left to his brother Victor Peirce to dispose of the body. Again it was Peirce who was the disposer. He took a chainsaw and, when that became jammed full of skin and blood, used a chopper on the legs so the body would fit in an oil drum. Filled with cement and Kenny, it was rolled into the Yarra River at Kew. 'Dennis was good as a killer but not as a disposalist,' said Jason Ryan, so adding a new word to the English language.

Robertson was charged and acquitted when Kath Pettingill told the court that Dennis had confessed to her that it was his finger on the trigger. By this time Allen was dead and so the jury was deprived of his testimony. Allen had had a heart condition and when his health deteriorated in 1987 he entered hospital, staying nearly two months. His drug intake was by then totally out of control and he would keep himself awake on drugs for up to a fortnight. He was, recalls Kath Pettingill's biographer Adrian Tame, 'a truly frightening human'. As Allen left hospital on 11 March he was arrested and charged with the murder of Wayne Stanhope. He could no longer walk and had to be moved in a wheelchair. His luck in the courts had run out. He was remanded in custody and returned to St Vincent's Hospital, where he died on 13 April.

By 1995 three Allens/Pettingills—Peter, Victor and Trevor—were serving sentences. Jason Ryan was surviving tenuously on the outside after being discharged from the witness protection scheme. After her last release from prison following a drugs conviction, Kath Pettingill moved to Venus Bay, a small town some three hours outside Melbourne where, perhaps surprisingly, she has become a pillar of the community, receiving a Community Service Certificate. 'She has a magnetism; you can't ignore her,' says Tame. In 2007, much to her joy, she featured in a photographic exhibition of crime and criminals in Melbourne. She was particularly delighted that one photograph was featured in *The Age*, taking up almost half a page.

But all was still not straightforward for the Pettingill clan. On 1 May 2002 Victor Peirce was shot as he sat in his car in Bay Street, Port Melbourne. Apart from a shoplifting charge, described by his solicitor as 'shitty little', he had not been in court for some years. Nevertheless it was thought that he was still heavily involved in the cocaine industry and that his execution was over a $29 000 debt. That or he was killed because he had accepted a contract and failed to deliver. His death drew a number of notices, including an oblique one from the robber Mark 'Chopper' Read: 'Don't worry, Vic, Kath will keep an eye on things.'

It was only after her husband's death that Wendy Peirce admitted that he had in fact told her he killed the Walsh Street policemen. Her apparent move to the prosecution and away from the family had been a ruse to weaken the case against him.

Over the Wall and into the Bank

11

One of the earliest of the major post-war robberies was at Cockatoo Docks, Sydney, when, at about 10 a.m. on 13 April 1946, three men armed with a Thompson machine gun and automatic pistols robbed five waterside employees of 12000 pounds. The money had just been collected from the Drummoyne branch of the ES&A bank and the armed employees were in the launch to take them to the wharf when they were held up by the machine gun-wielding masked man and his colleagues. The robbers left the waterfront in a highly polished stolen black Buick which was later found in Kalgoorlie Street, Leichhardt. Despite the offer of a reward of 1000 pounds and a free pardon to any informant provided he had not actually been on the robbery, the underworld remained staunch and no charges were ever brought. It was the first robbery in New South Wales in which a machine gun was used. Over forty years later, in 1987, the Sydney identity Abo Henry pulled off another robbery at the Cockatoo Docks, this time netting $300000.

There is, however, a maxim in the underworld that one's best partner in crime is oneself—and it is one largely followed by Australian identities. They have rarely banded together in large teams in the style of England's Great Train Robbers, Boston's celebrated 1950 Brinks-Mat hold-up, the 26 million pound gold heist at Heathrow Airport in 1983, or New York's 1978 Lufthansa robbery. Rather, they have often worked in pairs or in small family teams. Many of them have also been highly talented escapers.

One of the great robbers and escapers, who more or less operated solo, was Bernie Matthews, who began his career in 1969 when, at the age of nineteen, he was arrested on 13 October and charged with two armed robberies and possession of a sub-machine gun. It immediately established him as a cut above the average. He escaped from the Court of Appeal in June 1970 and, on his recapture, received ten years plus six months for the escape. Soon afterwards he escaped from Long Bay jail. (Perhaps he was not that successful as an escaper because, during his years in prison, he made some fifteen failed attempts.) This time he was recaptured seven weeks later, by which time he had robbed two banks and a payroll office. The money was spent on gambling, women and liquor and Matthews later said of career bank robbers, including himself: 'They've got no respect for money, you know, because it's easy come, easy go, so you might have $100000, you might have $10000, there's no respect there because you haven't earned it … It's the adrenalin rush of getting it.'

After his sentence Matthews made an effort to start his own business and settle down. Then, on 20 February 1991, he was arrested in Sydney by members of Task Force Magnum of the Sydney Major Crime Squad over a Brambles security van robbery at Sunnybank Hills in Queensland on 3 April the previous year. Petrol had been poured over the driver and staff to force them to open the back of the van, and $694000 was stolen. The evidence against Matthews was that of a police informer, and a police inspector who alleged Matthews had made an oral confession to him. Committed for trial, he remained in custody until, on 26 October, Garry Sullivan, a former Rugby League international, and William Orchard were arrested for an armoured car robbery the day before. They put their hands up and admitted to the Brambles robbery. Matthews was released two days later and the charges were finally dropped. His efforts to obtain compensation for the wrongful imprisonment came to nothing.

A robbery that brought pain, suffering and death to the protagonists was the Mayne-Nickless robbery on 4 March 1970 in Sydney. The raid itself was a simple one. Incredibly, the guards regularly parked in the Guildford shopping centre while they had their lunch inside their van before they made a delivery to the Commonwealth Bank. One of the security guards opened the van door to put out the rubbish at a certain time. In came the robbers and out went $587 890.

The pain and suffering came in the form of the much feared Sydney-based Toecutters Gang. Frank 'Baldy' Blair had his toes cut and testicles torched to persuade him to reveal where he had deposited his $90 000 share. Blair died from his injuries and his body was thrown into Sydney Harbour in the belief that it would be eaten by sharks. It was not and it washed up in Botany Bay. The blame for that misapprehension was laid at the doorstep of Jake Maloney who was shot by fellow Toecutter John Regan on 23 November 1971. According to underworld legend, just before Maloney was killed, Regan said, 'Sharks, hey Jake, I'll give you bloody sharks, you idiot.'

Meanwhile the Toecutters attacked the wharfie Stephen Nittes, who was also on the Mayne-Nickless raid. He handed over a substantial part of his share. Another robber, Alan Jones, escaped their attention but both he and Nittes received sixteen years for their troubles.

Former robber Mark 'Chopper' Read has a story about the Toecutters that tells how they kidnapped a robber to question him over a theft of $75 000. On his back the man had a tattoo of an eagle fighting a dragon and the Toecutters took pliers and slowly ripped off the tattoo. The man died halfway through the operation. They then took the view that no man would die in such pain for the sake of the money and reasoned that his wife must have it. They promised her they would return him if she paid over the money. She did this and was then told her husband had died.

* * *

Melbourne had its own share of 'high-class' robberies. By June 1970 the quota of robberies had matched the total for the previous year. Another robbery in Victoria which was also meticulously rehearsed and planned—possibly for up to a year—and the takings from which dwarfed the lower estimate of the bookie robbery, was the theft from an Armaguard security vehicle in Richmond on the morning of 22 June 1994. It was a deceptively simple operation. The van was stopped as it turned from Punt Road towards the South Eastern Arterial—apparently by a council road gang.

The whole set-up was a fake. The man with a stop sign halted the vehicle and another had a key which fitted the van doors. Two of the crew were dragged into the rear compartment and handcuffed. One of the robbers then drove the vehicle into a dead-end street and the gang escaped with a haul of more than $2.5 million. The team had been seen on a number of occasions rehearsing and carrying out their supposed roadworks and the operation was thought to have been financed by a series of smaller bank raids in and around Melbourne. Around $40000 was recovered when what was probably a second team began to change notes in Melbourne banks some two months after the robbery. None of the robbers was ever charged and the fallout among the players seems to have been negligible. One man who had been questioned but not charged was found dying on the pavement in Brunswick Street, Fitzroy, in December 1997. He had been beaten with a wheel brace.

That was a totally professional operation but the same could not really be said for the behaviour of the Melbourne robber Alex Tsakmakis, a man who struck fear in the hearts of lawyers and judges alike and who owned a company that made car ramps. In early 1978 Tsakmakis trussed up an athlete, Bruce Walker, with chicken wire and pitched him into the bay in an argument over money. He was given bail and took the opportunity to rob the Hawthorn Tattslotto agency of a paltry $1500. As he left he ordered the owner and his wife to the floor and shot them both in the head. They survived. On 17 March three jewellers were shot and killed in almost identical circumstances in a $30000 diamond robbery in the Manchester Unity Building in the city centre. Tsakmakis was convicted of the Tatts robbery and also the Walker killing and, while in prison, boasted that he was responsible not only for the diamond robbery and killings but also for the diverse deaths of Brian Finemore, the curator of Australian Art at the National Gallery of Victoria, on 23 October 1975, and Margaret Clayton, shot twice in the head in a North Fitzroy massage parlour in June 1979. He was also thought to be responsible for the disappearance of Willie Koeppen, owner of The Cuckoo restaurant in Olinda, on 26 February 1976. Koeppen apparently owed him money.

While in Pentridge, Tsakmakis set fire to Barry Robert Quinn, who was serving life for the murder of two men at the Car-O-Tel motel in St Kilda in 1974. Quinn had been taunting Tsakmakis over the rape of his girlfriend. The following day Tsakmakis threw industrial glue over his tormentor and then flicked matches on him until one ignited. The death notice from his fellow prisoners posted in *The Sun* read, 'Barry, We always stuck together.'

Tsakmakis lived only for a few more years. He had earlier made an enemy of Chopper Read, who stabbed him in the neck, so said Read, to teach him manners. In 1988 Tsakmakis wanted to try to take control of the prison and had been picking up $1000 weekly financing drug sales. Now he wanted Read to team up with him against the robber Craig Minogue, who had bombed Russell Street Police Headquarters, causing the death of young policewoman Angela Taylor. In June that year Minogue made a pre-emptive and terminal strike by crushing Tsakmakis's head with a pillow case stuffed with weights from the prison gym. Tsakmakis died in St Vincent's Hospital. Minogue received a sentence concurrent with the twenty-eight years he was serving for the Russell Street bombing. In prison he began to study politics. In June 1990 he told a newspaper reporter, 'It's not as though I have brutally struck down Mother Teresa in the yard.'

* * *

In November 2004 the *Herald Sun* ran a poll asking its readers whether they thought that Paul Steven Haigh, currently serving life imprisonment, should have early release. At the age of twenty-one he had killed six people, more or less anyone who stepped in his path during and after a series of botched robberies. On 21 September 1978, in a raid on a bookmakers in Chapel Street, Prahran, he shot Evelyn Abrahams in the back and on 7 December a pizzeria owner, Bruno Cingolani, in the stomach. Cingolani had refused to hand over his takings and tried to grab a knife from a drawer. On 27 June the next year Haigh shot Wayne Smith, the boyfriend of a St Kilda woman he believed was claiming he was a police informer. The next month he killed one Sheryle Ann Gardner and her nine-year-old son Danny. Later Haigh maintained he had not initially intended to kill the boy but, because Gardner had demanded that Danny go with them on a drive to Ripponlea, his death was inevitable. Gardner had been involved in one of Haigh's murders and had to be killed to eliminate any possible chance she, too, might inform. He went to their funerals and later commented that she had lived by the sword and died by it.

The sixth victim was his girlfriend Lisa Maude Brearley, whom he stabbed 157 times. He said he had lost count and therefore had to begin again. Sentenced to life imprisonment, on 14 November 1991 he helped in the death of an inmate, Donald George Hatherley. He maintained he had simply held his legs, so assisting the man to commit suicide, but he was convicted of murder.

And the result of the poll? Out of a total of 1579 calls, amazingly 2.9 per cent voted in his favour.

A robber who ended his life in mysterious circumstances was Aubrey Maurice Broughill, known variously as 'The Gentleman Bandit', 'The Beanie Bandit' and, later in life, as 'The Grandpa Harry Bandit'—because he caused no trouble when arrested; he always wore a beanie during his robberies; and, finally, because he was getting old and his handgun resembled that of Dirty Harry. His fifty year career had begun in 1938 when he was twelve. In 1961 he received eight years for a payroll snatch and then, after his release and a spell working as a boundary rider, he resumed his earlier career. Working alone he was caught in March 1979 when he used his own car to rob a bank in North Blackburn and the number plate was taken by an off-duty police officer. Released in 1986 he again resumed his career and by the time he was arrested in February 1987 he had netted some $50 000 in a series of armed raids. At the age of sixty-two he was sentenced to a twelve year minimum. He was released on parole in 1998 and the next year, now aged seventy-two, was charged with burglary. He was released on bail and on 17 February his body was found in a flooded quarry in Wodonga. His testicles were missing, and there has been considerable speculation whether they were eaten by the snake-neck tortoises that lived in the quarry or the operation had been carried out by humans. At the inquest an open verdict was returned and no charges were ever brought. Since there were no other wounds to his body the likelihood is that the tortoises were innocent and Broughill was killed to prevent him dobbing in younger and more violent associates from South Australia in return for a lighter sentence.

One of the more violent of the quasi-independents who regularly tried to shoot his way out of the slightest of troubles was James Edward Smith, brought up in the Colac district of Victoria, and who, because as a teenager he was apprenticed to a trainer, was known as 'The Jockey'. Early in his criminal career Smith, regarded as a bank robber's bank robber, teamed up with Ronald Ryan, who would become the last man to be hanged in Australia after killing a guard in an escape from Pentridge. This time, however, it was Smith who tried to shoot a police officer when the pair were caught burgling a shop. On this occasion, fortunately, the gun jammed. In 1973 the situation was repeated when a police constable, Russell Cook, was searching a car. Smith again tried to shoot and once more the gun jammed.

Charged with a string of robberies in Sydney, despite his escape attempts Smith was given bail. He skipped and was found in Melbourne. Sent to Pentridge, he was there only a matter of weeks before he obtained a visitor's pass and walked out. One thing he was good at was dealing with horses and now he combined the names of two of the country's top trainers, Tommy Smith and Bart Cummings, and set up as trainer Tom Cummings. He did well at country tracks but the life of a small trainer has never been an overflowing cup; in 1976 he shot and injured Jerry Ambrose in a robbery in Sydney and the following year he killed bookmaker and crime associate Lloyd Tidmarsh in another robbery. This time he was arrested in Nowra and tried to shoot Detective Bob Godden, who saved himself by putting his thumb between the breech and the trigger of the gun. In December 1977 he was charged with Western Australia's then biggest hold up, the Taxation Department's $176 000 payroll snatch in Perth on 1 May 1975. Smith was given life, of which he served fourteen years, for the attempted murder of the detective and on appeal was acquitted of the other charges after allegations were made that his confession had been fabricated.

He was released on 12 February 1992 and a day later was shot in the chest and left for dead outside his home in Curlewis Street, Bondi. He declined to help the police, who said that he was another with so many enemies it would be difficult to say who might have shot him. He was in hospital for a month and then on 12 June another figure, Desmond Anthony Lewis, was shot at Denison Street, Bondi Junction. The police said that, as a matter of routine, they would be interviewing Smith. No charges were brought.

Now, for a time, he made good money dealing in amphetamines and it was said he was so mean he would 'bite the head off a shilling'. But, over the months, according to his colourful solicitor, the column writing Chris Murphy, he became something of a recluse. In late 1992, another to break the rule of never shoplifting for oneself, he tried to steal an iron and kitchen equipment from Grace Brothers. Stopped by the store detective, he yet again produced a gun and hijacked a couple to drive him away. He hid in the bush for a while and later teamed up with Christopher Dean Binse—another escapee from Pentridge—in plotting a series of armed robberies.

Smith died in Victoria on 5 December 1992. About 8 p.m. he was seen speeding by Senior Constable Ian Harris, who followed him to the Farmer's Arms Hotel in Creswick. When asked for his identification, Smith pulled a gun on the officer. And when a man, Darren Neil, who had seen the incident, approached, he fired a shot into the ground. Neil retreated, drove his car a short way and dropped off his children. He then drove the car at Smith, distracting him. The constable pulled his own revolver and fatally shot Smith three times in the chest.

By the time he was fourteen, Smith's short-term bank robber companion, the self-styled 'Badness' Christopher Dean Binse, had been declared uncontrollable and sent to Turana Boys' Home. From then on his career was a revolving door of crime and prison. His ego was immense. After one bank robbery he took out an advertisement in the *Herald Sun* which read 'Badness is Back'. His home in Queensland, bought with the proceeds of robberies, was named Badness and that was also his personalised car number plate. In September 1992 he escaped from St Vincent's Hospital using a gun smuggled in for him. He was then arrested in Sydney and escaped almost immediately on 26 October from Parramatta jail. He was not long on the outside. Hours after Smith was shot dead, Binse was apprehended close to Daylesford. The next year, on 26 October, the anniversary of his Parramatta escape, he tried to escape from Pentridge and planned to kill the murderer Julian Knight, who was suspected of being an informer, a far more serious crime in the underworld.

By ill-chance for Binse, a prison officer was attacked the day before and a security crackdown followed. A search of Binse's cell turned up a homemade prison officer's uniform, six prison officers' shirt insignias, and blades and weapons. Also found were Binse's draft plans to release thirty inmates. The group to be involved in the escape included John Lindrea, a double murderer, and Paul Alexander Anderson, another noted escaper who had advised on tactics. During one part of his sentence Binse was shackled in leg irons and handcuffs for twenty-three hours a day. In 2001 he was transferred to a new maximum security jail in Goulburn. This prison is not regarded as a happy place, housing as it does a variety of serious offenders.

A little earlier identical twins Peter and Doug Morgan, known as the 'After Dark Bandits' and whose father had himself been an armed robber, kept the police on their toes after a raid on 7 April 1977 on a TAB at Doreen, 30 kilometres north-east of Melbourne, which netted $370. Dressed identically and giving each other alibis, for two years they robbed TABs and banks alike. They were finally arrested after Peter Morgan shot and almost killed Senior Constable Ray Koch during a bank hold-up in Heathcote in central Victoria on 27 April 1979. It was the second time they had robbed the bank. They received non-parole periods of eighteen and seventeen years respectively.

* * *

Over the years Queensland has had a number of serious robberies. In April 1974 a mail truck was forced off Beerburrum Road and robbers cut open mail bags, stealing around $480000. Then, in May 1994, $2 million in cash and gems was stolen from the showroom of Diamonds International in Edward Street, Brisbane. Four years later bandits stole around $2 million in cash, jewellery and designer clothing, using blowtorches to melt safes in a series of robberies in and around the city.

Then, in Brisbane's Sunnybank Hills Shopping Centre in the early hours of 9 March 1999, came the biggest hijacking of an armoured car in Australian history. Brinks Australia driver Matthew Kelly told police that he was forced to unload about twenty bags of cash totalling some $2.7 million from his truck and transfer them to the boot of the hijackers' car. He was in the van alone while his three colleagues went to make a cash transfer. Four white-hooded men dressed in black with white gloves and carrying long rifles surrounded the truck. Kelly, who said he feared the men might shoot him through the bullet-proof glass, allowed them into the cab. He was given directions to drive to Calamvale Community Hall, where he unloaded the bags. He was handcuffed and left inside the truck, where he was found around 8 a.m.

Kelly had been with the company for a bare and unhappy ten weeks. He had joined after being with a security company in Sydney but thought that the Gold Coast would be safer. Unfortunately, within days of coming to Brisbane, he had been on duty when nearly $165000 went missing. Later it emerged that he had been questioned over a series of thefts from ATMs while he was with the Sydney firm.

Kelly was suspended after the 9 March robbery and he later resigned. In August that year Kelly was said to be away on holiday but by December things had taken a more serious turn when he had not reappeared. Now it was feared he might have been murdered and the police thought his body might be in bushland at Captain's Flat,

40 kilometres from Queanbeyan, New South Wales, where his abandoned green Holden stationwagon was found on 26 September.

Further progress appeared to have been made in May 2001 when a number of addresses were searched in Sydney, and drugs, a stolen Mercedes and $200000 in cash were recovered. No one was arrested at the time but then, on 3 June, Ian Charles Guthrie was charged with money laundering. It was claimed he had been spending very substantial sums on cars, said to come from the Brinks robbery, and the purchase of 200 hectares of land near Kempsey. The allegation was that he had met Kelly in Queanbeyan in September and that Kelly had been murdered shortly afterwards.

On 18 April 2002 Ian Guthrie and his brother Patrick appeared in Sydney Central Court charged with Kelly's murder. The Crown's case had crystallised into an allegation that Guthrie had killed Kelly on a shooting trip on 7 September 2000 at Jerangle, south of Queanbeyan, and had returned a week later with his brother to dispose of the body. Some of Kelly's blood had been found near his car.

The case against the brothers was not strong but there to help things along was a man, now in the witness protection program, who had convictions for seven armed robberies and who had his jail term reduced from eighteen to five years for his co-operation with the police. Another witness from Jerangle claimed Ian Guthrie had borrowed a knife from him and lost it. He had written in his diary that he thought Guthrie had buried something on his property. The police found a collapsed wombat burrow with digging marks at the entrance, two plastic gas bottles, some burned timber and a glass bottle which contained some of Kelly's blood. The alleged motive for the killing was that Kelly was losing his nerve over the robbery and had been murdered to stop him confessing.

The problems for the prosecution were that juries don't like super-dobbers or 'no body' cases. There is always the danger that the supposed victim may not be dead and over the years a number of them have reappeared when it suited them. After two and a half days of deliberation, Ian and Patrick Guthrie walked free. A police spokesman said he was 'devastated' by the verdict. Ian Guthrie declined to comment on the suggestion that Kelly had gone to Britain and had undergone facial surgery.

One of the great non-violent robberies, known as the 'Chinese Takeaway', which may be the biggest ever in Australia, took place on the evening of 2 January 1988 when three tankmen, or safebreakers, squeezed through a gap in the wall of a construction site next to the Haymarket branch of the National Australia Bank in Sussex Street in Sydney's Chinatown. A window had been left open and with a 10 metre extension ladder they climbed through it to begin a systematic raid on the eighty-two safety deposit boxes in the bank. They were lucky because when they tried to blow a cash vault they had tripped a wire but security guards thought it to be a false alarm.

Just how much the thieves took will never be known because only half the people renting the boxes came forward to detail their losses, which were mainly in gold ingots and bars and jewellery. At the time gold was selling legally for $670 an ounce and estimates on the total haul have been put between $10 million and $100 million. Almost certainly much of it went abroad to Hong Kong and Singapore.

There was another similar raid in January 1991 on the Westpac Bank at the corner of Liverpool and Castlereagh streets. Again it is not known how much was actually stolen. It was probably carried out by a ten strong team put together by one of the unsung men of Sydney crime, a former member of the Kangaroos and described as 'a Grade A criminal almost unknown', who linked men who had never worked together before with out-of-town invitees. It says something for the man that he was able to combine these disparate elements and that there were no prosecutions. It is the exception that tests the rule that the criminal's best partner is himself. One name suggested for the mastermind has been the drug dealer Michael Hurley, who died in February 2007.

* * *

The trick for the escaper is not the escape itself, which is often relatively easy, but managing to stay out afterwards. The pitfalls are many; often the pleasures are few, and then only very temporary. First, there should be reliable contacts outside the prison to provide transport and safe houses. Unless they are relations or very close friends these people will require payment, often at extortionate rates. Money left in safe keeping with supposedly trustworthy sources often disappears during years in jail. A continuing life of crime is almost inevitable for an escaper without vast resources and the ability to get out of the country.

Over the years some escapers have managed to get quite a long way. John Parker escaped from the Darlinghurst lock-up in August 1928 when he had just been given four years for armed robbery in which he led a small team which included his girlfriend. He had a fretsaw and he stood on the shoulders of other prisoners as they covered the noise of his sawing by singing 'There's a long, long trail a-winding ...' He obtained a passport as a woman and left Australia for Europe on a wheat steamer. He was arrested when the ship docked at Bordeaux.

Others have stayed around. One of Australia's greatest serial escapers was Darcy Dugan. On 15 December 1949 he and William Cecil Mears escaped from Sydney's Central Police Court. It was Mears's second successful escape, Dugan's fourth. They were, at the time, serving ten years for the robbery of an elderly woman in Cascade Street, Paddington. Mears was at court to give evidence on behalf of Dugan who had been charged with possessing a pistol. During the lunch adjournment they cut through the cell bars with a hacksaw and ran into Central Lane where they boarded a tram.

They had both escaped three months earlier while on remand at Long Bay. Dugan had also escaped on 25 January 1946 when he forced his way out of a moving police van. He did not last long on the outside but in March that year he cut a hole in the roof of a prison tram on its way from Long Bay to Darlinghurst Police Station and was off again.

This time he and Mears were arrested in Alexander Street, Collaroy, on 14 February 1950. They were now charged with assaulting and robbing the well-known jockey John Thompson as well as shooting and wounding Leslie Nalder, manager of the Ultimo branch of the Commonwealth Bank on 13 January 1950. They made one final escape bid at the committal proceedings. Dugan slipped his handcuffs and made it through the court doors before being recaptured. At their trial they were sentenced to death but this was commuted and Dugan was released in 1985. He died in 1991 at the age of seventy-one.

George Savvas, jailed for twenty-five years in March 1990 over the importation of 80 kilograms of heroin, managed to stay out for ten months. On 6 July 1996 he put on a false wig, beard and moustache and walked out of the Long Bay prison visiting area in civilian clothes. It was not until May the next year that he was dobbed in by a caller telling the police he was in the Suntory Restaurant behind the Hoyt's cinema complex in Kent Street. When officers arrived they found him drinking red wine and eating beef fillets with two women companions who were left to settle the bill. He lasted in prison a bare two months. Two days after the discovery of an escape plan devised by him and Ivan Milat, the backpacker murderer, Savvas was found hanging from a bedsheet in his cell.

Alexander Robert MacDonald upped the ante after his escape in the autumn of 1995 from Queensland's Barellan Correctional Centre where he was serving a sentence of twenty-one years for armed robbery. Once known as the 'Corrie Bomber' after he bombed a hotel in Western Australia in an extortion attempt, he had, during his career, acquired convictions for robbery and kidnapping. In an effort to change his identity and get to live in Vanuatu, he advertised in a Melbourne newspaper for applicants for a job as a 'general hand geosurvey'. The prize was the opportunity of earning a fortune prospecting gold and the unfortunate successful applicant was a Ronald Joseph Williams. First, pioneering identity theft, MacDonald borrowed the unsuspecting Williams's birth certificate and Medicare and bank cards and used them to open an account with the Plenty Community Credit Union. Next, he told Williams to prepare for a two year trip to Western Australia. He would be paying him $500 a week. In February 1996, when the pair went fishing at Cheyne Beach, 400 kilometres south of Perth, MacDonald shot Williams and buried his body in the dunes.

With the proceeds of his various crimes he bought a boat for $32000 and spent another $40000 doing it up. He obtained a passport in the name of Williams and prepared to leave for Vanuatu. In complete contrast to the sophistication of his ploys so far, he was intercepted by police while hitch-hiking with his brother near Melbourne. He produced papers in Williams's name but when his fingerprints were taken the game was over. Sentenced to life imprisonment with a non-parole period of twenty-five years, he indicated that he did not think he would survive the sentence—one way or another.

Around the time MacDonald was being sentenced, 35-year-old Brendan James Abbott—known as the 'Postcard Bandit', because of his habit of sending cards from various cities and towns in Australia to the searching police—was leading the authorities in Queensland, and the other states for that matter, a merry dance. In November 1997, with the help of the then nineteen-year-old Brendon Luke Berrichon who hero-worshipped him, Abbott and four others escaped from the Sir David Longland prison in Brisbane.

Abbott had been sentenced to fourteen years after a Perth bank raid in 1987, which netted $112000. 'You are a thorough gentleman.

Thank you very much,' he told the judge. Along with Aaron Reynolds, he escaped from Fremantle prison two years later. They had used the prison workshop to make overalls similar to those worn by the guards and jumped 3 metres from a roof. A month later they robbed a TAB in Perth, firing at a pursuing police car. From then on Abbott criss-crossed Australia, robbing as he went, often hiding in a bank ceiling overnight ready to confront the staff when they arrived to open the vault. It was 1995 before this particular spree ended. A police raid in Perth on Abbott's younger brother Glenn turned up Abbott's post office box number on the Gold Coast. A search of the box produced his pager which, in turn, led to the unit where he was living.

This time he pleaded guilty to two robberies and, convicted of a third, was sentenced to twelve years. He stayed in prison until November 1997. For the first part he was in solitary confinement but once in Sir David Longland prison he began his escape plans, helped by the former prisoner Berrichon. Angel wire—often brought in, uncomfortably if not downright dangerously, by visitors *per vaginam*—had been smuggled in by another prisoner's friend, Natalee Hunter, who passed it through a small hole in a plastic screen in the prison visiting room. It was then used to cut through the cell-bars. For the escape, chairs were stacked to provide a makeshift ladder to get over the razor wire which surrounded Abbott's block and he and the four others ran 100 metres to the first perimeter fence. Bolt cutters and a rifle were thrown over and Berrichon and others pinned the guards down as Abbott cut through the fence. He left in his cell a prison transfer request with a smiley face.

The other four were caught within a month but in November Abbott carried out a robbery on a Commonwealth Bank on the Gold Coast. Then, in December, six weeks after the escape, Abbott, disguised as a businessman in a grey wig and a false moustache and brandishing a .45 Webley, took some $300000 from the Yirrigan Drive branch of the Commonwealth Bank in Perth.

Despite 'sightings' all over the country Abbott and Berrichon continued to remain a step ahead of their pursuers, living quietly in a brick terrace cottage at 41 Nicholson Street, Carlton, until they purchased a blue Toyota Landcruiser in Bendigo on 14 April 1998. On 20 April two transit policemen stopped the heroin-addicted Berrichon in the midst of what they thought was a drug deal in a shopping mall in Box Hill.

Berrichon produced a false driver's licence and was asked to empty his bag. It was found to contain a number of clean $50 notes. He then drew a gun and shot Constable Baltas in the hip and Sergeant Scott Roberts in the arm before forcing a woman to drive him home. When the police traced him the next day, the Nicholson Street cottage was empty. It was thought that Abbott would split from Berrichon as he had done from other former companions but, in an error of judgement, he remained loyal to the young man who had engineered his escape.

The Toyota was left at Melbourne Airport and Berrichon and his illegal immigrant girlfriend Ruang Khiankham, known as Michelle, drove to Adelaide and then on to Alice Springs. It seems likely Abbott also visited the Alice but then the trio definitely split. Berrichon and Michelle went to Darwin by bus, then flew to Broome before returning to Darwin and the Luma Luma holiday apartments. Abbott was booked in to the Top End Apartments there for 1 May. Through telephone monitoring and tip-offs the police traced Abbott, who had travelled from Queensland to the hotel. The capture of one of Australia's most wanted men of the time was low-key. As he left a nearby laundromat where he had taken his washing, officers from the Territory Response Group were waiting.

In March 1998 Natalee Hunter, the angel-wire girl, received a sentence of two years with an eight month minimum for her part in the escape. Berrichon received thirteen years, with a nine year minimum, for his attempt to kill the two police officers. Back in prison, the now heavily guarded Abbott, serving twenty-three years, took up painting. After he complained of chest pains there were, however, fears that he might be planning another escape and in the autumn of 2006 he was transferred out of the mainstream prison population in Woodford jail to the maximum security Arthur Gorrie Remand and Reception Centre. On Australia Day 2002 Berrichon was stabbed in a fight in Barwon prison's Eucalypt Unit. He survived.

* * *

It is always useful to have help from the inside. In March 1993 prison warden Heather Parker helped her lover Peter Gibb and another inmate, Archie Butterly, escape from the Melbourne Remand Centre by sliding down a line of knotted prison-issue sheets and blasting their way out. She had arranged a getaway car. Butterly, Gibb and Parker went to Gaffneys Creek Hotel, which burned down hours later, possibly to conceal the amount of blood shed by Butterly; he had leg and ankle injuries and deep cuts caused by falling from the sheet rope and crashing a motorbike in the escape. Gibb and Parker were captured a week later and Butterly was found dead after a fierce gun battle with the police at Jamieson in Victoria's north-east. He may have shot himself rather than be captured. Parker, placed in the security wing at Barwon prison, now claimed she was suffering from stress, arguing she was entitled to be paid sick leave from the prison service. She also appeared on Channel 9's *60 Minutes* program, for which she was paid $30000, later confiscated by the courts. In July 1994 she received a ten year sentence for her part in the escape.

In March 1999 John Killick escaped from Sydney's Silverwater prison in a helicopter organised by the Russian-born 41-year-old Lucy Dudko. Killick, a career criminal regarded by his fellow professionals such as Bernie Matthews, as a gentleman, had first been convicted in 1960 and served eight years for a series of TAB robberies committed in 1977 and 1978.

In August 1984 he had escaped in Brisbane while being taken to the Princess Alexandra Hospital for treatment of an injured eye. His then girlfriend, twenty-year-old Jacqueline Hawes, wearing an auburn wig, brought him a pistol and he held up his guards at gunpoint. While on the run he maintained that everything he had done had been for the benefit of his nine-year-old child. A year later Hawes received two months for aiding and abetting the escape. Killick was sentenced for three armed robberies committed while on the run.

A decade later, charmed by Killick, Dudko, who left her scientist husband Alex for him, hired the helicopter for what the pilot thought was to be a joyride over the Olympic Games site. Instead he found himself ordered at gunpoint to land in the prison exercise yard. He was later found bound with radio wires. The pair were thought to have left the state but were recaptured in a cabin at a caravan park six weeks later, on 9 May. Killick had apparently devised the escape after reading the novel *The Flight of the Falcon*.

On 21 December 2000 Judge Barry Mahoney handed Killick the maximum sentence of twenty-eight years for the helicopter escape and some related matters, rejecting submissions from a solicitor and a CSE case manager that Killick could reform. It was argued that he was well on the way to rehabilitation in the early 1990s when, after a series of personal reversals, he slipped back into a life of crime. Killick will be seventy-three when he can first apply for parole in 2014.

* * *

Perhaps the most celebrated escape, certainly from Pentridge, and the one that caused the most controversy, had been that of Ronald Joseph Ryan and London-born Peter John Walker in 1965. Ryan grew up in poverty but had later married a girl who was privately educated and whose father had been Mayor of Hawthorn. At the time of the escape Ryan was serving nine years for shop-breaking and Walker twelve for armed robbery. They took advantage of a warders' Christmas party to escape on 19 December with the ultimate destination being South America. They used knotted bedspreads to scale a wall to a catwalk and there they seized a warder's Armalite rifle. They then took a visiting Salvation Army brigadier hostage and made for Sydney Road with warders in pursuit. What exactly happened next was a subject of conjecture for some time to come. Certainly warder George Henry Hodson was shot and killed as he tried to grab Walker. The pair fled.

They made their way to St Kilda, from where, to obtain funds, they travelled to Hampton and held up the ANZ Bank. On the proceeds they threw a Christmas party where a guest, one Arthur Henderson, recognised Ryan and mentioned this to Walker, whom he had not recognised. A little later Walker suggested he and Henderson should go to a sly-grog shop to buy some more alcohol. The next day Henderson's body was found near a public lavatory on the beach. He had been shot in the head.

Ryan and Walker went to Sydney where they rented a flat at Coogee. Walker contacted an old girlfriend, a nurse, to set up a double date but in turn the girl contacted the police and a decoy policewoman was used. When Ryan and Walker arrived at Sydney's Concord Repatriation General Hospital they were arrested by the notorious detectives Ray Kelly and Fred Krahe. After he had seen Ryan and Walker back on a plane to Melbourne, Kelly remarked, 'I've shot brumbies. I've chased steers. But there's nothing to touch the thrill of a manhunt.'

The question that divided Australia was whether it was Ryan who had fired the fatal shot or whether the bullet had come from another warder's gun. All witnesses agreed that only one shot had been fired and a warder accepted that he had discharged his weapon. In the days when forensic testing does not seem to have overly troubled the courts, the jury found Ryan guilty and a string of appeals was rejected.

Since 1955 some thirty-five death sentences within the Australian legal system had been commuted to life, and in many circles it was thought Ryan's sentence would, and should, be, too. Ryan himself seems to have been more troubled by haemorrhoids than by his impending execution; that, at least, was the view of the prison psychiatrist. By the time all of Ryan's appeals had been rejected there was a great deal of public support for him, mainly from opponents of the death sentence. A crowd of some 3000 gathered outside the prison in the hours before his execution on 3 February 1967.

Walker was convicted of the manslaughter of Henderson. He served nineteen years before being released in 1984. He remained out of the public's eye until, in April 2002, he was convicted of cultivating marijuana and was sentenced to a year in prison and fined $12 000. He claimed the 6 kilograms were for his own use to relieve his asthma.

Sex from the Sixties

12

In the late 1960s a brothel war broke out in Sydney and appropriately it was the man at the top, the Maltese-born immigrant Joseph Borg, who was the first casualty. Borg, at his peak the undoubted claimant to the title 'King of Palmer Street Vice', was born in 1932 and arrived in Australia in the early 1950s. In June 1963 he opened his first brothel at Woods Lane, East Sydney, and four years later he owned a row of terrace houses as well as another twenty houses in East Sydney. His police records described him as gunman, thief, shop-breaker and pimp.

Perhaps the last was his greatest forte because he collected rent from fourteen houses that he let to girls in The Doors, the centre of Darlinghurst prostitution (it got its name from the fact that the girls would lean against their door jambs). In the 1960s the girls were charged a flat twenty pounds a shift and chose the comparative safety that the brothel bouncers provided in preference to the risks of the street. The girls wore no underwear and sex took place while they remained otherwise fully clothed.

A man with an eye to business, Borg also opened the Maltese Club, which provided rest and recreation for the mainly Maltese pimps, giving them a place to drink and play cards while waiting for their girls to finish their shifts.

Not all the brothels in the area were under Maltese control. At least one was under police supervision. In April 1965, at a stormy bankruptcy hearing, one alleged madam Aileen Patricia Donaldson was questioned about her relationship with Sergeant Harry Giles of the Vice Squad, who was alleged to have been her silent partner. It all ended in tears.

On 8 April Donaldson went to jail for fourteen days for 'repeated prevarications'. Sir Thomas Clyne, the judge, described her evidence as a 'farce from beginning to end'. She denied she had ever received a penny from Giles but other witnesses said he was paying her a weekly amount, limited to fifty pounds because of her gambling tendencies. Giles attempted to resign from the force, retiring to his house in Gymea where he was reported to be under sedation and consequently 'unavailable for comment'. His resignation was rejected and he was ordered to report for duty on 13 May. Donaldson promptly took an overdose in a motel and ended up in hospital.

Joe Borg, who clearly did not have the same close relationship with the police, earned his nickname 'The Writer' from the frequency with which he wrote to them complaining of harassment. At the time of his death he was due to appear on a charge of controlling prostitutes and was on bail while appealing against a conviction for attempting to bribe a policeman. Borg's troubles were not only with the authorities. He knew there was a serious challenge being mounted for control of Darlinghurst prostitution—an enterprise that was said to net him $10 000 a week—and consequently he slept with a loaded Biretta under his pillow.

On 28 May 1968 he left his home in North Bondi, turned the key in the ignition of his van and was blown up. A massive gelignite bomb weighing up to 2.5 kilograms had been planted under the van during the night. Borg's right leg was severed and he died before he arrived at St Vincent's Hospital. Borg's rivals cashed in on the changeover. Within a matter of days his houses were shut down and his rivals more than doubled the money they required to allow the girls to operate.

Devoted to his Alsatian Caesar and four cats, Borg had bequeathed his property to the RSPCA. While the Victorian branch declined to accept the wages of sin, the New South Wales branch had no such qualms, sending a wreath, 'In Gratitude from all the Homeless Animals'. In fact, despite reports, the charity did not do quite as well as hoped. While Borg did indeed own a number of properties, he had them mortgaged to the hilt. Three years after his death the RSPCA had received only some $25 000.

After Borg's death his Sydney associate Simone Vogel moved her innovative 'massage parlour' concept to Queensland where, she disappeared. The likelihood is that she, too, was killed.

One theory was that Borg's death was arranged by another Maltese, Paul 'King Joe' Mifsud, because of The Writer's tendency to steal from girls run by other men and also because he would not allow a greater share in his operations. Another is that Mifsud was not the prime mover and that certain members of Sydney's senior criminal hierarchy wanted him disposed of. They approached Keith Keillor, known as the 'Jitterbug Kid' because of his prowess on the dance floor in his youth, and in turn he recruited Mifsud and another Maltese, Paul Attard. A variation is that they approached Keillor in the Maltese Club in April 1968 and he sought the advice and help of the experienced explosives expert Jackie Steele, with whom Borg had quarrelled badly. They had clashed in the Mediterranean Club in the previous May when Borg had set Caesar on Steele, who had conveniently been heard by a prosecution witness to say, 'I will have that bastard put in orbit if it's the last bomb I make.'

Mifsud and Attard were prime suspects over the death of Borg but when they were arrested they failed to play by the rules and dobbed in Keillor. In turn he let the police know that he would tell all and was given reduced bail of $200 put up by crime associate Lennie McPherson. Mifsud and Paul Attard received sentences of life imprisonment. Keith Keillor was given seven years for showing them how to make the bomb. Steele had also been charged but died during the trial from the wounds he had received when he was shot in 1965. Despite the convictions there were underworld rumours that the principals had not been arrested.

A long-time associate of standover men Donny Smith and Ratty Clarke, Eric Williams (known as 'Monkey' because of his long arms and generally simian appearance), came to power after the death of Borg principally because he took up with Julie Harris, Borg's de facto wife. Williams later married her after he had served a two year stretch at Long Bay. On his own release John Regan, who had known Williams in prison, decided he would like to move in on the brothels. He engaged an old Canberra criminal to carry out a contract on Williams, who had declined to share the takings with him. Williams had the unfortunate habit of sticking to a set routine, never wise for a criminal. He could generally be found in the Maltese Club playing cards waiting for Julie Harris to shut up the shop. On one occasion when Williams went home alone, the contractor knocked on the door of his house and, when Williams came to the door, fired five times through the woodwork, hitting him every time. Williams was unable to reach the telephone to call for help and died in his hallway.

* * *

Community attitudes were reflected in changes in policing and prosecuting prostitution. Sydney's sex industry had been openly thriving for some time when, in 1967, there was a dramatic decline in rates of arrest for prostitution in New South Wales. Some police officers were tempted by the more relaxed attitude to exercise their 'discretion' as to which offences and individuals were prosecuted. This discretion became a marketable commodity.

Prostitution was alive and well all over the country, but it often masqueraded as something else. To get around existing laws in the 1960s and 1970s in Melbourne, so-called health studios and massage parlours became a common euphemism for brothels and there were so many men who needed a dose of health or a massage that the industry burgeoned. Permits, granted by local councils, offered some measure of protection and the parlours became attractive to sex workers who wanted to get off the streets. In 1966 a survey showed that St Kilda was the workplace of at least a hundred street prostitutes, and six St Kilda massage parlours employed many girls as well. Action by residential groups about parlours in their streets resulted in some legislative changes in the mid-1970s, but the parlour game flourished and by 1976 police counted 160 operations, 'more parlours than any other city in the western world [and] escalating like a bushfire out of control'.

In Perth, a young lesbian mother, Shirley Finn, began her career by finding a creative and even artistic way of extracting money from men for exercising their sexual fantasies. At country fairgrounds, they paid her well to watch or even participate in the body painting of naked ladies. In 1969 her 'studios' were raided and she was found guilty of prostitution. Soon afterwards she met up with, and was mentored by, a Sydney-based madam and began keeping her own brothel. However, this meant she was working in an industry where money had to be paid—to police and others who demanded a piece of her action—if she wanted to keep operating. In her heyday she ran a brothel of eight prostitutes and was making enough money to lavishly entertain Perth society members and distinguished guests at her South Perth home.

On 23 June 1975 the 33-year-old Finn was found by a passing patrolman in her Dodge Phoenix sedan—with its sticker 'Mafia Staff Car'—near the Royal Perth Golf Club. She had been shot in the head four times and had bled all over her pleated satin ball gown. Her jewellery was untouched, as was a diamond she wore in her front tooth. Her murder, unsolved after three decades, raised many questions: why had she dressed up, who did she meet the night of her murder, who so badly wanted her dead and why?

There was feuding among brothel owners in Perth at the time and they were also coming under pressure from east coast mobsters who were seeking to expand. Finn was also almost certainly laundering money. Perhaps most likely is that some of her girls were relaying pillow talk with their political clients and this was leading to blackmail, something which prompted a Commission into Policing of the Sex Industry in 1976. Given the diverse reasons offered for Finn's death it is not surprising that her murderer was never found. After a series of articles in *The West Australian* and calls from the public which indicated the callers believed there had been police involvement in the murder, an application was made to see certain materials held in police files. The application was refused. In 2005 the case was reopened in the hope that DNA evidence might lead to Finn's murderer. So far no arrests have been made.

* * *

In Sydney during World War II, Bondi was the home of back street abortionists, there to deal with women pregnant by visiting servicemen. The police targeted the abortionists who did not pay protection money and women were arrested as they left the clinics. Often there was a police photographer to record their humiliation. Obtaining the co-operation of the police was therefore a must for the clinic operators.

In Melbourne both during and after the war, abortion provided a lucrative income for organised crime as well as the police, the latter controlling the abortion racket for something like twenty years. Complaints could be disregarded and, as with sly-grogging, the clinics could be warned of any raids in time to bundle equipment, and if necessary patients, out of the premises. Just as detective Ray Kelly was part of the abortion rackets in Sydney so the police stood over abortionists in Melbourne.

Indeed the police not only stood over the abortionists, from time to time they took a more active part. One of the leading backyard operators was a former policeman known as Harry who had at one time also run an SP book. In the 1960s he persuaded an out-of-town doctor to teach him the rudiments of this trade. It is said that at his peak he was performing twelve abortions daily at $250 a time. When he wanted to move his clinic into his private house and train his nineteen-year-old daughter as his assistant, she and Mrs Harry shot through.

Throughout the latter half of 1969 the abortion reform advocate Dr Bertram Wainer, who had a practice in St Kilda, made allegations claiming that police officers were taking money from abortionists. On 9 December 1969 he handed in affidavits to *Truth*, which forwarded them to the solicitor general. They contained allegations that payments ranged from $600 to a lump sum of $1200, which would include cover for the 'possible fatality' of a patient. The chief commissioner was directed to investigate the complaints but five out of six officers refused to see him. The government then appointed an independent one-man board of inquiry in the form of William Kaye QC. The principal allegation was that, since 1953, some members of the elite Homicide Squad were paid $150 a week each to look after the interests of abortionists.

The next year the formerly highly regarded Superintendent Jack Matthews, Jack Ford and two other officers were in the dock. One was Fred 'Bluey' Adam, there on the allegations of Peggy Berman who was claiming he had stood over the abortion clinic where she worked in return for warning them of police raids. Berman, who was the godmother to a child of standover man Norman Bradshaw, claimed the doctors had been the victim of what she called a somersault. They had, she claimed, been paying Adam, who had passed them on to Ford, Matthews and the fourth officer Marty Jacobson, who demanded even more money.

Abuse was heaped on Berman throughout her cross-examination and the officers' evidence: apart from being a chronic liar, she was an hysteric who had herself had a series of abortions; she was doing this on political grounds; she had tried to poison her former lover Ford by sending him a bottle of whisky. He feared she had injected the poison through the cork with a hypodermic needle. She took the allegations well and it did not help the defence case when they called Joey Turner, the old standover man then serving a sentence in Adelaide, in a further attempt to discredit her. It was not a success because he deliberately identified a tax inspector in the public gallery as a man who had 'approached' him on Berman's behalf. An application to treat Turner as a hostile witness was refused.

The jury returned their verdicts late on 9 April. Adam, then an alcoholic and weighing 140 kilograms, was acquitted. He died just over a year later suffering from stomach cancer. During his career, which began in 1928, he had been instrumental in sending twelve men to the gallows. Jack Matthews and Jack Ford were convicted and released after serving less than half their five year sentences. Jacobson was released in May 1972 after serving thirteen months of his three years. Matthews was later given a job writing on consumer affairs at *Truth*, the newspaper whose campaign had led to his destruction. He was assigned the chair of Evan Whitton, the journalist who had exposed him. He took these humiliations in good part.

The growth of the sex industry in the 1960s and 1970s coincided with burgeoning drug use. At first marijuana use and supply, as part of the hippie counterculture, was a cottage industry, with dealers growing it on their rooftops and providing it from their homes or corner shops. Police activity in Melbourne in the early 1970s is said to have pushed the dealers and users south towards St Kilda and Prahran and provided an incentive for drug importation rather than home-growing. This saw the rise of organised criminals with business plans who ousted the hippies who had sold their dope at $30 for a one ounce bag.

The market for heroin, too, was growing fast and street prostitution was part of the distribution rackets. The sex–drug symbiosis evolved quickly. Prostitutes, due to their way of life, have always been vulnerable to drug dealers. In the mid-1970s money was invested in the importation of huge amounts of heroin. When provided by operators as part payment for the prostitutes' sex work, it increased their profits and chained the girls and boys to them.

Also, the average age of prostitutes was falling and in 1977, after an undercover raid in St Kilda, police concluded that, 'prostitution was becoming more closely tied with the drug trade and organised crime'. Standover tactics, murders and assaults provided evidence that organised crime was well into the multi-million dollar massage parlour industry on the east coast.

A spate of fires in the parlours, including Queens Road's Hawaiian Health Studio, and the murder in January 1977 of the owner of St Kilda

Road's Gentle Touch, were wakeup calls. James Kelly had twenty girls working at The Gentle Touch which, elegantly appointed with antiques and a classy discreet exterior, catered for businessmen. He was woken as usual that January morning by a phone call from the night manager of his parlour. As Kelly got into his luxury car outside his Kew home, about to head for work, he was shot and killed.

Around 1.15 a.m. on 9 February 1979, Victor Frederick Allard, the former Painter and Docker who was dealing heroin to prostitutes, was shot with a sawn-off shotgun in St Kilda's notorious Fitzroy Street. A woman who was with him at the time was unhurt. Allard had lasted a bare fourteen months since he was shot in the stomach in December 1977. It was known he was owed a substantial sum of money by dealers.

Another dealer for whom prostitute addicts were profitable customers, Peter Dale Russell, was shot and killed at his flat in Waterloo Crescent, St Kilda, in July 1980. Soon after, another drug courier who was to give evidence at his inquest was found dead. John Desmond 'Machinegun Fred' Gordon was a Kiwi who had also been expected to give evidence at the Zampaglione drugs ring trial (he had worked as a courier for the drugs ring). He had been advised to seek police protection and relocation in a safe house but had declined, believing that he was safest maintaining his regular pattern in the drug scene. Three months earlier, brothel keeper John James Elbert was shot in Melbourne. He had, it seems, been treading on more important toes.

From 1978 to 1982 in Victoria a major police protection racket operated in the brothel industry. By the late 1970s, Paul William Higgins, a former schoolboy athletics champion, who had joined the police force in 1965, was boasting to one brothel owner that he had the whole Consorting Squad and most of the Vice Squad under his control.

With Higgins as ring leader, the police officers had under their protection a well-known and wealthy brothel owner, Geoffrey Lamb, whose empire included an estimated twenty-five illegal massage parlours which afforded him a sweet lifestyle. It was one he wanted to maintain; with two luxury homes, in Hawthorn and Kew, and a Lamborghini, he had extremely expensive personal habits. His lavish informal parties involved recreational use of drugs as well as women. When Lamb came to the conclusion in 1977 that he could indeed use a little police protection, he got in touch with someone he knew in the New South Wales Police who, for a fee of $10 000, put him in contact with Higgins. He and other police officers were invited into Lamb's circle and girls were on the house, a facility of which Higgins regularly availed himself.

Lamb would regularly carry around up to $10000 in cash, which came in handy because he was soon paying police thousands of dollars each month as protection money. In exchange his sex empire flourished as the officers on his payroll would warn him about any raids planned for his various parlours on the city fringes. Money was handed over on the first of the month in the back room in the office of Higgins's squad. In return Higgins and others were able to stop investigations in their tracks, fabricate evidence if necessary and even lean on the working girls if they were thought to be taking it too easy.

Higgins would instruct junior officers in his squad to make false entries on running sheets when Lamb was visited. On one occasion an officer was taken by Higgins to one of Lamb's establishments at Rathdowne Street, Carlton, and sent in to pick up a gun from Lamb. Higgins then allegedly told him to record that the .32 revolver had been received from a Drummond Street dobber. Lamb himself alleged that he'd been told by Higgins that, if questioned by Police Internal Investigators, he was to say he was an informant.

The detectives who were part of Lamb's battalion were also prepared, for a price, to protect Lamb from competition. He was hardly the only brothel owner in town. One rival and enemy was James Robert Slater. Another was Joey Hamilton, of Station Street, Carlton, who had been a witness at the earlier Kaye Inquiry into abortion rackets. Hamilton was no shrinking violet. In 1973 he received eight years for armed robbery but was granted a new trial in November 1977. He was also the man shot at in mistake for Charlie Wootton years earlier.

On 1 August 1978, when a bomb went off at Joey Hamilton's home, he claimed police planted it. This was the third attack and second bomb in twelve months on his home. Asked by reporters when the violence would stop, he said, 'When people like you stop getting edited and start exposing organised crime—the police.' Two days later the Gaslight brothel blew up.

The brothel war continued when, on 9 August, five detectives under Higgins's direction paid a short visit to James Slater's home in Collingwood. Slater's brothel office had already been visited earlier in the day. A few hours later warrants to search both of Slater's premises were issued and police raids 'uncovered' gelignite under the brothel's filing cabinet. Explosives were also found, as was a tin of detonators inside a child's toy box at Slater's home. Higgins did not even attempt to make an appearance of conducting a proper investigation, nor did he interview people who had access to areas where the explosives had been found. Despite claiming to have a watertight alibi at the time of both bombings, Slater was duly charged on suspicion of being involved. The sting had stung and Slater went to trial where, courtesy of a traffic infringement booking he'd copped from the Transport Regulation Board, evidence showed that he had been driving around Mildura at the time. He was acquitted, closed down his brothel and no doubt quite happily paid his Mildura traffic fine.

Another significant soldier in Geoffrey Lamb's empire was the armed robber and killer Alistair Farquhar 'Sandy' MacRae, said to be Lamb's second in command and believed to be involved in up to twenty suspicious deaths or disappearances.

MacRae eventually left Lamb and tried to set up a massage parlour on his own in Mildura. After that he met Albert O'Hara and convinced him he would be able to make a profit out of buying and selling marijuana. Instead, on 21 December 1984, MacRae killed O'Hara by shooting him in the head, then cut up his car so it could be dropped into the Merbein tip.

The list of MacRae's other victims include standover man Michael Ebert, killed outside a Carlton brothel in April 1980. Apparently Ebert had beaten MacRae badly the previous fortnight and this slight, balding man was out for permanent revenge. In July 1980 police found the remains of a woman buried in the backyard of a home owned by an underworld figure's mother. It was thought to be a prostitute from South Australia, also killed by MacRae. Next there was his girlfriend Deborah Joy Fahey, found dead in a St Kilda motel in August 1981. She had been given a hot shot of almost pure heroin. Then came a prostitute known as 'Little Lisa'.

Higgins and Lamb finally fell out over an affair the detective had with Lamb's wife, Lorraine Goyne, who later died from a drug overdose. Lamb's empire began to crumble when he fell for a gorgeous ex-model turned prostitute who had also succumbed to heroin. He tried to help her break her addiction, but instead ended up using himself. In 1991 at the Higgins's preliminary hearing, Lamb meekly told the court he had blown $20000 a week on heroin and had used up all his brothel profits. Once MacRae, in one of the kinder acts of an untidy life, had chained him to a bungalow wall on his Mildura property in an effort to wean him off the drug.

Lamb eventually went to prison for living off immoral earnings and then gave evidence against Higgins, whose trial began in November 1991. It was not until late March 1993 that, considerably aggrieved that much of the evidence that convicted him came from MacRae, Higgins was sentenced to seven years' imprisonment with a minimum of five to be served. Lamb died, aged sixty-one, in an armchair in his modest West Heidelberg home in 2004.

Brisbane had its own wars decades later, when legalisation took place under the *Prostitution Act 1999*. (Before the Fitzgerald Inquiry, brothels had been under the active protection of the police for years.) The principal target was the illegal brothel The Love Shack on New Cleveland Road at Capalaba West. It had been running for eight years and numerous overdoses had been reported on the premises.

Bambi, the manageress, and her partner, a former boxer, claimed that a Mr Big of the prostitution world had been trying to take over brothels and run them with front men. They claimed that shots had been fired at the premises and their car, and then there had been 'bikie-types' with baseball bats harassing the staff. Then, in May 2000, the receptionist, Andrea Snowdon, was executed. She had disappeared when she was driving a prostitute home and her half-naked body was found nine days later with three shots to the head. Seven months later, in late December, Bambi herself was shot and killed on the doorstep of the brothel with a shortened .22 rifle. Her twelve-year-old daughter was abducted, tied to a tree and raped. A year later, a prostitute, Rhonda Karger, claimed she was being stalked and feared for her life because she knew too much about the killings. She had, she told a Brisbane court, left a tape recording in a bank vault for her protection.

Not all standover merchants in the sex industry go to prison. In 1988 Wayne Ronald Burrell took over seven suburban houses, part of Hector Hapeta's Queensland brothel empire, while Hapeta was under scutiny by the Fitzgerald Commission. Burrell avoided imprisonment despite repeated convictions for controlling prostitutes. His success was wholly due to the fact he was a paraplegic and the prison authorities were concerned about the cost of housing him. Burrell's injuries came from a truck accident in 1975 but he was still able to combine his profession with that of horse training. That hobby received a setback when, in 1987, one of his horses swabbed positive for performance enhancement drugs. In 1989 a court heard that he was offering prostitutes protection at a modest $500 a week. Burrell avoided prison until the end, dying after a heart attack at his home in Laidley on 13 May 2002.

South Australia, too, has had its fair share of sex–drugs–corruption scandals. In 1991 the National Crime Authority investigated illegal brothels in Adelaide and the involvement of senior police officers with major criminals. This investigation followed the conviction of the former head of the Drug Squad, Chief Inspector Barry Moyse, in August 1988, and the work of the Fitzgerald Inquiry into corruption in Queensland. Arrested in September 1987, Moyse received a twenty-seven year sentence reduced on appeal to twenty-one after pleading guilty to seventeen charges of taking part in the supply and sale of heroin, confiscating drugs from small-time dealers and passing them through a dealer named George Octapodellis, later found dead of an overdose in his car in Sydney in June 1989. Moyse was released in 1999.

The immediate trigger for the NCA was a Chris Masters television program, *Suppression City*, screened on the ABC on 6 October 1988, which looked at possible links between organised crime (including prostitution) and police corruption within the South Australian police force. There were other suggestions, including one that a senior politician had visited prostitutes and enjoyed being whipped and ridden like a horse.

The commission found that the allegations against the politician were unfounded but at a time when brothels were illegal, one witness, Patti Walkuski, had operated a brothel from 1972 to the mid-1980s. Another, the engagingly named Stormy Summers, had run Fantasy House from 1978 and a Geoffrey Williams had been involved in over seventy brothels from 1972, including some in New South Wales and Western Australia. One brothel, the Holdfast Health Clinic, had been run for an astounding twenty-six years.

During this era prostitutes (soon to be renamed sex workers) and their supporters were lobbying to change the laws regulating the industry. Ironically, while decriminalisation was promoted as making the prostitutes less vulnerable to exploitation, legalisation was opposed by the sex workers on the basis that it would force them into licensed brothels in specified areas. This, argued the lobbyists, would simply make prostitution more profitable for those who were already making money from it—including police, landlords, councils and organised crime, along with big business interests and those already running drug rings and off-loading stolen goods in massage parlours—in exchange for offering some protection and security.

Victoria's Prostitution Control Act, passed in 1994, licensed brothel premises but not individuals running them. As a result properties were being sold, with a licence attached, for four times their market value. About that time, a nephew of Robert Trimbole had a brothel on the market for $12 million.

Notwithstanding the new legislation, illegal street prostitution with ever younger girls flourished in Melbourne. Legalised 'commercial sex', including lap-dancing and the like, was more a boon for the large operators than the sex workers themselves. Although owning more than one brothel was illegal, licensing was not effectively monitored and one proprietor owned six brothels. Convicted criminals were heavily involved in running brothels which were fronted by cleanskins.

From the 1980s Fred Lelah was involved in the industry. Born in Singapore of Eurasian background, he settled in Melbourne. Although described by his barrister as, 'a benign, non-threatening type of individual', he had convictions in 1986 and 1989 for living off the earnings of prostitution, in 1994 for managing the brothel Exquisite Ladies and in 1997 for entering into an agreement for the provision of sexual services by a child and for being an unlicensed provider of prostitution services. Legalisation and regulation of prostitution had obviously deterred him but little.

In the early 1990s, a young barrister, Dominic Hickey, seduced by the demi-monde of St Kilda and Carlton, teamed up with Fred Lelah and his colleague Rosa Brcic. Hickey 'entered, indeed wallowed in, the world of prostitution' according to the trial judge. By the late 1990s Lelah and Brcic were running a licensed brothel, Sasha's, in Fitzroy and Hickey proved a useful friend, acting as something of an agent for the team, recruiting prostitutes to work either at Sasha's or privately for other clients. Sadly he was not particular enough about the ages of the girls he recruited or whose services he used. The girls, while not children, were, the court said, 'vulnerable by reason of their youth and their addiction to heroin'. Lelah and Hickey would offer the girls the drugs they needed in exchange for providing their services. They would kerb-crawl the St Kilda streets operating a mobile prostitute recruiting and drug supply business. One fifteen year old was persuaded to perform oral sex on five men at Hickey's flat in exchange for heroin and money.

In 2000 Hickey pleaded guilty to seventeen counts, including making an agreement for a child to act as a prostitute, and taking part in acts of sexual penetration of a child between ten and sixteen years. He was sentenced to seven years but on appeal his minimum was reduced to four years. On appeal Lelah's minimum sentence of three years six months was upheld.

* * *

Insiders say that another development over the last two decades has been the Asianisation of the brothel industry. Since the 1980s in Victoria's brothel district around South Melbourne, Asian brothels have proliferated. Some are licensed and more are not. Some Asian sex workers are legal residents who may be cashing in on the taste for Asian women; more are illegals who are cashing up their bosses. The combination of depressed economic conditions in many South-East Asian countries, particularly in rural regions, and Australia's relaxed prostitution laws, make it tempting for Asian girls to believe the promises of traffickers. Raids by Victorian police and immigration officers have uncovered hundreds of Asian women in brothels being paid merely a weekly allowance hardly adequate to buy them a lipstick and a blouse. Even once they worked off their debts they would not necessarily be free to go.

The importation of such women is a lucrative trade for Asian and home-grown organised criminals, who sell them in batches to brothel operators. In one 1988 case, six Thai women were found in a Port Melbourne brothel. One woman had had an encounter with a violent customer a few days earlier and her vagina was torn. Nonetheless she was compelled to continue working. They had been told that brothel work was a path to permanent residence in Australia, but their tourist visas had expired or been breached.

In 1999 immigration officials reported that an 'increasing irregular migration to Australia' was linked to the increase in Asian brothels.

Brokers operating in Sydney were said to be able to supply the sex industry with as many Asian girls as were wanted and could even select shape and size to order. The sex importation industry was estimated to generate more than $50 million a year.

A food importer, at the time suspected of being Australia's biggest people trader, was said to have imported more than a thousand Asian women to work in brothels in Sydney and Melbourne. The women were brought in on student or tourist visas and worked virtually as sex slaves to pay off their hefty debts. In turn the money they earned went into the casinos. Officially the owner of a takeaway, the food importer was said to have put $2 million through the high rollers' room at Sydney's Star City Casino in one month.

At the low roller end, in the 1990s the Vietnamese owner of an illegal brothel in Clayton, Victoria, was quietly wholesaling and retailing Thai girls to other brothels, taking most of their earnings. When Vietnamese gangsters stood over him demanding a cut, he refused. The gang broke into his brothel and kidnapped two of his girls, demanding money for their return. It was at this stage that the brothel owner decided to assist police with their inquiries. Two of the gangsters were convicted of aggravated burglary, kidnapping and false imprisonment and received sentences of six and four and a half years. It is unclear whether the brothel owner faced charges.

Local sex workers say that the presence of imported girls in the industry makes life more difficult and that they undercut the conditions and rights of sex workers. Those who traffic in illegals are in a position to insist that rougher, condom-free sex and other less acceptable practices are on offer. One such practice that Thai women are expected to perform is called 'a warm tea', where the woman holds hot tea in her mouth while performing oral sex without a condom.

The dangers faced by illegally imported sex workers go beyond oppression by organised criminals and unsafe sex practices. In March 2004 two Thai prostitutes were tied up and thrown alive to drown in the crocodile infested Adelaide River about 65 kilometres east of Darwin. Teenagers Phu Ngoc Trinh and Ben McLean were convicted and sentenced to life imprisonment, with the judge fixing a minimum non-parole of twenty-five years. No motive was ever established but McLean spoke of being forced to kill the women by Hells Angels and Phu Ngoc Trinh said he had witnessed their killing by an Asian crime gang. Another explanation offered, which the police did not accept, was that they had been forced to kill the women to repay a drug debt.

By 2005, after years of debate, laws criminalising possessing or trading in sex slaves were in operation; the Australian Federal Police had rescued fifty women but no one had been successfully prosecuted. A crackdown on the importation of Thai sex slaves resulted in traffickers turning to Korea as a source for women and girls. Insiders anticipate that the next trade will be in African women. 'Where there is a demand, someone will supply,' says the co-ordinator of Project Respect, Valli Mendez.

A report published by the project the previous year outlined hundreds of case studies and estimates that each year 1000 women were trafficked to Australia from Colombia, the former Soviet Union, Myanmar, China, Vietnam, Malaysia and Albania. The Russian *Mafiya* has involved itself in the trade since the end of the 1990s.

Internationally, it is acknowledged that only a minority of trafficking cases are reported and convictions of traffickers are extremely rare. One problem for authorities is that, while organised crime gangs control trafficking of women from Eastern Europe to the west, those trafficking Asian women to Australia are less likely to be part of organised crime gangs. More often they are elusive individual entrepreneurs or members of small semi co-ordinated teams such as the Boonthum and Nana gangs in Bangkok.

It was not until 2006 that a gang was finally successfully prosecuted in Victoria for owning and trading in what were found to be prostitution slaves. Surprising to anti-trafficking campaigners, if not to the more pragmatic, some of the owners and traders are women. A woman we shall call 'F' pleaded guilty and was sentenced in 2005. In her turn she had been a contracted prostitute who, when she had paid off her debt, had remained working, recruiting other women who were smuggled through immigration and placed in brothels in Sydney.

The first jury conviction under the new Act was against Wei Tang, an associate of 'F', who, in June 2006, was found guilty of five counts of possessing a slave and five counts of exercising power of ownership over a slave. Thai women, promised a better life, were accompanied on their flight from Bangkok to Sydney by escorts and then taken to Melbourne to work in her brothel, Club 417, in Brunswick Street, Fitzroy. While she did not actually put these women under lock and key, Wei Tang held their passports and tickets against debts of $45000 each. The trial judge found that all of the women were effectively restrained by the insidious nature of their contract: 'How could they run away when they had no money ... no passport or ticket, they entered on an illegally obtained visa ... they had limited English language ... no friends, they were told to avoid Immigration ...?' ·

The Wei Tang operations are clearly only the very tip of the iceberg. In 2006, soon after Wei Tang's sentencing, the Australian Federal Police invited local and international NGOs and police to Canberra to thrash out once again the problem of women imported for the sex trade. In June 2006 the AFP were reported to be investigating another fourteen cases of sexual servitude.

In 2004 researchers looking into the effect of legalisation on prostitution studied Melbourne and concluded that, after twenty years, 'the illegal layer still flourishes ... the number of unlicensed brothels has trebled and street prostitution in the St Kilda area has increased fivefold'. The research showed that many prostitutes did not want to register as sex workers because of the stigma attached and because they would then have to pay tax on their earnings. Others avoid brothel work because drug taking is prohibited under licence conditions. Significantly, more trafficked sex workers had been found in legal Melbourne brothels than in illegal ones.

In the top-end licensed brothels, sex workers say that their earnings have dramatically dropped since legalisation and the influx of foreign sex workers. One young woman, 'K', who has worked off and on in the sex industry since the early 1990s, says, 'It was common before 1994 to earn $8000 to $10000 per week; since legalisation a girl is lucky to make $1000'. This is confirmed by a survey of prostitution in Queensland: girls who answered a questionnaire said they earned an average of $1341 in the previous week. 'K' believed that the high-class establishments where she has worked must also be making a lot less. So how do they account for the palatial refurbishments which are evident? Her answer is, 'Perhaps their money comes from other activities.'

That was certainly the view of the National Crime Authority, which did not believe that customer-generated money could keep a brothel afloat. In 1990 it had found that criminal activity in some of Victoria's legal brothels included money-laundering, conspiracy to murder, trafficking in heroin, defrauding the Commonwealth Immigration Act and inducing a child into prostitution.

Life in the sex industry—legal or illegal—seems to come down to a choice between masters. In 2006 Sydney authorities began chasing sex workers in legal brothels for tax owed. This proved a disincentive to the workers, and numbers of available girls in some legal premises halved. Perhaps they traded masters and headed for one of the estimated 750 unlicensed brothels operating in New South Wales. Many would say little has changed; certainly not much has changed for the better.

Drugs and Ethnic Minority Crime

13

Shortly before midnight on 31 July 1996, six Vietnamese-born men, the eldest twenty, the youngest sixteen, drove towards the Endeavour Oval in Fairfield, New South Wales. The brothers in the front seat were senior associates of the Cabramatta Madonna Boys, also known as Madonna's Mob. They were talking tough about a job that 'had to be done'. It was the killing of a sixteen year old who had failed to pay a debt and was suspected of collaborating with a rival gang, 5T. He was taken behind a toilet block at the oval and shot four times in the head in what the Court of Appeal called, 'a cold-blooded execution … murder of the most heinous kind.' Welcome to the world of the ethnic crime gangs.

The first non-European immigrants to come to Australia in significant numbers were the Chinese, who had flocked to the goldfields in their thousands in the 1850s. By 1861 the census showed that Chinese made up almost 40 000 of a total population of 1.1 million people. They often suffered exploitation, oppression and blatant discrimination and many left Australia after the gold rush. Some moved to the cities, where the Chinese slums became known for opium dens.

Until the 1950s, Australian–Chinese with a taste for opium had little trouble acquiring the relatively small quantities needed. Then, however, Chinese addicts developed a taste for heroin, the derivative manufactured from opium in Hong Kong laboratories and imported into Australia by ethnic Chinese dealers. By the 1960s the suppliers saw emerging markets outside Chinatown, mainly in Kings Cross. With the patronage of US servicemen, the Cross evolved into a frantic scene, with everything the sexually frustrated soldier might want.

In December 1972 Gough Whitlam became Australia's prime minister and the next year he introduced legislation which, by abolishing all racial quotas, killed off the White Australia Policy. The first year in which potential immigrants officially stood on a level playing field, regardless of skin, colour or race, was 1974. The result was a huge surge in Asian immigration. In 1971 Australian residents who had been born in China, Singapore, Malaysia, Taiwan or Hong Kong numbered 43 100. By 1986 the numbers had reached 133 000.

During the late 1960s and early 1970s, crackdowns on secret societies gave Chinese criminals and gangsters in Singapore and Malaysia pause for thought—perhaps there were greener pastures not far south. It cannot have gone unnoticed that Australia, at that stage, had no national police force and state forces were preoccupied with their own duckhouses. It was not until 1979 that the ACT's police force became the Australian Federal Police.

During the 1960s Singapore's Triad gangs had been the subject of intense police scrutiny. Prime Minister Lee Kuan Yew's People's Action Party, with its reputation for taking an authoritarian approach to Singapore's social problems, targeted secret societies. Gang violence was tackled with increased police powers and detention without trial. In the early 1970s Malaysian authorities followed Singapore's lead and conducted a similar crackdown.

Triads closely resembled Mary's little lamb; wherever the Chinese community went, they were sure to follow. Soon half a dozen powerful gangs were thought to be operating in Sydney and Melbourne—among them the Wo Yee Tong, Sun Yee On, Wo Shing Wo, 14K and the Big Circle from mainland China. From Malaysia there were also the Sing Ma and Sing Wa.

By the 1980s law enforcement agencies accepted that ethnic Chinese were the major organisers of heroin imports into Australia. The NCA's Chinese liaison officer in 1988 reported that the Chinese had been linked to every major seizure of heroin in the preceding two years, that seizures totalled 63 kilograms and of those more that 85 per cent were estimated to be Triad-related. The Chinese gangs were primarily wholesalers, rarely involved at the local distribution level.

A key man in a 1988 importation of 31 kilograms of heroin was (John) Chai Nam Yung, the owner of an illegal gambling club in Sydney and also the head of the Australian branch of the Wo Yee Tong. For his role in the deal, he was sentenced in March 1991 to twenty-four years' imprisonment.

By now there were suggestions that cocaine was taking hold of the middle classes in Melbourne and some dealers would kill to defend their territory, however small. At the end of May 1985 Brendan Wilson, who ran a few prostitutes as an escort agency and dabbled in cocaine, was forced to kneel and then clubbed to death—a method of execution once common in China. His Asian flatmate was killed in a similar manner. It was thought that rather more organised criminals had decided to make an example of both him and an innocent bystander.

Interviewed on 10 October 2005 for the 'Dead Man Talking' episode of ABC Television's *Australian Story*, the corrupt New South Wales Police officer Trevor Haken said: 'The Chinese in Chinatown were virtually a law unto themselves. They were involved in all sorts of crime, from video pirating right through to heroin importations, illegal gambling, prostitution … Whenever you saw them, there'd be a handshake and you'd end up with a bundle of money in your hand.'

One Triad member who later received a heavy sentence was Jack Chen of the Sun Yee On. Chen, a well-known Sydney Chinatown identity who favoured smart cars and gambled at Crown Casino in Melbourne rather than on his home ground, received a forty year sentence for importing heroin, with a minimum of twenty-six to be served. He had changed his plea to guilty after listening to a four week opening statement by the Crown. The police had first become interested in Chen in 1995 and there were 11 000 legal telephone intercepts before he was arrested in 2000. In a six week period early that year he had organised the importation of 17 kilograms of pure heroin from mainland China. The break-up of his team was seen as a contributing factor to Sydney's heroin drought of the time.

And of course the Chinese were not the only wholesalers. Sociologist Bertil Lintner wrote: 'Some Lebanese drug dealers in Sydney buy heroin from Chinese wholesalers, but the drug also comes through their own contacts in Bangkok and is sometimes carried by African couriers to Australia.' Although Lebanese gangs are said to have been in Australia since the 1960s it was the civil war in the 1970s that forced Beirut's vice kings to close down their establishments and look further afield. They moved to India and eventually to Bangkok. Australia, with its large Lebanese communities in Sydney, Brisbane and other cities, was only a short sail away for the drug dealers who, instead of buying from Chinese wholesalers, now used their contacts in Bangkok.

By the 1980s the Bayeh brothers Louis and Bill had built up serious businesses, money and reputations. Initially minders for Lennie McPherson, they effectively became controllers of Kings Cross. Opinions vary over them. Some regard Louis as 'sharp as a cannonball', believing his more dapper and cosmopolitan brother to be the brainier. One journalist sees it differently:

> Louis Bayeh is considerably smarter. He pulled off a mafia don act when he was sentenced for the standover, behaving in court as if he was a halfwit. Originally McPherson smoothed his way. The cops weren't going to talk to a Lebanese who can't read or write but they'd deal with McPherson. Louis Bayeh was the man on the ground. He's more powerful than people give him credit [for].

Trevor Haken spoke about dealing with the pair: 'Bill Bayeh was the largest heroin and cocaine supplier in the Cross and I formed an arrangement with him to turn a blind eye to his operations and he supplied us with information and money. We used the information that he gave us to take out his competition.'

The Bayehs and their friend Fayez 'Frank' Hakim established a working relationship not only with the East Coast Milieu but also with government figures such as Sir Rex Jackson. Frank Hakim died aged seventy-four in January 2005. Known as 'Mr Fixit', he had come to Australia in 1952 and opened a delicatessen in Cleveland Street, Redfern, close to the old New South Wales Police Academy, which he supplied with rissoles. A way to police officers' hearts is often through their stomachs and as a deli owner Hakim made many friends as well as cultivating underworld acquaintances such as Louis Bayeh and the gambler 'Croc' Palmer. He once told Lennie McPherson, well down the pecking order of the Milieu, 'You are a flag and should be obeyed and should be respected'—which was a generous, if well-deserved, tribute.

Nevertheless, Hakim was able to both integrate and ingratiate himself so that he became an unofficial Godfather in the Lebanese community, offering (when needed) advice, help and introductions that would lead to withdrawn or reduced charges and consequently lighter sentences. Throughout the 1970s he was a Justice of the Peace, with the ability to sign warrants obtained by the New South Wales

Gaming Squad—something that gave him 'extraordinary power', said Barry Toomey QC in an Independent Commission Against Corruption (ICAC) inquiry of 1992.

Things went awry for Hakim in 1985 when his offices were raided and he was found to be in possession of a small amount of heroin. He claimed he had been framed but in 1987 he was fined $1000 both for the heroin and for possession of a sum of money suspected to have been illegally obtained.

There was worse to come because that year he became involved in a conspiracy to bribe the Minister for Corrective Services, Rex Frederick Jackson, to arrange early release for prisoners who were able to pay for the privilege. Jackson, who had a very serious gambling habit, was paid to arrange the release of Angelo Romeo, Tony Gioelle and Salvatore 'Sammy' Falvo who in 1982 had been sentenced to four years for growing marijuana plants. They were not due for parole until October 1983 but early in the year approaches were made—through racing identity and fixer for the underworld Keith Harris and the men's solicitor—for their early release. Much of the evidence was in the form of tape recordings, which showed the solicitor pressing the minister to act after telling Hakim (who had introduced the lawyer to Harris): 'The fuckin' goods were handed over. Results you know that, and I'm saying … it is not handed over without results.'

For his part Hakim received six years but he was released in 1989. Two years later he was convicted of a conspiracy to bribe a chief of detectives. Keith Harris, who for years managed to keep himself well out of the limelight, died in March 1991. Born in 1913 to wealthy parents and a successful businessman and horse owner, for his part he received a nine year sentence. Curiously his brother Neville had also been involved in an earlier prison scandal. In 1927 he had been sentenced to ten years with hard labour for a rape at Bondi. However, almost immediately, he was transferred to light duties on Tuncurry Prison Farm. In the ensuing political row, there were claims that his family had paid for the privilege and when the Lang government took office Neville was transferred back to Goulburn jail. As for Jackson, after his release he became the proprietor of a hot dog stall in Heathcote before a bad back forced him to hand over the business to his brother.

It was, however, the troubles of the Bayeh brothers during the 1990s that finally spelled the end of any interests, other than as landlords, that the East Coast Milieu and their immediate successors had in Kings Cross. From then on a very different breed of criminal took control of the decaying area. One Sydney detective recalls: 'I have never seen any intelligence with credibility that supported in any way Freeman, McPherson, Saffron's involvement in drugs. Their area of criminal activity was illegal gambling, prostitution, SP bookmaking, unlicensed alcohol.'

Not all would agree with that opinion but as the years passed the scene at Kings Cross changed noticeably for the worse. Lennie McPherson was no longer interested and left it to the Bayeh brothers. Now much of the Sydney drug trade took place in the area around Bill Bayeh's video and games parlours and 'shooting galleries' where for $6 addicts could rent a room for ten minutes in order to shoot up. It was thought that it was more effective for busy paramedics to go to the shooting galleries on Darlinghurst Road to treat any overdoses than to try to save lives on the street. The same Sydney detective remarked on the decline:

> What was once a wonderful bohemian environment became a cesspit of criminal activity revolving around heroin and property crime with assaults, robberies and break-ins to get money to buy heroin.
>
> Why not open premises as a pinball and pool hall or a second rate coffee shop for use as a commercial front to supply heroin? Legitimate business could not compete.

By the late 1980s the area had deteriorated into a sea of squalor. Now Chinese and other property investors had bought heavily into the area, owning buildings that were home for sex shops, erotic movie houses and shooting galleries. The Wood Royal Commission was told that, on the upper floors of one property in Darlinghurst Road, rooms could be let out as many as 200 times a day and prostitutes and their clients paid $10 a visit, with up to 150 visits a day. In 1989 there was a fire that killed six guests.

In the early 1990s Kings Cross was a Mecca for Korean gangs, one actually based in Korea and two in Sydney: the White Hawk Gang, the Kings Cross Gang and the Casino Gang, who were loan sharks and whose leader was seen in the Sydney Harbour Casino over 100 times in the first six months of 1997.

The Wood Royal Commission heard that another strip club, the Love Machine, run by Steve Stavrou, a Greek known as 'Skinny Steve', allowed its clients to pay for prostitutes on credit cards which he kindly put through as payments to Idemeno Clothing. His nickname distinguished him from Steve Armatas, 'Fat Steve', who told the commission he paid police monthly bribes of $2000.

In June 1990 Louis Bayeh was arrested outside a Kings Cross club and agreed to become an informant. Later he alleged that evidence had been fabricated and the charge against him was dismissed. He offered to give evidence to ICAC but the terms and conditions for his co-operation were set too high. In April 1993 he complained that a senior officer had taken out a contract on his life. Certainly on 12 July that year Louis Bayeh's home in Ermington, North West Sydney, was sprayed with bullets. He believed that it was done on the orders of Robert Daher, who at one time ran the Budget Hotel in the Cross. Two men were charged and later 'no-billed'. A police officer arranged to have a meal with Daher and Bayeh's other brother Joe at a restaurant, the Water's Edge. For the moment peace was restored.

Louis Bayeh's highest profile moment came when he gave evidence before the Wood Commission in 1995 claiming he had paid hundreds of thousands of dollars in bribes and naming the police officers involved. Two years later he was described by an acting judge as 'obese, illiterate, unable to find gainful employment, a hypochondriac, panic-stricken, of questionable morals and an author of his own misfortune'.

On 2 July 2000 Louis Bayeh was seriously injured in a shootout in the foyer of the El-Bardowny Restaurant in Narwee, south-west Sydney. Initially it was thought the incident had been part of a power struggle and detectives, following reports of threats in the hospital at Long Bay prison, investigated the possibility that a contract had been taken out on Bayeh. Perhaps disappointingly for aficionados, the shooting turned out to have been over a jacket. In January 2001, still suffering from his gunshot wounds, Bayeh pleaded guilty to standing over brothel owner Antoine Debruyne, beginning in October 1988. He also asked for a similar offence involving John Hundy to be taken into account.

According to Bayeh, over the years $180 000 had been shared with corrupt New South Wales Police officers. On 27 July Bayeh limped into the dock to receive sentences totalling three years with a minimum of two to be served. On 26 February 2002 he was acquitted of charges relating to the shooting and immediately after the hearing he was returned to prison to complete his sentence.

Louis Bayeh's explanation as to his wealth had been the usual one. His annual income of $36 000 was supplemented by his gambling winnings to such an extent that he was able to put $126 000 towards a $526 000 home in Gladesville. However, according to evidence given to the Royal Commission, Louis Bayeh acted as a standover man earning, with police protection, $20 000 a week.

Bill Bayeh and his successor Danny Karam had been keen to introduce heroin users to cocaine on the grounds that it was more profitable. By 2005 Bayeh could reflect from his cell that the use of cocaine was now rife among the general public and not simply the party-going rich. Under the Bayehs' regime things had been almost gentlemanly. As they faded, from then on things changed dramatically.

Karam, a former commando in the Lebanese Christian Army, had worked as a rigger after he migrated to Australia in 1983. He soon found drugs more profitable and his regular court attendances over the years included one when he was fined for possession of a pair of handcuffs that he explained were for sexual rather than criminal purposes. Now he ran DK's Boys, a gang that organised the supply of cocaine to their own street level runners but also stood over other dealers who paid them protection money known as 'rent', so that the competitor dealers could operate without fear of harassment in the form of robberies, beatings and shootings from DK's Boys. The rent collection business brought in around $30 000 per week.

DK's Boys were also encouraged to set up their own little networks of cocaine cappers, dealers and runners so long as 'rent' was paid up the line to Karam. In turn he was quite willing to cheat those with whom he dealt. On one occasion three submachine guns were obtained on his behalf but the vendor never received the promised $15 000. The gang was also early to recognise the benefit of mobile phones, regularly changing and swapping them to disrupt police surveillance.

It was in 1993, when Karam was said to be out of control and trying to feed a $1000 a day heroin habit, that he was slated to be the subject of an attack. It was arranged by the husband of a woman with whom he was having an affair and his shooting was designed as a lesson but not a fatal one. It went horribly wrong. Hired gunmen unfortunately went to the wrong address. Instead of Karam being shot in the legs at No. 50, on 23 February a sixty-year old citizen, Leslie Betcher, was shot by mistake in the stomach at No. 15 and died that night.

Shortly afterwards Karam was imprisoned for assault and he began to see if not The Light, at least that he needed to control his drug habit and he seems to have made efforts to do so. At the Wood Royal Commission he came out of the woodwork to talk about Kings Cross and his relationship with Bill Bayeh, with whom he had worked a version of the Murphy Game. Bayeh would find a client who wanted to buy drugs and Karam would then rob him. He was also earning $5000 for 'cleaning the streets' of any drug dealer who was not prepared to work for Bayeh. It was not clear why Karam decided to give evidence or why he gave evidence without taking a codename. If he had indeed seen The Light, it soon dimmed. He continued to lead his ten-strong gang, which was thought to have killed three innocent people in a drive-by shooting and to have carried out another twenty shootings over Sydney in a twelve-month period. The last had been a drive-by at the EP1 nightclub in Kings Cross when over fifty shots were fired.

DK's Boys included Michael Kanaan, Rabeeh Mawas, Wassim El-Assaad, Charlie Gea Gea and a number of others who were later given pseudonyms for their own protection. One of these, renamed Rossini, was close to Kanaan and the two of them were among those seriously dissatisfied with the boss. One thing a gang leader must do is keep his troops happy but Karam seems to have gone out of his way to foment trouble.

A select few members were provided by Karam with special 'inner group' gold rings with tiger heads, ruby eyes and a diamond mouth. A large D for Danny was stamped on each ring and inside the D the initial letter of the wearer's first name. Tellingly, the rings were not gifts; each wearer was asked to cough up $900 for the privilege. Karam's young acolytes Rossini and Kanaan were at one stage growing hydroponic marijuana at one of Karam's safe houses in Parramatta. On a couple of occasions, when crops were harvested and partially dried, Karam swooped in and took it all to his own Randwick home, refusing to share the proceeds.

Around 9.30 p.m. on 13 December 1998 Karam was executed outside a block of flats in Riley Street. When he left his Randwick home in his Toyota RAV4 to go to a meeting in Surry Hills four men were waiting for him. He was shot through the open window and at least five bullets hit him in the chest and body. The men ran away down Fitzroy Street to Central Station and, as they did so, another man ran over to the dying Karam and stole his wallet and mobile telephone. In his hurry he missed the 12-gauge pump-action shotgun on the back seat.

It took a little while to sort out just who had killed Karam and why. The answers, when they came, were that it was Michael Kanaan and other members of the gang, tired of doing the work while he took the profits. They were sentenced in 2002. By then the killers of the unfortunate Leslie Betcher had also been dealt with. On 18 December 1998, after three trials, John Leslie Baartman, the lookout, was sentenced to fifteen years' imprisonment. The gunman, Paul Thomas Crofts, had already pleaded guilty. The hit had paid only $1000.

Kanaan was in a wheelchair by the time he came to trial for Karam's murder. In December 1998 he was hit in the back and leg after shooting at police as he tried to escape when trapped in Rushcutters Bay. Constable Chris Patrech was shot in the wrist and Kanaan was hit seven times by another officer, Senior Constable John Fotopoulos. That little expedition caused a ruckus in the courts.

First, magistrate Pat O'Shane dismissed charges against him and Wassim El-Assaad, ruling that the police had no reason to chase them near Paddington's White City tennis complex, saying the police action had been 'stupid, reckless and foolhardy'. It was not a decision that appealed to the DPP Nick Cowdery and in a re-hearing on 16 December 1999 magistrate Michael Price said: 'It would be judicial naivety on the part of this court not to accept that the officer had been shot at, wounded, wounded to both the arm and thigh … a trauma that many might not survive.'

When he was shot and apprehended Kanaan had been looking for another of the more colourful Sydney identities, John Ibrahim. Ibrahim began his working life in Kings Cross as a driver cum bodyguard for Louis Bayeh, taking him to collect money from nightclubs, brothels and illegal casinos. In the early 1990s he became a part owner of The Tunnel nightclub in Kings Cross and was then briefly emotionally involved with a police officer, Wendy Hatfield. As the years passed he and his family became involved in more and more clubs in Oxford Street. At the Wood Royal Commission he was asked whether he was 'the new lifeblood of the drug industry in Kings Cross', something he cheerfully denied. The next year he was no-billed for murder.

For most of his life, after a teenage skirmish which earned him some criminal stripes, Ibrahim had retained a relatively clean bill of legal health. In 1997 he was charged with, but not convicted of, threatening a witness associated with the prosecution case of his brother Sam. By the late 1990s Ibrahim and his clan were well on their way to dominating the nightclub scene and in March 2001 he took over The Embassy nightclub from businessman Rene Rivkin and his then partner Joe Elcham.

In 2003 another Ibrahim brother, Michael, faced charges arising from the shooting of Pierre Malouf and his son Richard outside their Guildford home. The shooting occurred hours after another son, Roy Malouf, had been bashed by men with baseball bats. On 15 October, Roy and Richard Malouf were accosted at their kitchen joinery business by eight or more men wearing balaclavas and brandishing baseball bats. They were warned not to give evidence against Michael Ibrahim and the others and were attacked. The case against Michael was dismissed and, in his turn John Ibrahim was acquitted of threatening witnesses. After the case he told reporters that he had unfairly been branded a criminal.

In October 2004 John Ibrahim again faced charges relating to threats to a witness. At the bail hearing on 21 October 2004 police made submissions opposing bail which described him as a 'major organised crime figure' who had been the subject of no less than '546 police intelligence reports in relation to his involvement in drugs, organised crime and association with outlaw motorcycle gangs'. He was said to have a 'team of henchmen' at his beck and call. Bail was granted.

While the Bayehs and their associates were street level dealers and a couple of ranks above, drug transportation had become truly interstate by the late 1980s. On 19 October 1989 the Malkoun brothers Amad (known as Joey) and Elie pleaded guilty to dealing in $5.5 million worth of heroin, then the largest amount ever to come before a Victorian court. Their team had been betrayed by their former associate John Rajac, who agreed to co-operate with the authorities in return for a lighter sentence. As a result there were audio and visual recordings of deals taking place in a variety of places, including a playground opposite Pentridge prison.

Their dealing came to an end when two couriers, Alex Marotta and Robert Clare, were followed as they drove across the Nullarbor to deliver 1.3 kilograms of heroin to Amad Malkoun's nightclub Zuzu's in Northbridge, Perth. Malkoun was arrested at the club on 18 February. He and his brother had come to Australia in 1969 and had grown up in Melbourne. Both were keen bodybuilders and became nightclub bouncers, which introduced them to the drug trade. Despite Zuzu's books showing that the club was barely making a profit, Amad had a fine lifestyle with a mansion home, a $90 000 cabin cruiser, a variety of other properties and a share in the Whiskey au Go-Go, another nightclub in Rockingham, south of Perth. The brothers pleaded guilty and Judge John Howse, sentencing them to eighteen years with sixteen to be served, commented: 'The case presents a frightening degree of saturation of the Australian community with drugs. If it is not stopped, it will destroy our community and its culture.'

* * *

It is, perhaps, the Vietnamese who have had the highest profile in the rise of ethnic minority crime in Australia. The Vietnam War had an enormous impact on the demand and supply for drugs. Huge numbers of immigrants and refugees headed south and east from Vietnam, some waiting for years in Hong Kong refugee camps before admission to Australia.

Most of these post-1974 immigrants were hardworking people seeking a better life for their children. Naturally disguised in the crowd came many criminals and ambitious gang wannabes. Vietnamese refugees, including unaccompanied children, were initially placed in a camp at Villawood from where it was a short walk to Cabramatta, once the home of Italians, Irish and Yugoslavs but soon to be colonised by the new arrivals.

By the mid- to late 1980s there was some evidence of growth in Australia of organised criminal activity by Vietnamese. The *Sydney Morning Herald* of 2 January 1988 commented: 'Criminal gangs in the Vietnamese community are increasingly heavily armed, are moving into drugs and gambling, establishing links with Australian crime figures, and becoming involved in standover rackets in their own community.'

Lebanese gangs such as DK's Boys may have roamed Sydney, but they took care to avoid Cabramatta, of whose youth gangs the 5T has been the most recognised and vicious. The name 5T can stand just about any interpretation, with the most popular suggestion being that it comes from five Vietnamese words beginning with 't', meaning 'love, money, prison, death and conviction' or alternatively 'young people lack love and care'. Whatever the derivation, the gang employed the age-old rackets of any burgeoning community. Restaurant owners holding a wedding party would be asked, 'Can you give me $500 or there will be trouble on the wedding night?' This gang and others opened or controlled illegal gaming clubs and forced shopkeepers to install their poker machines. The money was recycled into the importation of prostitutes and drugs. In its heyday the gang was also seen as prepared to thumb its nose at the law. In 1994 it was said to have stolen all the Ts from the Cabramatta Police Station sign. 5T business developed from distributing heroin to importing high quality South-East Asian heroin which was 65 to 75 per cent pure. This trumped anything else on the market, was dangerously attractive to users and increased profits to down-the-line distributors. The Vietnamese networks were able to sidestep the Chinese bulk importers who had initially used them as distributors as well as to eliminate the middlemen. It was vertical integration exemplified.

The 5T enforced a prohibition on senior gang members injecting heroin but not on smoking it. They and other gangs provided what some sociologists saw as a family for youths, often from single-parent families. They clothed members, fed them, found girls and drugs for them and in return demanded loyalty and obedience. In 1992 two youths were killed because they had upset the 5T. One was beaten to death and a second, Duong Van Chu, was shot, a killing said to be witnessed by 200 people.

By the mid-1990s, there was a police crackdown, prompted by a huge increase in heroin overdoses and the 1994 murder of the federal MP John Newman. Police had mounted Task Force Coltsfoot and Operation Morrel and in 1994 there were 620 arrests and 897 indictable charges laid.

The 5T leader, Tri Minh Tran, was murdered on 9 August 1995 at the age of twenty, shot when he opened his front door in McBurney Road, Cabramatta. Bullets went through his hands into his nose and face. A second member of the 5T, Than Hao Nguyen, was shot twice in the face and head and twice in the stomach. A third, Hieu Dinh Trinh, who was asleep on the sofa and was shot in the thigh, survived when a bullet bounced off his belt buckle.

At the age of eleven Tran, who came from a relatively wealthy family, had spent six months in a children's institution after being found with a sawn-off rifle. It was thought that at the age of thirteen he killed two rivals, one with a machete and the other with a gun.

In October 1992 he was part of the crew that shot and killed Nghai Minh Hong of the Tuong Hai gang. Over the previous two years there had been shooting incidents between the rivals and after one, outside the Sweethearts Restaurant at the beginning of the month, Nghai Minh Hong went to Perth. He did not stay long enough and on his return to Sydney was involved in another incident at the Beyond 2000 disco. This time he was chased and shot on a stairway. The teenage Tran was acquitted. The same year he threatened his teacher with a machete. It was also said he had turned down the contract on Newman. At the time of his death the police estimated there were about forty 5T members and 100 wannabees.

Reprisals for Tran's killing came on 30 September when the 5T shot at least seven breakaway members outside the Jadran Hadjuk, a Croatian club at Bonnyrigg, which was holding a Vietnamese fashion show. No one was killed. Just as the Dockers had failed to notice the killing of Freddie Harrison some 280 patrons claimed they were in the four lavatories at 11.30 p.m. when the shooting took place. On 24 October *The Sydney Morning Herald* thought that if this was really the case the club should seriously consider changing its caterers.

As a result the gang splintered and, as with the Hydra's head, after 5T was cut back, new groups—including The Four Aces, the Black and Red Dragon gangs and the Madonna Boys—came into existence. Where there was one, now there were many. The prohibition against gang members injecting broke down, resulting in increased drug addiction and anarchy as the smaller gangs struggled for money and markets.

By the end of the twentieth century Sydney was recognised as the national gateway for the majority of illegal imports, and Cabramatta had been targeted as the centre for distribution, sale and purchase of drugs. There, 68 per cent of the population had been born in a non-English speaking country and 69 per cent spoke a language other than English at home.

One theory of crime control is that it should start at the bottom. Most of the drug houses were on premises next to the railway. They were, of course, like drug houses the world over—filthy with decaying food, no beds, littered with syringes, but equipped with state of the art televisions, stereos and play stations to entertain the waiting dealers.

So a 'Clean-Up Cabramatta' campaign began on 1 July 2001 and by the next year *A Report of Progress* detailed seventy-five drug houses eliminated, 532 charges of illegal firearm trafficking in New South Wales, and 209 people facing a total of 288 supply charges.

That has, of course, still left the nationwide Mr (and occasionally Mrs) Bigs. One early Mr Big Enough who imported his expertise and networking ability to Australia was Van Thanh Huynh. By the late 1980s Huynh, who lived in Sydney with his wife and three children, was boasting to friends about how he could make a million dollars with a kilogram of heroin, adding sugar to it for on-selling. Around this time, pure heroin was selling for at least $7000 an ounce.

Huynh, who spoke both Vietnamese and Cantonese, surrounded himself with a number of what he called 'disciples' most of whom were Vietnamese. He was also doing serious heroin business with at least one Chinese. At the peak of his heroin trafficking gang activity, Huynh claimed he was making $300 000 a month, after expenses 'while I sleep', with 'people to handle everything for me' and without supplying the up-front capital. Others supplied the cash and Huynh split his profits with them. In his thirties, he was highly placed in the racket hierarchy and spoke about his many underlings who on occasion respectfully called him 'paternal grandfather'. He held himself out as an expert in the game, reminiscing about his drug trafficking and other criminal activities back home in Vietnam and badmouthing fellow Vietnamese traffickers who were stupid enough to get themselves arrested.

Huynh was a braggart and a chatterbox, which was his eventual undoing. In late 1989 an extensive surveillance operation was mounted which included monitoring of the gang's various premises and movements. The most damning evidence came from secretly recorded conversations. Some months later, Huynh and his gang were hit with a number of charges of conspiracy to traffic heroin. Predictably he showed neither emotion nor remorse and was sentenced to a total term of twenty-four years.

In the mid-1990s London-based Hong Phuc Truong headed up an international network of Vietnamese criminals working across three continents. In February 1996 Hong, using an alias, flew into Melbourne from Hong Kong to rope in new gang recruits of Vietnamese origin. He planned to bring in a huge heroin shipment and needed assistance in Australia to get the profits out of the country. First, he enlisted his older sister Truong Thi Van, from Springvale in Melbourne's south-east. Mrs Van had a wealthy friend Ha Que Thi Mai who ran a successful clothing and footwear import/export business. Hong met Mrs Ha and asked her to help him both by transferring $400 000 cash overseas for him and using her consignments of clothing to stash and send in the heroin. Mrs Ha was reluctant but Hong became increasingly insistent that she help him, making it clear her family could face unfortunate consequences if she did not.

At the end of March, Hong went to Hong Kong from where he telephoned Mrs Ha saying if she refused to help, she would then have to pay $400 000 for protection because now she knew of Hong's trafficking. His sister also applied pressure and eventually Mrs Ha buckled to the extent that she was prepared to pay $20 000 to Mrs Van for Hong's use. The pressure continued into April as Mrs Ha was told more money was required.

Around this time, Hong's sister rented a house in Glendale Road, Springvale. At the same time two of Hong's Vietnamese thugs, the brothers Bui, who had been living in the United States, flew in to Australia. On 29 April 1996 two men matching their description kidnapped Mrs Ha's 21-year-old son Le Anh Tuan. He was first assaulted both inside and outside his Glen Waverley house, then thrown into the boot of a green Toyota and driven off to the Glendale Road house. A ransom note was found demanding that Mrs Ha pay the money within seventy-two hours.

In the days following the kidnap Hong continued with his long distance threats to Mrs Ha, but promised he could save her son if she would pay the $400 000. Desperate, Mrs Ha arranged to make the ransom drop at Spencer Street bus depot on 4 May. Four collectors turned up, but they twigged that officers had them under surveillance. The police were obliged to change plans and arrest the four men, rather than merely follow them.

On 7 June 1996 Le Anh's body was found in a drain aqueduct not far from Glendale Road. He had been shot in the head on or shortly after 3 May. Following police investigations, Hong was charged with murder, kidnapping, blackmail and threats to kill Mrs Ha along with charges relating to importation of heroin. By this time he was in London. He was extradited, tried and sentenced to nearly twenty-four years before being eligible for parole. One barrister recalls him: 'He was personable, respectful, not rude or demanding. But he was obviously more powerful and above all the others mentioned in the case. He was 1000 per cent classier than the usual drug-trafficking Viets.' As for the Bui brothers, they had fled the country and one is reported to have been killed in Vietnam.

Australian lawyers regard some of their Vietnamese clients as difficult to deal with. They are gamblers who make money from heroin dealing and then blow it away in the casinos. Duong Van Ia, known as 'Uncle Six' because he was the sixth of eight brothers, had a small barbecue shop as well as a butcher's. Commercially the food businesses were successful but in no way could they support his gambling.

When Duong was banned from Sydney Harbour Casino by Commissioner Peter Ryan—he had turned over $96 million in a six month period in 1996—the Casino Control Authority Chairman Kaye Loder said she was sorry to see the money go out of New South Wales. Her remarks created an immediate furore and she promptly resigned. Duong led an adventurous life. On one occasion he and his mistress, a dancer known as 'Miss Kim', were returning from a casino when they were the target of a robbery and attempted kidnap. He handed over $35000 in chips and cash while Miss Kim was taken hostage and ransomed for $200000. After fifteen hours he went to meet the kidnappers and the police were on hand to arrest them.

A multicultural casino based gang, this time in Melbourne, was busy in 1999 operating from an hotel room at the city's Crown Casino. Vinh Lac Lao, a Cantonese-speaking Hong Kong resident, obtained the heroin from mainland China and brought the shipments from Sydney. Casino high roller Ko Kon Tong, the lynch-pin of the group, was also staying there compliments of the management. Tong was assisted by his acolytes Lisa Vuong and Dat Thinh Ong, a Melbourne couple who fundraised, located wholesale purchasers, collected and distributed. Lower down the chain was Thanh Hung Nguyen, Tong's largest wholesaler. The money went up from Nguyen and the heroin came down to Nguyen. Both ways Tong profited. On one occasion Lao brought twenty blocks of heroin from Sydney. They stashed it in the boot of a car and parked, overlooked by Lao's hotel room. All was set for the exchange but for the fact that police had recorded telephone and face-to-face conversations in Cantonese and Vietnamese and were ready to pounce. At 6 p.m. on 3 August 1999, NCA investigators opened the car boot and Tong, Ong and Vuong were arrested within the hour. Lao's room was searched. Nguyen was arrested a couple of days later but Lao had skedaddled and was picked up a month later at Sydney Airport. Tong, as ringleader, received a minimum of twelve years for his pivotal role.

Another of the big heroin dealers of the period in Sydney was Chinese born Duncan Lam, known as 'Big Nose Cheung'. He ran the Golden Kingdom in Kensington as a cover for his heroin dealing. In 1985 he was seen delivering ceramic plates, which were found to contain heroin, to a motel in Randwick. This time he was acquitted but the end came in 1999 when he was found with $40 million in the boot of his car. He received a twelve year sentence.

* * *

Some see a direct connection between the expansion of casinos and the burgeoning of the drug trade so far as the ethnic dealers are concerned. One former detective sees a causal link between international casino gambling and a required explosion in the need to sell larger amounts of drugs more frequently:

> Before the advent of legal casinos compulsive Asian gamblers went to illegal casinos to gamble $5000 or $10 000. And that was substantial money. To cover the costs they would sell one or two kilos of heroin. With legal casinos a gambler can drop $1 million in a week or even a night and to cover those losses it is no longer enough to sell one or two kilos. They have to sell five or ten on a continuing basis.

The drug dealers may make hundreds of thousands but it never sees their lawyers' trouser pockets for they are almost always defended on legal aid. Lawyers say that Vietnamese clients charged with trafficking are quite shamelessly liable to change their story in mid-case and along with it their barristers and solicitors. They are regarded, possibly because of family ties and possibly because of the fear of retribution, as being extremely loyal to one another.

In the first years of the twenty-first century it was thought there were some fourteen bulk heroin importers resident in Australia. Victoria Police intelligence estimates there are now at least 10 000 Asian criminals in Melbourne; several hundred are believed to be active Triad members. In Queensland, Vietnamese heroin gangs operate as satellites for their friends and relations in Sydney with half a dozen families running operations in and around Inala and Darra. As the family grows, tentacles spread to include siblings and in-laws. On one occasion an ex-wife has been found co-operating happily with her replacement.

A shake and shootout in May 1999 in what was called the Mother's Day Massacre left Sun Trung Luu dead on the floor of the lavatory of the West End Cypriot Club in Inala. Two years earlier the civic centre at Inala was Queensland's equivalent of the railway station at Cabramatta. Luu had earlier been involved in the savage beating of a pawnbroker from whom he and friends tried to steal a ring in 1998. When the shopkeeper protested he was knocked to the ground and stripped. But he managed to reach the licensed Glock pistol that he held for his own protection and fired a round. His attackers vanished. Another of the team was found dead in Ipswich in 1999. He had been bound, beaten, strangled and then thrown off a cliff with a plastic bag over his head.

The teenager who killed Luu was eighteen-year-old Sydney-based Thi Dinh Nguyen, found in 2000 with a $100 000 block of white rock heroin under the passenger seat of his car. He pleaded guilty to Luu's manslaughter and received nine years as well as a five year sentence for the heroin. He claimed that there had been a quarrel with Luu and his mates, who had begun to attack his friend. He had fired a shot in an effort to frighten them off but unfortunately it had hit Luu.

With closer ties with Asian and other police forces over the years, there has been an increasing number of seizures of substantial amounts of hard drugs in Australia. In October 2002, 357 kilograms of heroin bound for Australia were intercepted in Suva, Fiji. One of the last big hauls of cocaine in Western Australia took place in July 2001 when 938 kilograms were seized. Two Americans and three Colombians were arrested and received sentences of between twenty-five years and life. A somewhat smaller but still significant seizure came in August 2003 when 317 kilograms were impounded in Adelaide.

In March 2003 one Chi Hung So appeared for sentence in his part in the importation of 80 kilograms of amphetamines and 184 kilograms of heroin with a total street value of up to $100 million. The reduction in the availability of heroin had a knock-on effect. Until then addicts had been stealing cars to get themselves to Cabramatta, but now car thefts and robberies were down.

The same year the authorities captured a North Korean freighter, the Tuvalu-registered *Pong Su*, which was seized carrying 135 kilograms of heroin when it anchored off the south-west Victorian town of

Lorne on 16 April. Four men pleaded guilty to helping to smuggle a commercial quantity of heroin into Australia but in 2006 the captain and three officers were acquitted. There were plans for the vessel to be broken up.

That, however, was the tip of the iceberg. Large hauls were no longer necessarily fashionable and entrepreneurs were also bringing in smaller parcels or even sending them by post or air cargo. Couriers were bringing in cocaine hidden in such varying devices as a door and cans of fruit and vegetables. One haul in 2003 found 750 kilograms of pseudoephedrine packed to resemble Plaster of Paris ornaments. The drugs had a potential street value of $1.4 billion. There was another success the next month when $24 million of heroin was seized at Port Botany found in fish paste from Cambodia and destined for a seafood company in Sydney's inner west. Four months later an Australian and four Cambodian men appeared in a Phnom Penh magistrates' court charged with exporting 24 kilograms of heroin to Australia.

In 2005 some progress continued to be made with halting major international drug deals when a man described as a criminal 'head honcho' of a new East Coast Milieu was arrested. It followed a five month investigation, known as Operation Mocha, involving the alleged co-operation of baggage handlers in smuggling drugs through Sydney airport. The haul had been loaded last on an Aerolineas Argentinas flight from South America. As a result it would be unloaded first and could be removed before it reached the baggage hall in Sydney on 8 October 2004.

In 2004–05 the Australian Crime Commission managed to dismantle twenty criminal syndicates and seized drugs with an estimated street value of $66.6 million, up from $19.9 million in the 2003–04 seizures. Operation Katakan had broken up a drug trafficking gang operating in Melbourne and Brisbane while Operation Schumaker had seized 800 000 ecstasy tablets and obtained restraining orders in respect of $2.3 million arising from proceeds of crime.

In early October 2006 police smashed an alleged $93 million drug trafficking and money laundering racket among Vietnamese communities in Sydney and Melbourne. Three weeks later the police found evidence of the continuing creativity of drug smugglers in an AFP/Customs operation. Metal pods chained to the hulls of incoming ships were found to contain cocaine from South America worth millions of dollars.

Bikers

14

On 11 May 2006, 39-year-old Russell Merrick Oldham shot himself as he stood knee deep in the sea at Sydney's Balmoral beach. Once considered a potential doctor, Oldham had taken another path as a violent member and office bearer of the downtown Bandidos. Jailed for manslaughter and released in 2003, Oldham was furious that a former friend, now rival, Rodney Monk had been elevated to Bandidos Downtown president and was intending to expel Oldham on suspicion of disloyalty. Monk had links with the powerful Sydney Nomads and this complicated his life when 29-year-old Milad Sande, an associate of both the Bandidos and the Nomads, was shot dead in November 2005 while delivering $2 million worth of pseudoephedrine to other Bandidos. The buyers, who had ripped off Sande, then endured weeks of painful and expensive payback at the hands of the Nomads.

In east Sydney's Bar Reggio on 20 April 2006, the Bandidos' internal battles boiled over and Rodney Monk was first embraced and then killed by Oldham with a shot to the head. It was thought by friends that Oldham, in hiding for three weeks, had no choice but to 'top himself' to avoid further painful retaliation.

Two months earlier, on a Saturday night in February 2006, one of half a dozen bearded men told a bouncer at the Sapphire Suite in Sydney's Kings Cross that they were Hells Angels. The bouncer made the mistake of refusing them admittance and was promptly shot in the leg. A woman in the queue was grazed with a bullet.

On 16 March 2006 a second shooting occurred, outside the Men's Gallery club in Pitt Street. Police alleged that that the victim was a member of the Nomads who had been shot by a former member of the Finks who had recently defected to the Angels. Police suspected that the shooting was a way of announcing that the Angels were back in town, sizing up the city for control of its highly profitable amphetamine trade. 'The Big Red Machine wants to roll into town', *The Sydney Morning Herald* reported on 21 April.

The resurgence in biker gang violence in 2006 and significant increase in gang chapters across the country prompted the Australian Crime Commission to set up a new task force in January 2007. Nationally it will examine the involvement of motorcycle gangs in drug trafficking, prostitution and money laundering, along with the possibility of motorcycle gangs selling weapons to terrorists.

The first and best known of the outlaw motorcycle gangs, the Hells Angels were founded by disaffected World War II veterans in 1947 in Fontana, a depressingly dull steel town outside Los Angeles. One gang of ex-soldiers travelled as a bunch of motorcyclists around California becoming known as the Pissed Off Bastards of Bloomington (POBOB). On 4 July, Independence Day, they rallied at Hollister, a backwoods small town. Fighting broke out with the townsfolk, leaving fifty citizens injured and, following the call-out of the state's Highway Patrol, nearly 100 bikers in prison. Two months later a ride into Riverside on the Labor Day weekend brought similar havoc when 6000 bikers turned up. Until then motorcycle rallies had been orderly events sanctioned by the American Motorcycle Association. Now, the 'Outlaw' bikers were banned. The Angels liked to refer to themselves as the One Per Cent, distinguishing them from the well-mannered 99 per cent of motorcyclists in the United States.

It was only a matter of time before other organisations across the United States applied to join the Angels. Almost immediately rival gangs such as the Outlaws, the Rebels and the Bandidos were formed and over the years chapters developed worldwide. Some writers put a Hells Angels chapter in Sydney as early as 1967 but the group was officially inaugurated in Melbourne and Sydney on 23 August 1973. The Rebels, with the biggest membership, had come to Sydney in 1969 and by the 1970s were at war with the Angels. The Finks were founded in Sydney in 1969, probably as a Hells Angels' offshoot.

Superintendent Fred Gere of the Western Australia Police, who has studied outlaw motorcycle gangs (OMCGs) for three decades, argues that biker gangs have evolved into worldwide organised crime syndications which in some ways (such as their global links) have even surpassed the Mafia. 'Like the Mafia, clubs have loyalty links back to the mother chapter and involvement in both high profile legitimate business and illegal global operations, such as prostitution and narcotics trafficking.'

Predictably, given their origins, the motorcycle gangs follow a military structure. Rules, regulations and orders are ruthlessly enforced and immediate obedience is expected from an inferior. Disobedience is dealt with harshly and privileges are earned from adherence to the gang's code over time. Recruits must be introduced or sponsored by an existing member and must pass tests and prove themselves over probationary periods. At the top of the pecking order are the president, vice-president, enforcer or sergeant-at-arms and road captain. Then come the fully patched or proven members, probationary members and those who simply hang around, hoping perhaps for eventual acceptance. Probationary members are required to do menial tasks around the club house and are matched in fights for the entertainment of the members. As tests of strength, buttons may be sewn on bare chests. Wannabes are also often required to undertake some major criminal activity which will bind them to the gang.

The club mottos are not for the faint-hearted: 'Three can keep a secret if two are dead,' say the Hells Angels. The Outlaws boast, 'God forgives—Outlaws don't!' The Bandidos, founded in Texas in 1966 (hence their Tex-Mex name), have a catchy motto: 'We are the people our parents warned us about' and the Mongols enjoin, 'Respect few— fear none!'

Today, Australia has chapters of the big four clubs—the Hells Angels, the Outlaws, the Bandidos and the Pagans—as well as the Coffin Cheaters, Gypsy Jokers, Nomads, Rebels and Finks. The Hells Angels spawned the Gypsy Jokers in Western Australia, who then came east, founding the Fourth Reich in Wollongong and later the Black Uhlans in Brisbane and Melbourne. The Comancheros have two chapters in Sydney and one in Brisbane. The lesser known Finks are a Gold Coast biker gang which took its name from the comic strip the Wizard of Id—'The King is a Fink'. They have a reputation for being the most multicultural of gangs, with both Christian and Muslim members, and also for being one of the most 'righteous', tending to finish a conflict with a show of force. After one Finks member had been badly beaten, a mass raid on the Hells Angels HQ in Mascot took place on 25 November 1972. In the fracas Angel Frederick Celovic was shot three times. Seven Finks were charged with the attack and Ralph Moran received life imprisonment for Celovic's murder.

Estimating the number of OMCG members is not easy. There is, of course, a high attrition rate—death, motorcycle accidents, drugs and arrests all take their toll. In 2003, Professor Arthur Veno of Monash University, author of *The Brotherhoods*, put the total number at between 2000 and 3000, down from 8000 in 1980. Recent Australian Crime Commission intelligence puts the number at 3500 fully patched members spread over thirty-five clubs plus many more associates and nominees. Twenty-six new chapters are said to have been opened by ten biker gangs in the last eighteen months. Other estimates are even higher: the Rebels, said to be Australia's largest gang, may have as many as 2000 members. Standards of entry to the Rebels—with a probation period of only three to six months compared with years for the Angels or Gypsy Jokers—are regarded as lax by other gangs. The Nomads and Bandidos compete for second place in terms of size, while the Finks and Comancheros come next, ahead of the Gypsy Jokers and the Hells Angels. In 2006 the Angels chapter in Melbourne was thought to be only thirty strong, with more probationers than actual members.

Over the years there have been countless small OMCGs, including the Galloping Gooses, God's Garbage, the Gladiators, the Brothers and Western Australia's Club Deroes. In the mid-1990s the police believed that internal efforts were being made to reduce the number of OMCGs in Australia to a maximum of six. Smaller gangs were to be taken over and subsumed or eliminated by force. The aim, as alleged by police but denied by the gangs, was to limit and control the amount of competition in illicit drugs. Some amalgamations were friendly takeovers, some were coercive, and serious turf warfare erupted. Certainly some smaller gangs were compulsorily absorbed—Satan's Cavalry were taken over by the Coffin Cheaters—but others such as the CUNTs fought off the Rebels in 1997.

Club Deroes also survived a 1998 feud with the Coffin Cheaters when Cheater Marc Chabrière was gunned down in Welshpool, Western Australia. The smaller club was back in the news in January 2006 when its president, Phillip William Rowles, was charged following a raid on his property at High Wycombe, Western Australia. Police, alleging they found cash, amphetamine production apparatus and shotgun ammunition, applied to freeze Rowles's assets, said to be worth $1.2 million. By February 2007 no date had been set for the trial and Rowles had not entered a plea.

* * *

In the early 1980s OMCG interclub rivalry reached a high with the notorious Milperra battle between the Bandidos and the Comancheros, originally another Texas-based club ruled in military fashion by William 'Jock' Ross. In 1983 Anthony Mark 'Snodgrass' Spencer formed the Bandidos in a movement to break away from the Comancheros. It was clear that there was bad blood between the groups and from then on the Bandidos became a predominantly New South Wales based club. Soon relations, which had always been fragile, completely broke down. On 11 August 1984 the Comancheros barricaded their clubhouse and put an armed sentry on the roof. In their turn the Bandidos posted guards.

On 2 September 1984 the Comanchero and Bandidos members decided to meet at the satellite town of Milperra on Sydney's wild west for a full-on confrontation. The venue was the car park of the Viking Hotel where a swap meet of around 1000 motorcycle enthusiasts was being held. At the end of the twelve minute gun battle, twenty people had been injured and seven killed, including four Comancheros, two Bandidos and a fourteen-year-old girl, Leanne Walters, who was caught in the cross-fire. The police charged forty-three men with the murders and associated offences. Before the trial, charges were dropped against eleven, one of whom, Bernard Podgorski, turned queen's evidence.

The trial of eighteen Bandidos and thirteen Comancheros before Mr Justice Adrian Roden lasted 332 days and cost about $12 million. On 28 April 1986 nine were found guilty of seven counts of murder and twenty-one of manslaughter. One was found guilty only of affray. Snodgrass Spencer later killed himself in prison.

The Milperra Massacre may be the best known Biker horror story in Australia but for sheer planned savagery an attack by members of the Coffin Cheaters on another gang, the Resurrected, in Morwell, Victoria, a decade earlier puts it firmly in the shade. The conflict started at a 1976 meeting at a hotel in Melbourne's bayside suburb of Hampton when the Coffin Cheaters attempted to stand over the Resurrected, first by demanding a $10 a head levy per member and secondly by demanding that they should change their name. Neither suggestion appealed to the representatives of the Resurrected and as they set off on their return journey to their clubhouse the vice-president of the Coffin Cheaters, Scurvy Stephens, appeared to try to force some of the bikers off the road. In fact, all he succeeded in doing was killing his passenger, the club's president, Shades Marshall. Stephens in turn became president and, in a curious and twisted way, blamed the Resurrected members for Marshall's death.

On 5 November, a few months later, Stephens and a number of other Coffin Cheaters rode for revenge. They attacked Glenn 'Pig' Harrison at his home in the presence of his girlfriend. When he answered a knock on the door he was knocked down and his clothes were cut off him. Cigarettes were stubbed out on him, pigs eyes were stuffed into his mouth and the spike of a German World War I pickelhaube was rammed into his anus. One biker defecated on him. His girlfriend was raped, both as a punishment and to make her divulge the address of other members of the Resurrected. When the Coffin Cheaters left her, she telephoned other Resurrected members to tell them they were on their way. By the time the Cheaters arrived at the home of Terrence 'Dactyl' Coady, their targets had barricaded themselves inside. They were still savagely beaten but one of the girls in the house managed to shoot Gorilla Snot Stevenson and the bullet passed through him into the side of Stephens. When the police arrived they handcuffed Stephens to a lamppost while they tried to sort things out and an hour later he told them he had been shot, showing them a gaping wound in his side.

In March 1977 Judge Leo Lazarus sentenced Stephens to a minimum of ten years, and five others to lesser terms. Two were acquitted. Sentencing them, Lazarus commented on biker clubs:

> They dehumanise their members and those with whom they associate, they enshrine sacrosanct rules and customs, a code of conduct which is at its best puerile and at its worst bestial, degrading and depraved in the extreme. Their attitude towards women and girls is at least as vicious and despicable as that of any cult, past or present, of which I am aware.

It is hard to please everybody. Two days after sentencing, a police motorcycle club criticised Lazarus for generalising and the Auto Cycle

Union of Victoria demanded an apology for his comments. As for the Resurrected, they disbanded. The Coffin Cheaters have gone from strength to strength.

* * *

In 2003 it was estimated that biker gangs controlled 75 per cent of the Australian methamphetamine trade, with one in five clandestine laboratories directly linked to OMCGs. Other laboratories are suspected of being run on the gangs' behalf. They are also involved in cannabis dealing, vehicle theft, car rebirthing, currency counterfeiting and fraud. There is evidence that gangs—or some of their members—run guns and prostitutes, stand over bars and work as contract killers.

Some bikers, such as Dr John Smith of God's Squad, whose ordained members marry, christen and bury bikers and their families, deny gang members are the mass criminals they're painted by authorities and the media to be:

> there are some real myths ... and to say this is some huge massive organised mafia is simply untrue ... The bike clubs are a strange mixture between medieval pageantry and partly a blokey thing, 'you insult my woman and you better get on your horse, grab your lance and we'll have it out' ... but there just isn't one size fits all ...

Arthur Veno has pointed out that, while individual club members have been found guilty of manufacture and distribution of illegal drugs, there has never been a successful prosecution of a biker club in Australia. But given that a chapter may consist of barely a dozen members, of whom half may be involved in drugs, this fact makes little difference.

In 2003 a Hunter Valley amphetamine network of over twenty people linked to the Nomads came before the courts in the New South Wales city of Newcastle. Club members got their methyl amphetamines from a couple of Nomads, including Johnny Skyrus who cut and distributed the drug. Richard James Walsh, who had joined the Newcastle Nomads in 1995, then began to help with distribution. When in 1997 Skyrus was killed in a motorcycle accident Walsh moved into his position as cutter and distributor, obtaining supplies from Queensland. Walsh soon after became the Newcastle Nomads' sergeant-at-arms.

Walsh and his de facto Melinda Love enlisted the assistance of dozens of others to help cut the drug or act as couriers or distributors.

His new manufacturer from 1999 was Todd Douglas Little, who lived eight hours' drive north of Newcastle and had methyl amphetamine labs set up in Murwillumbah which had earned him an estimated $2.5 million. Between March 1997 and September 2001, Walsh admitted purchasing 50 kilograms (110 pounds) of around 77 per cent pure methyl amphetamine for around $50000 to $60000 per pound. After cutting it with other compounds, Walsh distributed about 450 kilograms of the drug to some seventy-five Nomad members and associates. To put the size of this operation in perspective, one kilogram qualifies as a 'large commercial quantity'. Walsh was also in the business of stealing trucks to harvest their parts, and also rebirthing vehicles used in his construction work as a concreter. Both Walsh and Little had caches of firearms including machine guns and silencers. Walsh's cleaner, Anne Chapman, and her husband, Paul, also got in on Walsh's business, as lab tester and courier respectively, but following a dispute Paul Chapman lost his position. He and Melinda Love later became indemnified witnesses. The courts that heard the various cases were extremely conscious that 'a number of persons who were otherwise law-abiding citizens in the community became entangled in Mr Walsh's enterprise and as a consequence have committed criminal offences'.

Walsh and Little pleaded guilty to the drugs and firearms offences and were sentenced in 2005. Walsh received thirty-two years with a minimum of twenty-four and Little twenty-two years with a minimum of sixteen and a half.

Judges and juries are invariably concerned when biker gangs recruit cleanskins into their illicit transactions in order to avoid trouble themselves. One former associate of the Coffin Cheaters, who he says 'make Hells Angels look mild mannered', recalls:

> Some years back the Cheaters got me and some other young surfies to move around forty garbage bags full of cannabis for them through WA. They'd chosen us and the van carefully and I suppose we were pretty pleased that they trusted us with their gear to go off on our own.
>
> We got pretty stern instructions on how to avoid the coppers: no alcohol or drugs, no speeding, nothing to draw attention. Off we went, not a Cheater in sight. Then I suppose we relaxed too much and I started speeding near a small town. The only cop car in the place is now on our tail. I accelerated. He accelerated. All I could hear was a rumble in the distance. Then the rumble turns into a roar and there

in the side mirror I can see a Coffin Cheater on a Harley cutting in front of the cops and giving the finger and kicking off his mirror.

That's it. He's lost interest in me and our clapped-out panel van and he's off after a real honest-to-God bad guy, sirens blaring.

When we delivered, a huge, patched rider comes up and says, 'You owe me a hundred bucks. That's what that bastard copper fined me.' I couldn't get the money out fast enough.

Gang members have certainly been used as contract killers, with varying degrees of success. One such job in 1997 was sloppily executed: Jane Thurgood-Dove, a Niddrie housewife, was chased and shot in front of her children at her home by Rebels biker Steven John Moody. The true target of the hit was another blonde woman in the same street and Moody, who later died of a drug overdose, had mistaken his quarry.

Another unsuccessful attempted contract killing was revealed to be drug related when the Australian Institute of Criminology published *Contract Killings in Australia* over a decade after the event. Two men, one a member of a biker gang, arrived to inspect a boat for sale. The shipwright, when asked for a test run, ran the boat up the river. One of the men, telling the shipwright that he had been paid 'to do a job', shot him twice at close range in the stomach and groin with a homemade firearm. The shipwright managed to disarm his attacker and threw him overboard. The shooter drowned and an inquest found that the shipwright, who survived, had acted in self defence.

* * *

Biker gangs sometimes use bombs as warnings or weapons. Most clubhouses are fortified against bomb attacks from rival gangs, but this didn't deter recent bombings of the Gypsy Jokers' headquarters in Newcastle, and the clubhouses of the Bandidos in Geelong and the Rebels in Adelaide. In 2003 Western Australia Police obtained powers under the WA Corruption and Crime Commission Act to issue 'tear-down' orders for heavily fortified premises used by those reasonably suspected of involvement in organised crime. The Gypsy Jokers were not happy. Their lawyers argued that clubhouse security was needed to protect patrons' machines, worth upwards of $30000, and that the changes demanded by police would cause safety traps and fire risks. Clubhouse fortifications came under constitutional challenge in the

Supreme Court of Western Australia in 2006 when the Gypsy Jokers took on their long-time enemies, the state police. In early 2007 parties were still waiting on a Court of Appeal decision on jurisdiction.

In 2005 a tear-down order permitted South Australian police to remove iron window and door grates, steel doors and razor wire at the Adelaide Hills premises of Hells Angel Eugene Osenkowski. Osenkowski ran a test case challenging the order, but in November 2006 the Supreme Court upheld it. In January 2007 Osenkowski avoided a showdown with police by removing the fortifications in what he maintains is his parents' home.

When the notorious Perth police officer Don Hancock retired as head of the CIB in the late 1990s he went back to the Kalgoorlie goldfields where he had grown up and opened a pub in the remote town of Ora Banda. On 1 October 2000 he met with trouble from the local Gypsy Jokers. William Grierson was banned from the hotel after he and other bikers swore in front of Hancock's daughter. Later that night the biker was shot dead at a nearby campfire—hit in the shoulder and spine. Hancock was known as a fine shot and over the next few weeks, his home, store and hotel were firebombed or blown up. He returned to Perth where he declined to assist with police inquiries.

In the spring of 2001 the police heard that some Jokers were mounting surveillance on Hancock's home and warned him there was a plot to kill him at a Kalgoorlie race meeting. Ignoring the warning, on 1 September he and his friend Lou Lewis went to Belmont racetrack in Perth. After the races, as Lewis was driving Hancock home, a powerful bomb was remotely detonated, killing the men and blowing a large crater in the road. The bomb was presumed to have been planted while Lewis and Hancock watched the races.

On 28 March 2002, 38-year-old Sidney John Reid, a full member of the Gypsy Jokers, pleaded guilty to the murders. After a long police investigation he had been persuaded to roll over and break the bikers' code of silence. Now he implicated another Joker, Graeme 'Slim' Slater, as being with him when the bomb was planted. Reid, who came from a broken home and was estranged from his own children, had come to regard the Jokers as his family. In return for his co-operation he was given fifteen years, instead of the twenty-five he might have expected.

Reid also gave evidence in the prosecution of Gary Ernest White, who was found guilty of the execution-style killing of Anthony David Tapley, a drug user who owed money. On 19 August 2001 White shot Tapley six times—in the shoulder, buttocks and head—and then incinerated his body in a bonfire. Later he boasted to Reid that 'the barbecue went well'. White's conviction survived a 2006 appeal to the High Court.

Despite Reid's evidence against a number of other bikers, all were acquitted of the bombing campaign against Hancock. Slater, who had earlier been acquitted of the car bomb murders, admitted four charges relating to the bombing campaign and received a three year sentence— which, since he had been in prison awaiting trial, meant his immediate release. Mrs Hancock received $40 000 in compensation for the death of her husband. In April 2006 a coroner's inquest found insufficient evidence to conclude that Hancock had been involved in the murder of the biker Grierson.

Giving evidence against OMCGs is an extremely dangerous occupation, as Adelaide woman Vicki Jacobs found to her cost. The Crown's case against Gerald Preston, in another life a marijuana salesman, was that in 1996 he was contracted to murder car repairer Les Knowles as a favour to a Melbourne Hells Angel and for a fee of $10 000. He allegedly recruited Kevin Gillard as his driver.

Preston phoned Lee's Auto Repairs, at Donegal Road, Lonsdale, in Adelaide to confirm that Knowles would be in. He was not alone. A friend Tim Richards had dropped in to do some casual work and Knowles also had a couple of mechanics there. Just after midday on Thursday 15 August a masked Preston strode into the workshop and headed for the office carrying a Lüger. Both Knowles and Richards were in the office and Preston demanded to know which was which. Not getting an answer, he shot Knowles through the head. When Richards stammered he was not Knowles, Preston shot him as well.

Outside the office, working on a car, were the two mechanics, Traeger and Leane. As Preston left the office he saw Traeger near the car but failed to see Leane, who remained under the vehicle. Traeger was hit in the arm. The getaway car was set on fire at Christies Beach but Preston did not get rid of what was an easily identifiable gun.

When Preston was charged with the murders of Knowles and Richards in November that year, and his former wife, Vicki Jacobs, said she had seen Preston purchase the Lüger pistol on a visit to Melbourne in 1994. He was sentenced to life imprisonment. Gillard, seemingly terrified of repercussions from the Angels, was later found unfit to stand trial.

After Preston's trial, Jacobs changed her name and went to live on the outskirts of Bendigo. On 12 July 1999 she was shot to death as she slept on a fold down bed in Wood Street, Long Gully. Her killing was believed to be on the orders of the Angels. In October Michael 'Bags' Lane, a member of the Hells Angels East County Chapter was killed when a branch hit him as he was cutting down a tree. He was thought to have driven the Darwin based hitman to Bendigo.

Bikers attract women in large numbers. Some are sent out to make money as waitresses in cocktail bars, topless barmaids, strippers and prostitutes. They can find employment in police agencies, financial institutions, government offices, licensing departments or within the justice and corrections systems. There they can obtain information which is invaluable to the OMCGs: birth certificates, drivers' licences, police records, financial information and so forth.

Intelligence gathering is an integral part of OMCG culture and, with access to an endless supply of money, no expense is spared as new technology becomes available. Miniature recording devices are used by law enforcement officers and OMCG members alike. An Adelaide raid in 2003 targeting OMCGs seized, along with sawn-off shotguns, rifles and drugs, a sophisticated listening device. Superintendent Fred Gere says that no law prevents the bikies from conducting surveillance on police, as was done from a backpackers' hostel adjacent to the rear entrance of one WA police headquarters. 'More disturbing,' he says, 'is the photographing of individual police officers and support staff by the gangs.'

Some members of the wider community assist OMCGs in their counter-intelligence gathering and surveillance. If locals living close to clubhouses and headquarters come to believe that gang members are simply rowdy weekend bikers, bonds start to form. The bikers support local businesses, pay cash and deal with any offences in the neighbourhood. In return sympathetic locals act as the gang's eyes and ears—all neatly symbiotic.

Nor have OMCGs ever had much trouble getting their hands on weaponry. After the 1996 Port Arthur massacre, the availability of firearms was dramatically reduced but this has not deterred those biker gang members who like to have a gun handy. A cache was found by police at the Gypsy Joker clubhouse in Adelaide in 2001. In 2003 police raids on Northern Territory Hells Angels premises supposedly unearthed Glock pistols and a rocket launcher. Gere says that when biker premises are the subject of search warrants, in 99 per cent of cases weapons are found.

In raids on properties connected to the Brothers Motorcycle Club in north and western Melbourne suburbs in 2003, Organised Crime Squad detectives found drugs, a stolen Harley Davidson and a stash of weapons including a nifty mobile phone pistol, loaded by splitting the phone and inserting ammunition under the screen. Recent Sydney raids netted fourteen firearms, including semi-automatic pistols and an SKS assault rifle plus a bullet-proof vest.

* * *

In 2003 the Australian Crime Commission reported that biker gangs were behind the flood of illegal amphetamines onto Australian streets and were suspected of forming alliances with other crime groups, such as ethnic gangs, to distribute amphetamine-type stimulants and ecstasy. Hundreds of secret drug labs were discovered or raided around the country. In Queensland 162 labs were found; in New South Wales seventy-two labs had been uncovered along with a seven-lab Nomad drug network which resulted in fifty-one arrests. At the time there may have been a war over the control of amphetamines but, when necessary, inter-club rivalry, particularly in the eastern states, is put aside in the interests of a high profit making venture.

In 2003 it was suspected that drugs were being transported between South Australia and Queensland following a trucking route through Dubbo. At dawn on 26 May 2004, some 350 police officers arrived at twenty-eight premises in Dubbo, Sydney and various addresses in South Australia and Queensland armed with dozens of search warrants obtained after months of surveillance and a year long investigation. No fewer than five different biker gangs were alleged to have teamed up and transported $22 million worth of amphetamines and quantities of cannabis between South Australia, New South Wales and Queensland. After the raids, twenty people were arrested.

In 2005 there was another setback for the Rebels when, after raids in Perth and Busselton, members Raymond Washer and John Dilena were found guilty of conspiracy to possess drugs with intent to supply. Their clubhouse in Malaga was shut following Operation Gallipoli. Washer and Dilena were found to have been involved in transporting amphetamines from Queensland to Perth and both were sentenced to seven years.

In early 2006 Australian Federal Police raided a remote property near Murwillumbah in northern New South Wales. The AFP claimed to have found a secret underground room, firearms, cash and enough chemicals to produce 300 kilograms of speed or 'ice'—crystal methyl amphetamine. Chinese criminals, alleged to have joined forces with an Australian biker gang, were suspected of being behind the operation. Police were seeking a Chinese man who had come to Australia in late 2005 bringing palladium, a metal used in the manufacture of amphetamines. The tip-off to the AFP had come from Hong Kong police. Seven were arrested in April 2006, one of whom was said to be a member of the Rebels.

Despite the ability of the gangs to co-operate for profit, in recent years territorial disputes and ambitions to expand have resulted in tension between the gangs. Western Australia's Coffin Cheaters have spread their tentacles nationally and internationally, even establishing two Norwegian chapters, presumably with the tacit approval of Hells Angels. The Outlaws have moved into Perth. Around Christmas 2004 the Rebels, the largest club in Sydney, formed a Queensland chapter without consulting the local Nomads, something that led to disturbances. Sam Ibrahim, a Kings Cross nightclub owner like his brother John, as well as being president of the Nomads' Parramatta chapter, said that he would take on Rebel Alex Vella, known as the 'Maltese Falcon', with 'guns or fists anywhere, any time'. This would, said Ibrahim, stop innocent members of opposing clubs getting hurt. Police thanked him for his suggestion but announced they would broker a peaceful meeting.

In Adelaide, the Hells Angels and Rebels have been feuding since 1998, after the beating of a Hells Angel that year. In July 1999 the Rebels clubhouse in Brompton was bombed and three Rebels were killed at their Wright Street clubhouse a few months later. Part of the issue appears to have been who should provide security guards at Adelaide nightclubs. The last incident in this long-running row was in 2005.

By the autumn of 2006 it was clear the Angels had their sights on a Sydney base. On Saturday 18 March Angels and Finks fought at a kickboxing tournament at the Royal Pines Resort on the Gold Coast amid a crowd of 1600 spectators. According to police, tensions between the two gangs had been ignited by the defection of a senior Finks member to the Angels and incidents including a drive-by shooting. Twenty to thirty bikers arrived at the venue at about 10.30 p.m., armed with guns and knives smuggled in past venue security. One Angel was shot in the throat and stomach and another two were stabbed. A Fink was shot in the shoulder and a spectator received a foot wound. Police said afterwards they were fearful that an all-out biker war was not far away.

Ten days later an Adelaide kickboxing tournament was cancelled on police advice that violence could erupt between rival gangs. Back in Sydney, on 26 March, another men's club in Kings Cross, Showgirls, played unwilling host to a biker squabble which resulted in the shooting of the Nomads' national sergeant-at-arms. Although reports said the shooter was not a patched Hells Angel and the dispute concerned a woman not turf, the incident was taken as further evidence that biker gang members were 'armed and dangerous' in inner Sydney.

Operation Avatar, a South Australian police operation set up in 1999 to deal with OMCGs, has arrested hundreds of gang members, bikers and their associates. Numerous labs have been busted and millions of dollars in drugs have been seized, along with weapons and criminal proceeds. In the autumn of 2006 four key members of the Hells Angels North Crew in South Australia left the state and another went overseas.

It is not only the Angels who are moving into Sydney. One Comanchero who survived the Milperra battle was Raymond 'Sunshine' Kucler, who later deposed Jock Ross, the founder and president. Two decades on from Milperra, the Comancheros are on the rise again. Reports are that this gang was recruiting around Sydney during 2006 and the members are younger and mainly Lebanese–Australian. Passing are the days when OMCGs were white supremacists. Now relationships are being formed with Middle Eastern and Asian crime gangs and Mafia-type groups. In Perth the Coffin Cheaters have links with the Scorpions and the Sword Boys, once a local street gang recognisable by the miniature scimitars they wore and now alleged to be running drugs for the Cheaters.

There has clearly been some dispute between the Coffin Cheaters and a faction in the Scorpions. On 23 January 2005 Troy Desmond Mercanti, a Coffin Cheater and an old friend of some Melbourne identities, who was alleged to have been present at the beating of Tony Mokbel in Melbourne, was stabbed in the basement of Perth's Metro nightclub by Nabil Dabag, a Scorpion. Dabag was dragged away and allegedly shot and wounded by Mercanti. The prosecution later claimed that, under the supervision of west coast identity John Kizon, there was then a massive attempt to cover up what had happened—walls were hosed, an effort was made to clean Mercanti's hands and so defeat a residue test and the security tape was got at. Denying any involvement, Kizon told reporters, 'This is fantastic and youse knows it.'

Eighteen months later the suspects had been acquitted of all charges: first, Dabag in February 2006 and then, on 12 May, Mercanti, Kizon and the others. Kizon had explained to the jury that he had removed the weapon: 'I wasn't leaving no gun on no floor with those two gentlemen.' Mercanti was charged with possession of the gun with which Dabag was shot, something he considered really unsporting. Naturally, there were squeals of protest both about this and the acquittals themselves. Suggestions from the prosecution of jury tampering were rejected both by the defence and two of the jurors. Late in 2006 a magistrate permanently stayed Mercanti's charges relating to the firearm on the grounds that it was an abuse of process.

On the east coast, the Rebels and Bandidos spent a year in fierce battle over disputed takeovers of various chapters. In April 2007, Rebel chief Alex Vella returned from a visit to Japan, where his son Adam had been boxing, to find a serious escalation in the feud. The day he had left for overseas, the Rebels' clubhouse in Newcastle had been firebombed. At the end of March the Rebels' headquarters in Brisbane were also firebombed.

There have also been internal troubles among the east coast Nomads as well, apparently over the welfare of a member currently serving more than thirty years. The national president and several other officials were charged with attempted murder, grievous bodily harm and affray. The charges followed the defection into the arms of the police of the one-time Newcastle sergeant-at-arms after he had allegedly been shot at the clubhouse in September 2004.

* * *

A new national taskforce under the Australian Crime Commission will supplement the work done by Operation Avatar in South Australia, the Gangs Squad in New South Wales and Western Australia's Gang

Response Squad. Fred Gere says that in recent years some authorities have 'been behind the eight ball' in respect of biker investigations. Hence the growth in clubs and members. Now the national approach will even up the contest.

Various state governments are now attacking outlaw bikers by seizing their assets. Les Hoddy, the co-founder of the Gypsy Jokers, died a broken man. His property had been seized under Western Australia's 'unexplained wealth' laws. Hundreds may have turned out for his Perth funeral but he had been reduced to driving a car left unused following the conviction of Gary White for the Tapley murder eighteen months earlier. Since Hoddy's death meant that he was deemed to have absconded, all his assets were subject to confiscation.

But in the twenty-first century OMCGs are attempting some serious image tweaking—long sleeves hide tattoos, business is done wearing suits and from vehicles less obvious than motorbikes, and leathers are for the weekend. Expansion among the gangs is being conducted much as a fast food chain might expand its markets, with franchises using identical or similar operating procedures. The Hells Angels have even globally patented their skull logo.

While politicians have been distracted by national security and terrorism, OMCGs have quietly moved into South America, South Africa, and countries such as Thailand, Italy and Greece. Fred Gere explains that the alarming global expansion of the illegal activities associated with OMCGs is largely due to the fact that:

> the smart ones are changing the way they deal with the community and are forming strategic partnerships with other organised crime groups, politicians, police officers and lawyers—there are no exceptions or areas that they will not try to get into through the use of money, intimidation or force.

Further muddying the waters is the fact that, in the last few years, accountants, stockbrokers, lawyers and doctors are buying Harley Davidsons and donning leathers and bandanas to hit the road for recreational runs and they are indistinguishable from bikers. Police biker gangs such as the Wild Pigs and Blue Knights are also expanding from the United States.

Ironically, in the outlaw motorcycle gang of the future, the distinguishing features may be even less apparent. There might be no evident tattoos, patches or colours. Gang clubhouses may become even less visible and perhaps even motorcycles will be considered redundant.

The Best that Money Can Buy

15

There is a widely held belief among criminals that the police worldwide are the most villainous of all gangs, and over the years there have been cases and statistics to back up their admittedly biased theory. There is bound to be some corruption in any force in any major city but, from time to time over the years, Australia's state police forces in general and the New South Wales Police in particular appear to have raised it to an art form. Anyone who thinks a high percentage of the New South Wales and Queensland Police have in the past been rogues has the support of the colourful Sydney solicitor Christopher Murphy, whose father was an officer:

> Lennie McPherson and George Freeman may have been the Mr Bigs of Sydney crime but in truth the real Princes of the City were the police. When they came back from the Second World War the uniform seemed attractive. By the 1960s they had started networking criminals and they got lazy. In the end, by the late 1980s, they were using criminals to kill people.

There is naturally a great deal of argument among sociologists about what is corruption and where it starts. Is it expecting free bacon and eggs every morning at the same café, or is that simply a good example of keeping one's finger on the pulse of the local community?

After looking at patterns of police corruption in New York, Marseille, Hong Kong, Bangkok and Sydney, sociologist Alfred McCoy suggested that the first of a five stage model of police corruption is what he calls honest graft, such as receiving bungs from tow-truck drivers when they give them work. In other words, getting an informal bonus for doing their job of keeping the roads clear. What harm is there in that?

Probably not a great deal, except that it can be turned into a business—and also that it leads to step two, which is taking a bribe not to report a speeding offence. It may then mean sharing the proceeds of an armed robbery or splitting the drugs with a dealer, either to be resold for the officer's profit or to be given to his informers.

The third step is obtaining a regular fee from club and brothel owners or illegal gamblers to allow them to continue unmolested or to warn them of impending raids. The fourth step is a giant leap. Now officers at senior level become criminal entrepreneurs, licensing certain criminals to commit serious offences. The fifth stage is the one reached in the Royal Hong Kong Police in the late 1960s when drug dealers, brothel keepers and gambling palace owners paid to senior officers a fixed share of their income, which was then divided among themselves and junior officers. In the ensuing investigation around forty Chinese officers left the colony, taking between them something in the region of $80 million. Over the years some Australian police, in the New South Wales and Queensland forces in particular, have operated on levels three and four.

Given the origin of the various forces around the world it is not surprising there have been continuing troubles. In London the police had initially been made up of ex-soldiers, and the Commissioners there had troubles enough. In Australia convicts were encouraged to become constables and there was a high turnover. In their first seventeen years in Victoria the police were paid less than road labourers, there were no standards of entry and there was no code to govern police conduct.

In New South Wales in the 1840s three consecutive chiefs of police in Sydney were dismissed for a variety of indiscretions; one because of 'irregular practices' when he had been a visiting magistrate at Darlinghurst Gaol. By 1850 the New South Wales police force was described as being at an all time low, with scandals, drunkenness and bribery prevalent among the constables and with itching palms throughout the force.

In 1851, after Victoria separated from New South Wales, a fine-sharing policy was introduced in an effort to recruit constables. Naturally, this had disastrous consequences. The police were keen to weed out sly-groggers, whose convictions produced fines, while serious assaults, which would not result in a fine, went undetected.

It was after the April 1852 robbery of the barque *Nelson*, when some 232 kilograms of gold were stolen, that arrangements were made to recruit police from England and the first of the many commissions and committees was appointed to examine policing in Victoria.

After the 1852 inquiry the first chief commissioner, William Mitchell, was appointed. Unfortunately for the force, he lasted little more than a year before he resigned due to deteriorating health. *The Argus*, never a supporter of the early police force, paid tribute:

> Nothing could be worse than its condition when he took the reins ... corruption, perjury, ruffianism of every description were rife throughout the force, till it had become a public nuisance, not a safe-guard. In a few short months, with the aid of a strong will, a sense of duty and a competent intelligence, all this has been so far reformed, that to calm observers like ourselves, it appears little short of miraculous.

Unfortunately the first long-lasting commissioner, the gambler/drinker/womaniser Captain Frederick Charles Standish, was not such a success. Born in England in 1824 he was one of the most popular men on the local racecourse until, in 1852, he was forced to sell his mortgaged properties to pay his gaming debts and he set sail for the Colonies. He was appointed assistant commissioner of the goldfields and then, in September 1858, chief commissioner of police in Victoria at a salary of 1200 pounds. In 1853 he had previously been rejected for an appointment when he applied under an assumed name.

He was not a good choice. Standish certainly undertook some reforms, including the use of the telegraph and the railway for communication and transport, but his control was lax and he did not believe in any formal training for officers. There was preferment for Irish Catholics (82 per cent of the force) and from 1860 to 1863 there were no fewer than three select committees looking into Standish's administration; the third suggested he be replaced. He survived.

Standish did not, however, survive the Ned Kelly outbreak. Legend has it that the hunt for Kelly was suspended while the weights for the Melbourne Cup were declared. After his resignation Standish continued his rackety ways. In 1882 he was nearly thrown through the window of the Melbourne Club by Colonel Craigie Helkett whom he had called by a 'provocative name'. His legacy is the Standish Handicap run at Flemington on New Year's Day.

After Kelly's capture in June 1880, there were serious concerns about the inefficiency of the country police and, more importantly, the corruption among those in Melbourne. In particular, one superintendent, Fred Winch, who had conducted a system of organised corruption, had allowed sly-grog shops, prostitution and gambling to flourish over a twenty year period. He had also blocked honest Melbourne police trying to stamp out these pursuits. He was allowed to retire without charges, his pension intact. The Detective Branch was seen by the Longmore Commission of 1881 as a 'standing menace to the community'. It was institutionally corrupt and there were also complaints about the uncontrolled use of informers. It recommended that the Detective Branch be disbanded. Nevertheless, the force was still the place to be. In 1888, 500 young men applied for the fifty positions available.

Even the great successes of the Melbourne police were not above suspicion. The well-known thief-taker John Christie was thought to have lived with the wife of the skeleton key maker Levi Walker while Walker was in Pentridge. Worse, he had 'dressed her like a lady'. Christie, who resigned in dubious circumstances, was not a fan of the efforts of the force. It may have been a bit of sour grapes when he wrote: 'One does not expect the genius of a Sherlock Holmes for comparatively small wages but the pretensions of the Victorian force are such as to warrant the public in expecting a high average of successes.'

In Queensland there were suggestions that a constable was taking money to allow gambling—suggestions repeated for the next hundred years—as well as the case of Constable Walker who was accused of standing over one Kate Brooks in Albert Street, Brisbane, arresting her for obscene language and then having sex with her and refusing to pay. Despite the fact that her complaint was supported by Walker's sergeant, the woman was still fined two pounds. In the wash-up Walker was transferred to the remote north Queensland settlement of Normanton. Again, one hundred years later only the amounts involved have changed.

Over the next quarter of a century things did not improve. In 1915, at a Select Committee on the Prevalence of Venereal Diseases, Sydney physician Ralph Worrall gave evidence that police were regularly accepting bribes from brothel keepers and were operating a de facto licensing system. Unsurprisingly the police denied this.

In November 1923, following a long struggle to obtain better conditions, the badly underpaid Melbourne police staged a three day strike. The city fell into the hands of criminals who mugged, looted, and set fire to trams. The situation was remedied with a thousand 'specials' brought in to quell the rioters and after four hours of fighting the streets were once again under control. By the end one ex-soldier had been killed and 237 civilians were in hospital.

Distinguished military man Thomas Blamey began and ended his police career as chief commissioner in Victoria in scandal. His appointment on 1 September 1925 at the age of forty-one was generally well received by property owners and police alike. It also averted the possibility of an inquiry into allegations of corruption in the force, particularly the Licensing Branch. Now that Blamey, with his fine war record, had been appointed, the 'right man' was in the post and things would soon be cleaned up.

Indeed Blamey had many suitable qualities. He looked on the force as a military operation and was innovative in matters such as training, man management and organisation. He also increased wages. Unfortunately he held the view that liquor was an adult version of mother's milk and should be available to all, with as little let or hindrance as possible. He could be found in smart hotels drinking after hours on a regular basis, something which provided, for the right people, a cast iron guarantee against police raids.

Worse, on 21 October 1925, within weeks of his appointment, someone who carried the commissioner's police badge Number 80 was found in a brothel in Bell Street, Fitzroy, run by Mabel Tracey, who masqueraded as a teacher of elocution. When the place was raided by three constables from the Licensing Branch, one of the catch had an explanation, 'It's all right, boys, I'm a plainclothes constable. Here is my badge.' All the constables agreed that it was not Blamey who held the badge, although it was definitely his.

Blamey maintained the badge must have been removed from his key-ring the day before the raid and that he found it three days later in his locker at his club. However, his next in command, Superintendent Daniel Lineham, said quite specifically he had seen the badge on Blamey's desk only seven hours before the raid. A public inquiry was refused and instead Lineham was accused of disloyalty. Now Blamey produced a witness, an old army friend, who said he had been with Blamey and his family from 9 p.m. until just before midnight on the night of the raid.

The best and most likely explanation is Blamey lied to protect a married friend who had met him after dinner at the club and asked him if he had any grog in his locker. Blamey had handed over his key ring with his badge on it, telling the man to drop it back later. Many rather admired him for his refusal to betray his friend but it was hardly a good example to the lower ranks. Indeed it is a classic example of how corruption spreads in a police force.

While Blamey restored morale among his officers, he lacked judgement, and importantly he dismissed a series of allegations of corruption and brutality—thirty in 1933 alone—against officers.

His career ended with another fudged cover-up. On Saturday 23 May 1936 the head of CIB, Superintendent John O'Connell Brophy, was in St Vincent's Hospital suffering from a gunshot wound. Brophy was highly regarded by the underworld and celebrated in the couplet 'Ashes to ashes and dust to dust; if Brophy don't get you then Piggott [his colleague] must.' He had accidentally shot himself in the right arm while handling a pistol. Unfortunately those who visited him in hospital could see that he had also been shot in the face and the chest. 'Injuries [that], even for the most persistent pistol cleaner, it would have been difficult to receive,' said L.E.B. Stretton, counsel at the subsequent inquiry. It was time for a revision of the facts. Now the heroic officer had been shot while chasing car bandits near the zoo. The press did not give up and on 5 June the county court judge Hugh Macindoe was appointed as royal commissioner to investigate the shooting of Brophy and the subsequent press statements made by Blamey.

What was quite clear was that Brophy had been with a chauffeur and two women that night. All sorts of lame explanations—such as meeting in the dead of night with an informer—were offered as to how he came to be chasing dangerous bandits with innocent spectators at risk. Forty-four witnesses, including both Blamey and Brophy, were called and much of the time was spent trying to refute 'scandalous' allegations that Brophy had been shot by an 'enraged' husband. Later there were allegations that Brophy was half naked and practising cunnilingus on his companion when the gunman approached.

On 2 July, Macindoe submitted his report, which many saw as a whitewash. Unfortunately for Blamey he said of the commissioner: 'I cannot accept his evidence that he believed it was an accident ... [he] gave replies which were not in accordance with the truth, with the sole purpose of secreting from the press the fact that women were in the company of Superintendent Brophy.'

Blamey was finished and on 9 July he was required to submit his resignation. At first he tried to bluster his way out but he was told that if he resigned he could have a pension of 260 pounds per annum but not otherwise. He resigned. The official police history *Police in Victoria 1836–1980* also whitewashes him: '... his only crime being a desire to preserve the reputation of his Force'. Blamey returned to the army where he served with great credit in World War II, becoming Australia's first field marshall.

One of the great detectives of the Sydney police immediately after the war was Ray Kelly. After his retirement in February 1960 *The Sydney Morning Herald* thought 'he deliberately made friends in all walks of life because he knew that was the way to be a successful detective'. Kelly was also probably one of the most corrupt of policemen worldwide. He was a good friend of Tilly Devine, Kate Leigh and Dulcie Markham and a close associate of Dr Stuart-Jones. Richard Reilly and Paddles Anderson were more than just his informants; they were his partners in abortion and other rackets.

For a time Kelly, born in New South Wales in 1906, worked as a jackeroo, but he craved excitement and came to Sydney in 1929 where he joined the police. He worked with the Riot Squad and in 1931, during the Depression, his skull was fractured in the eviction riots at Newtown.

Recovered from his injuries, he began to make his name that same year. He was on bicycle patrol when he saw three men in a stolen car and followed them into a dead end. They tried to run him down and he leaped on the running board, grabbing the steering wheel. The car crashed into a shop window and the driver again tried to shake Kelly off by reversing at high speed. Instead Kelly shot all three, hitting one in the head and the others in the back. Swann, a known standover man, died in hospital.

From then his career was onward and upward. He went into detective work in 1936, equally at home, said his colleagues, with bankers and standover men. Although some of the photographs of him appear to show a small, bespectacled, almost dapper little man, he was more than 2 metres in height and weighed nearly 90 kilograms. A keen golfer and surfboarder, he didn't drink or smoke.

On 15 March 1953 Kelly killed a criminal, Lloyd Edward Day, who with two companions had spent a weekend dealing with the safe of Marcus Clark in Central Square. The police had heard there was to be a major job and Kelly and others had been on a seventeen hour stake-out. When the men emerged, two got into a truck said to have been driven by Lennie McPherson, although he was never charged. The other three got into a car driven by Day. They were chased down College Street, Drummoyne, and Kelly called out for them to stop. When they didn't, Kelly, leaning out of the window, fired a number of shots, hitting Day.

He was involved in the repeated captures of the gunman and escaper Darcy Dugan, on one occasion in 1958 using his informants to tell him Dugan was waiting patiently in a 1.3 metre hole for the chance to move over the prison wall. That same year he confronted James Hackett, who had fatally shot Marlene Harvey in her home and wounded two other men. The next year he was part of the team that tracked down Kevin Simmonds and Leslie Newcombe, who had clubbed an Emu Plains prison warder to death as they were searching for food following their escape. He was in the Arthur Street, North Sydney, shoot-out with Tony Martini and Edward Garland for which the pair were sentenced to death and later reprieved.

That was Kelly's public side; but he was also quite capable of arranging that criminals such as Dugan took the blame for some robberies he and his colleagues set up—indeed that was said to be his speciality. He was one of three senior detectives who, questioning applicants for the plain-clothes division, asked them if they were prepared to load up a suspect. If the answer was no, they would be rejected and Kelly was apt to remark derisively, 'Give him back to the Cardinal. He's no good to me'. 'The Cardinal' was the incorruptible uniformed officer Brian Doyle, a practising Catholic.

Kelly's retirement party on 3 February 1960, a five-pounds-a-plate buffet with unlimited drink, was attended by 874 people and included luminaries such as Robert Askin, Commissioner Norm Allen, judges, horse trainers, criminals and gambler Perce Galea.

It was with Kelly that Fred Krahe groomed a young officer, Don Fergusson, to be their bagman in the abortion rackets of the 1960s.

Krahe had joined the police as a cadet in 1940 and, although another talented detective, he also organised abortion rackets, armed robberies and the extortion of prostitutes and criminals. In 1971 he was exposed by Shirley Brifman, a girl in the Kings Cross area, who said she paid him a regular $100 a week. When she was arrested for allegedly procuring a fourteen-year-old girl, something she bitterly denied, she went public, maintaining that Krahe had helped organise a theft of bonds from a bank and that he and a Queensland officer 'exchanged' criminals—one of whom was Donny 'The Glove' Smith—so that they could work in each other's state without fear of recognition.

Detective Superintendent Donald Fergusson, former chief of the CIB, had been Krahe's partner in the 1950s and both had worked regularly with Kelly. With exposure of the abortion business about to break, Fergusson was found dead in the lavatory of his office at Sydney's Police Administration Centre in Campbell Street. He had been shot through the right temple. A verdict of suicide while suffering severe mental depression was returned but there were many who thought Krahe had held the trembling hand.

During his career Krahe was also involved in another curious case, the murder of Alan Burton, who disappeared in February 1972. He had been involved in a huge car stealing racket with the one-legged Reg Varley, who was accused of paying two New South Wales detectives $5000 to dispose of his partner. The Varley–Burton combo stole cars worth $1.5 million in seven months, the lion's share of which, said Varley, was received by Krahe. In January 1972 a series of raids began on the Varley chop shops and on the night of 7 February Burton disappeared. Much of the evidence against Varley came from another member of the gang, Paul Hos, who told the Central Criminal Court that Varley said he went to Burton's house with some detectives, one of whom hit Burton with a cosh. Allegedly Varley also then hit him and the body was taken 320 kilometres down the coast and dumped at sea. Varley told the court that Krahe had called on him at his Blakehurst home that night and told him they were going to give Burton a hiding. He had, it was said, swindled them out of $20000. When Varley protested he was hit on the ankle and his aluminium crutches were smashed. Burton and he were taken for a drive and then Burton was taken from the car and Varley heard shots. However, Varley was convicted of manslaughter and sentenced to fourteen years. He served nine and after his release he constantly tried to have his case re-opened. A week after Burton's supposed abduction and killing someone who gave his name as Alan Burton was involved in a car accident in a vehicle rented in the name of Paul Hos. The address and age corresponded with those of Burton.

Shirley Brifman fled to Queensland where she was found dead in her Brisbane flat in March 1972. She died of either a heart attack or a drug overdose but there have been persistent rumours among the police that Krahe, with or without the active assistance of a Queensland officer, forced the pills down her throat. Krahe was allowed to retire that year at the age of fifty-two with a thrombosis in the leg. He was later involved in the Nugen Hand bank affair and was charged with conspiracy to defraud the group but was acquitted on all counts. He died, aged sixty-one, in 1981.

If there was corruption in the senior or lower levels in the New South Wales Police during those years, it was not surprising. The corruption went straight to the premier's office and the belief is that both the commissioner of police, Norman 'The Foreman' Allen, and the premier, Robert Askin, were on the take from illegal casinos, abortion rackets and prostitution. Askin died a rich man, leaving something over $3 million. Could he have acquired this legitimately? There is little doubt that Norman Allen acquired his money dishonestly but there is possibly room for a chink of doubt in Askin's case. Mr Justice Moffitt, in his 1973 inquiry, took a charitable view:

> There was no evidence against him in my inquiry, never any solid proof. I always thought he got money by being put in on the Stock Exchange. There was a smell about his selling knighthoods but there was no evidence. It's a false assumption that a person who ends up wealthy has been getting it in a brown paper bag.

Under Allen's successor, Frederick John 'Slippery' Hanson, the New South Wales Police were known as 'the best police force money could buy'. Hanson began his working life as a railway porter, joining the force in 1936. Two years earlier he had been rejected as undersized and had gone on a bodybuilding course. After the war he was a founding member of 21 Division, set up to deal with the young bashers who were robbing demobbed servicemen of their pay.

But one good deed deserves another and Hanson, who disliked his nickname, declined to go after casino owners such as the highly popular gambler Perce Galea, said to be pushing $5000 a week all the way to the top. Unbelievably Hanson claimed the police did not have the authority to go into the clubs. His appointment coincided with the growth of organised crime in New South Wales and if there is not clear evidence against him, there is the deepest suspicion that he protected those people like his duck-shooting friend Robert Trimbole.

By 1974 Hanson was slacking off, working only 47 per cent of his official hours and in February 1976 he brought and settled a libel action against a newspaper which implied he had an interest in an illegal casino at West Gosford. But with the action his days were literally numbered. He agreed to retire early if he could appoint his successor and sat on the three-man committee to appoint his nominee Merv Wood. He died of carbon monoxide poisoning in October 1980 and many believe it was suicide.

Mervyn Wood had had a most successful rowing career, representing Australia in the 1936 Berlin Olympics, and over the years he won a gold medal, two silver medals and a bronze medal. In 1950 he won the single and double sculls, this time partnered by another policeman, Murray Riley, later a convicted drug smuggler.

Indeed Murray Stewart Riley was one of the earliest post-war senior officers to go astray in a public way. He had been a police officer since 1943, resigning in 1962 after an incident in which he was alleged to have taken a communication to a serving prisoner. He then went into the security business and at one time was an adviser to South Sydney Juniors. He was convicted in New Zealand of attempted bribery of a police inspector to obtain bail for Sydney criminals who had been arrested in a pyramid-selling fraud, and was sentenced to twelve months' imprisonment before being deported back to Australia on 1 March 1967.

In both 1973 and 1974 he managed to avoid being called to give evidence before the Moffitt Inquiry. Despite reports of sightings in the neighbourhood, Riley could not be found by the police and Justice Moffitt recorded that he had been treated with undue favour by them. At that time Riley had clearly put behind him his earlier mistake of attempted bribery, for a police account of his behaviour presented to Moffitt was: 'The overall situation in relation to this man is that he could not even be reputed to be a criminal.'

From then on at the very least, Riley flirted with organised crime. He was to be seen with the Californian *Mafioso* Jimmy 'The Weasel'

Fratianno in San Francisco in November 1976. Two days later, his briefcase was stolen from his room while he lunched in a Hilton hotel in the city. Fratianno was his luncheon partner that day. In June 1978 Riley pleaded guilty and received ten years in Sydney for importation of 2.7 tonnes of cannabis. In 1980 he received a further seven years on charges of possessing an unlicensed pistol and conspiracy to cheat and defraud the American Express Company of $274000. Shortly before his release in May 1984 he was made bankrupt, owing more than $132000 to the Nugan Hand (Hong Kong) Bank, which was, by this time, in liquidation. In 1985 he was named in an inquiry by Justice Bredmeyer of the Papua New Guinea Supreme Court as being part of a ring to import $40 million of heroin from Bangkok.

He moved to England where he was jailed in July 1991 at Bristol Crown Court after he and an accomplice were convicted of a plan to defraud British Aerospace of approximately $93 million by means of computer fraud. In 1990 they had applied to open a bank account on the Isle of Man but the manager became suspicious when Riley could not provide references. Less than six months into a five year sentence he walked out of Spring Hill prison, Aylesbury. He was recaptured at Harlow in Essex on 31 January 1992. During his eight weeks out he travelled to Northern Ireland, Spain and Belgium.

Overall, Police Commissioner Wood's attitude was one of live and let live and, until he was forced to do otherwise, that was the way policing was conducted. His first clash with Premier Neville Wran came in December 1977. At last, after years of tolerance, illegal casinos were to be closed but Wood stated publicly that he did not intend to close them before Christmas because of the hardship it would cause to the 300-odd employees who would lose their jobs. The next and more serious came in March when a report linking George Freeman and Lenny McPherson to the upper echelons of the American Mafia was not passed to Wran. The third came at the beginning of May when Wran appointed Bill Allen to the post of chief superintendent ahead of recommendations by Wood and did not inform him.

It was not a good month for Wood. In the face of mounting criticism of the police and leaked allegations—which he denied—he resigned on 5 June. The allegations included an association with casino owner George Zirios Walker, George Freeman and Abe Saffron and, more specifically, that a senior policeman had been at the Wentworth Hotel on

7 November 1977 with a casino operator. It was there that two women, Joanna Coman and Erica Scott, were killed two days later. There were also allegations that Wood was linked to a drug conspiracy case with the one-time Chief Stipendiary Magistrate Murray Farquhar, the dishonest Sydney solicitor Morgan Ryan and a convicted drug trafficker, Roy Cessna. The case had been heard in May 1979 when Farquhar dealt with Cessna most leniently. Originally he had been charged with the importation of cannabis valued at $1.5 million. In court the value was more amorphously given as 'some value'. Farquhar fined him a nominal amount. The allegations were that Morgan Ryan had pressed his old friend Wood for help. Wood died in 2006, aged eighty-nine.

Jim Lees, a devout Christian, was the commissioner next up to bat but he simply could not cope and lasted only two years. During his time, however, he had to deal with the corrupt Bill Allen still clawing his way to the top and it was at the end of 1981 that the lid blew off. As was often the case the problem arose over gambling and the plans for a casino at a time when Allen was the assistant commissioner for licensing. There was a separate allegation that on five occasions that year Allen had given Warren Molloy, then chief of the Special Licensing Squad, $500 cash in an envelope. There was also a problem caused by the regular visits of Abe Saffron to Allen's office.

What is absolutely clear is that on 6 June 1981 Allen, his wife and 23-year-old daughter flew First Class on Pan Am, first to Hawaii where they met another of Allen's daughters and her husband. There they stayed free of charge at the home of Lori Yip, the daughter of the chief of the Macau Trotting Club. On 11 June they went on to San Francisco, staying again free of charge in the Holiday Inn at Union Square, courtesy of 'representations' by the Sydney bookmaker Bill Waterhouse. Then it was on to Las Vegas where once again they were in luck because, this time, the tab was picked up by Jack Rooklyn, the head of the Bally poker machines in Australia, a man who had come under heavy fire from Mr Justice Moffitt. Allen had known Rooklyn from earlier in the year and had been not only to his office but also twice to his home and once on his yacht. Not only had the Allens been paid for but happily Bill Allen had won $1000 on the machines.

This was the second freebie in as many months; earlier in May, Allen, his wife and daughter had been in Macau, guests of the *Sociedade de Turismo e Diversoes de Macao*, run by the Yip family. Allen was a man who liked cash. He told the inquiry he was a regular winner at the races. He bought his house for cash, paid off his American Express card in cash and, he said, he kept $10000 in cash at home. In turn the inquiry told him that by accepting hospitality and associating with the likes of Saffron and Rooklyn he had acted in a manner likely to discredit the police. By paying money to Molloy he had tried to compromise him. Allen resigned.

Tony Lauer, back from exile in the Blue Mountains, was appointed in 1991. He just could not accept that there was corruption in his force until it was too late for him to save his career. He argued against a Royal Commission, claiming that reports that 'corruption was entrenched' were 'figments of the political imagination' — this in the teeth of evidence to the contrary.

* * *

By the mid-1980s on any account certain police officers were not only out of control but also, as it was said of Lord Byron, 'mad, bad and dangerous to know'. Once a shooting star, Roger Rogerson had aligned himself with a major criminal and was taking an active part in the drug war which was running in Sydney at the time.

It was during these drug wars of the 1980s that some members of the New South Wales Police really appear to have shown their true colours. Roger Rogerson, who served under both Krahe and Fergusson, had a most unhealthy relationship with Neddy Smith, much of which would be revealed, along with a picture of Rogerson in his underwear, in Smith's book *Neddy*. In 1990 Smith was given a sentence of life imprisonment for what amounted to the road rage killing of Glen Flavell. He had stabbed the truck driver to death in a Coogee street. In 1993 he went into segregated confinement as he became a principal witness at the Independent Commission against Corruption hearing conducted by Ian Temby QC, which led to a Royal Commission.

Chaired by Mr Justice Wood, the commission sat for more than 450 days and heard 640 witnesses. Its broad terms of reference were to inquire into the existence of corruption and misconduct within the police service and into the efficacy of its Internal Affairs Branch. As an immediate result, eighty-two police officers were dismissed. It was, even its critics agreed, the most thorough and far-reaching of all the inquiries into the police. The star witness was the corrupt former Detective Trevor

Haken who had worked with the Joint Commonwealth–State Drug Task Force (JTF) for two years from 1983. At an early stage he had been persuaded to roll over and, provided with a mini-camera, taped and filmed his dealings with other corrupt colleagues. On 12 September 1995 he gave evidence about his dealings, including the New Year's Eve 1983 divvying up of $200000 taken by officers from drug dealers.

In June, Wendy Hatfield, an apparently shining young probationary officer, described how she had felt compromised by the behaviour of her male and senior colleagues. On one occasion she had been at the Downunder Motel in Kings Cross and was told by a 'Mr Ibrahim', who seemed to be the manager, that there was between $1500 and $1800 behind a wood panel in a bedroom. When she returned to the motel some hours later there was only $100 to $200 and she presumed, she told the Wood Royal Commission, that the rest had been taken by corrupt police. Unfortunately Ms Hatfield fell from grace when it was alleged she had been romantically involved with John Ibrahim, covering for him over a driving offence and holidaying with him. In December 1995 *The Sydney Morning Herald* placed her at No. 6 on its table of losers for the year.

As the weeks went by the commission's investigators found it apparent that Mr Justice Wood was quite prepared to be ruthless with police officers who initially followed the golden rule that provided they all stuck together they would be all right. They were swiftly disabused of the usefulness of this approach.

In December 1995 Wayne Eade, the former head of the Gosford Drug Squad, faced questioning by Virginia Bell, assistant counsel to the inquiry. Yes, he thought he was an officer 'of impeccable integrity'. No, he did not have an interest in child porn videos. Nor had he tried to buy ecstasy for colleagues; he knew that was an illegal drug. He had certainly never visited a witness code-named GDU7, a former prostitute and drug dealer, while on duty.

It was a classic piece of cross-examination. Eade was then invited to look at a film taken when he was on duty at 10.40 p.m. on 27 August that year. Up on the television screens in the room appeared a film of GDU7 pouring a line of cocaine on the officer's penis and then proceeding to lick it off. She then started to talk about a shipment of cocaine before they moved to a couch where he began masturbating and talking about buying ecstasy and a porn video of children. The screen went blank as GDU7 was about to provide more oral sex.

Wood asked Eade if he wished to see more of the film, adding: 'I'm not saying that by way of a threat. I'm not suggesting I want to show it publicly, but you and your solicitor are free to view the entirety of the tape, including the sexual relations depicted, if you wish to do so.' Eade did not. Before the end of the day the man about whom there had been suspicions for the previous ten years and who had survived a number of internal investigations, had been dismissed by the beleaguered Commissioner Tony Lauer. That half hour broke the resistance of corrupt officers. Who could tell who was on film and in what position? No longer a question of solidarity, it was more one of all hands to the life raft.

Historically few investigations had gone further than officers being asked to resign and, if they did not, being dismissed. The commission was no exception. At the end of 1995 an amnesty was offered to corrupt officers if they agreed to tell all and provided evidence against their colleagues. This was, said Mr Justice Wood, a once-and-for-all amnesty. Those who did not take advantage of it would not get a second chance. They had until 9 February 1996 to come out of the locker room. Resignation would be required but they would be allowed to keep their superannuation, pension and ill-gotten gains.

With the Wood Royal Commission winding down, in mid-January 1996 Lauer resigned as commissioner. Unfortunately not only had he been quite unable to recognise that there were corrupt officers in the force, but he was also given to making statements that would rebound on him. In 1993 he said, 'In New South Wales we are at the cutting edge of policing as far as our ability to act on corruption among officers.' The next year there was another statement that would come to haunt him: 'It ought to be my responsibility that this service never again has working among it another Roger Rogerson.'

In June 1996 Peter Ryan, a lecturer at Bramshill Police College in England, was called in at a salary of $400000—rather more than that of the premier—to drink from the poisoned chalice. The job had been hawked around senior officers in Britain and although he had been chief constable of rural Norfolk, Ryan had never commanded a city force. From the start he was isolated and was fed contradictory advice and information. At his first press conference on 11 June he asked, 'Who is Roger Rogerson?' The press conference came to a hurried end.

Some 200 officers were known to have criminal records when Ryan took over. It was proposed he should have power of dismissal without appeal. Unsurprisingly it was an unpopular move and on 20 November there were demonstrations with calls to 'send the Pommie back'. Seventy per cent of officers sacked for having criminal convictions won reinstatement at industrial tribunals. In fact, after the Royal Commission only one person went to jail.

When he was interviewed shortly after his appointment Ryan had been keen to dismiss suggestions that he did not have the depth of experience to deal with city detectives bent on hiding their misdeeds. 'People have overlooked the fact that there is a determination to clean up the act. It rests not only with me but with a widespread group of people.' There was now in place a Police Integrity Commission, established in January 1997 to root out corruption.

On 7 February 1997 Ryan launched a new code of conduct, including the banning of free gifts and drinking on duty, and the threat of dismissal for any criminal offence such as drink driving. It did not go down well, particularly when it was immediately disclosed that he had earlier accepted a ticket for the Grand Final and another for the opening night of *Crazy for You*.

On 28 June that year the drug dealer Ron Levi was shot by officers Rodney Podesta and Anthony Dilorenzo on Bondi Beach. Two years later Podesta admitted he had dealt in cocaine. Another problem was when former stripper and prostitute Kim Hollingsworth was dismissed after eight weeks at the police academy. Some of her stripping performances had been for police functions. Ryan was quite unwilling to let her stay but he was overruled and she was reinstated prior to dropping out of the course.

Ryan announced in 2001 that his reformatory mission was now complete. In his earlier years in New South Wales he had faced a good deal of sniping on a professional and personal level but he had weathered the storm. In his first months he had dismissed twenty officers and 150 had been suspended. 'When it was seen I was dismissing officers, there was a rush to hand in resignations,' he said. The force was now clean.

Unfortunately at hearings of the Police Integrity Commission that same year, Operation Florida, a three year sting mounted by the force's internal anti-corruption unit, told something of a different story. Microphones and cameras had been planted in lavatories in the North Shore suburb of Manly and the police were filmed as they met and dealt with drug dealers. One detective was filmed pushing banknotes down his trousers. He had found the money while searching the home of a cannabis dealer. Another clip of film showed three officers taking $40000 and laughing as they chorused 'Happy Days'. At an operation in Manly in 1992 it was alleged $100000 plus had been shared among officers.

Much of the evidence came from a former officer, known as M5, who had been trapped and persuaded to roll over. For six months he recorded what he did on a daily basis. Six officers were later convicted of offences. Forty former officers and three serving officers were said by the commission to have been guilty of a variety of offences but because of the lack of corroboration they were never prosecuted. One Sydney solicitor was acquitted of bribery and acting with intent to pervert the course of justice. Nevertheless, the Law Society cancelled his practising certificate. Ryan, who had just negotiated a new $400000 a year contract, was said to be very angry about the affair, as well he might be. Putting on a brave face, he told his force to, 'Wear your uniform with pride.' But on the roads drivers who had stopped for speeding were asking the police 'How much?'

Ryan said that the operation showed his reforms were working. In fairness to him a good deal of the evidence heard by the commission pre-dated his appointment. It was a long uphill struggle in which he was eventually totally isolated. He resigned on 3 April 2002 amidst scenes of recrimination on all sides. There are very mixed views on the likely legacy of his tenure. Some feel he was a major influence in stamping on corruption. Others, including senior officers, believe he was not sufficiently firm on ethnic gang crime.

* * *

In Victoria there seems to have been a belief that while corruption thrived in New South Wales, when it came to the Murray River it drowned. In 1975, following more allegations by Dr Wainer, Barry Beach QC held a fifteen month long inquiry at the end of which he made adverse findings against fifty-five officers. Thirty-two were charged and all acquitted.

Nor does it appear that the lesson of Wayne Eade and the video tape travelled interstate. At a Police Integrity hearing in September 2006 witness A100 told how he had asked to be allowed to make a telephone call. A videotape apparently showed an officer hitting the suspect with the telephone saying, 'Here's your ******* call.' Questioned about the tape he said, 'I don't know who it is … I'm denying it.'

Perhaps the biggest of the police and political corruption scandals has been in neither New South Wales nor Victoria but in Queensland. In the late 1980s allegations of corruption reached to the very, very top there, engulfing even the Premier, Joh Bjelke-Petersen. Apart from Police Commissioner Sir Terence Lewis and senior police officers, five Cabinet ministers were ultimately charged. Four were convicted—the fifth died while facing the charges. Also convicted were three business magnates, including Jack Rooklyn, along with a variety of identities including brothel owners Hector Hapeta, Geraldo Bellino and Ronald 'The Pom' Kingsnorth.

It was the culmination of decades of shady policy dealing. In 1957, when Frank Eric Bischof became commissioner, he shut down the brothels in the Brisbane inner city by the old expedient of padlocking the doors. One of the best known brothels, Killarney, employed Shirley Brifman who, along with two other women, Val Weidinger and Lilly Ryan, were police informants. Very quickly an arrangement was made with hotel managers to allow these women to solicit in the lounges.

In 1963 came a Royal Commission, chaired by Justice Harry Gibbs, into allegations of police protection of prostitution and after hours drinking at the National Hotel during the previous five years. Although the police bagman Jack Herbert was mentioned, along with a number of others who would feature in the Commission of Inquiry fifteen years later, soon it was back to business as usual. Herbert did not retire for another eleven years and that was when he was arrested and charged with corruption. He was acquitted in 1976 and then took up work in the gaming industry. But he was soon back acting as bagman for police officers, collecting from those involved in SP bookmaking, prostitution and gambling generally.

Bischof had retired in 1970 and fell from grace when he was charged with shoplifting in 1974. He was actually committed for trial before the charges were dropped. It was only after his death that allegations began to surface that he had been involved in massive graft involving SP bookmakers. In 1982 the state treasurer revealed that as long ago as 1964 bookmakers paid protection ranging from $80 000 in large towns to $20 000 in small country ones. Additionally, and this is what riled them, top-ups were demanded.

When Shirley Brifman was found dead in her flat in Clayfield on 4 March 1972 she had also been due to give evidence against Detective Senior Sergeant Tony Murphy who had been charged with perjury relating to his evidence to the National Hotel Royal Commission. He had told the commission that he had been unable to establish whether she was a prostitute. With her death the charges against him also died.

The position of Bischof's successor, Commissioner Ray Whitrod, described by one newspaper as 'The Last of the Honest Cops', was consistently undermined and he resigned in 1976. Now the Queensland Police had its own Rat Pack, which included Terry Lewis—whose promotion from sergeant to commissioner had been meteoric—Tony Murphy, Jack Herbert and Glenn Hallahan. They were firmly behind the Premier Joh Bjelke-Petersen and equally firmly against 'undesirables' such as homosexuals, Aborigines, students and hippies, not necessarily in that order.

The wheels were grinding slowly, very slowly. In 1986 the Director of Public Prosecutions, Des Sturgess QC, conducted a limited inquiry into police corruption. By the middle of 1987 Phil Dickie of the *Courier-Mail* was calling for an investigation into police corruption in the state. Following the footage shown on Chris Masters's 'Moonlight State' documentary for the ABC's *Four Corners*, the National Party government set up an inquiry presided over by Tony Fitzgerald QC. In theory the terms were narrow—the remit was the previous five years—but Fitzgerald manoeuvred the position to a far wider ranging investigation. At its centre was the one time English policeman Jack Herbert who in 1947 emigrated first to Victoria, then, not finding things there to his liking, trekked to Queensland and joined the force in 1949. It was nine years before he joined the Licensing Branch and became involved in taking bribes—a process known as 'The Joke'—from SP bookmakers, casino operators and brothel owners. He maintained he had only started to slip from the path of righteousness when he had to pay heavy medical bills following his wife's illness. He would always deny he was involved in the drug trade but there is little doubt that drugs were washing around the Herbert-protected massage parlours owned by Hector Hapeta, later jailed for life for heroin trafficking.

The Fitzgerald Inquiry's live hearings began with a bang. On 27 July 1987 the commissioner of police, Sir Terence Murray Lewis, said that policing prostitution was a low priority for the Queensland force. On 31 August, Sergeant Harry Burgess admitted corruption and was given immunity. He now implicated Herbert and also the assistant commissioner, Graeme Parker, and the Licensing Branch chief, Noel Dwyer. On 17 September, Parker admitted corruption.

A few days later Sir Terence Lewis was stood down. In November, the premier, Sir Joh, stood down after reports that he would be removed as parliamentary leader by his National Party colleagues, and the following month he announced his retirement from politics.

In March 1988 Herbert and his wife were retrieved from England, to where they had fled, and that September he became the inquiry's principal witness, detailing payments totalling $1.5 million paid to senior officers including Sir Terence, known as 'Big Daddy' or 'The Shark'—'because he took the biggest bite'.

Before then, on 20 June, Ann Marie Tilley admitted that her husband Hector Hapeta ran a $30 million vice empire and paid Herbert $38000 a month and Harry Burgess another $2000. On 31 August Herbert agreed that over the years he had given Lewis $600000. On 11 October, Lewis, who had been commissioner from 1978 to 1987, said that, in his forty years as a policeman, he had never known or suspected there was corruption in the force.

On 3 July 1989 Tony Fitzgerald released his report making wide-sweeping recommendations but being careful not to make accusations, instead saying that it was not the guilt or innocence of any individual that was the concern but the 'pattern, nature and scope of the misconduct that has occurred and the lesson it contains for the future'.

However disappointed some observers may have been with this, the fallout was immense. In 1991 Lewis stood trial on twenty-three counts of perjury, forgery and corruption. He was acquitted of the perjury allegations but convicted of accepting $700000 in bribes as well as forging the premier's signature on an official document. Although he had denied he ever met the poker machine identity Jack Rooklyn, there were entries to show that he had done so on a number of occasions. Lewis was never charged with this particular lie, something many thought would be easy to prove. Throughout he protested his innocence. Lewis was sentenced to fourteen years, complaining bitterly that much of the evidence against him came from Herbert. He was released after serving ten and a half years and was stripped of his knighthood. Former premier Sir Joh's trial for perjury ended in controversy and a hung jury. On 25 May 1992 Jack Rooklyn, then aged eighty-four, was spared prison because of his age. He was fined $35 000. Herbert died on 7 April 2004.

Over on the west coast the deaths of two retired officers on 1 September 2001 led to yet another re-examination of a case that had long caused problems for the Perth police. The deaths were those of Don Hancock, one-time head of the Perth CIB, and his friend Louis 'Lou' Lewis, which followed the fatal shooting of Gypsy Joker biker William 'Billy' Grierson. The case that was re-examined was the Perth Mint robbery of 1982 and the convictions of the Mickelberg brothers, Peter, Ray and Brian.

On 22 June 1982 three different couriers, each with false cheques, arrived at the Mint in the middle of the city and took away gold bullion weighing 68 kilograms and worth $653 000. (In today's terms it would be valued at around $1.5 million.) The couriers then delivered the gold to an office several kilometres away and promptly vanished. In many ways it was an impressive crime—daring, well thought through and best of all there was no violence involved. In charge of the investigation was Detective Sergeant Don Hancock, one of many officers worldwide who revelled in the soubriquet 'Grey Fox'.

High on the list of suspects were the Mickelberg brothers, who worked as abalone divers and pilots. Ray Mickelberg was a former SAS commando in Vietnam and, given the military precision with which the raid had been carried through, was regarded as the mastermind. They had only one previous conviction between them: Peter had been fined $50 for possessing an unlicensed firearm.

On 26 July that year Peter Mickelberg was driving home to the northern suburbs of Perth when a police car pulled in front of him, forcing him to stop. He was taken to Belmont Police Station where he was interviewed by Hancock and Tony Lewandowski. This was regarded as an odd choice of police station as there was a headquarters in the city specially set up to deal with the robbery. Other odd features of the arrest are that all other officers save one attached to Belmont had left the station by the time Mickelberg arrived. The one remaining officer, Bob Kucera, later the Western Australian health minister, left shortly after.

According to Peter Mickelberg, first Lewandowski told him that no one knew where he was and that as far as others were concerned he could be dead, then Hancock told Lewandowski to make the prisoner strip and punched Mickelberg in the solar plexus and throat. Years later Lewandowski claimed he told Hancock that they really had no evidence but Hancock replied, 'Don't worry, it will get better.' According to Hancock and Lewandowski, Peter Mickelberg confessed to his involvement and implicated his brothers. The confession was, as is often the case, unsigned. The prosecution also claimed that a fingerprint matching Ray Mickelberg's was found on one of the fraudulent cheques. The defence claimed that, since one of his hobbies was casting hands it would have been easy for the police to obtain a mould of Mickelberg's finger. There were about twenty casts found when his home at Marmion Beach was raided. In 1983 Ray Mickelberg received twenty years and his brother Peter six. Brian served nine months before his conviction was quashed.

Over the years Peter and Ray Mickelberg made a total of seven appeals—six to the Western Australian Court of Criminal Appeal—and all were rejected. In 1989 some 55 kilograms of the gold was left in a Perth suburb, which certainly cannot have been done by the brothers. Brian Mickelberg had died in a helicopter crash in 1986 and the other two were still in prison. A bar and two containers, later tested and identified by the Perth mint, was sent to a local television station together with a note that the Mickelbergs were innocent and had been framed. It also claimed that a prominent Perth businessman was behind the swindle.

After an appeal was rejected in November 1989 the police commissioner, Brian Bull, told the press that the decision 'totally vindicates the actions of the police in their investigation into the Perth mint swindle'. Peter Mickelberg was released that year and Ray two years later, when each had served his sentence.

Regarded as a man who knew how to get results, Don Hancock became the head of the Perth CIB on the back of the successful prosecution of the brothers. One officer said he was a 'take no prisoners sort of bloke' and described him as 'the Roger Rogerson of West Australia without the criminality'.

It was after Hancock's death that Tony Lewandowski, now estranged from his wife and son, swore an affidavit admitting that he had lied and had taken part in the beating of Peter Mickelberg. While Lewandowski admitted fabricating evidence he said he still believed the brothers to be responsible for the robbery, and asked the DPP for immunity. But while it was being considered he left the country.

He returned to give evidence by video-link on 27 September 2002 at a preliminary hearing of a further appeal by the brothers. On 2 July 2004, by a majority of two to one the court allowed the appeal, quashed the conviction and indicated there would be no retrial. It is difficult to see how there could have been. Hancock was dead and so was Lewandowski, who had committed suicide at his Perth home in May of that year. The chief justice, David Malcolm, and Justice Christopher Steytler were in favour of allowing the appeal. Justice Michael Murray was not, holding that no miscarriage of justice had occurred. Western Australia Police were unwilling to accept the verdict. Assistant Police Commissioner Neil Hay said there was an abundance of evidence linking the brothers; and the brothers, in turn, claimed $11 million compensation.

The perennial problem for police and their handlers is the high level of temptation on offer. As Norman Gulbransen, one-time acting commissioner of the Queensland Police (who died in August 2006) said, 'The rewards for dishonesty are greater than for honesty.'

Some Bent Briefs

16

One of the wishes of crime bosses is that their children should take up a profession and so become at least semi-legitimate. In Melbourne, Gaetano 'Tom' Scriva, grandson of the old hardman from the 1960s Michele Scriva, was one such. He became a solicitor. In 1986 he had defended, among others, Claudio Crupi, charged with shooting with intent to murder the police officer Gerard Michael Wilson. Crupi was also questioned and cleared over the bombing of Russell Street Police Headquarters that year. Over the years Scriva acted for major criminals such as Victor Peirce, for whom he laundered the proceeds of the ANZ Bank robbery in Ringwood in January 1988. A friend of the Benvenutos, he had his licence to practice withdrawn after he claimed to witness signatures on statutory declarations and fraudulently completed a certificate of identity. He would have been able to apply for reinstatement in 2009 but, in the months before his death following a heart attack on 13 July 2000, he had allegedly been acting as a loan shark and had embarked on a very successful campaign to raise $6 million. The bait was interest of 18 per cent and Scriva took a cut of the lending margin as well as a fee from each duped investor. One source said, 'I think he honestly believed he was still a lawyer.' Most of the money he raised was never traced. The same applied to the remainder of the money he was holding for his underworld clients. Perhaps his death was timely.

It is impossible for career criminals to flourish over a long period without the active help of lawyers. On the professional side bail must be obtained, inadmissible evidence excluded, impassioned speeches made to juries, sentences kept to the minimum possible. On the unprofessional side lawyers are needed to fabricate defences, create false alibis, bribe police officers, suborn witnesses and look after the proceeds of crime either by laundering the money or acting as a banker.

Criminal lawyers, or lawyers who undertake criminal cases as they prefer to be known, generally receive a poor press. If their client is acquitted, then the police and public think that it is their trickery rather than defaults in the prosecution's case which has allowed a murderer, a kidnapper or a rapist to go free. Nevertheless there are some who, over the years, appear to have gone out of their way to give their profession a bad name. For instance, in the 1970s in New South Wales, it was suggested that some defence lawyers were 'buying briefs', with the police making their evidence available in advance of the hearing, so allowing the defence to tailor its case to the material supplied.

Lawyers are no different from other men and women in society. One expects them, possibly because of their education and the calling they have answered, to perform on a higher plane of ethics than, say, car salesmen or estate agents. The same is true of doctors and clerics but there is no reason why lawyers, doctors and clerics should not suffer venereal itch or sticky fingers, tiresome wives or importunate boyfriends any less than stock car racing promoters or fire fighters.

As a general proposition lawyers are not at risk from their clients unless they step over the boundaries and get into business with them. Then life for a bent lawyer can be extremely dangerous and indeed short, as Max Green found out. He had once been a partner in the Melbourne firm Shugg & Green and then another firm from whom he embezzled some $42 000, money belonging in the main to wealthy Jewish clients. It appears that he then invested part of the money in Gem Mining Leo, a sapphire mine in Laos. In 1998 his body was found in his room at a Phnom Penh hotel. He had been hit on the head with a tile and then strangled. There was no sign of forced entry to his room and the local police concluded he knew his killer. The Victoria Police indicated they would like to interview a Bangkok identity who had known Green back in Melbourne before the embezzlement. It was thought he had siphoned from clients a total of $9 million, converting it into Swiss francs.

* * *

Corrupt police officers always like a bagman to act as the intermediary between themselves and the criminals from whom they are extracting favours, money or both. In the 1980s there were three main squads of detectives in Sydney: the Special Breaking Squad, or the 'Breakers' as they were known, the Armed Hold-Up Squad and the Drug Squad, which had only recently been formed. Some members of the first two had been trading with criminals over the years. A major problem for a police officer who accepts bribes or leans on a criminal is that one day, if it suits him or he feels the officer is taking more than his fair share, the man may turn on him. The authorities may well then be prepared to offer a lesser sentence if he informs on the corrupt officer. A facilitator is therefore an extremely welcome addition to the game. He provides some guarantee of fair treatment to the criminal and some degree of protection to the officer.

Brian Alexander was a solicitor's clerk who filled this position admirably. Born in Sydney in 1939, he was ten when his parents separated and he went to live with his father's sister. Although he often referred to himself as a solicitor, he was not qualified; indeed he had not done particularly well at St Anne's Marist Brothers School in Bondi. Initially he worked for a solicitor with a practice dealing with lower level criminals and prostitutes in the Cross area. During this time he took correspondence courses to qualify as a solicitor or a barrister but never completed them. He also became the associate of criminals (convicted and not) and also a group of detectives in the New South Wales force.

After nearly twenty years Alexander then joined John Aston, a solicitor who had a mainly commercial practice but was looking to acquire high quality criminal work. This was unusual. Normally a solicitor with a commercial practice would regard criminal work to be beneath him, with the possible exception of high-class fraud. Aston must have come to regret his decision.

One of the men with whom Alexander dealt was the notorious Neddy Smith, who would later serve a series of life sentences for murder and became regarded as a killing machine. He had been charged with receiving, something which was not of itself too much of a problem. His difficulty was that he was still on parole for his 1968 rape offence. In his book *Catch and Kill Your Own*, Smith recalled his first meeting with Alexander: 'He was standing there looking like a combined advert for top brand-name fashions, like Simon Ackerman suits, Yves St Laurent shirts and Gucci shoes. He was decked out to impress, and impress he did. But still there was something missing.'

Alexander took some $3000 from Smith to obtain bail on the receiving charge and later came to his aid when Smith fell foul of Roger Rogerson and the Armed Hold-Up Squad and was charged with shooting with intent to kill and armed robbery. Despite Smith's quite appalling record and the seriousness of the charges, he was given bail and later acquitted of all the counts against him. Alexander later put himself about when Smith was found to have some $39000 for which he could not account and which the police said came from drug smuggling. Smith's half-brother had also been arrested and Alexander sold Smith the statements his brother had allegedly made against him.

Smith then allegedly bought the whole of the evidence against him for $4000 and was asked for $50000 for the case to be dropped against his wife, who was about to be charged. He paid the money but the next day conspiracy charges were preferred. He sent for Alexander who refunded $25000, saying the rest had gone to two police officers.

Alexander was, however, involved not only with Smith but also with some seriously heavy players in international drug smuggling. What emerged at the 1980–83 Stewart Royal Commission into Drug Trafficking was that Alexander was a tried and trusted man on drug dealer Terrence John Clark's staff with valuable contacts in the Narcotics Bureau. Witnesses told the inquiry that if a member of the syndicate was arrested Alexander would be contacted and would not only provide legal representation but would also report back to Clark whether they were remaining staunch. On a legitimate income of $32000, Alexander earned $130000 in the year before his death.

On 25 March 1981 Alexander was arrested and charged with conspiring with two federal narcotics agents. The allegation was that the three of them had disclosed confidential information about the drug couriers Douglas and Isabel Wilson to Clark, who had promptly had them killed. The case was dismissed at the committal proceedings because the Crown could not prove beyond doubt the source of the leaks. It was, however, the end of Alexander's 'legal' career. He was effectively unemployable and drifted into drink and working out of hotels. Now it was learned that he was likely to give evidence to the Stewart Royal Commission and name names, dates, places and amounts. On 21 December 1981, shortly after Alexander was seen drinking with three men in the King's Head Tavern near his office on Park Street, Sydney, he disappeared. Two weeks later his car was found abandoned near The Gap at Watsons Bay, a place known for suicides.

According to Smith, however, Alexander was too much of a coward to commit suicide in that way and he heard a story that the clerk had been driven to the Darling Street wharf in Balmain and, handcuffed behind his back, was thrown from a launch with an old gas stove tied around his body. He was apparently still alive and crying when he went in the water. Smith concludes this moral tale: 'But I had no part in it. That was something I wouldn't wish even on someone like Brian Alexander.' The Crown decided not to proceed with the prosecution of Smith for the murder.

The early 1990s saw a new role for Smith—that of assistant to justice. He had become an informer and was now the star witness at hearings conducted by the Independent Commission against Corruption. Much of his evidence was directed at the solicitor Graham Valentine 'Val' Bellamy, with whom he had had such a working relationship in the past that a Mercedes-Benz and a Rolls-Royce which belonged to him had conveniently been registered in the solicitor's name. One incident they shared, according to Smith, was the snatching of a bag containing $60000, not once but two times in almost as many minutes. Around 3 p.m. on 17 September 1984 a black vinyl bag that contained money withdrawn from a safety deposit box at the Commonwealth Bank in Castlereagh Street was snatched from Bellamy as he walked through Martin Place. A passer-by—some say it was Bellamy's own father—chased after the thief and retrieved the bag with the help of an off-duty policeman and returned it to Bellamy. The theft was repeated successfully almost immediately. This time the solicitor was punched in the stomach.

Smith's version of the matter was that the robbery was a put-up job to cover Bellamy's withdrawals from the box on his own account. A fee of $10000 was, he claimed, paid to a police officer to help fake a report on the robbery.

Another man who claimed to have worked with Bellamy was the former police officer Trevor Haken. He maintained that he had been speaking with Bellamy at a police court and had mentioned that the prosecution was going to drop the case against Bellamy's client because a witness had failed to appear. The solicitor, alleged Haken, had seen this as a singular opportunity to make money and had told the client that the police would drop the case for $5000. The satisfied client drew the money from the bank and Bellamy and Haken split it.

Then there was the question of a tape which appeared to suggest that Bellamy and Smith had chatted about the disposal of some stolen gold coins. Bellamy was sure the voice was not his but he agreed that he knew about them. Indeed, he had accepted them as part payment of his legal fees. Poor Bellamy was also accused of faking statements from a number of witnesses which exculpated Smith in a fight at the City of Sydney RSL Club back in December 1984. He said he had no recollection of them although he presumed he was acting for Smith at the time.

He was not pleased with ICAC, seeing himself as the only person to be bitten by it. An application for his evidence to be heard partly in private and for his name to be withheld was refused. He went on television to explain his position, commenting as a sort of trailer for the program: 'That's the difficulty with being a criminal lawyer. I lost the murder trial; he turned on me.' Curiously he did not seem to hold this ratting against Smith. 'He's a very likeable bloke, a very intelligent bloke. He's lived a very impressive life and he was always good company.'

The ICAC reported in 1994 and recommended that consideration should be given to preferring charges of stealing, perjury and possibly conspiracy to steal against Bellamy. It also enjoined the Law Society to consider disciplinary action.

Bellamy was not, however, without a sense of humour. At the time applications for the post of the new commissioner of ICAC were being considered and he put his name forward. The firm of head-hunters employed to sift the candidates declined to say whether he had been interviewed, but he did not get the appointment. Shortly afterwards he was served with summonses alleging he had lied to the commission and that he had misappropriated money.

In September 1998, now suffering from Parkinson's disease, Smith was back in court and convicted of another murder, this time of drug dealer Harvey Jones. By now he had recanted his apparent confession and said that his cell mate, known as 'Green', might have been paid to tell his story through a solicitor enemy of Smith. His loyal wife said that all she knew to the detriment of her husband was that he might have been an illegal bookmaker: 'People say I must have been so naïve, but Ned could have been leaving home at eight in the morning, coming home at five and said he was a doctor. I never asked, and he would tell me what I wanted to know.'

In May 1999 Smith appeared in the Glebe Coroner's Court when an inquest was held into the disappearance of male model and cocaine dealer Mark Johnston. What was definitely known was that the last sighting of Johnston was on 1 September when he had called on Val Bellamy to collect $60000 which the solicitor had been holding for him. Johnston's hired Holden Commodore was found eight days later at Maroubra after a tip-off by an anonymous woman. There were over 500 grams of cocaine in the car and some loose change. When Bellamy was seen by the police he told them he was constrained by client confidentiality and could not discuss the matter. However, he agreed that Johnston had been to his home and had stayed about fifteen minutes before leaving with his money.

What was less clear was what had happened to Johnston whose father, Arthur, had spoken to Bellamy a week after his son's disappearance. Mark had told his father that he had tried to arrange three meetings with Bellamy to collect his money.

It all came back to those cell confessions. It was alleged that Smith had told his cell mate that he had killed Johnston at the solicitor's request. In the confession he said that he had handcuffed and then garrotted the drug dealer rather than stab him, as a stabbing would have spoiled the carpet in the solicitor's new $3.5 million home at Dover Heights.

Detective Sergeant Neville Smith told the court that he believed Bellamy knew full well what had happened to Johnston and found it difficult to accept that the money had been returned to him. In turn the coroner ruled that Johnston was dead and that he had been killed at Dover Heights. He ordered the papers to be sent to the Director of Public Prosecutions.

After the hearing Arthur Johnston—who had told the court that he believed Bellamy, 'motivated by greed and avarice', had taken his son's money—said that he felt a sense of sorrow for Smith. 'As to Bellamy, however, I feel total repugnance.'

On 5 May 1999 Bellamy, now working as a telephone clerk, was charged with fraud involving nearly three quarters of a million dollars, including one charge of obtaining $350000 from Broadway Credit Union. On 11 October 2000 he was sentenced to four years with at least two to be served. He had pleaded guilty and in mitigation blamed his downfall on Smith. Justice Blanch took the view that he would be at risk from Smith in the prison system and recommended that on his arrival Bellamy be transferred into protective custody.

* * *

Mario Condello was a lawyer who had a long and interesting career on both sides of the fence. His father, a painter and decorator from Calabria, had been captured in Libya during the war and sent to work on a farm near Warrnambool. After the war he returned to Italy, married, then emigrated to Australia. Condello was born in 1952 and educated at Fitzroy High before going on to study law at the University of Melbourne. Almost from the start of his legal career he was involved in laundering and extortion.

In December 1982 he was sentenced to six years' imprisonment after a marijuana crop was found on land he leased near Ararat. A fortnight earlier he had been struck off the roll by the Supreme Court. After his release from prison he owned a restaurant in Bourke Street and, says one of his former lawyers, 'also had an interest in the cemetery business'. The next year he was found guilty on two counts of arson.

On 5 March 1985 Condello stood trial for the attempted murder of Richard Jones, a businessman who had upset another. Condello had been called in to deal with the recalcitrant Jones who was shot in the stomach through a doona as he lay in bed. Amazingly, Jones survived because feathers plugged the wound. Condello was found not guilty after a confession he had made was ruled to be not under caution.

In 1986 he received four years for conspiracy to defraud an insurance company. His company bought 120 000 prints for $2.40 each and arranged a sham sale in Italy which valued the prints at $1.4 million. The prints were said to have burned in Naples during a riot. Happily for art collectors worldwide this was not the case.

Outraged at the 1982 charges, Condello hired a hitman to dispose of the trial judge, the prosecuting lawyer and the main prosecution witness. His plan was foiled when the police arrested the proposed hitman on an entirely different matter and documents relating to the attempt were found at his house.

Condello was fined in 1993 for being in an illegal gaming house and again in 2003, this time for the possession of a variety of weapons, which included a stun gun, a hunting knife and a pool cue. Throughout his career he was suspected of providing a link between the Honoured

Society and other criminal enterprises, including Romanian drug dealers. He was said to have been present when a solicitor was pistol-whipped in the cellar of a Lygon Street restaurant. He was quite prepared to order beatings, even if he did not deign to carry them out himself. The man's client had been likely to give evidence against protection racketeers. By now Condello was a senior member of Melbourne's Carlton Crew, a loose-knit confederacy which since the mid-1990s had battled other groups such as the New Boys for control of the drug market. Regarded as a lender of last resort, like all sharks Condello could keep a debtor on the hook for years. One man to whom he lent $2.3 million had to repay $10 000 weekly. A great gambler, Condello was barred from Melbourne's Crown Casino in 2004.

Far from being a solicitor, Condello should be regarded as a truly international Calabrian *Mafioso* with links to the Neapolitan N'Dranheta, of whom even the violent Alphonse Gangitano was afraid.

Times have changed in criminal legal practice. Gone are the days when clients were never spoken to outside the confines of their cases. Now clients expect their lawyers to socialise with them and some solicitors and barristers dine happily with often charismatic senior identities, so courting the ever present danger that they will be irrevocably drawn into the webs spun by their clients.

Those who ignore the dangers of becoming too close to criminal clients do so at their own peril. It is far more difficult to decline an offer from someone with whom one has just eaten dinner or been to the races. One Melbourne lawyer who became far too close to his clients for his comfort and paid the penalty was Andrew Roderick Fraser. His roster of clients ran the gamut of criminals—from some of the Hells Angels to the disgraced tycoon Alan Bond, the footballer Jimmy Krakouer and the scion of the Pettingill family, Dennis Allen, known as 'Mr Death'.

Fraser also acted for Anthony Leigh Farrell over the killing of the two young policemen in Walsh Street in 1988 when his robustly expressed advice to 'keep your fucking trap shut' was caught on tape and widely criticised. But it was the correct advice for a defence lawyer to give in the circumstances, if somewhat crudely expressed.

Although he was looked at askance for his apparent willingness to be what amounted to an in-house lawyer for Mr Death, available around the clock, Fraser's downfall actually came from his involvement with the drug importer Werner Paul Roberts. Fraser, educated at Wesley College, had shown great promise as a young athlete. He might not have been good enough for the Olympics but he certainly could have had a shot at the Commonwealth Games. Although he continued to run and train for another twenty years, by the beginning of the twenty-first century he had become a cocaine addict. However, by the time he appeared in the County Court, pleading guilty to his part in a conspiracy to import 5.5 kilograms of cocaine and trafficking in the drug, he had been through drug rehabilitation. Altogether he had spent some $100 000 on cocaine in the twelve months before his arrest.

Roberts, his wife Andrea Mohr and Carl Henze Urbanec were found guilty of importing the drug from Benin in Western Africa using an innocent former girlfriend as the courier. Fraser's part had been to act as legal and practical adviser, on call as the drugs came through Customs. He had also suggested that to give the unfortunate girl too much money for the unwitting risks she was taking might attract attention. By the time of their arrests Fraser had been buying drugs from Roberts for several years and had been selling a gram at a time— at no profit to himself—to a psychologist friend who had, he claimed, dobbed him in. Fraser received a seven year sentence, Roberts received thirteen, Urbanec nine and Mohr six.

One South Australian solicitor who became far too close to his clients was Justin Birk Hill, who for a time rode with the now defunct biker gang The Mobshitters and later the Gypsy Jokers. He was jailed in 1996 for eight years for financing an amphetamine operation from his home. It had been expected to gross around $600 000. He had not practised since 1992. Earlier he had swindled an eighty-year-old man out of his life savings, offering 16 per cent interest and guaranteeing that his funds were safe. In May 2005 he was named as a person of interest in the deaths of Anthony and Frances Perish, aged ninety-one and ninety-three respectively, both of whom had been shot. He had visited their farm shortly before their deaths on 14 June 1993 with his client, their son. Earlier a crude firing device had failed to ignite at their property.

* * *

The killer Lewis Caine, also known as Sean Vincent (among other names), who was shot and killed in a cul-de-sac in Brunswick, Melbourne, on 8 May 2004, must have had good qualities. In 2002, after his release following the killing of David Templeton in a nightclub fight on 18 September 1988, he took up with a solicitor, Zarah Garde-Wilson, of Pryles & Defteros, who had been qualified a relatively short time. According to a psychologist's report it was her 'first intimate relationship' and a court was later told it was 'one of integrity and love'. They both began to study reiki with a view to their becoming qualified healers. Garde-Wilson had grown up in rural New South Wales and took a law degree at the University of Western Australia. She had been articled to the firm when she represented Caine on a driving charge.

In 2004 George Defteros, a partner in Pryles & Defteros, voluntarily surrendered his practising certificate after being accused of conspiracy to murder a Melbourne identity. The case against him was dropped but by then Ms Garde-Wilson had established her own firm using her name and that of her dead lover Caine. She took with her a clientele that would be the envy of many a criminal lawyer. She also applied to have Caine's sperm taken and frozen.

The dangers of acting for the underworld have never been clearer than in the case of Ms Garde-Wilson, who was inexorably dragged into a completely untenable position over the death of Caine and paid a heavy penalty. On 7 October 2005 she was called by the Crown to give evidence in the trial of two men for the murder of Caine. She had apparently been with Caine on the afternoon before his death and knew of his finances. She applied unsuccessfully to enter the witness protection program and was fearful of what might happen to her if she gave evidence against the hitman. Con Heliotis, QC, who appeared for her, said that she would claim the privilege against self-incrimination and, if that was not successful, she would stand mute and take whatever the court meted out, 'I tell your Honour that Ms Garde-Wilson is frankly terrified for her life.' She was convicted of contempt of court but no penalty was imposed. However, her conduct was reported to the Law Institute. In June 2006 she abandoned an appeal against her conviction for contempt when it was pointed out that the court had power to reconsider the sentencing aspect of the case. Nevertheless the Director of Public Prosecutions pursued an appeal against what he regarded as an overly lenient disposition of the case.

On 20 December 2006 the Court of Appeal ruled that the Director of Public Prosecutions had no power to appeal against a contempt-of-court sentence. The previous week the Legal Services Board had refused to renew Garde-Wilson's certificate, deeming her unfit to practise as a solicitor. Her appeal against the decision failed in June 2007. In March 2007, she was committed for trial on charges of giving false evidence to the Australian Crime Commission and of possessing an unregistered gun, allegedly given to her by Caine. Her problems did not stop her maintaining a substantial clientele including some of the cream of Melbourne criminals such as drug dealer Tony Mokbel, whom the police have alleged to be her on-and-off lover, something she denies. Those who think kindly of her believe she regards everyone as innocent.

But lawyers are not the only professionals to fall for the fascination of crime; accountants are just as vulnerable. In prison serving a four year sentence for fraud, Anthony William Corrigan, once one of Brisbane's leading accountants, became friendly with Hector Hapeta, who rose to public prominence in Queensland's Fitzgerald Inquiry. When Corrigan was released on 30 May 1997 he took up a new profession cooking methyl amphetamine for Hapeta, working happily for just over a year producing one bake a week and being paid $150 000 for his year's work. Unfortunately, just as lawyers and accountants suffer from writer's cramp and repetitive strain injury, an occupational hazard for drug cooks is side-effects from the fumes. So he passed his new skills to Ann Marie Tilley, the long time mistress of Hapeta. Naturally it all ended in tears. Hapeta died in prison and Tilley received nine years. Corrigan was a trifle more fortunate. The Court of Appeal knocked a year off his sentence, reducing it to seven.

The New Century

17

In recent years, with the profits to be made from drugs, particularly amphetamines, the crime scene has changed radically. There are, of course, still traditional standover and protection rackets in the inner suburbs of capital cities but these are now relatively small operations. The Kings of Crime are now the drug barons.

One of the reasons for the rise of gang violence in Melbourne stems, at least in part, from the high-risk policy adopted by the police in Victoria during the 1990s, of using their own purchases of pseudoephedrine in an attempt to break into the city's network of dealers.

Amphetamines, which are relatively easy to produce, were being cooked in small illegal laboratories. There were even instances of people cooking amphetamines in the back of their car while they slept in the front. The profits were substantial and the dangers slight. A conviction for a major trafficking in heroin could earn twenty years and upwards; for a similar amphetamine conviction the penalty was a quarter or a third of that. By 1990 Melbourne had become the amphetamine capital of Australia. Two years later producers, rather than distributors, were to be the main target of the police. Demand for amphetamines as a recreational drug was to increase tenfold in the next decade.

There were other changes to policing practice around this time. The Victorian Drug Squad, far from being enlarged to try to stem the tide of heroin flooding the markets in 1992, was divided into three units. The first unit was to investigate the Asian heroin syndicates, the second the Romanian drug gangs and the third the local amphetamine market.

By the middle of the decade a system had been devised whereby the police would buy chemicals from wholesalers and, under a system of controlled deliveries, officers or their trusted informers would sell the chemicals on to the producers, providing evidence for prosecutions.

In the three years from 1998 nearly sixty clandestine laboratories were discovered. In 1999 John William Samuel Higgs, regarded as Australia's biggest amphetamines manufacturer, was arrested and sentenced to four years and Melbourne identity Tony Mokbel was charged with conspiracy involving a shipping container of chemicals. But then the wheels began to fall off. There were allegations that chemicals were being stockpiled by the police; a secret bank account was opened and sometimes chemicals went missing. In December 2001 the Drug Squad was disbanded and replaced with a major drug investigation division. But the damage had been done.

Opinion over the cause of the violent troubles in the city varies but everyone agrees that drugs have been the catalyst. The violence stems from either Higgs's arrest or the murder of Melbourne gang figure Alphonse John Gangitano in Templestowe in 1998, or possibly both. Speaking about the gangs, a former friend of Gangitano recalls: 'At the beginning they weren't divided. It was all one big gang. Monday we'd be at Billboard, Tuesday at Chasers and another night at Sheiks. There was always somewhere to go. Drugs changed it all. That's what split them up.'

As a result there has been a long-running turf war as the Sunshine Crew, sometimes known as the New Boys, from the inner western suburbs, co-led by Carl Williams and (doing most of the dirty work) his henchman Andrew 'Benji' Veniamin, struggled for power against the more established, if loose knit, Carlton Crew whose members included Gangitano, Jason and Mark Moran, and Graham Kinniburgh. Since 1998 there have been more than thirty gangland killings in Melbourne, many of which can be linked to the power struggle between the rival bosses. Had he still been alive, the contract killer Chris Flannery would have been a rich man.

Gangitano was shot dead at his home on 16 January 1998. Known as the 'Robert de Niro of Lygon Street', he had no visible means of support and in his will he gave his occupation as 'Gentleman'. The leader of the Carlton Crew was regarded as unstable. 'One minute he'd be charming, polite and the next he'd go psycho on you. He'd drive along the pavement knocking over dustbins,' recalls one former friend. In 1991 Gangitano believed that a contract had been taken out for his execution by Mark

'Chopper' Read; he retreated with his family to Italy. He returned only when Read was jailed in October 1992 following his conviction for the attempted murder of Sid Collins, a biker and drug dealer in Tasmania.

Gangitano was said to be involved in horse race fixing and to have connections with west coast identities. At the time of his death he was awaiting trial on a charge of affray but he had previously faced far more serious legal challenges. He was confidently suspected of the killing of the popular gangland figure Gregory John Workman. The two went to a wake together on 7 February 1995 and had then gone on to a party to raise bail for an alleged robber. Gangitano became abusive and he and Workman went outside. Two sisters saw the shooting and made detailed statements of seeing Gangitano with a smoking gun in his hand. The women went into a form of protective custody, living in a caravan, dining on takeaway food and collecting their clothes at a roadside stop. Unfortunately, thanks to the authorities, it was not all that protective. The sisters were contacted by Carlton Crew stalwart Jason Moran who told them that if they gave evidence they and their families would certainly be killed. They were taken to see a lawyer and made statements withdrawing their evidence, after which they absented themselves from Victoria, spending a year in Europe on a trip paid for by Gangitano. Inevitably the charges were dismissed and Gangitano's lawyer, George Defteros, put in a bill to the police for $69975.35. At the time it was thought highly probable that East St Kilda criminals would exact revenge for Workman's death, but none came immediately.

Three years later Gangitano had other problems. He had fallen out with the Moran brothers who now controlled a large part of the drug dealing organised from Lygon Street in Carlton. He was almost certainly killed by Jason Moran, who, despite limited earning capacity in the outside world, was able to send his children to private schools. Despite his balding hair and paunch, Moran was seen as a wise guy in the American tradition. 'He was like a cat on the prowl, clicking his fingers as he walked. When he entered a room he took control,' says one of his admirers. Moran, in a link with history, was married to docker Leslie Kane's daughter.

Gangitano's solicitors thought of him as 'a respected businessman, devoted family man and loyal friend'. They inserted a death notice in the *Herald Sun* which read: 'In loving memory of a loyal friend that we now entrust to God. Together now with your dear parents. Partners and Staff, Pryles & Defteros.' Other lawyers were not so sure. One remembers him as a man who 'never ran anything, never was involved in the big money networks … he had everyone conned but he was really a gambler, never paid his debts and bills'.

Mark Read may have had little time for Gangitano but his admirers included the bail justice Rowena Allsop who knew both him and his great friend Dominic 'Mick' Gatto. In turn Allsop came under some criticism for being as close to Gangitano as she had been. Only a few hours before his death they had been drinking together before his curfew came into effect for the night. Prevailed upon to speak at his funeral—held at the underworld's favourite church St Mary's Star of the Sea, West Melbourne—Allsop, dressed in turquoise and her voice trembling with emotion, spoke of the departed's wit, his love of Oscar Wilde and his passion for Dolce & Gabbana aftershave lotion.

Another tribute placed in the *Herald Sun* was more ambiguous: 'The impression you left on me will stay eternally in my heart.' It purported to be from Jim Pinakos, whose headless and dismembered body—with a steel arrow through the chest—had been found buried in packages on Rye beach in July 1989. Ronald Victor Lucas, who was convicted of the murder, always denied his guilt and linked Pinakos's death to a friend of Gangitano.

The police believed that the scenario of Gangitano's death ran more or less as follows. Jason Moran was involved in an argument and shot him. Although he denied it, also present when the 'Lord of Lygon Street' was killed was Graham 'The Munster' Kinniburgh who saw what was happening and ran out through a security mesh on the front door, cutting himself. Later he went upstairs to see what the security video had recorded. On the sound principle that lies should be as close to the truth as possible, he told the police he had indeed been to see Gangitano who was on the telephone speaking to his west coast friend John Kizon, who was having dinner with a barrister in Perth. Gangitano had asked Kinniburgh to leave as he was due to have a meeting with an unnamed man. Kinniburgh went to buy some cigarettes and returned half an hour later only to find his host dead. The coroner had no doubt that both he and Moran were implicated.

On 23 January, Moran posted a touching eulogy in the *Herald Sun*: 'Words can't express how I feel. There will never be a man such as yourself. Whatever I asked of you was done 110 per cent. I will love you always. Your little mate Jase.'

.   Gangitano's death was followed in rapid succession by other killings—beginning, on 23 November 1998, with that of 'Mad' Charlie Hegyalji in Bambra Road, Caulfield South. A one-time standover man turned amphetamine dealer, the Hungarian-born Hegyalji was either extremely careful or paranoid. He filled notebooks with the numbers of cars he thought might be following him. His house was surrounded by thick hedges and a security camera covered the front door. On the night of his death he had been touring bars and hotels in Caulfield and St Kilda and had made a call to Dino Dibra. About 12.40 a.m. he arrived home in a cab which he ordered to drop him off a little way from his house. Hegyalji was shot in the head four times as he walked down his garden path. A fifth shot missed, not that it mattered. It was not until morning that his de facto, Michelle Newman, discovered the body. His life in the underworld had been one of hits and misses. He was shot in 1989 in South Caulfield and, in return, shot the gunman in a car park in St Kilda. In 1997 there was another inconclusive gun battle.

Two days after Hegyalji was killed, Raymond Mansour, who had convictions for a gamut of offences—including burglary, theft and assault as well as possessing heroin—survived an attempt on his life when around 2 p.m. he went to a meeting near his Brunswick home and was shot five times with a small-calibre weapon. Mansour staggered to a milk bar in Albion Street and was taken to Royal Melbourne Hospital.

The following year Victor Peirce's one-time employee Vince Mannella died shortly before midnight on 9 January 1999 when he was shot and killed outside his home in Alister Street, North Fitzroy. Mannella, regarded as a personable man, had interests in nightclubs and coffee shops and convictions going back to 1971 when he was found carrying a dagger. On 20 February 1981 he shot the owner of a café in Nicholson Street, North Fitzroy, hitting him seven times. For this he received a minimum sentence of seven years. Almost immediately after his release he was found in one of Gangitano's casinos in Fitzroy along with the speed merchant Higgs, and he was under scrutiny by Operation Phalanx, the Drug Squad's investigation into Higgs.

In late 1998 Mannella was the receiver for a group that stole wholesale quantities of foodstuffs and it is possible that his death stems from problems with that involvement. The preferred and more likely version is that his death was ordered by the same cartel that disposed of Gangitano. Another suggestion is that he was taken out as a pre-emptive strike before the killing of his brother Gerardo on 20 October 1999.

* * *

Gangitano's death could not possibly be left unremarked in the underworld. On 15 June 2000 Jason Moran's half-brother, designer drug dealer and standover man Mark, was shot dead as he was getting into his car outside his luxury home in Aberfeldie. Two blasts from a shotgun were followed by one in the head from a revolver. At the time the killing was thought to be over a quarrel with Carl Williams, who had been shot in the stomach by Jason Moran in 1999 as part of an ongoing war. On that occasion, the wounded man gallantly made no complaint and claimed not to know the identity of the shooter. One lawyer described Williams as 'Chubby with designer sportswear. I truly believe his own publicity sort of got to him. He started believing it and he thought he was bullet proof and immune.'

Between the deaths of Gangitano and Mark Moran, eight other identities were killed in Melbourne. Not all of them were necessarily involved in the drugs war. A year after Gangitano's death the fraudster Jim Belios was killed in an underground car park in St Kilda Road on the evening of 9 September 1999. He had been shot in the back of the head. In the days before his death he had been trying to pass fake diamonds as real and he was known to be heavily in debt. The fake diamonds are a more likely reason for his death. Recalcitrant debtors usually receive a beating; debt, in the underworld, tends to die with the debtor.

Frank Benvenuto, shot on 8 May 2000, may have died as part of a long-running struggle for control of the Footscray Wholesale Fruit and Vegetable Market. It is true, however, that shortly before his death he had quarrelled with the Moran brothers. His killer was probably Dino Dibra, highly placed in the Sunshine Crew, whose activities ranged from growing hydroponic marijuana, car re-birthing, kidnap and extortion to the drug dealing that brought the gang into conflict with the Carlton Crew.

The year 2000 was definitely not a good one for the uncommitted and unprotected. First, Richard Mladenich—who liked to be known as 'King Richard' but who was often known as 'Spade Brain' because of injuries he received in an incident in Pentridge prison—was killed in room 18 of the Esquire Motel in Acland Street, St Kilda, at 3.30 a.m. on 16 May. The distinctly odd Mladenich, who allegedly had once been walked off the pier at St Kilda by an infuriated detective, dealt in drugs but had also been the minder for Mark Moran. A long line of identities might have wished him harm, but his killer was thought to be Dino Dibra. The murder was witnessed by Andrea Davies who was talking with Mladenich while her boyfriend Rocky Jabbour slept. In April 2003 the inquest on Mladenich was told that Jabbour thought Dibra's friend Rocco Arico was also in the motel at the time. In June 2001 Arico was convicted of the attempted murder of Vincenzo Godino and received a minimum seven year sentence.

Dibra did not last the year. He was shot outside a house in Krambruk Street, Sunshine, on 14 October. His trio of killers was thought to include Benji Veniamin and another drug dealer Paul Kallipolitis.

The next year saw the end of George Germanos, shot in a park. Germanos, a power lifter known for his bad temper, had worked both as a nightclub bouncer and in the drug trade. Shortly before his death he had beaten a well-connected boy who was admitted to hospital. As a result, his death was almost inevitable. On 22 March 2001 he was shot and killed when he went to a meeting in a park in Armadale.

Four months later, on 1 May 2002, Victor Peirce went down in Port Melbourne and later that year, on 15 October, Paul Kallipolitis was shot and killed at his home in Sunshine. Benji Veniamin was again a suspect in his death.

In late 2002 the Melbourne drug wars escalated after what was intended to be a peace meeting at La Porcella restaurant on the corner of Faraday and Rathdowne streets in the Little Italy district of Carlton. Present were representatives of the Carlton Crew and the New Boys as well as west coast biker Troy Mercanti and the major independent amphetamine dealer Tony Mokbel. The meeting quickly degenerated into violence. Mokbel upset Nikolai 'The Russian' (sometimes 'The Bulgarian') Radev and, after his bodyguards had been taken out, Mokbel was beaten within an inch of his life. Carl Williams was ordered to take him to a doctor to be patched up and it was then that Williams changed sides. None of the Carlton Crew had intervened to prevent the beating and now he felt vulnerable.

Once more the body count began to mount. Sometimes it was personal, but more often it was business. The veteran crime reporter

John Silvester, who thought there were simply too many people in Melbourne trying to deal in drugs, saw it as a game of musical chairs in which the loser was usually shot.

Arsonist, extortionist and drug dealer Radev died in the afternoon of 15 April 2003, shot after he met with what has been described as 'a group of criminal identities' at the Brighton Baths Café. They met in the café and then drove to Queen Street, Coburg, where Radev was shot. Two men who were with him ran away and so could not identify his killer, believed to be Veniamin allegedly acting on orders from Williams. Nor has the contractor been identified although it was suggested that Tony Mokbel paid for the hit. Regarded, even in the circles in which he moved, as a violent and dangerous competitor, Radev was thought to have killed a man and taken his identity until his own naturalisation papers came through. His funeral was not well attended.

In May 2003, Operation Purana, a team of some sixty detectives, was set up to solve the Melbourne underworld murders and possibly to make pre-emptive strikes towards stopping the feuding. But almost immediately, on 21 June, Jason Moran was shot dead in front of his and other children in the car park of the Cross Keys Hotel in Essendon North after they had been to an Auskick football clinic. Down with him went Pasquale Barbaro, his bodyguard. With the second of the Moran brothers gone, it was probably only a matter of time before a move was made on Graham Kinniburgh. Over the decades, the modest, influential and shadowy Kinniburgh, once a member of the dying breed of safebreakers, rose to become a kingpin of the city's crime scene. Kinniburgh, whose career spanned three decades, was one of the relatively few mobsters who have bridged the gap between the underworld and respectability and was well known for his discreet connections to Melbourne's establishment. On one occasion he rather diffidently told his barrister after a successful defence, 'There's not much a feller like me can do for a feller like you but if you ever need a feller like me ...'

Born in a slum in Richmond, he was regarded in his early days as having a razor sharp temper and the ability to back it up with his fists. He began his career as a fringe member of the Kangaroo Gang and was then a member of the so-called 'Magnetic Drill Gang' which was responsible for stealing $1.7 million from a New South Wales bank, a jewellery haul from a Lonsdale Street office, and a raid on safety deposit boxes in Melbourne. He was also thought to have been the organiser of a bullion snatch in Queensland.

Early in his career he was charged with receiving stolen property from a burglary at the home of trucking magnate Lindsay Fox. When the police raided Kinniburgh, he was found to have a unique pendant owned by Mrs Fox in a coat pocket as well as $4500 in cash in a drawer. He offered the police the cash if they did not charge him but they declined. He was charged with both the burglary and the bribery but he had an identical pendant made in Hong Kong, so planting sufficient doubt in the minds of the jury that the pendant was, in fact, unique.

Over the years the lantern-jawed Kinniburgh, known as 'The Munster' because of his facial resemblance to the television character, refined his public image. He was seen with barristers and solicitors around the law courts and with owners and jockeys at Caulfield and other Melbourne racetracks where he was a genial and successful tipster as well as being privately regarded as a race fixer. He was said to have been kind enough to help a jockey pay an $80000 tax bill. Although he claimed to be a simple rigger, he lived in the well-heeled suburb of Kew, could be seen in fashionable restaurants such as The Flower Drum, and was well able to mix socially with the fraternity, the police and straight people alike. He was, said one Melbourne barrister who knew and socialised with him, 'One of the three top crims I ever met.' 'Graham was a gentle, gentle man, a beautiful quiet soul,' says one friend. 'I don't know why they had to kill him.'

In 1994, when Kinniburgh's son married into one of the city's established families, the wedding was held at St Peter's Anglican Church, East Melbourne, and the reception was at the oldest of the Melbourne establishments, the Windsor Hotel. In a scene that could have been taken from *The Godfather*, intelligence police snapped not the bride and groom but the guests, so updating their files. Many of the guests wore Ray-Bans throughout the evening and Kinniburgh's speech was said to have resembled one by Marlon Brando. A few months before his death, his barrister daughter Suzie married the son of a former Attorney-General.

In the month before Kinniburgh died he took to carrying a gun, something he had not done since his early days. Shortly before midnight on 13 December 2003, he was shot in the chest as he left his car outside his home and walked to his drive carrying a bag of groceries. It is thought he managed to get one shot off from his own gun.

It was said that no gangland killing could be regarded as such until Mick Gatto, the semi-official newspaper epitaph writer and tribute payer to so many of the city's underworld figures, had inserted a flowery death notice in the *Herald Sun*. His tribute to The Munster is a fair example of his work:

> You were a true Chameleon, you could adapt to any situation, rubbing shoulders with the best of them and being able to talk at any level about any topic. I was so proud to be part of your life. This has left a void in my heart that can't be replaced. I love you 'Pa' and I will never forget you.

Unkind people thought Kinniburgh's ability to talk to the police on many topics may have helped to keep him out of prison in the years before his death. The week before he was shot he held a series of meetings in Carlton restaurants with the cream of the local villains. Indeed the day before his murder he had been seen having coffee in Lygon Street with a detective from Carlton CIB. Others would have none of it, believing Kinniburgh of all people to be staunch.

* * *

Earlier in the year, two relatively minor figures had left the game. First, Willy Thompson, nightclubber, kickboxer and dealer, was shot and killed in Waverley Road, Chadstone, on 21 July as he sat at the wheel of his Honda S-2000 convertible. He had been followed from a martial arts class at the Extreme Jujitsu and Grappling Gym. Thompson, who had also appeared in films such as the low budget *The Nightclubber* filmed at the Tunnel nightclub and the Men's Gallery, may have been a comparatively small player but it had been worthwhile for Nik Radev to firebomb his car eighteen months earlier.

On 25 October his friend Michael Marshall, who trained at the same gym and who sold lollipops and drugs, was gunned down in front of his son outside the family home in South Yarra as he returned from buying hot dogs. It was a planned killing and a stolen Ford, believed to have been used by at least one gunman, was found burnt out in Port Melbourne.

The killings climaxed early in 2004 when, on 23 March, Williams's bodyguard Andrew 'Benji' Veniamin, now regarded as dangerously erratic, was shot in the head at lunchtime in a back room of La Porcella.

He had gone there for a meeting with Mick Gatto. The heavily tattooed Veniamin, a small man who was said to have lively soft brown eyes and was believed to receive $100000 per hit, arrived at the restaurant at 2 p.m. in a borrowed silver Mercedes which he double parked. At the time he was disqualified from driving and in the months before his death had racked up some forty speeding and parking tickets.

Gatto was at his usual table. A former heavyweight professional boxer who was regarded as a great fixer, Gatto demanded a fee of $5000 from anyone wishing to sit with him. The Royal Commission into the Building Industry had described him as a standover man; he preferred 'industrial consultant'. An early girlfriend of his has described him as having 'beautiful skin and eyes'. 'He was gorgeous, dressed in alpaca jumpers. He had the best style I ever saw on any man. Very old-fashioned with perfect manners. Everything had to be done with "respect". He took care of things with one phone call.'

Gatto and Veniamin went into a back room and within minutes Veniamin was dead. Later it would be said that Veniamin was on the verge of giving up his criminal enterprises but was reluctant to do so in case it was thought he was a quitter. Quitter or not, at the time of his death the police had him in their sights over five murders, including those of Frank Benvenuto, Dino Dibra, Paul Kallipolitis and Nik Radev.

Veniamin died after 'an altercation'. As Gatto waited for the police he apologised to the restaurant owner for the undoubted inconvenience caused by the shooting. His good manners could not turn back the clock and the restaurant closed down shortly afterwards. It was said the price on Gatto was now $400000.

The word on the street was that Carl Williams would be killed before he arrived at the church for his best friend's funeral. On this occasion, as indeed on many another, the word was wrong. Over the years there had been a number of attacks on Williams and his demise had been confidently and regularly, if erroneously, predicted.

Now the deaths and attempted hits came faster. The next to go was Lewis Moran. The decision to kill Jason's father and Mark's stepfather, a man with strong ties to the Painters and Dockers, was said to have been taken at the wake for Veniamin. Lewis Moran had been in the cross hairs, if only because he had offered a mere $50000 for the killing of Williams. It was just thirty hours after Veniamin was buried that Moran was shot in the Brunswick Club on Sydney Road. Two men, one with a handgun, the other armed with a shotgun, came into the main room of the club, shot and injured the man with whom Moran was drinking and, with Moran running in a panicked circle, killed him at close range.

When Lewis Caine was killed in Brunswick in 2004 it was thought he had accepted a contract to take out Carlton Crew member and former lawyer Mario Condello as a reprisal for the death of Veniamin. Of Caine, an observer said appreciatively, 'I thought he was trying to go lead a normal life, I don't think he was a gangster or a big timer.'

* * *

In spring 2004 police foiled an attack on Mario Condello as he walked his Jack Russell terriers close to his home near Brighton cemetery. Perhaps foolishly he then went into print on the subject of the gang wars and within a matter of weeks, along with his own solicitor George Defteros, he was arrested for conspiracy to murder Carl Williams. He was said to have offered $150 000 a head to kill Williams, his father George and a bodyguard. There was to be a bonus of $50 000 on completion.

Again Condello went into print saying that the enquiries he was making into the value of contracts, and so on, was simply to find out how endangered a species he was himself. Defteros, who adamantly denied any involvement, voluntarily gave up his practising certificate until things were sorted out. Although he was committed for trial, the magistrate indicated that she thought the evidence was slender at best, and later a no bill was entered. Defteros now said he would apply for the restoration of his practising certificate. In 2007 Defteros began proceedings against his former partner for his share of money earned by the firm. He was still considering a return to practice.

In March 2005 Condello was given bail on the grounds that he was going 'stir crazy'. He was offered round-the-clock police protection but declined.

Defended by Robert Richter QC, Mick Gatto went on trial in May 2005 for the murder of Andrew Veniamin at La Porcella the previous year. Gatto maintained that it was Veniamin who had attacked him, and not vice versa, and that while they struggled five shots were fired from Veniamin's gun, which Gatto had managed to turn on him. An expert witness, pathologist Dr Malcolm Dodd, agreed that it was difficult to determine individual reactions to particular injuries and that even people shot in the brain could remain active for a brief time.

This produced the unkind comment in *Melbourne Underworld News* on 17 May that, since 'Ol' Benji was brain dead from birth', this was a difficult call to make. Gatto was triumphantly acquitted and after the trial his wife Cheryl Gatto told journalists, 'An innocent man has been vindicated and we couldn't be happier.'

By then there had been no Purana-related murders for more than a year—the last had been that of Lewis Caine in May 2004—and as the months wore on the police became more confident that the Melbourne underworld war on the streets was over. (It may, of course, have transferred to the prisons, where a number of the former participants were now lodged.) The police were wrong and the newly re-appointed police commissioner, Christine Nixon, became a hostage to fortune when on 7 February 2006 she told reporters that the 'gangland issue' was under control. It was certainly not under control so far as Mario Condello was concerned. His trial for inciting murder, in which Condello had been expected to give evidence relating to allegations of police corruption, was due to start the following day. But now he was a seriously endangered species.

Instead of Condello making the allegations, his barrister Robert Richter QC told the court: 'Unfortunately, I announce my client won't be answering bail. He was murdered last night,' adding, 'He died confident of his acquittal.' Around ten o'clock the night before his trial Condello was shot at his Brighton East home as he was talking on the telephone. At about the same time, career criminal Lee Patrick Torney vanished. In the 1980s Torney had killed Sidney James Graham in a dispute over the proceeds of a bank robbery in Hawthorn. Now released from prison, in March 1999 he had been found in possession of twelve rifles and a shotgun. Later he turned informer and became a Crown witness. He was last heard of in April 2005 and fears for his safety increased when he did not appear at his brother's funeral later in the year. One suggestion was that he had been entrusted with a large amount of money to pay a solicitor and somehow was unable to account properly. For some weeks, searches at Golden Point near Castlemaine, an area with a large number of abandoned mines, failed to produce his body. It was eventually found badly decomposed at the bottom of a mineshaft and a forty-year-old man was charged with his murder. Unfortunately the coroner's office forgot to return Torney's head with the body, which his family had already cremated before the omission was discovered.

His son generously took the mistake in good part, saying his father would have 'laughed his head off'.

Amphetamine dealer Tony Mokbel's career came to either a temporary (police) or permanent (underworld) halt in March 2006. A man regarded by the lawyers who knew him as 'a good bloke, talkative, affable, who paid his bills' and sent them work, had convictions for assault, threats to kill and resisting arrest. In 1992 he received six months for attempting to bribe a County Court judge. In 1998 a conviction on charges of conspiracy to traffic in amphetamines was overturned and the next year he was also cleared of a perjury charge. He had been building fashion and property enterprises when, on 24 August 2001, he was arrested and charged with the importation of pure cocaine worth $2 billion hidden in candles and statues from Mexico. When the court was told the case might take two years to come to trial, and this might cause Mokbel's business interests to collapse, his application for bail was granted.

Mokbel had, according to the stories in the underworld, set up a seven-figure fighting fund to deal with witnesses and a potentially vulnerable co-accused. In October 2001 his bail was revoked by the Supreme Court.

Mokbel's trial proceedings were seriously delayed because of the arrests of two Drug Squad officers involved in the case, Stephen Andrew Paton and Malcolm Rosenes. Then Mokbel's committal proceedings were adjourned in June 2002, a charge of threatening to kill a prison officer was dropped the following month and in September that year he was once more granted bail. There were also problems with prosecution witnesses. In 2003 a supergrass witness was jailed for eighteen months after a plea bargain and in October 2003 Rosenes was jailed for a minimum of three and a half years for drug trafficking and Paton for a minimum of three years. In February 2004 the supergrass was allowed to travel overseas on parole on his promise to return to give evidence against Mokbel. Three months later the man decided he wanted $500000 to return to Australia. Despite his refusal to reappear, the case went ahead and Mokbel was committed for trial over the importation of cocaine.

In October 2005 he was charged with inciting others to import drugs and the court was told that the police believed he had been having an affair with his solicitor, Zarah Garde-Wilson, something she denied.

He was bailed the next month with his sister-in-law Renate standing surety and in February 2006 his trial for importing cocaine finally began. He had already agreed to plead guilty to trafficking in ecstasy, speed and cocaine. Indeed for some time it seemed as though Mokbel was well on his way to an acquittal on the importing charge. Despite prosecution objections his bail was continued and, after reporting to the South Melbourne Police Station on Sunday 21 March, Mokbel disappeared.

Immediately there were suggestions in the underworld that he had become another body in the gang wars. He was certainly suspected of financing the deaths of Radev and Lewis Moran and his death might have been a reprisal. Not so, said the police; he had definitely flown. But to where? It was possible he was still lying low in Australia but the heavier money was placed on a return to his birthplace of Lebanon. Or there was Central America or Mexico, or Domenica, which had once given a passport to the disgraced financier Christopher Skase. Another suggestion is that he was tipped off that he was to face a murder charge over Radev's death and fled as a result.

Assistant Police Commissioner Simon Overland vowed that, even if it took five years, Mokbel would be found and brought back to Australia. On 29 March 2006 he was found guilty in his absence and sentenced to a relatively modest twelve years. There were unconfirmed reports that for a fortnight he had hidden out in a farmhouse near Nicholson on the Gippsland Lakes and had then slipped away on a yacht bought in a friend's name. Then it was suggested that an escape plan had been sold to him years ago by the late Lewis Moran, who had devised it for himself and courteously made it available to others. If this is correct, Mokbel went from his apartment to Essendon airport from where he flew in a private plane to North Queensland, refuelling at remote airfields. He was then picked up by boat and taken to Malaysia from where, using forged documents, he flew to Turkey and went into hiding in a remote village. It is as good a version as any. 'He's larger than life. If he's alive, he'll show up,' said one lawyer. Meanwhile, there were skirmishes over the forfeiture of his $1 million bail money put up by Renate Mokbel. In April 2006, Justice Bill Gillard ordered her to pay the surety or face two years in jail. In September 2006 jewellery and cash totalling around $1 million, which the police claimed was part of the Mokbel treasure, were dug up at a house in Alma Road, Parkdale.

In the winter of 2006 there was a surprising development in Melbourne's long-running gang wars. A man pleaded guilty to the murder of Lewis Moran and was sentenced to life imprisonment. He claimed he had been promised $150000 by Mokbel for the hit but was paid $10000 less.

There were more surprising developments over the summer and early autumn of 2007. First, in February, Mokbel was charged in his absence with the killing of Lewis Moran; and then, at the beginning of March, Noel Faure junior pleaded guilty to Moran's murder. Noel Faure junior's grandfather was standover man and Squizzy Taylor associate Norman Bruhn. His father, Noel senior, had been a talented safecracker working on commission and a ranking member of the Painters and Dockers. In late life he abandoned his criminal career and became a slaughterer in a Footscray meatworks. A diabetic, he died in 1999. In 1990, Noel Faure junior, who had worked in the slaughterhouse with his father, had killed a Frank Truscott—something that, according to a witness at the trial, he likened to killing a sheep.

Then, days later, Carl Williams, still very much alive despite the threats made against him, pleaded guilty to the murder of Jason Moran and also that of Lewis Moran. In 2006 he had been convicted of the murder of Michael Marshall but there had been a suppression order banning the reporting of his plea. He also pleaded guilty to the murder of Mark Mallia. Designer drug dealer Mallia, a friend of Nik Radev, and whose family had emigrated from Malta, was killed and stuffed into a wheelie bin in West Sunshine in August 2003. For the Marshall murder Williams had been sentenced to a non-parole period of twenty-one years. (In June 2007, allegations were made public that Mokbel was also involved in Marshall's murder.)

Williams had left school at the age of eleven and was soon selling amphetamines, moving steadily up the criminal hierarchy as he quarrelled with the Moran family. As for his regular work, he considered himself to be a 'commissioner'—that is, he bought and sold jewellery on commission. In 2004 he received a minimum five year sentence for a drug trafficking operation. By the time he appeared in court to plead guilty to the murders, his wife Roberta, who had also served a short sentence for drug dealing, had left him; she was reportedly thinking of converting to Islam. There was, said the newspapers, a potential new Mrs Williams in the offing.

On 7 May Justice Betty King sentenced Carl Williams to life imprisonment with a minimum of thirty-five years to be served, meaning his earliest release would be in 2042. He was less than pleased, hurling abuse at the judge and labelling her a 'puppet of Purana'.

Outside the court Jason's mother, Judy Moran, said she was too upset to comment, while Williams's estranged wife Roberta said that she and the couple's daughter loved him as much as they did before and would be there for him. 'He's still her dad and she'll always love him,' Roberta said. Williams's mother Barbara thought the sentence unfair because Jason Moran had shot her son first and had tried to shoot him another three or four times.

Williams has appealed against what he sees as the severity of his sentence. He had apparently hoped that he would be released before his seventieth birthday.

* * *

As winter 2007 approached there were suggestions that Tony Mokbel was now in Dubai, which has no extradition treaty with Australia. His girlfriend, Danielle McGuire, who allegedly had been leading the police in a merry dance, had arrived in the country in time for the racing season. However, of Mokbel there was no sign at the Dubai track. Meanwhile, it appeared that he had been laundering his fortune through what was called the Tracksuit Gang—men who attended the races placing huge cash bets and, if the horse won, demanding clean notes. Mokbel's sister-in-law Renate was less fortunate. She was carted off to jail to begin her two year sentence over the forfeited bail money. The hunt ended, perhaps surprisingly, in Greece, when on 5 June Mokbel was arrested in a seaside café in Athens. The Australian government promptly announced it was preparing extradition proceedings. Mokbel was alleged to have been in disguise and carrying fake documents.

There was also plenty of activity going on outside the overall Melbourne gang wars. On 9 February 2006, Nicholas Riad Ibrahim was momentarily convicted of the murder of Sam Zayat—standover man and close friend of Nik Radev—with whom he had quarrelled over the purchase of his share in the Chokolat nightclub for $200 000 with $20 000 down. The pair had been friends and the previous week Ibrahim had arranged $50 000 bail for Zayat. Both Zayat and Ibrahim had drug related convictions. In 1994 Zayat was charged with the murder of his lover and the attempted murder of her sixteen-year-old son. He was convicted of the latter. In 1998 Zayat and his friend Nik Radev had been charged with a home invasion in which a 71-year-old man was beaten and his five-year-old granddaughter threatened with a handgun.

On 10 September 2003 Zayat went with his pit bull terrier and a former solicitor's clerk, Ali Aydin, to meet Ibrahim out in the country near Tarneit, west of Melbourne. Aydin told the Magistrates' Court at the committal proceedings that, when Zayat conducted negotiations, 'It was not your average settlements in the security chamber of the Commonwealth Bank.' The allegation was that Ibrahim had a pump action shotgun and after words were exchanged he chased the unfortunate Zayat over a barbed wire fence before fatally shooting him. Aydin ran some 12 kilometres to the Sunshine Police Station.

Ibrahim was right to be shocked by the murder verdict. The foreperson had made a mistake and had intended to say 'Not guilty but guilty of manslaughter'. The error was corrected and Ibrahim was duly convicted of manslaughter. There had been evidential problems in the case, with Aydin refusing at one stage to give evidence. Ibrahim received a minimum thirteen year sentence but he was later given leave to appeal against his sentence. In early February 2007 Zayat's brother Haysam Zayat, also known as 'Sam' and another suspected drug dealer, was found stabbed to death in a house in Noble Park. It was not a lucky family—a third brother, Mohamad, had hanged himself in prison in 1999.

With the death or imprisonment of most of the warring Melbourne parties, it may well be that Christine Nixon was only one out when she said, before Condello's death, that the gang wars had been halted. But, to mix a few metaphors, pendulums continue swinging and where one door shuts another opens. Crime abhors a vacuum.

* * *

The full disaster of the 1990s drugs policy of the Victoria Police became brutally clear on 18 October 2006 when, after three years on remand, a senior Drug Squad member, Detective Senior Sergeant Wayne Strawhorn, was convicted of trafficking 2 kilograms of pseudo-ephedrine to the late Mark Moran. It was Strawhorn who had helped introduce the chemical diversion program. He was acquitted on three of four other charges, including trafficking the chemical to members of the Bandidos outlaw motorcycle gang. He was sentenced to a maximum seven years' imprisonment but he continues to maintain his innocence and has lodged an appeal. It soon emerged that, in previous months, officer Ian Ferguson had received a minimum of eight years for conspiracy to traffic heroin and money laundering. Detective Senior Constable David Miechel, who had been the handler for the drug dealer and informant Terrence Hodson—found shot dead in bed with his wife Christine at their home in Kew on 16 May 2004— received a minimum of twelve years after convictions for burglary, theft and trafficking a commercial quantity of drugs. Hodson had been expected to give evidence in forthcoming trials of police officers.

The charge of burglary followed the theft of drugs from another dealer's house in East Oakleigh. Unfortunately for Miechel and Hodson, they had been seen throwing bags over the back fence and were promptly arrested. In November 2006 two other officers, Stephen Cox and Glenn Sadler, received seven and ten years respectively for drug offences. Sadler has also appealed against his conviction.

After this spate of sentences, Sergeant Bill Patten, an original member of the Ceja anti-corruption task force, claimed that up to two dozen officers had escaped corruption charges and that the only proper investigation would have been a Royal Commission. Other officers in difficulty at the time included Matthew Bunning—a former member of the Drug Squad—who was sentenced to a minimum of three years for providing information about intercepts, and former Victorian officer James McCabe, who failed to appear in Sydney to answer charges of armed robbery; he was thought to be in Cambodia, with which Australia has no extradition treaty.

In February 2007 the Office of Police Integrity told Commissioner Nixon that it had evidence against dozens of officers who had been involved in drug dealing, theft and associating with criminals. The office maintained that another Royal Commission was not necessary and that the OPI was the best way of dealing with corruption.

* * *

By no means as high profile as the Melbourne gang wars of the period but just as lethal were the ethnic-based groups operating in Sydney. By the end of the 1990s at least six such groups had been engaged for some eighteen months in tit-for-tat blood lettings, with more than 115 drive-by shootings, knee cappings and killings—the worst for some four decades. Indeed one-third of all Australian firearm homicides in the period 1999–2000 had occurred in New South Wales. It was far easier and cheaper to buy a semi-automatic weapon than a sawn-off shotgun in the city.

Over the first years of the twenty-first century the violence escalated. The first victim was a presumed drug dealer, Michael Collins, who was shot dead and wrapped in a blanket at his home in Darlinghurst Road, Roselands, in May 2001. His death was followed a month later by that of another relatively small-time dealer Bassam Mansour who was stabbed and then dropped off at the Long Jetty Medical Clinic where he died. Then, on 13 December 2002, Dimitri Debaz, a senior member of a gang known as the Bronx Boys, was shot in a Sefton hotel in what the police claimed was a drug-related killing. He died outside in the car park. His brother Aleck was shot in the leg. Sandro Mirad was charged with the murder and warrants were issued for the arrest of two other men. Three days before Christmas, Aleck was alleged to have shot at Hendrick Chekazine, pulling up at an intersection in the outer western suburb of West Hoxton after each had left separate memorial services.

The Bronx Boys originated at a housing estate in Villawood, known as the Bronx. They first emerged in the late 1990s, graduating from petty crime and vandalism to more serious crimes. By 1998 they were said to be dealing in $40 000 of cocaine weekly, as well as in cannabis, stockpiling weapons and acting as armourers for other gangs. At one time they had occupied the home of a terminally ill woman and were dealing cocaine from her front yard, divvying up the proceeds in her bedroom. Applications by police for surveillance equipment and outside assistance were rejected. The estate was knocked down that year but by then it was too late to stop the gang's burgeoning activities.

It might have been a financially rewarding life but it was a dangerous one. The Bronx Boys were having troubles with the Assyrian Kings—or Spenser Street Boys, also known as 'The Last Hour'—a rival gang from West Sydney whose members have a fist tattooed on their backs. In the period between May 2001 and October 2003 there were nine murders, four drive-by shootings and ninety-nine arrests, and eighteen weapons were seized. Another senior Bronx Boy, Ali Elrich, was doused in petrol in Mandarin Street, Villawood, in February 2003. He died almost two weeks later.

In October 2003 Task Force Gain was established in Sydney with a specific brief to deal with Middle Eastern gangs. Predictably the move did not appeal to everyone, with more radical elements of the press even going so far as to suggest it was an 'Anti-Arab' squad. On 12 October 2003, Amar Slwea was shot four times, bound, gagged and, after being doused with petrol, was set on fire and put in the boot of a car. Amazingly he survived. He had been charged with being an accessory after the fact to the murder of Dimitri Debaz. The same day another man was stabbed. Dimitri Debaz's father Pierre and brother William were charged over the incidents. Both were acquitted. It was not until June 2006 that a man who had been on the run for three years was arrested over the killing of Dimitri Debaz.

On 6 November 2003 half the strength of Task Force Gain swooped on houses in south-western Sydney trying to bring an end to the wars between gangs in Fairfield and Liverpool. But the Task Force was being hampered by a lack of Arabic speaking officers and by the sheer weight of evidence it was accumulating. In the meantime Victoria was being used by the gangs as a dumping ground for stolen white goods, prestige car parts and cigarettes. A quite separate five-year-long war began around Liverpool in Sydney, between Adnan 'Eddie' Darwiche and Bilal Razzak when, in June 2001, Razzak was shot in the stomach and legs by an unknown gunman. Two years after the shooting, on 27 August 2003, the home of Farouk 'Frank' Razzak in Yanderra Street, Condell Park, was sprayed with more than sixty bullets by two men with semi-automatic assault rifles. Two days later Ali Abdul-Razzak was shot ten times in the head and chest by masked men as he sat in his car outside the Lakemba mosque. On 1 September gunmen opened fire on a home in Boundary Road, Liverpool, and four hours afterwards another house, in nearby Lurnea, was also shot up. On 22 September a house in Greenfield Park was targeted.

Ali Abdul-Razzak's nephew, 24-year-old Ziad Abdul-Razzak, was shot through the back of the head at a friend's home in Lawford Street, Greenacre, on 13 October when the house was sprayed with up to a hundred bullets. His friend's sleeping wife, 22-year-old Mervat Hamka, died after she was hit by a stray shot.

The fallout from these gang wars continued unabated, but many other unrelated feuds were running at the same time. On 30 October, Ahmad Fahda, an associate of the Razzaks, was killed as he was filling his car with petrol at a service station in Punchbowl and on 7 December Sayeh Frangeih was killed at his home in Merryland. The police thought the latter was a case of mistaken identity and the intended victim had been one of his sons, released earlier in the year after convictions for drug dealing. The same night there was a shoot-out near the Kings Head Tavern in South Hurstville and this was followed four days later by another shoot-out, this time in the early evening at Wattle Grove.

On 9 August 2006, Eddie Darwiche, along with three other men, was found guilty of the murders of Ziad Abdul-Razzak and Mervat Hamka, the malicious shooting of Bilal Razzak and the attempted murder of Frank Razzak. Darwiche was sentenced to life imprisonment and then gave the authorities information of how he had been dealing in rocket launchers which had apparently gone missing from the Australian Army.

Earlier in 2006, Sydney had experienced yet another outbreak of shootings, mainly among warring Middle Eastern gangs. On 25 March Marcus and Adam Saliba were shot and wounded at the Roxy nightclub in Parramatta and four days later Bassam Chami and Ibrahim Assad were shot and killed in South Granville.

On the first Sunday in April, Ashoor Audisho, a disc jockey at the Assyrian Australian Association Ninevah Sports and Community Club at Edensor Park, left the club after taking some calls on his mobile phone. About 7 p.m. the unarmed man was shot in Hamilton Road, Fairfield West.

In recent years these new gangs have been considered more violent than the old-time criminals. 'They'll tell you they're going to fuck your mother. Normal crooks will have a bit more respect,' said one detective.

Another officer recalled:

> One sixty year old told me, 'We would go round and say if you don't pay we'll break the place up. Now they go round, shoot you and say to the next person "Look what happened".'
>
> There was one fellow shot as he came out of the Mosque. The killer had waited, 'So [the victim] would be clean. I had bits of him all over me. I couldn't eat my dinner.' And the man had been a friend in a drug deal gone wrong.

One observer believes :

Things are very different. The old fashioned criminals went to Boys' Homes and then after a bit and a few jobs, they graduated to Parramatta. These [Lebanese] kids have skipped all that. They have grown up on a diet of hydroponic cannabis and video games. Whilst they were still at school they were making $10000 a week.

Where does all this sit on the scale of things? While some commentators continue to maintain there is such a thing as ethnic crime, there are suggestions that Asian crime is still the more dangerous. In Victoria, Vietnamese crime is proliferating. Bikers remain prominent around the country, particularly in Western Australia. The Romanian gangs, regarded as big in heroin and major stolen goods scams, were never popular with their lawyers—'absolute liars who never told the truth and would change their stories in the witness box at the drop of a Bible,' recalls one lawyer. As for Albanian criminals, they have been regarded as even lower down the criminal hierarchy: 'Bad blokes, amateurs doing it for the money—no moral code, no scruples, no class.'

One group that has generally been keeping a low profile has been the Russian *Mafiya*. There have been occasional sightings, although none of the mastermind Alex Nuchimov since he was extracted from a dentist's chair by a gunman and spirited away from the clutches of prison guards while awaiting trial for his involvement in George Savvas's in-prison drug dealing empire.

One high profile incident occurred on 24 July 2000 when a former KGB colonel, the 41-year-old Gennadi Bernovski, was killed by one or more frogmen who emerged from a canal near his home on the Gold Coast as he went out to empty the rubbish in Sir Bruce Small Boulevard, Benowa. He was shot five times with a .32 automatic, allegedly by his former business partner Oleg Kouzmine, who swam away.

Bernovski had a small distribution company with Kouzmine in West Burleigh, Queensland, but he was also thought to have been handling (or rather mishandling) substantial amounts of money that other Russians had given him to invest. Something approaching $1 million was missing at the time of his death, including $400000 of Kouzmine's money. Bernovski was said to have been a regular and unsuccessful player at the local casino. After his funeral a wake was held at Spargo's restaurant in Southport, but significantly, say the police,

Kouzmine was not there. He returned to Russia where he claims he was arrested and held for some eight months over the killing before being released. Later he wrote complaining that there was an arrest warrant against him in Queensland.

On 10 July 2002, Ukraine-born Michael Goldman attempted to kill Alexander Kudryavstev who was suspected of being an informer. When Kudryavstev went to the door of his flat Goldman shot him in the stomach and then in the forehead. Amazingly Kudryavstev survived. He and Goldman had been half of a four-man team that had committed nearly 150 burglaries in Melbourne. Now Kudryavstev wanted out and it was feared he would become an informer. Goldman, who was jailed for a minimum of eleven years, claimed the killing had been ordered by Nik Radev.

On 22 October 2003, Istvan 'Steve' Gulyas and his Thai wife were executed at their home in Wildwood, north of Melbourne. They had been running a dating agency, Partner Search, introducing Victorian men to Russian women (which some saw as a scam), as well as running an illegal under-age brothel.

Recently there have been suggestions that the *Mafiya* or *Organatiza* which, in Melbourne, operates principally from St Kilda and Caulfield, has been buying luxury properties and other real estate holdings across the country. There are signs it has been taking a more active interest in the community, establishing bases for white collar crime, money laundering and drug trafficking as well as abalone poaching. One scam operated by the *Mafiya* has been 'Trojan', the collection of personal details of bank customers and then illegal transference of money into the accounts. This is then passed on, less a percentage, to Russia.

In March 2007 Australian Federal Police's Taskforce arrested 24-year-old Southbank, Melbourne, resident Edy Kuswoyo, an alleged leader of a multi-million dollar identity theft syndicate operating over four Australian states. Extradited to Sydney, he was one of twenty-two people charged with 500 identity crime offences which had netted more than $2.5 million. The police alleged members had numerous mobile phones in false names, including that of the actor Robert de Niro.

As the Melbourne identity Joey Turner said to journalist Tom Prior nearly half a century ago, 'There'll come a time when the police will wish they still had only us locals to deal with.' Will the Carlton Crew, the New Boys and their counterparts and cronies in other states survive the spate of deaths, arrests and imprisonments? In November 2004 reporter John Silvester thought, 'The survival of the Carlton Crew will depend on the acquittals of some of their senior members'. And as for the New Boys? 'There'll be the New, New Boys.'

And even if they did not survive, on 17 May 2005 the *Melbourne Underworld News* was quite sure:

> The vacuum we've been talking about is growing day by day and rest assured folks—the current crews are in strife but let us say this right fucking now lest there be any confusion:

> THIS IS NOT THE FUCKING END.

Notes

Abbreviations used in Notes

A Crim R	Australian Criminal Reports	SASC	Supreme Court of South Australia
MEPO	Metropolitan Police Office Records, National Archives (UK)	SLV	State Library of Victoria
		VCC	County Court of Victoria
NSWCCA	New South Wales Court of Criminal Appeal	VPRS	Victorian Public Record Service
NSWLR	New South Wales Law Reports	VR	Victorian Reports
		VSC	Supreme Court of Victoria
NTCCA	Northern Territory Court of Criminal Appeal	VSCA	Victorian Supreme Court of Appeal
QSC	Supreme Court of Queensland	WASCA	Western Australian Supreme Court of Appeal

Preface

Page xi, 'The criminal has no hates or fears': Karpis, p. 8.

1. Early Days

Page 4, Joseph Samuels was 'The Man They Could Not Hang': There is a story that two years earlier a similar situation occurred when a soldier was due to be shot for desertion. It rained so heavily that the muskets would not fire, and after it poured for a further five days the authorities took the view that this was a divine message and the man should be reprieved. **Page 4, The Bank of Australia:** For accounts of the theft and trials, see, for example, *Blackman v. MacVitie*, [1930] NSWSC 20 (19 March 1830); *The Australian*, 25 November 1828, 25 November 1830; Brown (ed.), *Australian Crime*, pp. 26–8. **Page 6, One of the earliest planned urban armed robberies:** *The Argus*, 3–10 April 1852, 5–9 June 1852, 5 August 1852. **Page 6, Bushrangers occasionally ventured into town:** *The Argus*, 18–29 October 1852; Nixon, pp. 62–3. **Page 6, Robberies of miners:** *Ballarat Times*, 21 October 1854; Nixon, pp. 74–5. **Page 7, From the earliest days:** R. Frances, 'The history of female prostitution in Australia' in Perkins et al., pp. 27–52. **Page 7, In 1831 came Tasmania's first sex scandal:** For an account of the case and similar ones, see Daniels, *Convict Women*, pp. 200–3. **Page 8, Naturally there was also sex to be bought:** Lahey, p. 21. The visit is described in Standish's private diary in the State Library of Victoria. **Page 8, At the other end:** Pearl, pp. 202–3. **Page 9, Dismissing the charges against the trio:** VPRS 937:306; *Truth* (Melbourne), 10 March 1906. **Page 9, 'women who have been in a state of menial servitude':** [Anon. A pupil of the late Professor John Woolley DCL], pp. 42–6.

Notes

Page 10, In Queensland major centres of prostitution: Dickie, 'Civilising the sex trade', p. 2; *The Argus,* 28 March 1893. Page 11, In the late 1860s: VPRS 937/183/6 SLV1515 Mss 114. Page 12, The professional thief: [Anon. A pupil of the late Professor John Woolley DCL], pp. 67–9. Page 12, A correspondent in the *Adelaide Advertiser*: For this and other letters and comments on prostitution in the city, see *The Advertiser*, 8 September 1884. Page 12, One illegal trade that flourished: *R v. Makin* [1893] ·14 NSWLR 1; K. Laster, 'She killed babies didn't she?', in Lake and Farley, pp. 148–56; Fitzgerald, *Studies in Australian Crime*, second series, pp. 272–91; There is a story that Jones the executioner cut his throat rather than hang Mrs Knorr and a replacement had to be found. Page 14, The fight lasted for some two hours forty minutes: What is curious is that while fights among gangs for supremacy were usually knock-down and kick affairs, the Foley–Ross contest was fought under London Rules and is recognised by prize-ring historians as a genuine match. Foley, who was never defeated in the ring, was, however, badly beaten in his last bout with 'Professor' William Miller, a strongman and wrestler, on 28 May 1883 for a 500-pound purse. Although he was ageing and Miller was heavier, Foley should have had the skill to defeat him, but Foley was saved when the crowd invaded the ring in the fortieth round. He later conceded the match, and although it was recorded as a draw, Miller received the purse. Foley died on 12 July 1917. *Australian Dictionary of Biography*, vol. 4, p. 193. For an account of Foley's life, see Roberts. For an account of Black Perry, see *Bell's Life*, 18 March 1846. Page 15, Over the next twenty years others pushes: For a full account of the Hicks's case, see Clune, pp. 1–50. Page 15, In Melbourne in 1880: *Collingwood Mercury*, 18 December 1880. Page 15, By the mid-1890s: *Truth* (Sydney), 8 April 1894. Pages 16–17, Jones and Grand trial: For an account of the trial, see Fitzgerald, *Studies in Australian Crime*, second series, pp. 316 *et seq.* Page 17, 'I have to tell you': He was correct. The judge he mentioned had indeed died friendless and away from home. Sir William Windeyer, deeply unpopular after his conduct in the trial of the Mount Rennie and Dean cases as well as his part in the resignation of the Chief Justice in 1886, died in Italy on 11 September 1897. He was on his way to take up a temporary appointment in Newfoundland. Page 18, During the war single bets: Birmingham, p. 471; Hickie, *Chow Hayes*, pp. 196–200. Page 19, In 1919, instead of going to the Melbourne Cup: *The Argus,* 7 November 1919; *The Age,* 31 October 1927. Page 19, It was in the spring of 1914: *The Sydney Morning Herald,* 11 June 1914.

2. From John Wren to Squizzy Taylor

Page 22, It was just one example: Much of this information was provided by one of Wren's daughters. In 1950, Mrs Wren brought an ill-advised libel action against Hardy on the grounds that she had been defamed in the chapter where West's wife, an otherwise rather saintly character, is driven by her husband's behaviour to have an affair with a workman. The problem for the prosecution was that neither Wren nor his wife gave evidence, leaving it to one of their sons, something that must have alienated the jury. Wren junior was forced to admit that he considered the allegation of his mother's adultery to be worse than the repeated allegations of corruption and murder made against his father. Nevertheless, it was to Hardy's surprise that he was acquitted. He later published *The Hard Way* describing his struggle. He died on 28 January 1994. Over the years there has been a considerable division of opinion over the role of Wren, with supporters distancing him from the accusations of financial and political chicanery. In particular, Hugh Buggy wrote a very supportive biography, *The Real John Wren*, as did Niall Brennan, *John Wren: Gambler*. For a view of Frank Hardy, see Hocking, *Frank Hardy*. Page 23, Cases against gaming clubs: A criminal lawyer in both senses of the word, David Gaunson, born in 1846 in Sydney, defended Ned Kelly. He was also the legal adviser to the brothel owner Madame Brussels and was no

doubt her client as well. He believed that a man should get drunk once a month for his health's sake and was said to overdo his own maxim. He might have been bound for greatness but for 'his utter instability, egregious egotism, want of consistency and violence of temper'. He died in 1909. *Australian Dictionary of Biography*, vol. 4, p. 23.
Page 23, In May 1906 he turned his attention: In 1912, stricken with cancer, William Judkins died, leaving a wife and a thirteen-year-old daughter. Wren was a substantial donor to funds set up for the reformer's family. Gillott died after a fall down a flight of stairs in Sheffield, England, on 29 June 1913. His body was brought back to Australia for burial. He left an estate of nearly 300000 pounds, much of it to charity. John Norton, increasingly alcoholic, died in 1916, leaving his fortune to his 'niece'. His wife negotiated a settlement with the girl. Norton, 'Lechery and lucre'; Pearl, ch. 16. **Page 24, Joseph Leslie Theodore Taylor:** For an account of Taylor's life and death, see H. Anderson. **Page 25, Taylor was moving into bigger:** 'The trotter tragedy', and 'Murder mystery still unsolved'. **Page 27, There were good descriptions:** *Victoria Police Gazette*, 2 and 9 March 1916. **Page 33, Any gang has to have a tame doctor:** Conversation with SL and JM, 21 February 2006. **Page 33, On 24 August 1923:** *Victoria Police Gazette*, 30 August 1923; Dower, p. 9. **Page 35, It all did Murray no good:** *R v. Murray and Taylor*, Victorian State Archives, Case No. 29, 1924. For accounts of the build-up to the hanging of Murray and of the search for Buckley, see *Truth* (Melbourne), 5 and 12 January 1924, 5 and 19 April 1924. At one time *Truth* (Brisbane) was convinced Buckley had been killed by the underworld, only to interview him for a later edition.
Page 36, In June 1924 all four men: Perhaps Brennan's most celebrated case was his unsuccessful defence in 1922 of Colin Campbell Ross, hanged for the rape and murder of twelve-year-old Alma Tirschke in Gun Alley, off Little Collins Street, Melbourne. Brennan was convinced that his client was convicted on the evidence of witnesses bought by the corrupt police officers Piggott and Brophy and wrote *The Gun Alley Tragedy* in defence of Ross. Brennan died in 1944. **Page 37, He was released in 1946:** By no means were all ageing and sick criminals released to die. The abortionist 'Dr' Bob Bruce died in Fremantle prison, Western Australia, in May 1928. He had been ill for some years and was due to be released after twenty-three years of a life sentence for the murder of a girl who died after an abortion. It was never established whether he had qualified as a doctor, but he was certainly an incompetent one. He had already served two terms for botched abortions. *Truth* (Perth), 27 May 1928. **Page 37, In June he, along with his brother Tom:** Caylock. Some believe that Tom Taylor was no re-lation to Squizzy. **Page 38, Describing the scene of the shooting:** *Truth* (Melbourne), 5 November 1927; *The Age*, 28, 29 and 31 October 1927. Another name in the frame for the killing has been that of the Melbourne identity Leslie 'Scotland Yard' Walkerden. This seems unlikely given that Walkerden's heyday was some fifteen years later. **Page 40, Ida Pender was twenty-two years old:** McCalman, p. 113. **Page 40, In January 1929 Mona Ryan was shot:** *The Argus*, 22 and 26 January 1929, *The Age*, 20 April 1929, 4 and 5 October 1930; *Truth* (Brisbane), 3 February 1929. **Page 42, Stokes had an immediate solution:** Dower, pp. 13–15.

3. Exports

Page 45, With these two as bait: It cannot have been Chicago May Sharpe. By this time she had returned to the United States after serving her sentence for the 1906 shooting of her former lover, Eddie Guerin, who was said to have eaten his colleagues in his successful escape from the French penal colony on Devil's Island. **Page 45, 'In fifty years of profligate living':** Davis, p. 34. **Page 45, Undoubtedly, one of the most talented:** Over the years there have been a number of very high-class Australian cat burglars, one of them being Vernon George Budge, also known as Blake, who maintained that no crib was too hard to crack and no drainpipe too dangerous to climb. He had, it was said, the ability of a trapeze artist. Perhaps because of this, the police knew just who was responsible for a particular burglary, and he was convicted on a number of occasions beginning in 1928. He died on 5 September 1940, when he fell 56 feet to his death in Foxton Street, Melbourne, after losing his grip on the top of a wall. He had been released from prison on 24 August after serving three years for safe blowing. *Truth* (Melbourne), 21 September 1940. **Page 46, The noted English cat burglar:** Sparks, p. 21; Greeno, pp. 58–62. **Page 47, Another Australian who worked in England:** Davis, pp. 139–40. **Page 47, Billy Hill:** Hill, p. 78; National Archives (UK) MEPO 8/41, 8/68; Illustrated circular of confidence tricksters and expert criminals. **Page 49, The very talented Australian conman:** National Archives (UK) MEPO 8/31. For an account of Australian conmen in London, including Biggar, see Leach, pp. 153–7. **Page 50, *et seq.*, From time to time:** All the quotes in this chapter, unless otherwise stated, are from conversations with JM, 2004–06. **Page 52, When in the 1980s Warren was caught:** Conversation with SL and JM, 1 March 2006. **Page 53, In the late 1990s there were signs:** Age may slow down criminals, but until they cannot actually stand, the lure of the money and the thrills generally prove too strong for them to retire. In Melbourne, on 19 May 2005, 65-year-old Murray James Perrier was given a second life sentence with no minimum term. Perrier is believed to have been the first person to receive a life sentence with no parole for a drug offence. In 1989 he had been the first to receive a life sentence for a commercial drug importation but had been released in November 2001 after thirteen and a half years. *Herald Sun*, 20 May 2005. **Page 53, In 2001 Levidis had his five year sentence:** *Sunday Mail* (Brisbane), 17 June 2001.

4. Between the Wars

Page 54, She and Leigh: In Melbourne, the brothel owners of the era co-existed rather more peacefully. In February 1925, between them Ruby Lynch and Maude Guenter had twenty-eight houses in the slum centre, including fourteen in Little Lonsdale Street. Sarah Brenner, known as Sal Redan, owned The Poplars in Exhibition Street, a supper house that catered for senior police officers. Even so, she was obliged to pay fifty pounds a month protection money. **Page 58, Asked what she saw in the disagreeable Bruhn:** Writer, p. 60. **Page 60, His downfall came in February 1929:** ibid., p. 37. **Page 61, It was a time when smugglers:** For an account of the Shark arm case, see Castles. For accounts of the trials, see *The Sydney Morning Herald*, 26 April 1935, 13 and 18 May 1935, 15 June 1935, 11 September 1935, 11 October 1935, 13 and 14 December 1935. **Page 65, It was not all Devine/Leigh:** In April 1930 another Sydney standover man who survived was Arthur Messenger (he boxed as Arthur Walker). He was shot four times, and one bullet hit his waistcoat button. A crowd pleaser in his contests, but a man with considerable woman troubles throughout his life, he drowned in Sydney Harbour in November 1945. Over the years he had become punch-drunk from the punishment he took in the ring. On the ferry from Luna Park he quarrelled with some servicemen, who threw him overboard. They immediately threw him a life belt, but he swam in the other direction. *The Sydney Morning Herald*, 23 April 1930; *Truth* (Sydney), 2 December 1945. **Page 70, Jeffs had organised his contacts:** New South Wales, *Parliamentary Debates*, pp. 22–6; McCoy, pp. 150–1. **Page 74, On 8 October, with T. S. Crawford appearing:** Crawford also prosecuted in the celebrated 1936 Lavers murder, a 'no body' case in which Frederick McDermott was convicted ten years later. His conviction, based on a contested partial confession and the wrong identification of a motor car, was quashed in 1952. It was another case used over the years by *Truth* to berate the police commissioner, criticising the efforts of his force to find the body and the murderer. Clegg, ch. 4.

5. The War Years

Page 80, War is a good time for criminals: Fraser, pp. 26–7. **Page 80, When the first seven vessels:** On 11 December that year, Adelaide experienced its most notorious murders when three men were bashed at 177a Hindley Street and the building was then set on fire. The house had been used by an SP bookmaker, and although no one was charged, the motive was robbery. The killer was almost certainly the standover man George 'Spadger' Bray, also known as Watson or Fimeri, who exercised his right not to give evidence at the inquest. On 4 November 1950 the trussed-up Bray, an associate of the gambling king Louis Zammitt, was found near Morphettville, shot twice in the head. It was thought he had been having an affair with the wife of another criminal. No charges were ever brought. **Page 81, There was the opportunity to work variations:** Sometimes the ginger game turned out very badly. On 5 May 1942, 5-foot, 15-stone Barbara Phyllis Surridge (who worked under the unfortunate name of Stella Croke) was involved in the death of Ernest Hoffman, who was variously described as a sporting man and a chef at the Royal Sydney Golf Club. She took him to a ginger joint in Langley Street, Darlinghurst, and while he was there he caught another woman going through his pockets. When he struggled with the women, two men rushed in and beat him unconscious before dumping him in an allotment in his shirt and singlet. He died in St Vincent's Hospital ten days later, but not before identifying Surridge. She, her husband William and the other man James Harris, known as Skinny Jones, were all convicted of murder. The trio were sentenced to death but were reprieved and given life sentences. For a time Phyllis Surridge was in the prison next door to her husband, and they were allowed to meet once a year in the men's chapel. After her release from prison in 1956 she was given a coming-out party by Tilly Devine. It was not the happiest of events, because she was shot through the bottom by another guest. The wound healed, and she returned to prostitution and the ginger game. She died a year later as a result of an infected cut on her finger. A whole room is devoted to the case in the Justice and Police Museum, Sydney. Tilly was clearly fond of Surridge, because Tilly once took a cauliflower and chicken to prison for her. Told she could not hand them in, Tilly threw the chook at the prison gates and the cauliflower at a warden. **Page 85, Meanwhile, in Brisbane, vice did a roaring trade:** The references to Curtin are from Ross, p. 268, and J. H. Moore, p. 216. **Page 86, In Sydney there was a special brothel:** Kelly, *Rugged Angel*, p. 68; J. H. Moore, pp. 131, 192. **Page 88, He served a ninety day sentence:** The so-called Peanut Farm is an acre or so of public gardens fringed with palm trees near Luna Park. At the time, on a Sunday morning, it was a home away from home for two-up players, conmen and SP bookmakers. The name may have come from a police officer who divided humanity into 'tired peanuts', 'worried peanuts', 'sly peanuts', and so on. Others suggest it was because people 'gambled for peanuts'. **Page 92, The black market bit was certainly right:** 'Is there a crime wave in Sydney?'; *The Sydney Morning Herald*, 16 January 1945, 23 February 1945; *The Argus*, 31 May 1946. **Page 93, The year 1945 started with remarkable claim:** *The Sydney Morning Herald*, 5 January 1945. **Page 94, When it came to it:** For an account of the quarrel, killing and subsequent trial, see Hickie, *Chow Hayes*, pp. 174–93. **Page 96, Joe Taylor:** The house rake-off in two-up games in Sydney after the war was four shillings in the pound. It was thought the turnover of the big game was 40 000 pounds a week.

6. After the War Was Over

Page 99, Stuffy Melbourne was now really rather proud: 'Melbourne, too, has an underworld'. **Page 102, Down south, the Melburnians:** Conversation with SL and JM, 22 February 2006. **Page 106, He again returned to Melbourne:** Some years earlier, in a murder trial in Melbourne, the detective Fred 'Bluey' Adam, who was known as 'Thumper' to colleagues and underworld identities alike, was asked to tell the court if he had a nickname. He agreed he had, telling the jury it was 'Honest Fred'. One former judge describes him as 'an old bastard, a thug-style copper'. **Page 111, They included William John O'Meally:** The evidence against O'Meally was strange. Before he died, Howell said the man who had shot him called him a 'fucking walloper' (Silvester and Rule, *Tough*, p. 94), an unusual expression for the time. Another officer recalled that on an occasion when he had chased O'Meally he had used the same phrase. O'Meally maintained his innocence long after his release on 4 July 1979. Apart from being taken hostage by Walker, he tried to escape twice. The second time a prison officer was shot in the leg, and O'Meally became the last man to be flogged in a Victorian prison. **Page 111, Meanwhile, in May 1952:** Hansen, pp. 108–9. **Page 113, Then, at 4.40 p.m. on 6 February:** 'The late Freddy Harrison'. **Page 113, Lawyer Frank Galbally:** F. Galbally, pp. 116–17. **Page 115, The police learned that:** *The Age*, 16–18 October 1961.

7. Italian and Other Connections

Page 123, In early December that year: *The Argus*, 20 December 1930. **Page 124, In October 1927 a French syndicate:** In 1929 the French white slaver Jean Georges Vigneron was arrested in Paris. After his deportation from Australia in 1927 he had sent out more than forty girls from France to work in Queensland. **Page 125, At the time of her death:** For rival theories about Morris's death, see Haney; Bottom, *The Godfather in Australia*. **Page 125, In November that year Antonio Cavalto:** *The Sydney Morning Herald*, 16 November 1932. **Page 127, There are some grounds:** For detailed accounts of the case, see Ayling; Clegg; Evans; Kelly, *The Charge Is Murder*. **Page 128, One report has him saying:** *Courier-Mail*, 15, 17 and 18 January 1938. **Page 128, The trial judge directed:** *Truth* (Melbourne), 3 November 1945, 1 December 1945. **Page 129, *Truth* took a close interest:** *Truth* (Melbourne), 7 April 1951. **Page 132, Insurance broker and money launderer:** Also killed was Pasquale 'Il Principale' Barbaro, the alleged boss of the Calabrian Mafia in Canberra. He had become an NCA informer and had named twenty-eight of the Calabrian bosses. **Page 133, In the afternoon on Monday 8 May 2000:** *Herald Sun*, 11 May 2000; Silvester, 'Coming clean'; Moor and Wilkinson, pp. 31–120, in particular pp. 89–90. **Page 137, Adrian Neale:** Conversations with JM, 22 August 2003, 23 January 2006. **Page 138, Without help he was effectively a dead man walking:** *Sun Herald*, 19 May 1991, 19 January 1992; *The Sydney Morning Herald*, 25 January 1992. **Page 139, In 2006 the respectable Costa family:** Moor and Wilkinson, pp. 31–120, in particular pp. 72–8.

8. Some Painters and Dockers

Page 140, In March 1980: Richards, 'Australia's most dangerous criminal tells all'. **Page 141, On paper Bazley's early career:** Conversation with JM, 24 October 2006. **Page 142, The MSS robbery:** Conversation with JM, 24 October 2006. **Page 143, The year after the robbery:** On 26 March 1972, Thomas Connellan was shot but survived. He was a principal witness in the case, but the police announced the attack was not connected with the case or the Dockers' war. Collingburn's widow, Rae Elizabeth, was convicted of the manslaughter of her de facto, former Kangaroo member Tom Wraith, on 14 September 1983. She served a year before her release and died shortly afterwards. Wraith, who had been struck with a tomahawk, was said to have killed a woman, Grace O'Connor, in England during his time there. Tame, pp. 154–5. **Page 143, Retribution was swift:** In Hillier's hagiography of the union, Nelson is described as 'one of the most respected persons who ever worked on the Melbourne Waterfront'. His untimely death is not even mentioned. Hillier, p. 61. **Page 144, What was amazing:** *The Herald* (Melbourne), 11–13 December 1971. The underworld is full of stories such as the one about the death of Costello. When the London criminal David Elmore was about to be executed in the Kalehi Restaurant in Barking on St Valentine's Day 1984, he began reciting the Lord's Prayer. When he reached, 'Thy will be done' his killer said, 'It will, son, it will.' **Page 146, The week after Shannon was shot:** Richards, 'Australia's most dangerous criminal tells all'. **Page 150, Bennett had learned:** In the late 1960s, Smalls led a team of robbers who raided London banks, usually on the day cash deliveries were made. He was arrested on an unrelated customs matter and rolled over, giving evidence against his former friends and so giving rise to the word 'supergrass'. His 'friends' received long sentences, but he was allowed to go free and share in some of the reward money. Morton, *Gangland*, pp. 272–82. **Page 150, The next problem faced by Bennett:** On 26 May 1971, Peter Pasquale Macari telephoned Qantas to say there was a bomb on their flight to Hong Kong, which would explode if the plane dropped below 35 000 feet. There was also a disabled bomb in an airport locker, which was found by officials. Qantas paid a ransom of $500 000 before being told it had been hoaxed. Macari and his associate, barman Raymond Ponting, drew attention to themselves by buying fast cars and a penthouse flat. More than $100 000 remained missing, and when Macari's counsel told the judge his client was remorseful, he received the tart reply that restoration of the money would show repentance. Macari received ten years and on his release was deported to England. *The Australian*, 27 May 1971. **Page 152, Mikkelsen and Pendergast went straight into hiding:** Some thirty-five years later Tony Mokbel, accused of importing drugs, was excused from attending the Melbourne Magistrates' Court until the end of his committal proceedings. It was argued, possibly with some justification, that he felt at risk from his enemies when so publicly exposed.

9. The Seventies

Page 155, 'No city in the world': McCoy, p. 199. **Page 156, There was also Karl Bonnette:** On 14 November 1957 a mass meeting of North American Mafia chiefs was held near the town of Apalachin, New York. It was observed by an astute police officer, who had them rounded up. Senior underworld figures fled in disarray, and it was thought the bust set the Mafia back some years. Morton, *Gangland International*, pp. 116–17. **Page 172, At the Street Inquiry:** Freeman had no love whatsoever for Bottom, a prolific author, journalist and editor, who was, for the period from April to September 1978, a special investigator into crime attached to the Attorney General's department. Freeman blamed Bottom for many of his misfortunes and in his autobiography, Freeman devotes considerable space to an attack on him. This may be one of the reasons why the book was privately published. **Page 179, The always immaculate:** Conversation with JM, 11 October 2006.

10. Two Wars in the Eighties

Page 189, It was a police officer: For an account of Egan's career, see Hickie, *The Prince and the Premier*, pp. 301–6. **Page 190, The first killing linked to the Australian heroin trade:** For an account of the Mr Asia connection and the drug killings ordered by Clark, see Royal Commission of Inquiry into Drug Trafficking, *Report, February 1983*. **Page 193, Career criminal Arthur Stanley 'Neddy' Smith:** Along with Smith, Chapman went on to a career as an armed robber before, in 1976, Smith dobbed him in and he received thirteen years. On 14 April 1995 he was shot, beaten up and left to die outside a brothel in Ingleburn in Sydney's south-western suburbs. At the time he was facing heroin and cocaine charges following another undercover operation. After his last release from prison he had husbanded his assets well, purchasing a penthouse at Noosa Heads and a share in a $200 000 racehorse. For a full, if self-serving, account of Smith's activities, see Smith, *Neddy* and *Catch and Kill Your Own*. **Page 193, Smith had a wide variety of friends:** On the death of Biber, see chapter 3. **Page 194, First a folk hero:** On an account of Rogerson's career, see McNab, *The Dodger*. **Page 198, 'McCann was getting more vicious':** Conversation with JM, 10 October 2006. **Page 201, Present at his home:** On 23 March 1986, James William 'Bill' Duff was dismissed from the force over allegations of offering a bribe in relation to a drug deal. In 1997 he was jailed for eighteen months for heroin trafficking. See Whitton, pp. 38–9, 274; Silvester and Rule, *Tough*, p. 14. **Page 201, 'There's no real question of Flannery':** Conversation with JM, 10 October 2006. The tree-shredder story is from robber and standover man Mark Read, *Chopper 2*. Read, whose nickname comes from the self-mutilation of his ears, has written a series of highly popular books in which he is the hero of the underworld. He came to prominence when, in an effort to secure the release of his friend Jimmy Loughnan, he kidnapped Judge Martin. He received thirteen years and was later convicted of the attempted murder of Sid Collins, a biker in Tasmania, something he bitterly denies. **Page 202, After all, as Sydney identity Jackie Steele:** see Smith, *Catch and Kill Your Own*, pp. 176–7. **Page 203, After a ten week trial:** Fife-Yeomans, 'No more Mr Bigs'; Smith, *Catch and Kill Your Own*, pp. 148–50. **Page 205, Throughout the trial:** see *Kidd v. Chief Executive, Department of Corrective Services* (2000) QSC 405; *The Sydney Morning Herald*, 5 July 2003; *Sunday Telegraph*, 12 December 2004. **Page 205, They included, on 25 March 1987:** His case, along with that of Jensen and Jedd Houghton, is recounted in Flemington/Kensington Community Legal Centre et al., *Police Shootings in Victoria 1987–1989*. **Page 206, Around 4 a.m. on the day after Jensen's death:** For a full account of the case, see Noble, *Walsh Street*. **Page 212, 'Dennis was good as a killer':** As quoted in Anderson, *Shotgun City*, p. 167.

11. Over the Wall and into the Bank

Page 214, One of the great robbers and escapers: Cohen, 'Interview with Bernie Matthews', 2004. **Page 215, The pain and suffering:** According to some accounts of the Toecutters, they were led by the corrupt Sydney policeman Fred Krahe along with an Englishman, Linus or Jimmy 'The Pom' Driscoll. It was said that Driscoll (or O'Driscoll) had been the personal bodyguard of the IRA deputy leader Joe Cahill, as well as serving in the Congo under 'Mad' Mike Hoare and being a friend of the Kray twins. London criminals of the period discount this and claim to have no knowledge of O'Driscoll, who does not appear in any Kray literature. It may be that he knew them as children. He was convicted of the Maloney murder, but released on appeal, he was later deported after being convicted on a weapons charge. See also Read, *Chopper 2*, pp. 90–2. **Page 217, That was a totally professional operation:** Anderson, *Dirty Dozen*, pp. 79–82; Read, *Chopper: From the Inside*, pp. 127–34. **Page 217, While in Pentridge:** Another standover man, John William 'Piggy' Palmer, was acquitted. Later he was convicted of rape and, on his release in 1986, of a fresh series of robberies. **Page 219, A robber who ended his life:** Silvester and Rule, *Tough*, pp. 259–63. **Page 220, Smith died in Victoria:** After his death, tributes were divided. The police thought he was a hostage taker, but solicitor Christopher Murray thought he had protected the young and vulnerable while in prison. An associate commented, 'Like so many of us, he was getting too old to go back to jail.' *Sun Herald*, 20 December 1992; Silvester, *Leadbelly*, ch. 28. **Page 221, The next year, on 26 October:** Around 9.50 p.m. on 9 August 1987 nineteen-year-old Julian Knight opened fire on motorists driving along Hoddle Street between the Eastern Freeway overpass and the Clifton Hill railway station in Melbourne. By the time he was arrested he had killed seven and wounded another seventeen. He received seven life sentences and 460 years on forty-six attempted murder charges. His twenty-seven year non-parole period was seen by some as merciful. On Binse, see also Silvester and Rule, *Tough*, pp. 55–9. **Page 223, The problems for the prosecution:** The dangers of both the evidence of dobbers and the absence of bodies were apparent in 2003 when evidence was given that Leonard John Fraser had confessed in prison to murdering Natasha Ryan, who had been missing for some five years, smashing her head and dumping her body in a pond. In fact, she had been alive and well and living with her boyfriend in Rockhampton, Queensland. *The Age*, 22 April 2003. **Page 226, Sentenced to life:** MacDonald was by no means the first to advertise for victims. In 1872 George Robert Nicholls and Alfred Lester were executed. They had placed advertisements in *The Sydney Morning Herald* seeking 'A steady man required for country store, drive repair wagons, houses. TYC'. The successful applicants were taken up-river and thrown overboard. TYC was said to mean 'take your chance'. **Page 228, In March 1998 Natalee Hunter:** In January 2005, while still in prison, Berrichon married Rhiannon, the daughter of former AFL player James Krakouer, who was jailed in 1995 for drug trafficking. On Abbott's career, see Pedley, *No Fixed Address*; Anderson, *Dirty Dozen*, pp. 83–118. **Page 229, In July 1994 she received a ten year sentence:** Her relationship with Gibb continued after her release, but in March 2007, after Parker pleaded guilty to assaulting a love rival, her counsel described it as 'a living hell'. She received eighteen months' imprisonment wholly suspended for thirty months. *Herald Sun*, 18 April 2007. **Page 230, Killick will be seventy-three:** *R v. Killick* [2002] NSWCCA 1; *R v. Dudko* [2002] NSWCCA 336. **Page 230, The question that divided Australia:** Bartholomew, letters to Crown Solicitor and Secretary to Law Department, 10 March 1966 and 10 December 1966 respectively; Richards, *The Hanged Man*; Silvester and Rule, *Tough*, pp. 100–4; Ayling, ch. 9. Ayling gives a very personal account of the escape, the hunt and the execution of Ryan, for whom he had a great deal of sympathy.

12. Sex from the Sixties

Page 233, After Borg's death: see Dickie, 'Civilising the sex trade'. **Page 235, Community attitudes:** see Grabosky, p. 194. **Page 235, Action by residential groups:** Longmire, pp. 209–11; Bottom et al., pp. 75–6. **Page 237, One of the leading backyard operators:** *Truth* (Melbourne), 11 October 1969. **Page 237, One was Fred 'Bluey' Adam:** Berman and Childs, pp. 46–53. **Page 238, An application to treat Turner:** Turner was killed when his car ran off the road and hit a tree in Nyora in January 1995. **Page 238, The growth of the sex industry in the 1960s and 1970s:** Longmire, pp. 221, 255–7, 262; Bottom et al., p. 76. **Page 239, He had been advised:** *R v. Zampaglione* (1981) 6 A Crim R 287. **Page 239, By the late 1970s:** Tame, 'Findings of lengthy probe sparked officer outrage'; Wilkinson, 'Former brothel king dies'. **Page 240, On 1 August 1978:** *The Age*, 2 August 1978. **Page 241, MacRae eventually left Lamb:** For an account of MacRae's career, see Silvester and Rule, *Tough*, p. 205. **Page 243, Arrested in September 1987:** *The Advertiser*, 19 January 1999. **Page 243, The commission found:** National Crime Authority, *Operation Hydra*. **Page 244, This, argued the lobbyists:** F. conversation with SL, 22 May 2006. **Page 244, As a result properties were being sold:** K. conversation with SL, 15 October 2006. **Page 244, From the 1980s Fred Lelah:** *R v. Dominic Patrick Hickey* [2001] VSCA 75 (23 May 2001); *R v. Lelah* [2002] VSCA 96 (27 June 2002). For an account of Lelah's career, see Noble, ch. 5. **Page 245, Insiders say that another development:** F. conversation with SL, 22 May 2006; Valli Mendez, conversation with SL, 19 June 2006; see also Project Respect, *One Victim of Trafficking is One Too Many*; Birnbauer, 'Migrants lured by sex ring'; Birnbauer, 'From Russia for love'; Birnbauer, 'Prostitutes caught in debt servitude'. **Page 245, In one 1988 case:** Bottom et al., p. 73. **Page 246, A food importer:** McClymont and Clennell, 'Brothel boom'. **Page 246, At the low roller end:** *R v. Nguyen & Anor* VSCA [1997] (28 November 1997). **Page 246, Local sex workers say:**

K. conversation with SL, 15 October 2006. **Page 246, The dangers faced by illegally imported sex workers:** *R v. Trinh* [2006] NTCCA 19 (27 September 2006); Murdoch, 'Teenagers threw prostitutes off bridge'. The young men were convicted in the Northern Territory Supreme Court and on 19 March 2005 were sentenced to life imprisonment—twenty-five years without parole. **Page 247, More often they are elusive:** Chaiyakorn Bai-ngern, 'Police investigate three alien smuggling gangs'. **Page 247, It was not until 2006:** *R v. D.S.* [2005] VSCA 99 (12 April 2005); *R v. Wei Tang* [2006] VCC 637 (9 June 2006). **Page 248, In 2004 researchers looking into the effect of legislation:** Bindel, 'Streets apart'. **Page 248, This is confirmed by a survey:** Woodward et al.

13. Drugs and Ethnic Minority Crime

Page 250, Shortly before midnight on 31 July 1996: see *R v. Phong Ngoc Pham; R v. Vu Ngoc Pham; R v. Minh Hoang Nguyen* [2003] NSWSC 1261 (13 January 2003). **Page 251, During the late 1960s and early 1970s:** Lintner, pp. 319–23. **Page 252, One Triad member:** 'Kingpin's high life from heroin trade ends in a cell'. **Page 253, 'Louis Bayeh is considerably smarter':** Conversation with JM, 10 and 11 October 2006. **Page 253, The Bayehs and their friend:** Brown, 'Death of a one-time Godfather'. **Page 254, There was worse to come:** Jackson was known as 'Buckets' because of the way he showered abuse on his political opponents. **Page 257, Bill Bayeh and and his successor:** see *R v. Bayeh* (Bill) [2000] NSWCCA 473 (21 November 2000). **Page 257, He soon found drugs more profitable:** see *R v. Kanaan* [2005] NSWCCA 354, *Kanaan & Ors v. Regina* [2006], NSWCCA. In 2007, an application for special leave to appeal to the High Court was pending. **Page 259, When he was shot:** see McClymont, 'Secret eyes on Rivkin and Sydney's drug trade'. **Page 262, In 1994 it was said to have stolen:** see Allbeury, 'Asian crime wave'. **Page 264, One early Mr Big Enough:** see *R v. Van Thanh Huynh* [1996] NSWCCA (13 May 1996). **Page 264, In the mid-1990s:** see *R v. Hong Phuc Truong* [2002] VSCA 27 (26 March 2002). **Page 265, One barrister recalls:** Conversation with SL, 16 August 2006. **Page 266, Australian lawyers regard:** Conversation with JM, 9 February 2006. **Page 266, When Duong was banned:** *The Sydney Morning Herald*, 25 April 2000; see also Dermott, 'Winner takes all'. **Page 266, A multicultural casino based gang:** see *R v. Ko Kon Tong, Dat Thinh Ong & Le Phan Vuong* [2003] VSCA 15 (26 February 2003). **Page 267, Some see a direct connection:** Conversation with JM, 9 February 2006. **Page 267, The drug dealers may make:** Conversation with SL, 16 August 2006. **Page 268, A shake and shootout in May 1999:** Callinan and Targett, 'The powder trail'. **Page 268, In October 2002:** *The Age*, 8 October 2006; *Herald Sun*, 27 October 2006. In the three years to 2006, more than $1 billion dollars' worth of crystal methamphetamine—known as 'ice', the party drug—had been found in Asia and the Pacific, including more than a tonne of ice destined for Australia, which was seized in Suva in June 2004. See Kidman, '$2 billion drug hauls as Australian agents tackle a new ice age'. **Page 269, There was another success:** Nothing really changes. In 1929 customs officials in North Queensland discovered gutted fish had been repacked with tins of opium.

14. Bikers

Pages 270–87: We have referred to outlaw motorcycle gangs as 'bikers' (as this is the term they generally use for themselves), rather than using the popular term 'bikies'. **Page 270, On 11 May 2006:** O'Neill, 'Deadly toll of bikie turf war'. **Pages 271–2, Superintendent Fred Gere:** Conversation with SL, 7 February 2007. **Page 276, Some bikers, such as Dr John Smith of God's Squad:** see Shand, 'Outlaw nation'. The God's Squad Christian Motorcycle Club was founded in Tasmania in 1972. According to the God's Squad webpage on the Concern Austalia website, its 'primary ministry …is to the "Outlaw" motorcycle club sub-culture where it plays an important chaplaincy role'. **Page 276, In 2003 a Hunter Valley amphetamine network:** see *R v. Walsh & Little* [2005] NSWSC (28 February 2005). **Page 277, Judges and juries are invariably concerned:** Conversation with SL, 20 October 2006. **Page 279, In 2005 a tear-down order:** Moscarlito and Williams, 'Bikies without borders'. **Pages 279–80, Reid also gave evidence:** *White v. The Queen* [2006] WASCA 62 (7 April 2006). **Page 280, Giving evidence against OMCGs:** *R v. Gillard & Preston* [2000] SASC 454; *R v. Gillard* [2006] SASC 46 (23 February 2006). **Page 281, Intelligence gathering is an integral part:** Conversation with SL, 7 February 2007. **Page 282, In 2003 it was suspected:** 'Police raid bikies over $23 million drug ring'; Kennedy, 'Bikies arrested over drug ring'; see also 'Bail for only one of 18 on drug ring charges'. **Page 283, In early 2006 Australian Federal Police raided:** Mercer, 'China link to bikie amphetamine lab'. **Page 284, Operation Avatar:** Moscaritolo and Williams, 'Bikies without borders'. **Page 284, Passing are the days:** In 2007 police are watching for further biker wars, fuelled by ethnic influxes into biker gangs and a more violent style of conflict. Stewart and Edwards, 'Attacks create bikie war concerns'. **Page 285, On the east coast:** Lawrence and Fife-Yeomans 'Landing in a war zone'; Crawford, 'Police fear national bikie war'. **Page 285, A new national taskforce:** Conversation with SL, 7 February 2007. **Page 286, Further muddying the waters:** In May 2007 the close friendship between distinguished Melbourne-based QC Peter Hayes and the once Gypsy Joker biker-turned-businessman Anthony John Sobey came under some media scrutiny. Hayes, briefed by Sobey in a civil matter, had dined with his client in a posh Adelaide suburb. Some hours after Sobey dropped Hayes at his hotel, Hayes collapsed following a heart attack and was later put into an induced coma at the Royal Adelaide Hospital. He died several days later. See McGarry and Hughes, 'Riddle of the ex-bikie and the drugged QC'.

15. The Best that Money Can Buy

Page 288, 'Lennie McPherson and George Freeman': Conversation with JM, 6 November 1996. **Page 288, After looking at patterns:** McCoy, pp. 32–3. Other writers, including the American E. R. Stoddard, have suggested there may be as many as ten stages, but McCoy's five-point plan seems to provide an eminently workable structure. **Page 290, 'Nothing could be worse':** As quoted in Haldane, p. 39. **Page 291, After Kelly's capture in June 1880:** Over the years the use of informers by the police in all countries and cities has been the subject of disapproval and disappointment. It was not until 2003 that an Informer Management Unit was introduced in Victoria. **Page 291, In 1888, 500 young men:** see Davison et al. (eds), *Austalians 1888* p. 367. **Page 291, 'One does not expect':** Christie, undated entry, probably 1897. **Page 293, The best and most likely explanation:** Haldane, p. 197. On Blamey's life, see Hetherington. **Page 294, Blamey was finished:** Royal Commission on the Alleged Shooting at and Wounding of John O'Connell Brophy, *Report*, VPRS 3992. A transcript of all the evidence in the Blamey–Brophy case can be found under VPRS 2570. There were apparently written police reports on the Brophy matter under VPRS 3992, unit 2561, file M4589, but the file is missing. Hardiman, in his paper 'Police accountability', confirms that the destruction of so many sensitive files is unique to Blamey's era. **Page 295, Kelly's retirement party:** Farewell dinners attended by politicians and criminals alike were common at the time. Sweeney, the retiring metropolitan superintendent, was feted by 600 vice traders and received a cheque for 600 pounds. Inspector Noonan, the metropolitan licensing inspector, did rather better on his retirement, pocketing a cheque for 1000 pounds presented at the Australia Hotel. The 1951 Royal Commission on Liquor Laws in New South Wales found that these practices were simply 'indiscreet' rather than illegal. **Page 296, During his career Krahe**

was also: Maguire, 'The case of the missing victim', pp. 280–300. **Page 297, Shirley Brifman fled:** For an account of the careers of Kelly, Krahe and Fergusson, see Hickie, *The Prince and the Premier*, pp. 280–300. **Page 297, 'There was no evidence':** Conversation with JM, 11 November 1996. **Page 303, In June 1996 Peter Ryan:** For Ryan's thoughts shortly after his appointment, see Morton, 'Ryan's war'. For an account of Ryan's time with the New South Wales police, see S. Williams. **Page 305, Much of the evidence came from a former officer:** New South Wales, Police Integrity Commission, *Operation Florida*. **Page 309, Herbert died on 7 April 2004:** For accounts of the problems leading to the Fitzgerald Inquiry and the subsequent fallout, see Herbert; Sturgess. **Page 309, On 22 June 1982:** In 2006 another, even larger, attempt on the Perth Mint nearly succeeded. Using fake deeds to claim ownership of the Australian Rugby property in North Sydney, conmen obtained a $14.4 million cheque from a church fund as a purported bridging loan. One of them, claiming to be a lawyer, then contacted a city bullion dealer to buy gold. The innocent bullion dealer ordered 605 1-kilogram gold bars from the Mint, and the bullion was actually flown to Sydney before the couriers, Brinks Security, became suspicious and contacted the police. *The Sydney Morning Herald*, 22 July 2006.

16. Some Bent Briefs

Page 313, For instance, in the 1970s in New South Wales: On the practices of the time, see Delaney. **Page 313, He had once been a partner:** *The Australian*, 6, 8 and 9 January 2001; see also Conroy. **Page 316, According to Smith:** Smith, *Neddy*, p. 115. **Page 319–20, Mario Condello:** For an account of Condello's career and influence, see Wilkinson and Moor, *Mugshots*, p. 2. **Page 320, His roster of clients:** Krakouer received sixteen years for his part in amphetamine transportation in January 1994. It was in sharp contrast to the lenient four years given to drug dealer John Higgs, who had persuaded him to undertake the run. **Page 321, Roberts, his wife Andrea Mohr and Carl Henze Urbanec:** *R v. Fraser* [2004] VSCA (27 August 2004); *R v. Roberts, Urbanec* [2004] VSCA 1 (6 February 2004). **Page 321, One South Australian solicitor:** *R v. Justin Birk Hill* [1996] SASC 5975 (24 December 1996); *The Sydney Morning Herald*, 21 September 2005. **Page 323, Her problems have not stopped her:** *The Age*, 22 November 2005.

17. The New Century

Page 325, In the three years from 1998: Silvester, 'Cops, robbers, drugs and money'. In December 1999 Higgs's deaf son Craig and his wife were savagely attacked in their home by a gang looking for drugs and money. Curiously, three of the four members of the gang were also deaf. **Page 325, 'At the beginning they weren't divided':** Conversation with JM, 25 October 2006. **Pages 325–6, He returned only when Read was jailed:** Read was released in 2000. Sid Collins, a former president of the Black Uhlans, later ran a Russian mail-order-bride business. In August 2002 he went to the Gold Coast to collect money that was owed to him and disappeared. **Page 326, He had fallen out with the Moran brothers:** Silvester, 'Death of a gangster'. **Page 326, Despite his balding hair and paunch:** Conversations with SL and JM, 18 October 2006. **Page 327, 'never ran anything, never was involved in the big money networks':** Conversation with SL, 16 August 2006. **Page 327, Ronald Victor Lucas:** *R v. Lucas* (1992) 2 VR 109. For full accounts of the deaths of individuals in the gang wars, see *inter alia* Anderson, *Shotgun City*; Silvester and Rule, *Leadbelly*; see also Shand's highly entertaining reporting in *The Bulletin*: 'Burial ground' and 'Piece talks'. **Page 329, 'Chubby with designer sportswear':** Conversation with JM, 18 October 2006. **Page 331, Down with him went Pasquale Barbaro:** Barbaro's death has had an unlikely postscript. Mark and Cheryl McEachran, frustrated by their inability to conceive a sixth child, snatched Montana Barbaro, a three-week-old baby, in Brimbank Centre shopping mall before dumping her in an abandoned house. Their choice attracted more than the usual publicity. The baby was that of Barbaro's cousin Joe, a drug dealer with links to the upper echelons of the crime scene. When the pair were remanded, it was Joe who was in the public gallery mouthing threats. The McEachrans were finally jailed for a total of nineteen years. The story had something of a happy ending, because Barbaro says the kidnapping changed his life. He had been a drug dealer but now thought, 'How could I have put another parent through that sort of agony?' This conversion must have helped his sentence because in August 2006 Barbaro received a modest five year minimum to go with the four and a half years he had received in March 2005. **Page 331, 'There's not much a fella like me can do':** Conversation with JM, 18 October 2006. **Page 332, 'One of the three top crims I ever met':** Conversation with SL and JM, 25 October 2006. For the record, the others were Bertie Kidd and Joe Turner. **Page 332, 'Graham was a gentle, gentle man':** Conversation with SL and JM, 22 February 2006. **Page 333, Earlier in the year, two relatively minor figures had left the game:** It was often dangerous to attend martial arts clubs. On 5 July 1973 Andrew Donnelly, a black belt judo instructor in Brooklyn, Sydney, was lured out of the club where he was teaching and shot in the back of the head at point blank range. The police said the likelihood was that it had been a contract put out by a group of Pentridge prisoners. The killing was thought to have related to an interstate incident two years before. **Page 334, An early girlfriend of his has described him:** Conversation with JM, 26 October 2006. **Page 335, There was to be a bonus of $50 000 on completion:** This was one of the less remarkable bonuses on offer. In 1988 in Detroit, Harry Kalasho had two of his rivals, Salem Munthir and Salem Gago, killed by hitman Buck Lavell. The payment was $5000 each and a further $10 000 if their heads were deposited on the disputed turf of Seven Mile, a road that runs through the middle of the city. Lavell completed the contract but did not deposit the heads. He was later convicted but never gave up Kalasho. In his turn Harry Kalasho was killed, on 3 February 1989, in the long-running feud. **Page 338, Or there was Central America or Mexico:** The corrupt financier Christopher Skase began his career as a financial journalist. In 1987 he bought the Seven Network and later tried to buy the American studio MGM. When he failed to pay, his pyramid of companies collapsed and it was found he had been siphoning money for his own account. He declared himself bankrupt to the tune of $170 million and, facing fraud charges, fled to Spain, from where he fought off attempts to extradite him until his death in Majorca on 6 August 2001. **Page 339, (In June 2007,:** see Silvester, 'New Mokbel murder charge'. **Page 340, On 7 May Justice Betty King:** R v. Williams [2007] VSC 131; Harrison, 'Williams jailed for 35 years'; The Age, 8 May 2007. **Page 340, 'He's still her dad':** Rennie and Berry, 'Roberta stands by her man'. **Page 340, Williams has appealed:** Butcher, 'Gangland killer Williams to appeal sentence'. **Page 340, As winter 2007 approached:** Munro and Butcher, 'Williams confesses'. On 25 May 2007, a suppression order banning the identification Michael Ronald Thorneycroft, a police witness against Carl Williams, was lifted after Thorneycroft died on 24 May 2007 following a suspected drug overdose. It was reported that there were no suspicious circumstances surrounding his death. Thorneycroft, who was charged with conspiracy to murder Condello, had turned Queen's Evidence and was given a three year suspended sentence and a new name. **Page 340, She was carted off to jail:** Silvester, 'The untold, bloody story of Melbourne's underworld war'. **Page 340, The hunt ended:** Shanahan, 'Disguised Mokbel grabbed at seaside cafe'. **Page 341, The full disaster of the 1990s drug policy of the Victoria Police:** The Age, 19 and 20 October 2006, Herald Sun, 19 and 20 October 2006. **Page 342, It soon emerged:** Protection of witnesses and informers has always been a problem. Sometimes they lose heart in the conditions.

Sometimes it is all a blind—Wendy Peirce in the Walsh Street shootings, for example. There may be attempts to get at them. Sometimes they get bored with the tight security and go off on dangerous frolics of their own. Sometimes there are leaks that put them at risk. The Western Australian Police had some problems of their own with internal and costly leaks. On 11 September 1995, Andrew Petrelis, supposedly in a witness protection program, was found dead at Caloundra in Queensland. His body was hunched over a CD player on repeat. He had been due to give evidence against a Perth nightclub owner and identity, John Kizon, a friend of Alphonse Gangitano. Petrelis, a heroin addict, had at one time worked as Kizon's driver. His body had been discovered after he failed to appear for a flying lesson. The coroner found that he died of a heroin overdose, but Petrelis's family and friends believe that it was a question of forcible feeding. In 1994 Petrelis had been instructed—it was never wholly clear by whom—to dig up bags, expected to contain cannabis, in Perth's Kings Park. He complied and took them to a self-storage unit that he had rented, putting a padlock on the door. The owners became suspicious, broke open the door, discovered $150000 worth of drugs and called the police. Petrelis rolled over. Grass cuttings were substituted for the cannabis, and one Michael Rippingdale picked up the bags on 22 November 1994. Following surveillance and phone taps he and Kizon were arrested and charged over the drugs. Kizon, who was in hospital at the time of Petrelis's death, complained bitterly, suggesting the arrest was a slur on his character and that he had only been arrested because of his associates. In November 1999 he and Rippingale were acquitted. Unfortunately, even before he left Western Australia, Petrelis's cover had been blown. A police constable looking on the web for information about Elvis Presley's manager stumbled on confidential details of his new identity. Worse was to come when a second officer also came across the details and passed them on to Western Australian criminals. The second officer resigned. **Page 343, Indeed one-third of all Australian firearm homicides:** Jones, *Firearm Restrictions*. **Page 344, Predictably the move did not appeal to everyone:** Kim, 'NSW cops to set up anti-Arab squad'; see also Stephen, 'The myth of ethnic crime'. **Page 345, 'One sixty year old told me':** Conversation with JM, 8 February 2006. **Page 346, The Romanian gangs:** Conversation with SL, 4 October 2006. **Page 346, One high profile incident occurred:** *Gold Coast Bulletin*, 23 July 2005.

Bibliography

Books

Allen, J. A., *Sex and Secrets: Crimes Involving Australian Women since 1880*, Oxford University Press, Melbourne, 1990.

Anderson, H., *Larrikin Crook: The Rise and Fall of Squizzy Taylor*, Jacaranda Press, Melbourne, 1971.

Anderson, P., *Dirty Dozen*, Hardie Grant Books, Melbourne, 2003.

——*Shotgun City*, Hardie Grant Books, Melbourne, 2004.

——*Another Dirty Dozen*, Hardie Grant Books, Melbourne, 2005.

Annear, R., *Nothing but Gold: The Diggers of 1852*, Text Publishing Company, Sydney, 1999.

[Anon.] *The Life and Adventures of Isaac Solomons*, The Unusual Pamphleteer, London, n.d.

[Anon. A pupil of the late Professor John Woolley DCL], *Vice and its Victims in Sydney*, privately published, Sydney, 1873.

Asbury, H., *The Barbary Coast*, Robert Hale, London, 1937.

Australian Dictionary of Biography, ed. D. Pike, vol. 4, Melbourne University Press, Melbourne, 1972.

Aveling, M. and J. Damousi (eds), *Stepping out of History*, Allen & Unwin, Melbourne, 1991.

Ayling, J., *Nothing but the Truth: The Life and Times of Jack 'Ace' Ayling*, Ironbark Press, Sydney, 1993.

Barry, P., *The Rise and Rise of Kerry Packer*, Bantam, Sydney, 1993.

Berman, P. and K. Childs, *Why Isn't She Dead?*, Gold Star Publications, Melbourne, 1972.

Birmingham, J., *Leviathan: The Unauthorised Biography of Sydney*, Random House, Sydney, 1999.

Blaikie, G., *Remember Smith's Weekly*, Rigby, Sydney, 1966.

——*Wild Women of Sydney*, Rigby, Sydney, 1980.

Bottom, B., *The Godfather in Australia*, A. F. & A. W. Reed Pty Ltd, Sydney, 1979.

——*Connections*, Sun Books, Melbourne, 1985.

——*Connections 2*, Sun Books, Melbourne, 1987.

——*Shadow of Shame*, Sun Books, Melbourne, 1988.

Bottom, B., J. Silvester, T. Noble and P. Daley, *Inside Victoria*, Pan MacMillan, Melbourne, 1991.

Brennan, N., *John Wren: Gambler*, Hill of Content, Melbourne, 1971.

Brennan, T. C., *The Gun Alley Tragedy: Record of the Trial of Colin Campbell Ross*, Gordon & Gotch, Melbourne, 1922.

Bridgeman, H., *Hanging Matters*, Invincible Press, Melbourne, n.d.

Brown, M., *Rorting*, Lansdowne, Sydney, 1998.

Brown, M. (ed.), *Australian Crime*, Lansdowne, Sydney, 1993.

——*Bombs, Guns and Knives*, New Holland Publishers, Sydney, 2000.

Buggy, H., *The Real John Wren*, Widescope International Publishers, Melbourne, 1977.

Burgess, R., *Guilty Wretch that I Am*, Macmillan, Melbourne, 1984.

Cannon, M., *Life in the Cities: Australia in the Victorian Age*, vol. 3, Currey O'Neill Ross Pty, Melbourne, 1983.

——*The Woman as Murderer*, Today's Australia Publishing Co., Mornington, Victoria, 1994.

Carlyon, N., *I Remember Blamey*, Macmillan, Melbourne, 1980.

Cash, M., *The Bushranger of Van Diemen's Land, 1843–44: A Personal Narrative of His Exploits in the Bush and His Experiences at Port Arthur and Norfolk Island*, J. Walsh & Sons, Hobart, 1972.

Castles, A., *The Shark Arm Murders*, Wakefield Press, Adelaide, 1955.

Caylock, G., *Charlie: As Game as Ned Kelly*, self-published, Melbourne, 1998.

Chicago Crime Commission, *The New Faces of Organised Crime*, Chicago Crime Commission, Chicago, 1997.

Christie, J. M., *The Reminiscences of Detective-Inspector Christie*, related by J. B. Castieau, George Robinson, Melbourne, 1911.

Clark, C. M. H., *Select Documents in Australian History (1788–1850)*, Angus & Robertson, Sydney, 1950.

Clegg, E., *Return Your Verdict*, Angus & Robertson, Sydney, 1965.

Clune, F., *Scandals of Sydney Town*, Angus & Robertson, Sydney, 1957.

Collins, D., *An Account of the English Colony in New South Wales*, vols 1 and 2, A. H. & A. W. Reed, Sydney, 1975.

Conroy, P., *Lawyers, Gems and Money: The Max Green Murder and the Missing Millions*, Information Australia, Melbourne, 2000.

Crowe, C., *One Big Crime*, Ross's Book Service, Melbourne, 1920.

Daniels, K., *Convict Women*, Allen & Unwin, Sydney, 1988.

Daniels, K. (ed.), *So Much Hard Work: Women and Prostitution in Australian History*, Fontana/Collins, Sydney, 1984.

Davidson, J. (ed.), *The Sydney–Melbourne Book*, George Allen & Unwin, Sydney, 1986.

Davis, V., *Phenomena in Crime*, John Long, London, n.d.

Davison, G., D. Dunstan and C. McConville (eds), *The Outcasts of Melbourne*, George Allen & Unwin, Sydney, 1985.

Davison, G., J. W. McCarty and A. McLeary (eds), *Australians 1888*, Fairfax Syme & Weldon Associates, Sydney, 1987.

Delaney, B., *Narc!: Inside the Australian Bureau of Narcotics*, Angus & Robertson, Sydney, 1979.

Dempster, Q., *Honest Cops*, ABC Enterprises, Sydney, 1992.

Dettre, A., G. Keith and P. Walker, *Infamous Australians*, Bay Books, Sydney, 1985.

Dickie. P., *The Road to Fitzgerald and Beyond*, University of Queensland Press, Brisbane, 1989.

Dower, A., *Deadline*, Hutchinson, Melbourne, 1979.

Dunstan, K., *Wowsers*, Angus & Robertson, Melbourne, 1968.

Evans, R., *The Pyjama Girl Mystery*, Scribe Publishing, Melbourne, 2004.

Felstead, S. T., *Shades of Scotland Yard*, John Long, London, 1950.

Ferguson, G., *High Climbers: Askin and Others*, John Ferguson, Sydney, 1989.

Fitzgerald, J. D., *Studies in Australian Crime*, Eagle Press, Sydney, 1924.

——*Studies in Australian Crime*, second series, Eagle Press, Sydney, 1924.

Fraser, F. with J. Morton, *Mad Frank: Memoirs of a Life of Crime*, Warner, London, 1994.

Freeman, G. D., *George Freeman, an Autobiography*, George Freeman, Sydney, 1988.

Galbally, A., *Redmond Barry*, Melbourne University Press, Melbourne, 1995.

Galbally, F., *Galbally for the Defence*, Penguin Books, Melbourne, 1994.

Grabosky, P. N., *Sydney in Ferment*, Australian National Press, Canberra, 1977.

Greeno, T., *War on the Underworld*, John Long, London, 1960.

Griffin, J., *John Wren: A Life Reconsidered*, Scribe Publications, Melbourne, 2004.

Haken, T. and S. Padraic, *Sympathy for the Devil*, ABC Books, Sydney, 2005.

Haldane, R. *The People's Force: A History of the Victoria Police*, Melbourne University Press, Melbourne, 1986.

Hall, R., *Greed: The Mr Asia Connection*, Pan Books, Sydney, 1981.

——*Disorganised Crime*, University of Queensland Press, Brisbane, 1986.

——*Tiger General: The Killing of Victor Chang*, Pan Macmillan, Sydney, 1995.

Haney, J. R., *Black Hand Vengeance*, Invincible Press, Melbourne, n.d.

Hansen, B., *Awful Truth: The Inside Story of Crime & Sport*, Brian Hansen Publications, Melbourne, 2004.

Hardy, F., *Power without Glory*, Angus & Roberston, Sydney, 1982.

——*The Hard Way*, Mandarin, Melbourne, 1992.

Harvey, S. and L. Simpson, *Brothers in Arms*, Allen & Unwin, Sydney, 2001.

Herbert, J. with T. Gilling, *The Bagman: Final Confessions of Jack Herbert*, ABC Books, Sydney, 2004.

Hetherington, J., *Blamey*, F. W. Cheshire, Melbourne, 1954.

Hickie, D., *The Prince and the Premier*, Angus & Robertson, Sydney, 1985.

——*Chow Hayes: Gunman*, Angus & Robertson, Sydney, 1990.

Hill, B., *Boss of Britain's Underworld*, Naldrett Press, London, 1955.

Hillier, L., *The Painters and Dockers*, Lew Hillier, Melbourne, 1981.

Hirst, J. B., *Convict Society and its Enemies: A History of Early New South Wales*, George Allen & Unwin, Sydney, 1983.

Hirst, W., *Great Escapes by Convicts in Colonial Australia*, Simon & Schuster, Sydney, 1999.

Hoban, L. E., *New South Wales Police Force 1862–1962*, Government Publisher, Sydney, n.d.

Hocking, G., *Bail Up: A Pictorial History of Australia's Most Notorious Bushrangers*, Five Mile Press, Melbourne, 2002.

Hocking, J., *Lionel Murphy*, Cambridge University Press, Cambridge, 2000.

——*Frank Hardy: Politics, Literature, Life*, Lothian Books, Melbourne, 2005.

Hughes, R., *The Fatal Shore*, CollinsHarvill, London, 1987.

Inglis, K., *Australian Colonists*, Melbourne University Press, Melbourne, 1974.

Jackson, R., *In Your Face: The Life and Times of Billy 'The Texan' Longley*, ABC Books, Sydney, 2005.

Jenkings, B., *Crime Reporter*, Horowitz Publications, Sydney, 1966.

Karpis, A., *The Alvin Karpis Story*, Coward, McCann & Geoghegan, New York, 1971.

Keating, C., *Surry Hills: The City's Backyard*, Hale & Iremonger, Sydney, 1991.

Kelly, V., *The Bogeyman*, Angus & Robertson, Sydney, 1956.

——*Rugged Angel: The Amazing Career of Policewoman Lilian Armfield*, Angus & Robertson, Sydney, 1961.

——*The Charge Is Murder*, Rigby, Adelaide, 1965.

——*The Shadow*, Mayflower-Dell, London, 1967.

Knightley, P., *A Hack's Progress*, Jonathan Cape, London, 1997.

Kohn, G. C., *Dictionary of Culprits and Criminals*, Scarecrow Press, Metuchen, New Jersey, 1986.

Lahey, J., *Damn You, John Christie*, State Library of Victoria, Melbourne, 1993.

Lake, M. and F. Farley (eds), *Double Time: Women in Victoria*, Penguin Books, Melbourne, 1985.

Leach, C. E., *On Top of the Underworld*, Marston & Co, Sampson Low, London, n.d.

Lintner, B., *Blood Brothers*, Allen & Unwin, Sydney, 2002.

Locke, D., *Watching the Detectives*, ABC Books, Sydney, 2003.

Longmire, A., *St Kilda: The Show Goes On: The History of St Kilda, vol. 3, 1930 – July 1983*, Hudson Publishing, Melbourne, 1989.

Lovell, A., *The Mickelberg Stitch*, Creative Research, Perth, 1985.

Luck, P., *This Fabulous Century*, Lansdowne, Sydney, 1980.

Mackenzie Clarke, F., *Early Days of Bendigo*, ed. F. Cusack, Queensberry Hill Press, Melbourne, 1979.

Main, J., *Murder Australian Style*, Union Books, Melbourne, 1980.

Manderson, D., *From Mr Sin to Mr Big*, Oxford University Press, Oxford, 1993.

Marsden, W. and J. Sher, *Angels of Death: Inside the Bikers' Global Crime Enterprise*, Hodder & Stoughton, London, 2006.

Matthews, B., *A Fine and Private Place*, Pan Macmillan, Sydney, 2000.

——*Intractable*, Pan Macmillan, Sydney, 2006.

McCalman, J., *Struggletown*, Melbourne University Press, Melbourne, 1984.

McCarthy, P. H., *The Wild Scotsman*, Hawthorn Press, Melbourne, 1975.

McCoy, A.W., *Drug Traffic*, Harper & Row, Sydney, 1980.

McCullough, L., *Packing Death*, Floradale Productions and Sly Ink, Sydney, 2005.

McNab, D., *The Usual Suspect: The Life of Abe Saffron*, Pan Macmillan, Sydney, 2005.

——*The Dodger*, Pan Macmillan, Sydney, 2006.

Mendham, R., *Dictionary of Australian Bushrangers*, Hawthorn Press, Melbourne, 1975.

Miller, I. and T. Koch, *Joh's KO*, Boolarong Publishing, Brisbane, 1983.

Moffitt, A., *A Quarter to Midnight*, Angus & Robertson, Sydney, 1985.

Moor, K., *Crims in Grass Castles*, Pascoe Publishing, Apollo Bay, Victoria, 1989.

Moor, K. and G. Wilkinson, *Mugshots 2: A Compelling Line-up of Murders, Madmen and the Mafia in Austalia*, News Custom Publishing, Melbourne, 2006.

Moore, J. H., *Over-sexed, Over-paid and Over Here: Americans in Australia 1941–1945*, University of Queensland Press, Brisbane, 1991.

Moore, L., *Shot for Gold*, Jim Crow Press, Daylesford, Victoria, 2002.

Morgan, K., *Gun Alley*, Simon & Schuster, Sydney, 2005.

Morton, J., *Gangland*, Warner Books, London, 1993.

——*Gangland International*, Warner Books, London, 1999.

——*Gangland: The Lawyers*, Virgin Publishing, London, 2001.

——*Gangland Today*, Time Warner, London, 2003.

——*Gangland: The Contract Killers*, Time Warner, London, 2005.

Mouzos, M. and J. Venditto, *Contract Killings in Australia*, Australian Institute of Criminology, Canberra, 2003.

Mullen, J. K. J., *Dangerous Strangers: Minority Newcomers and Criminal Violence in the Urban West, 1850–2000*, Palgrave MacMillan, San Francisco, 2005.

Murray, J., *Larrikins*, Lansdowne Press, Melbourne, 1973.

Nixon, A. M., *Stand and Deliver!: 100 Australian Bushrangers 1789–1901*, Lothian Books, Melbourne, 2001.

Noble, T., *Untold Violence: Crime in Melbourne Today*, Kerr Publishing, Sydney, 1989.

——*Walsh Street*, John Kerr, Melbourne, 1991.

Owen, J., *Sleight of Hand: The $25 Million Nugan Hand Bank Scandal*, Colporteur Press, Sydney, 1983.

Paterson, A. B., *An Outback Marriage*, Angus & Robertson, Sydney, 1904.

Pearl, C., *Wild Men of Sydney*, W. H. Allen, London, 1958.

Pedley, D., *No Fixed Address: The Hunt for Brenden James Abbott*, HarperCollins, Sydney, 1999.

——*Australian Outlaw: The True Story of Postcard Bandit Brenden Abbott*, Sly Ink, Smithfield, New South Wales, 2006.

Perkins, R., *Working Girls: Prostitutes, Their Life and Social Control*, Australian Institute of Criminology, Canberra, 1991.

Perkins, R. et al. (eds), *Sex Work, Sex Workers in Australia*, University of New South Wales Press, Sydney, 1994.

Porter, T. J., *Executions in the Colony and State of Victoria 1842–1967*, Wednesday Press, Adelaide, 1999.

Pring, J., *Abo: A Treacherous Life: The Graham Henry Story*, ABC Books, Sydney, 2005.

Prior, T., *The Sinner's Club: Confessions of a Walk-up Man*, Penguin Books, Melbourne, 1993.

Pudsey, J., *Snowtown*, HarperCollins, Sydney, 2005.

Read, M. B., *Chopper: From the Inside: The Confessions of Mark Brandon Read*, Floradale Productions, Kilmore, Victoria, 1991.

——*Chopper 2: Hits and Memories*, Floradale Productions, Kilmore, Victoria, 1992.

Rees, P., *Killing Juanita*, Allen & Unwin, Sydney, 2004.

Reeves, T., *Mr Big: The True Story of Lennie McPherson and His Life of Crime*, Allen & Unwin, Sydney, 2005.

Richards, M., *The Hanged Man*, Scribe Publications, Melbourne, 2002.

Roberts, K., *Captain of the Push*, Angus & Robertson, London, 1963.

Robson, L. L., *The Convict Settlers of Australia*, Melbourne University Press, Melbourne, 1965.

Roope, C. and P. Gregson, *An Organised Banditti: The Story behind the 'Jewboy' Bushranger Gang*, Colin Roope and Patricia Gregson, Lake Macquarie, New South Wales, 2002.

Ross, L., *John Curtin*, Macmillan, Melbourne, 1977.

Ryan, P., *Redmond Barry*, Melbourne University Press, Melbourne, 1980.

Sadleir, J., *Recollections of a Victorian Police Officer*, George Robertson, Melbourne, 1913.

Searle, G., *The Golden Age: A History of the Colony of Victoria 1851–1861*, Melbourne University Press, Melbourne, 1977.

Silvester, J. and A. Rule, *Tough: 101 Australian Gangsters: A Crime Companion*, Floradale and Sly Ink, Melbourne, 2002.

——*Leadbelly: Inside Australia's Underworld Wars*, Floradale Press, Melbourne, 2004.

——*Underbelly*, vols 1–11, Floradale Press, Melbourne, 1997–2007.

Smith, J., *On the Side of the Angels*, Strand, Sydney, 2006.

Smith, N. with T. Noble, *Neddy*, Kerr Publishing Pty Ltd, Sydney, 1993.

——*Catch and Kill Your Own*, Ironbark, Sydney, 1995.

Sparks, R., *Burglar to the Nobility*, Arthur Barker, London, 1961.

Sprod, D., *Alexander Pearce of Macquarie Harbour: Convict–Bushranger–Cannibal*, Cat & Fiddle Press, Hobart, 1977.

Steketee, M. and M. Cockburn, *Wran: An Unauthorised Biography*, Allen & Unwin, Sydney, 1986.

Stephenson, R., *Milperra: The Road to Justice*, New Holland Publishers, Sydney, 2004.

Sturgess, D., *The Tangled Web*, Bedside Books, Brisbane, 2001.

Sullivan, B. *The Politics of Sex: Prostitution and Pornography in Australia since 1945*, Cambridge University Press, Cambridge, 1997.

Swanton, B., *A Chronological Account of Crime, Public Order and Police in Sydney 1788–1810*, Australian Institute of Criminology, Canberra, 1983.

Tame, A., *The Matriarch: The Kathy Pettingill Story*, Pan Macmillan, Sydney, 1996.

Ullathorne, W.B., *Autobiography of Archbishop Ullathorne*, Burns & Oates, London, 1891.

Veno, A. with W. Gannon, *The Brotherhoods: Inside the Outlaw Motorcycle Clubs*, Allen & Unwin, Sydney, 2002.

Victoria Police Management Services Bureau, *Police in Victoria 1836–1980*, Victoria Police Force, Melbourne, 1980.

Weidenhofer, M., *The Convict Years*, Lansdowne Press, Melbourne, 1973.

Whitburn, D., *Penthouse History of Crime in Australia*, Horowitz, Sydney, 1988.

Whitrod, R., *Before I Sleep: Memoirs of a Modern Police Commissioner*, University of Queensland Press, Brisbane, 2001.

Whitton, E., *Can of Worms*, The Fairfax Library, Sydney, 1986.

Wilkinson, G. and K. Moor, *Mugshots: A Classic Collection of Thugs, Drugs and Mugs*, News Custom Publishing, Melbourne, 2006.

Williams, D., *This Little Piggy Stayed Home*, Panorama, Perth, 1989.

Williams, S., *Peter Ryan: The Inside Story*, Viking, Sydney, 2002.

Wilson, D., *Big Shots*, Sun Books, Melbourne, 1985.

——*Big Shots II*, Sun Books, Melbourne, 1987.

Wilson, P., *A Life of Crime*, Scribe Publishing, Melbourne, 1990.

Wilson, P., D. Trele and R. Lincoln, *Jean Lee: The Last Woman Hanged in Australia*, Random House, Sydney, 1997.

Woodward, C., J. Fischer, J. Najman and M. Dunne, *Selling Sex in Queensland 2003*, Prostitution Licensing Authority, Brisbane, 2004.

Wright, R., *Who Stole the Mace?*, Victorian Parliamentary Library, Melbourne, 1991.

Writer, L., *Razor: A True Story of Slashers, Gangsters, Prostitutes and Sly Grog*, Macmillan, Melbourne, 2001.

Bibliography

Articles, Pamphlets, Reports, Unpublished Manuscripts, etc.

'The abortion file', *The Age*, 16–17 April 1971.

Advertiser, The, 8 September 1884, 19 January 1999, 30 January 2007.

Age, The, 28, 29 and 31 October 1927, 20 April 1929, 4 and 5 October 1930, 16–18 October 1961, 2 August 1978, 22 April 2003, 22 November 2005, 8, 19 and 20 October 2006, 8 May 2007.

Allbeury, J., 'Asian crime wave', *Penthouse Australia*, November 1994.

Argus, The, 3–10 April 1852, 5–9 June 1852, 5 August 1852, 18–29 October 1852, 28 March 1893, 7 November 1919, 22 and 26 January 1929, 20 December 1930, 31 May 1946.

Arnold, J. and M. Shiels, 'Outlaw motor cycle gangs', *Policing Issues and Practice Journal*, vol. 1, January 2000.

Australia, Parliament, *Asian Organised Crime in Australia: A Discussion Paper by the Parliamentary Joint Committee on the National Crime Authority*, The Committee, Canberra, 1995.

Australian, The, 25 November 1828, 25 November 1830, 27 May 1971, 6, 8 and 9 January 2001.

Bai-ngern, Chaiyakorn, 'Police investigate three alien smuggling gangs', *The Nation* (Bangkok), 9 June 1999.

'Bail for only one of 18 on drugs charges', *Daily Liberal News* (Dubbo), 2 July 2004.

Ballarat Times, 21 October 1854.

Bartholomew, A., letters to Crown Solicitor and to Secretary, Law Department, 10 March 1966, 10 December 1966.

Bearup, G. and K. McClymont, 'Uncle Six: from refugee to high roller', *The Sydney Morning Herald*, 27 October 1997.

Bell's Life, 18 March 1846.

Bindell, J., 'Streets apart', *The Guardian* (UK), 15 May 2004.

Birnbauer, B., 'Migrants lured by sex ring', The Age, 29 March 1998.

——'From Russia for love', *The Age*, 29 March 1998.

——'Prostitutes caught in debt servitude', *The Age*, 30 March 1998.

Bottom, B., 'Faceless big shot', *The Independent Monthly*, July 1989.

Brown, M., 'Death of a one-time Godfather', *The Sydney Morning Herald*, 28 January 2005.

Butcher, S., 'Gangland killer Williams to appeal sentence,' *The Age*, 17 May 2007.

Callinan, R. and T. Targett, 'The powder trail', *The Courier-Mail*, 26 May 2001.

Carswell, A. and K. Lawrence, 'Warring bikies lose their guns', *Daily Telegraph*, 4 May 2006.

Cohen, J., 'Interview with Bernie Matthews', *Four Corners*, television program, ABC Television, 23 February 2004.

Collingwood Mercury, 18 December 1880.

Cornford, P., 'Juanita's lament', *The Sydney Morning Herald*, 1 July 1995.

Courier-Mail, 15, 17 and 18 January 1938.

Crawford, C., 'Police fear national bikie war', *Daily Telegraph*, 6 April 2007.

Daily Telegraph, 2 April 2007.

Dappin, M., 'Hitmen', *Penthouse Australia*, December 1997.

Delianis, P., 'Saying goodbye to a colourful crook', *Herald Sun*,
7 January 1995.

Dermott, D., 'Winner takes all', *Four Corners*, television program,
ABC Television, 24 April 2000.

Dickie, P., 'Civilising the sex trade', Brisbane Institute website, <www.
brisinst.org.au/resources/dickie_phil_prostitution.html>, 25 July 2001.

Doyle, B., 'The Hoffman murder case', *Australian Police Journal*, July 1949.

Duffy, J. H., 'Rogue cop', *Australian Penthouse*, October 1993.

Fife-Yeomans, J., 'No more Mr Bigs', *The Australian*, 22 October 1998.

Flemington/Kensington Community Legal Centre et al., *Police Shootings
in Victoria 1987–1989: You Deserve to Know the Truth*, Fitzroy Legal
Service, Melbourne, 1992.

Forbes, M. 'Our secret slave trade', *The Age*, 21 August 1999.

Gibbs, S., 'Now the streets go to hell', *The Sydney Morning Herald*,
22 April 2006.

Gold Coast Bulletin, 23 July 2005.

Hardiman, B., 'Police accountability', in Victoria, Ombudsman, *Annual
Report of the Ombudsman*, Government Printer, Melbourne, 2003.

Harrison, D., 'Williams jailed for 35 years', *The Age*, 7 May 2007.

Hazak, M. K., 'Crime club', *Penthouse Australia*, May 1998.

—— 'Crime in the Cross', *Penthouse Australia*, July 1998.

Heary, M., 'Gangs death nell', *Daily Telegraph*, 13 March 2001.

Herald (Melbourne), *The*, 11–13 December 1971.

Herald Sun, 11 May 2000, 20 May 2005, 19, 20 and 27 October 2006,
18 April 2007.

Illustrated Circular of Confidence Tricksters and Expert Criminals, Receiver
of the Metropolitan Police Division, London, 1935.

Illustrated Circular of Confidence Tricksters and Expert Criminals, Receiver
of the Metropolitan Police Division, London, 1947.

Irwin, M. P., 'Policing organised crime', paper presented to 4th National
Outlook Symposium on Crime in Australia, Canberra, 21–22 June 2001.

'Is there a crime wave in Sydney?', *The Sydney Morning Herald*,
31 January 1945.

Jarratt, P., 'The life and crimes of Murray Riley', *Penthouse Australia*,
August 1991.

Jones, R., *Firearm Restrictions*, Briefing Paper no. 3, Parliament of New
South Wales, Sydney, 2004.

Kennedy, L., 'Bikies arrested over drug ring', *The Sydney Morning Herald*,
27 May 2004.

Khazar, M., 'Chopper's whoppers', *Penthouse Australia*, December 1994.

Kidd, B., 'Who shot Mr Rent-a-Kill?', *Penthouse Australia*, March 1993.

——'The life and crimes of Neddy Smith', *Penthouse Australia*, June 1993.

Kidman, J., '$2 billion drug hauls as Australian agents tackle new ice age', *The Age*, 1 October 2006.

Kim, I., 'NSW cops to set up anti-Arab squad', *Green Left Weekly*, 28 January 2004.

'Kingpin's high life from heroin trade ends in a cell', *The Sydney Morning Herald*, 28 September 2002.

'The late Freddy Harrison', *Truth* (Melbourne), 15 February 1958.

Lawrence, K. and J. Fife-Yeomans, 'Landing in a war zone—Rebels boss rushing home as bikie feud spirals', *Daily Telegraph*, 2 April 2007.

Lozusic, R., *Gangs in New South Wales*, Briefing Paper no. 16, Parliament of New South Wales, Sydney, 2002.

Maguire, T., 'The case of the missing victim', *The Bulletin*, 19 January 1982.

Masters, C., 'On the take', *The Sydney Morning Herald*, 1 July 1995.

McClymont, K., 'Bashing, robbing, drinking: a day in the life of a bent cop', *The Sydney Morning Herald*, 4 July 1985.

——'Secret eyes on Rivkin and Sydney's drug trade', *The Sydney Morning Herald*, 22 May 2004.

McClymont, K. and A. Clennell, 'Brothel boom: the Asia connection', *The Sydney Morning Herald*, 31 August 1999.

——'Trapped into a life of prostitution', *The Sydney Morning Herald*, 31 August 1999.

McClymont K. and L. Kennedy, 'A violent man takes his last victim', *The Sydney Morning Herald*, 13 May 2006.

McGarry, A. and G. Hughes, 'Riddle of the ex-bikie and the drugged QC', *The Australian*, 19 May 2007.

'Melbourne, too, has an underworld', *Argus*, 15 June 1946.

Mercer, N., 'China link to bikie amphetamine lab', *Daily Telegraph*, 16 April 2006.

Miles, W. L., 'City of fear', *Penthouse Australia*, August 1995.

Moor, K., 'Mafia's dark secrets', *Herald Sun*, 30 October 2006.

Morton, J., 'Ryan's war', *Police Review* (London), 29 November 1996.

Moscaritolo, M. and M. Williams, 'Bikies without borders', *The Advertiser*, 30 January 2007.

Munro, I. and S. Butcher, 'Williams confesses', *The Age*, 1 March 2007.

'Murder mystery still unsolved', *Truth* (Melbourne), 18 January 1913.

Murdoch, L., 'Teenagers threw prostitutes off bridge', *The Age*, 10 February 2005.

National Crime Authority, *Operation Hydra: South Australian Reference No. 2*, National Crime Authority, Canberra, 1991.

New South Wales, *Parliamentary Debates*, 4 August 1937.

New South Wales, Police Integrity Commission, *Report to Parliament: Operation Florida*, vols 1 and 2, Parliament Integrity Commission, Sydney, 2004.

Norton, 'Lechery and lucre', *Truth* (Sydney), 29 November 1906.

O'Brien, N., 'Cold war', *The Australian*, 18 December 2004.

O'Lincoln, T., '"The most outrageous conduct": convict rebellions in colonial Australia', *Marxist Interventions*, <www.anu.edu.au/polsci/marx/interventions/convicts.htm>.

O'Neill, M., 'Deadly toll of bikie turf war', *Sunday Telegraph*, 11 February 2007.

Pearce, A., 'Narrative of the escape of eight convicts from Macquarie Harbour', MS in Dixson Library, State Library of New South Wales, c. 1824.

'Police raid bikies over $23 million drug ring', *The Sydney Morning Herald*, 26 May 2004.

Priest, T., 'The rise of middle-eastern crime in Australia', *Quadrant*, vol. XLVIII, no. 1, January–February 2004.

Project Respect, *One Victim of Trafficking is One Too Many*, Project Respect Inc., Melbourne, 2004.

Quine, B., 'Police framed brothel owner', *Herald Sun*, 12 November 1991.

RED: *A Magazine for the Sex Industry*, vols 1, 2, 3 and 9.

Rennie, R. and J. Berry, 'Roberta stands by her man', *The Age*, 7 May 2007.

Richards, D., 'Australia's most dangerous criminal tells all', *The Bulletin*, 11 March 1980.

——'How the government condones waterfront graft', *The Bulletin*, 18 March 1980.

Royal Commission on the Activities of the Federated Ship Painters and Dockers Union, *Final Report*, (F. X. Costigan, commissioner), Government Printer, Canberra, 1984.

Royal Commission on Allegations of Organised Crime in Clubs, *Report*, (A. R. Moffitt, commissioner), Government Printer, Sydney, 1974.

Royal Commission on the Alleged Shooting at and Wounding of John O'Connell Brophy, *Report*, VPRS 3992.

Royal Commission of Inquiry into Drug Trafficking, *Report, February 1983*, (D. G. Stewart, commissioner), Australian Government Publishing Service, Canberra, 1983.

Royal Commission of Inquiry into Drugs, *Report*, (E. S. Williams, commissioner), Australian Government Publishing Service, Canberra, 1980.

Shanahan, L., 'Disguised Mokbel grabbed at seaside cafe', *The Age*, 6 June 2007.

Shand, A., 'Burial ground', *The Bulletin*, 6 April 2004.

——'Piece talks', *The Bulletin*, 22 June 2004.

——'Outlaw nation', *Sunday*, television program, Nine Network, 12 March 2006.

Shand, A. and J. Davies, 'Killing time', *The Bulletin*, 15 June 2004.

Silvester, J., 'Death of a gangster', *The Sunday Age*, 18 January 1998.

——'Cops, robbers, drugs and money', *The Age*, 18 March 2003.

——'The anatomy of a suburban hit', *The Age*, 31 August 2004.

——'Coming clean', *The Age*, 1 October 2005.

——'The untold, bloody story of Melbourne's underworld war', *The Age*, 1 March 2007.

——'New Mokbel murder charge', *The Age*, 22 June 2007.

Smiles, S., 'Police move to curb sex slavery', *The Age*, 30 June 2006.

Stackhouse, J., 'Tax rackets lead to death threat', *The Bulletin*, 9 February 1982.

Stephen, S., 'The myth of ethnic crime', *Green Left Weekly*, 4 February 2004.

Stewart, J. and M. Edwards, 'Attacks create bikie war concerns', *Lateline*, television program, ABC Television, 3 May 2007.

Stoddard, E. R., 'The informal code of police deviancy: a group approach to blue coat crime', *Journal of Criminal Law, Criminology and Police Science*, 1968.

Stolz, G. and P. Doneman, 'Police prepare for biker gang warfare', *Courier-Mail*, 20 March 2006.

Sullivan, M. L. and S. Jefferys, 'Legislation: the Australian experience', *Violence against Women Journal*, vol. 8, no. 9, September 2002.

Sun Herald, 19 May 1991, 19 January 1992, 20 December 1992.

Sunday Mail (Brisbane), 17 June 2001.

Sunday Telegraph, 12 December 2004.

Swanton, B. and L. Hoban, 'William John MacKay, New South Wales' 7th Commissioner of Police', *New South Wales Police News*, vol. 70, no. 6, June 1990.

Sydney Gazette, 17 September 1828.

Sydney Morning Herald, The, 11 June 1914, 23 April 1930, 16 November 1932, 26 April 1935, 13 and 18 May 1935, 15 June 1935, 11 September 1935, 11 October 1935, 13 and 14 December 1935, 5 and 16 January 1945, 23 February 1945, 25 January 1992, 31 August 1999, 25 April 2000, 5 July 2003, 26 May 2004, 21 September 2005, 22 July 2006.

'Sydney's racketeers pay their taxes', *The Age*, 31 May 1946.

Tame, A., 'Findings of lengthy probe sparked officer outrage', *Herald Sun*, 18 November 2001.

Tedeschi, M., 'History of the New South Wales crown prosecutors 1901–1986', *The Forbes Flyer*, no. 11, autumn 2006.

'The trotter tragedy', *Truth* (Melbourne), 11 January 1913.

Truth: (Brisbane), 3 February 1929; (Melbourne), 10 March 1906, 11 and 18 January 1913, 5 and 12 January 1924, 5 and 19 April 1924, 5 November 1927, 21 September 1940, 3 November 1945, 1 December 1945, 7 April 1951, 11 October 1969, 13 December 1969; (Perth), 27 May 1928; (Sydney), 8 April 1894, 29 November 1906, 2 December 1945.

Verrender, I., 'The informer', *The Sydney Morning Herald*, 24 June 1995.

Victoria Police Gazette, 2 and 9 March 1916, 30 August 1923.

Victoria, Obudsman, *Ceja Task Force Drug Related Corruption: Second Interim Report of Ombudsman Victoria*, Government Printer, Melbourne, 2004.

Walsh, D., L. Kennedy and J. Gibson, 'Bandidos deadly fall out', *The Sydney Morning Herald*, 21 April 2006.

Wilkinson, G., 'Former brothel king dies', *Herald Sun*, 24 April 2004.

Zedner, L., 'Wayward sisters: the prison for women', in N. Morris and D. Rothman (eds), Oxford History of the Prison, *Oxford University Press*, Oxford, 1998.

Index